The Mbeki Legacy

The Mbeki Legacy

BRIAN POTTINGER

ZEBRA

Published by Zebra Press
an imprint of Struik Publishers
(a division of New Holland Publishing (South Africa) (Pty) Ltd)
PO Box 1144, Cape Town, 8000
New Holland Publishing is a member of Avusa Ltd

www.zebrapress.co.za

First published 2008
Reprinted in 2008

3 5 7 9 10 8 6 4 2

Publication © Zebra Press 2008
Text © Brian Pottinger 2008

Cover photographs: Mbeki © Gallo Images/Rapport/Brendan Cockcroft;
squatter camp © Logan Hicks

PUBLISHER: Marlene Fryer
MANAGING EDITOR: Robert Plummer
EDITOR: Marléne Burger
PROOFREADER: Lisa Compton
COVER DESIGNER: Michiel Botha
TEXT DESIGNER: Natascha Adendorff-Olivier
TYPESETTER: Monique van den Berg
INDEXER: Mary Lennox
PRODUCTION MANAGER: Valerie Kömmer

Set in 10.5 pt on 14 pt Minion

Reproduction by Hirt & Carter (Cape) (Pty) Ltd
Printed and bound by CTP Book Printers, Duminy Street, Parow 7500, South Africa

ISBN 978 1 77022 028 7

www.imagesofafrica.co.za

IMAGES OF AFRICA
PHOTO LIBRARY

Over 40 000 unique African images available to purchase
from our image bank at www.imagesofafrica.co.za

To Lucie Myriam

Contents

Preface

THIS BOOK HAS ITS ORIGIN IN A QUIET MOMENT IN MY LIFE between one career of thirty years as a corporate and editorial executive in the African media and entertainment sector and another as an active consultant. In my role as the manager of a number of businesses across the continent between 2003 and 2007, I was obliged to spend up to a third of my time out of South Africa. I began to gain the uncomfortable feeling that whenever I visited countries like Nigeria, Uganda, Tanzania, Ghana or Kenya I had a sense of progress, as hesitant as it may be and however subject to the occasional spectacular reversal, such as the snatched Kenyan elections. Yet whenever I returned home to South Africa I had the sense that things were going the other way. The citizens were becoming more querulous, irritable, cynical and despairing. Infrastructure was deteriorating, security worsening, public probity eroding. I had the sense that the country's rulers were losing grip and that policies, even good ones, were being subverted through corruption and incompetence.

I began to feel an increasing alienation from what was happening at home compared to what I had prayed for when my country enjoyed its triumphant political liberation a decade and a half earlier. I initially sought to rationalise it away. It was merely the effect of receiving relentlessly negative publicity about the ruling party and the president by a clearly unfettered media. It was the delayed result of the near-death experience my wife suffered in an armed robbery at a Johannesburg shopping mall at the hands of a gang of bandits operating with impunity. But I soon learnt that I was not alone. Many black and white fellow citizens were equally disillusioned by their political leadership and the state institutions. They were confused and angry. What, they asked, had happened to the miracle?

The Mbeki Legacy is my attempt to make some sense of what has transpired in this extraordinary country in the past decade. It cannot pretend to be a great work of history – we are all still writing that – but it does try to identify what we have done right and what wrong, sometimes catastrophically so, since Nelson Mandela left office. This book may not leave my readers more encouraged, but I do hope it leaves them more informed. Only with knowledge can we make the difference.

I owe a host of thanks – to Brian Wootton, CEO of Avusa's Books Division, Marlene Fryer and Robert Plummer of Zebra Press, and Marléne Burger, who was my editor. The latter was a colleague during tumultuous days on the *Sunday Times* in the eighties and nineties, and I was pleased to see she has lost none of her wit or perspicacity.

My sincerest thanks to all those who made their time available to me in researching this book. My regret is that its subject, President Mbeki, did not participate. My requests to his media office for access were ignored, whether because of discourtesy, time pressures or for the want of anything to say about his legacy, I cannot know. If the final product is weaker by his absence, I must assume the responsibility but not the blame.

Finally, my thanks to Susan, my wife of thirty-one years, who had to endure the long absences of a writing partner and suffer the endless discussions around this intriguing and challenging topic.

BRIAN POTTINGER
Kloof, KwaZulu-Natal
August 2008

Abbreviations

ABET:	Adult Basic Education and Training
AMIB:	African Mission in Burundi
AMIS:	African Mission in Sudan
AMPS:	All Media Products Survey
ANC:	African National Congress
APRM:	African Peer Review Mechanism
AsgiSA:	Accelerated and Shared Growth Initiative for South Africa
AU:	African Union
BBEE:	broad-based black economic empowerment
BEE:	black economic empowerment
CASE:	Community Agency for Social Enquiry
CIA:	Central Intelligence Agency
CPIX:	consumer price index excluding mortgage rate changes
CSVR:	Centre for the Study of Violence and Reconciliation
DA:	Democratic Alliance
DRC:	Democratic Republic of Congo
DSO:	Directorate of Special Operations
DTI:	Department of Trade and Industry
EPA:	Economic Partnership Agreements
EU:	European Union
FET:	Further Education and Training
FIFA:	International Federation of Association Football
GDP:	gross domestic product
GEAR:	Growth, Employment and Redistribution programme
GFCF:	gross fixed capital formation
HDI:	human development index
HIV/AIDS:	human immunodeficiency virus/acquired immune deficiency syndrome
ICASA:	Independent Communications Authority of South Africa

ICT:	information and communications technology
ICU:	intensive care unit
IT:	information technology
JIPSA:	Joint Initiative on Priority Skills Acquisition
JIT:	Joint Investigating Team
LINK:	Learning Information Networking and Knowledge Centre
MDC:	Movement for Democratic Change
NALEDI:	National Labour and Economic Development Institute
NATO:	North Atlantic Treaty Organisation
NEC:	national executive committee
NEPAD:	New Partnership for African Development
NERSA:	National Energy Regulator of South Africa
NGO:	non-governmental organisation
NPA:	National Prosecuting Authority
NPI:	National Productivity Institute
NSF:	National Skills Fund
OAU:	Organisation of African Unity
OBE:	outcomes-based education
RDP:	Reconstruction and Development Programme
SABC:	South African Broadcasting Corporation
SADC:	Southern African Development Community
SAPS:	South African Police Service
SCOPA:	Standing Committee on Public Accounts
SETA:	Sector Education Training Authorities
SME:	small and medium enterprise
SMEDP:	Small and Medium Enterprise Development Programme
SMS:	short message service
TB:	tuberculosis
UDF:	United Democratic Front
UN:	United Nations
US:	United States
USAID:	United States Aid
WHO:	World Health Organisation
WSDSP:	Workplace Skills Development Support Programme
WTO:	World Trade Organisation
Zanu-PF:	Zimbabwe African National Union – Patriotic Front

Introduction

O N 19 DECEMBER 2007, SOUTH AFRICA'S PRESIDENT THABO Mbeki was ousted as leader of the ruling African National Congress (ANC) by the votes of three out of every five delegates at the party's annual conference. It was an expected yet stunning defeat. The victor was an unschooled former guerrilla, facing the prospect of criminal charges for corruption, tax evasion and racketeering.

To the urbane and cosmopolitan Mbeki, the chaotic conference and the crushing of his bid for a third term as leader of the party was his worst nightmare come true. Not only had he lost his power within the party, but there were also questions as to how he could continue to govern the country until his term as president expired in 2009. Was his party, indeed his country, at risk of becoming another post-colonial cliché – turbulent, beset by personality feuds, riddled with corruption and incompetence and losing its competitive edge in the global economy day by day?

How did it all happen? And what is the future for sub-Saharan Africa's most powerful and wealthiest nation?

The transfer of power to the ANC had been achieved a scant thirteen years earlier. To those closely involved in the process over many decades, it was nothing less than a miracle. The new leader of the country, President Nelson Mandela, also appeared miraculous. Under his inspirational and reconciliatory leadership, the country survived its first five years of liberation, much to the disappointment of the infant state's direst cynics.

But Mr Mandela's style of administration was *sui generis*. His successor would have to be a tough-minded pragmatist, who would need to deal urgently with the numerous and daunting challenges confronting this newly liberated society with its many traditions, cultures and expectations. Mere patrician charm and the mantle of the ANC's struggle traditions were no longer enough.

At its December 1997 conference, the ANC appointed Thabo Mbeki the new party leader, thus effectively anointing him as the next South African president after general elections were held in 1999. Mbeki was a loyal servant of the revolutionary opposition to white minority rule, a well-read, complex, contradictory, tortured and authoritarian man. He had sat at the feet of some of the movement's icons and had often written their speeches. He was an unreconstructed intellectual in a country of bruisers and brawlers, a constituency of tough and unforgiving people. His style was academic, elusive and opaque in a nation of straight-talkers, people who liked songs with titles such as 'Umshini Wam' ('Bring Me My Machine-gun').

His defeated rival was Cyril Ramaphosa, who was well regarded by Mandela. Ramaphosa had once led the most powerful trade union movement in the internal resistance to the apartheid regime, and was a key architect of the political consensus that led to liberation and a successful businessman in his own right. By choosing Mbeki, the ANC irrevocably set the country on a course for the next decade and beyond.

This book does not presume to explore Thabo Mbeki's innermost being. Others have done that, some at extraordinary length. Neither does it wish to become entrapped in the endless bickering and manoeuvring of the ruling elites. There are few issues of principle to be found here: only power, profit, patronage and the age-old fight over them. Least of all does it set out to be an apologia for Mbeki. Those who have offered one have little benefited either his reputation or their own.

Rather, this book seeks to answer some simple questions. Is the South Africa left by Mbeki better or worse than the one he inherited? Did his stewardship add to or detract from the image of this nation in the making? What future has he laid out for South Africa – and indeed the continent – by his policies and his conduct?

Those seeking a simple answer will be disappointed. In some respects Mbeki and certain of his senior officers performed miracles, worthy postscripts to the great drama of 1994. He undoubtedly created macro-economic stability through managers of surpassing aptitude. He also established political stability on a broad front. Impeccably run elections ushered in three successive terms of ANC government with overwhelming majorities. No South African seriously challenged the outcomes or the process. In infant democracies, as Nigeria and Kenya showed in 2007, that is not something to be taken for granted.

He also presided over a dramatic reapportionment of wealth, income and opportunity between a traditional wealth-holding class and a new wealth-seeking one. The former was largely white, the latter black. This transformation took place without violence, within the law and largely with the consent, albeit grudging, of the elites. Rarely has this scale of wealth and income redistribution occurred within such a short space of time outside of a revolution.

Mbeki has also left his tracks abroad. He put Africa at the centre of many of the global debates. As the inheritor of a comparatively successful and modern state, he was taken seriously until the latter part of his tenure, when some of his positions left both opponents and friends bemused. His repeated failure to persuade Robert Mugabe to end the crisis in Zimbabwe also transformed him from a Goliath of Africa into a figure of ridicule, or worse, pity. Yet he relentlessly pursued his vision of a successful and modern continent, although all too often his interventions rested more on utopian ideals than reality. This led to failures that were grist for his many rivals among African leaders. Nevertheless, he did make a difference in terms of *institutions* if not *events.*

Yet, tragically, his legacy will probably not be celebrated for any of this. It will be remembered for his judgements on key issues affecting society: his ambiguity on HIV/AIDS; his refusal to take a strong and moral position on human rights abuses on the continent; his tolerance of epic incompetence and amorality among party colleagues; his introduction of an acrimonious, petty, race-based style of national discourse, so much at odds with the sentiments of the majority of his fellow citizens. He will be remembered as the African leader who pursued bizarre personal constructs relating to disease among his own people and human rights violations among his immediate neighbours.

Mostly, however, he will be remembered as the man whose judgement on his own stature, posterity and power led him to make the worst call of all – to stand for a third term as leader of his party. Not for sixty years had the ANC witnessed such bitter and divisive internal tumult as accompanied the contest for the 2007 party leadership elections. No leader in the ANC's near-century of existence had been as comprehensively humiliated as Thabo Mbeki.

Ultimately, however, the major charge against him will be that he was unable to manage the impact of that most maverick of forces: *the unintended consequence.* In researching this aspect I was reminded of my earlier writings on one of Mbeki's predecessors, the irascible PW Botha, president of South Africa from 1978 to 1989. The personalities, ideologies and backgrounds of these two men are – not surprisingly – utterly different.

Botha was a limited, crass, forthright tribalist, whose base was the most powerful army on the African continent. Mbeki is an educated, cosmopolitan dreamer, steeped in a mix of revolutionary theory and modern economics. The only similarity, perhaps, is that they both nursed a bottomless sense of grievance at the past injustices visited on their people and a crippling suspicion of those whom they held responsible.

The white president began a process of political and social reform and then became overwhelmed by the momentum of those changes in all sorts of ways. In the face of this confusion, this ambiguity, he retreated to what he knew best: the hard fist of the security despot. Mbeki's refuge in the face of the same tumult, the very messiness of political and social transition, was in the guile, subterfuge, disinformation and clandestine plotting of the revolutionary. It helped little. Both styles were in conflict with constituencies that had moved away from their leaders emotionally and intellectually. Their administrations in latter years became isolated, wounded and glowering. Both men were toppled by palace revolt. And both damaged their legacies terribly. It is too late for Botha to do anything about it. There may yet be time for Mbeki.

The South Africa bequeathed to us by Mbeki is different from the one he inherited. It has moved forward in all sorts of exciting ways. Favourable international economic circumstances and the skill of his economic managers gave the Mbeki administration the opportunity to guide a real improvement in the living standards of a considerable number of South Africans, overwhelmingly black. His administration witnessed a new confidence and growth among people who had once been repressed and marginalised. In the interstices of politics lay the *real* South Africa: a story of private triumphs and quiet victories within the ambit of a democratic, free nation.

Yet Mbeki had to dig deeply into national resources to achieve this moment. How deeply, we have not yet begun to comprehend. Still, when he leaves office, Mbeki will at least have the comfort of knowing he left strong, if now weakening, financial indicators and took his best shot at extending a sizeable chunk of national wealth to the previously disadvantaged.

Ironically, he was often hanged for the wrong reason. His left-wing critics accused him of being pro-business and anti-poor, surely the gravest calumny that can be laid at the door of an ANC leader. It is untrue. He has poured billions of rands of national, social and emotional resources, directly and indirectly, into the hands of both the poor and a new client class of black elites. His redistributive policies have created potentially unaffordable long-term liabilities for South Africa and huge dependency among swathes of the population. We may debate the wisdom of this course, but it is mischievous to accuse him of not acting within the ANC mandate. Betrayal of ANC policy is surely not one of Mbeki's sins.

This book will argue that, for all the pragmatism in the macro-economic sphere, the Mbeki administration will be remembered as one of the most ideological in the country's history. The motive force of Mbeki's vision was the correction of what he saw as race-based injustice. This sense of injury pervaded everything the administration did, underwrote all policies, tainted all judgement and infused all debate. It was because of this towering mission to correct the past, to confront the stereotypical images of Africa as the hopeless continent, that so much of Mbeki's judgement will be questioned: not for the correctness of the *objective* but for the *methods* of its achievement.

So what are President Thabo Mbeki's core legacies? Stripped of all irrelevancies, they lie in three baleful and long-term consequences.

The first is the growth of the dependency society. More than a third of all South African households now believe, correctly or not, that only state aid can ensure their survival. This group is becoming more dependent on subsidy, not less so, despite considerable efforts by the government to create paths to self-sufficiency. Additionally, a new black middle class, variously numbered as being between 400 000 and two million souls, depending on definitions, has emerged on the back of a growing economy and aggressive affirmative action. Half of these, again correctly or incorrectly, believe their improved fortunes are due almost entirely to affirmative action policies.

These dependent groups, then, rely on two things. The first is a state with the *capacity* to effectively intervene to support them without crippling the economy. The second is an economy growing at a rate sufficient to *fund* them. Both these propositions are doubtful in the light of a second overarching Mbeki legacy – an arrested state formation.

This means that the state left by Mbeki is currently incapable of underwriting the establishment of a truly successful modern state. Despite all the macro-economic successes and the credit-led economic boom of the early 2000s, the reality is that the institutional and physical core of the country is withering away, and has been for a long time. It is as simple as that.

A decade has effectively been squandered on grand visions, ideological dispute, feudalistic personality rows between political barons and a huge diversion of effort aimed at the salvation of Africa. The back garden, by contrast, was not tended. What was needed was work in building the infrastructure, teaching children, instilling professionalism in public servants, strengthening all instruments of the constitution from courts through to parliament, retaining skills, brokering a workable *modus operandi* between labour, state and capital, and building a long-term economic future.

The third legacy flows from the second. It is what I have called the rise of the proxy state. As the South African state administration began to falter for myriad reasons, a host of private interests interceded at all levels to ensure the continuation of state function, usually to their personal benefit. Indeed, in some cases these forces *became* the state function. Sometimes the interventions were legitimate and legal, and in others quite illegal. In most cases, however, they trespassed into grey and disquieting regions that no modern state should allow. The effect of the proxy state was twofold: a weakened locus of control for the state and yet another ratchet of the growing inequality between the citizens. The division was no longer merely between privileged and unprivileged; it was between those forced to stand in line in *front* of state counters and those who had infiltrated *behind* the counters.

In some cases South Africa is much advanced from where it stood in 1999; in many other critical instances it is no further forward, and in some cases it is way behind.

Why should this be? Why should a country with a profusion of blessings, physical and human, be sliding down the scale of international competitiveness, even against societies much less endowed than our own?

The answer is simple: a 'big man' political culture and policy overreach.

The first characteristic derives its name from the Nigerian political and economic personalities who wield inordinate and often subterranean power in that semi-feudal state. It is these self-perpetuating *ogas* who call the shots and operate with a combination of arrogance, guile, manipulation and ruthlessness, whether in or out of public office. They are the antithesis of the modern democratic leader who rules by consensus, transparency and within clear limitations.

Policy overreach is a consequence of the ANC elites, many of them disconnected exiles, choosing a dream rather than a reality. They over-elaborated policy, ignored the fragility of the institutions called upon to implement their rich imaginings and – worse – pursued as a matter of policy institutional discontinuity and the marginalising of key skills. They sought to re-engineer the state and society with little knowledge of what actually constituted either, let alone the long-term impact of their actions. And they compounded it all by making the bureaucracy an adjunct of the ruling party, thus condemning it to the same dysfunction as the movement itself.

The results are everywhere: a factionalised political leadership, a unionised and underproductive civil service, uneducated children, lack of skills, a hard-wired culture of indiscipline, grievance, entitlement and enrichment, internal dissent, social pathology and a growing scepticism by serious people at home and abroad that it can ever be pulled right.

The ruling party is in disarray, having splintered into what I call ANC Classic and ANC Lite, and in the short term virtually every institution of the constitution is at risk of being poisoned by a roiling power play between two struggle-era *ogas*, one a president without power, the other a power without a presidency.

It is possible to blame apartheid for all this, as the ANC ceaselessly does. This has some validity. Apartheid caused enormous damage to social relationships and economic prospects and criminally demeaned the confidence and dignity of black South Africans. The challenges left by the departing *ancien régime* were certainly severe, but no more so than in many other societies emerging from war, subjugation, economic collapse and cultural imperialism. And yet so many of them have fared better than South Africa. A criticism directed at my book[1] on PW Botha's imperial presidency was that I attributed too much power and influence to one man, that I was not cognisant enough of the multiplicity of forces, historic and contemporary, that drive modern states in one direction or the other. I acknowledge the criticism and have sought to avoid the same error in this book. It would be wrong to lay all the praise or blame on Mbeki the individual, or even on his coterie of advisors and ministers.

But it is nevertheless true that leaders, by the very nature of leadership, have the capacity to exert considerable influence with the decisions they make, the prisms through which they view the world, the people they choose, the discourse they encourage and the vision which they espouse. Modern South Africans are thirsting for a national conversation that goes beyond division, rectification, redistribution, justification and blame laying. They are looking for a clear-eyed vision of what can be achieved by a nation that should be moving beyond the travails of the past, accepting the challenges of the present and looking to the future.

Such vision, tragically, did not knock on South Africa's door during the Mbeki era, or not in a way that found anybody at home. Instead, there were endless policy documents, superbly crafted soliloquies and numerous bureaucratic interventions, nearly all of them failures. The discourse between white and black did not soften in the Mbeki years – it hardened, became more exasperated, vitriolic, divisive, zero-sum and entitlement driven, reaching always to the past for justification or explication. It had none of the vaunting generosity, enthusiasm and inquiry of the earlier years of the democracy. With it, inevitably, came high-level corruption.

In preparing the research for this book I sought views from many sources, including the head of one of the country's foremost business schools. A wise man, he advised me that African politics can best be understood if one accepts that politics drives economics. I have therefore shaped the book to consider first Mbeki's Political Kingdom: the structures and protocols he put in place to secure power and execute policy through a highly centralised decision-making process. It was this structure and style that was rudely shattered in December 2007 when the grassroots of the party – ANC Classic – rose up to take back power and challenge the aloof and authoritarian methods of their leader and his ANC Lite supporters.

From there I have considered Mbeki's Economic Kingdom, which, far from being written in stone as some have suggested, swerved from a rugged form of semi-Thatcherism in the early years to a hand-me-down version of the developmental state in the dying, desperate days of his presidency. His social and economic policies led directly to the creation of the dependency society. The obvious next question is, can what Mr Mbeki wrought survive? Here it was necessary to look at the various aspects of arrested state formation during Mbeki's years and the formidable challenges this has created for the maintenance of a national economic growth rate, sufficient to attain a lastingly successful modern state, let alone sustain the dependency society.

In this regard I argue that there has been a social, political and economic roll-back from the heady early days of liberation. I have suggested that the high point of South Africa's modernity might well have been in the decade between liberation and roughly the end of Mbeki's first term as president. Since then, the country has embarked on a trajectory of demodernisation or regressive governance – call it what you wish – that will require urgent and radical measures to correct.

The final part of the book wanders recklessly into a discussion of some potential South African futures. Here one moves beyond diagnosis and into the realm of faith. One either believes that this extraordinary country and its remarkable people will be able to rise above the misspent years and resume the march to a comparatively successful middle-tier country, or one takes the apocalyptic view that we are beyond the point of tip-over: that the soufflé option, in which the country slowly collapses from the centre as the heat rises, is our inescapable destiny. I subscribe to the first option, for these simple reasons. South Africa is not short of leaders. They just happen to be in the wrong places. Mbeki saw to that. Secondly, the country's economy is still strong and deep enough to withstand the wasted years if the correct signposts are followed *now*.

Finally, South Africans have shown time and again that under inspirational leadership they are capable of extraordinary resilience, flexibility and innovation. In the last section of this book I presumptuously advance some proposals as to how we can again begin playing to our strengths rather than to the endless succession of weaknesses we have courted so assiduously in recent years.

PART I

The Political Kingdom

CHAPTER 1

Life and soul of the party

In politics, what begins in fear usually ends in folly.
— SAMUEL TAYLOR COLERIDGE[1]

A S PRESIDENT PW BOTHA APPROACHED THE LAST MONTHS of his tenure in 1989, the pressure for him to move on became intense from within and without his party. He refused. A cartoon of the time shows him looking out of a window at a gathering of citizens waving placards saying 'goodbye', '*totsiens*', '*hamba kahle*'.

'Why are they here?' he asks an aide.

'They have come to say goodbye, Mr President,' responds the aide.

'Why, where are they going?' PW asks.

There was a dreadful sense of *déjà vu* in 2007 as Thabo Mbeki moved towards his closing months as leader of the ruling African National Congress. The parallels with PW Botha were painfully apparent. Here was a leader with a divided following, peering uncomprehendingly through the window as his vision, hopes and legacy slowly crumbled.

The story of Mbeki's term as president of South Africa is fraught with contradictions. Purportedly a pragmatist, he followed a zealously ideological position in nearly everything he did. Supposedly a reformist, he bent to his will the carefully crafted constitutional consensus that was the basis of the new nation. An intellectual man, he was also a calculating operator. Described alternatively as 'business friendly' or 'betrayer of the working classes', he was neither. His interests lay in power and the achievement of his urgent vision of what South Africa, indeed Africa, should be about.

Under the guise of what was called a national democratic revolution, Mbeki carefully and skilfully consolidated his power through the constitution and all the institutions of state. His objective was control of the political processes in South Africa, and he set out to eliminate or marginalise opposition. His was not a democratic project. It was a power grab.

His long-term objective, this book will controversially propose, was always the creation of a *de facto* one-party state run by the ANC. In this he succeeded. It might also have been his intention from the beginning to create his *de facto* extended presidency, or it might merely have been expedient when he saw power within the party shifting to a detested rival. It is unimportant. As Mbeki approached the end of his office at both party and constitutional level, he was fully committed to outstaying his welcome – a not unusual event on the continent.

How was this extended presidency to be achieved?

His first objective was consolidation of his personal power at all levels and through all the interstices of private and public life. Thus we will trace his systematic programme of centralised control of the party, seizure of the bureaucracy and the relegation of parliament to an adjunct of executive power. Next we will look at his challenges to the pillars of the constitution: the courts, media and independent investigative bodies. Parallel with this was the introduction of a nursed culture of insult and belittlement regarding critics, black or white, diffident or strident.

While securing or diminishing the institutions, his tandem focus was the co-option of what he considered to be key allies. On the one hand was the seduction of the business community: successful in the early days of his tenure but less so as his economic and political kingdom came under mounting challenge. On the other hand was the creation of a broad client base consisting of, firstly, a new black 'middle' class created by a growing economy and the racial re-engineering of the economy, and, secondly, the one-third of South African households that were poor and dependent on state handouts for survival.

These allies, believed Mbeki, would be bulwarks against the opponents he most distrusted: an autonomous militant unionist movement, uncontrolled local-level 'populist' civil movements and the omnipresent communists.

With this programme completed, Mbeki and his allies believed, the way would be open for an extension of his personal power – either through a constitutional amendment to give him a third term as president or, more nuanced, the continuation of the exercise of power by remote control, through the party. Here, I will suggest, were two possibilities: the Putin Option or the Obasanjo Option.

The Putin Option was the restructuring of the state to create a powerful new position of prime minister, so as to allow Mbeki to continue controlling the levers of power. This idea was floated in 2006 and then with greater urgency in 2007 by the Mbeki inner circle. The Obasanjo Option was more nuanced and therefore more dangerous. In essence, it involved the transfer of effective control of the state from a constitutional locus of power to the party itself. The scheme, however, required a pliant constitutional head of state prepared to play second fiddle to the party leadership. This he sought in the bevy of faithful but largely quite ineffectual women ministers he had cultivated.

Subsequent to the schism in the ANC between the Mbeki and Zuma factions, the Mbeki supporters sought to explain his desire to retain influence on the party for longer than two terms as a response to the risks posed by the accession of a 'populist' Jacob Zuma to office, with all the implied perils of financial indiscipline, capital flight and corruption. This is not correct. The Zuma opposition was the unanticipated and unwelcome creature spawned by the Mbeki plan, not its catalyst.

Yet the grand Mbeki plan came to nothing. In one of the most remarkable developments in post-liberation South Africa, Mbeki was repudiated by the majority of his own membership at a watershed party conference in Polokwane on 19 December 2007. The rejection was particularly galling when the ANC Women's League ignored his long record of advancing gender rights and voted narrowly to reject him. If he had been relying on some residual ethnic solidarity from the Xhosa-dominated Eastern Cape, he was disappointed. The ANC alliance under Zuma, a Zulu, made material inroads in the ANC structures there as well.

After Polokwane, Mbeki's cabinet was effectively purged from the senior decision-making bodies of the ANC, and his appointees to the public service found themselves in the firing line. When Mbeki created his one-party state, he never anticipated that he would lose control of that one party and that this, in turn, would split the bureaucracy. It did, as so often happens in such systems. In 2008, then, South Africa was in the uncomfortable position of having an ANC in power, represented by the constitutional president, and an ANC in opposition, represented by the party president.

Why did this happen? How *could* it happen after all the planning and manipulation by an otherwise very astute politician with all the levers of power at his disposal for an unbroken period of eight years prior to Polokwane?

At a technical, catalytic level it can be explained by a series of events that triggered a mass revolt within the ANC. These included the manifest failure of the Mbeki government to rise to the challenges of creating a modern state that could deliver on its promises. This translated into the catch-all phrase of 'failure of service delivery' (dealt with in detail in Part II).

The precipitators of revolt also included the suppression of internal critics; the widely perceived abuse of state power to advance personal political agendas; the aloofness and quasi-intellectualism; the failure to get to grips with the major issues of concern to ordinary South Africans; and, above all, the serial failure of his administration to meet any of his key targets regarding growth, jobs and poverty reduction.

But underlying it all was a more elemental conflict between what I would call ANC Classic and ANC Lite. This battle culminated at Polokwane. Classic routed Lite and the country was set on an even more uncertain path to the future.

ANC Classic represents the true heart of the movement. It is the poor and the dispossessed. It is the privileged labour elite represented by the trade unions. It is the civic organisations, youth movement, traditionalists and some elements of the old internal resistance, the foot soldiers of the United Democratic Front (UDF). To this lobby – it is too inchoate to be called a movement – certain business personalities, academics and the communists, eternal fishers in troubled waters, attached themselves. It is a broad front, riven even now with personality disputes and entirely bereft of a unifying ideological position, other than a vaguely defined socialism and the dread necessity of denying power to Mbeki in order to prevent him exercising it.

ANC Lite is a smaller, more focused group. It consists of the new elites created by Mbeki's aggressive system of affirmative action and state patronage. It operates in the spaces created by the opening up of the economy to black South Africans and the appropriation of the state organs by Mbeki's faction of the ANC. It has little intrinsically in common with the poor. It has behaved with reckless ostentation, much to Mbeki's despair, and has alienated significant sectors of the broader society. So out of touch was ANC Lite with the feelings of ordinary black South Africans that until very late in the day its representatives, including some of the brightest black analysts in the media, dismissed Zuma as an aberration in the modern history of the ANC rather than what he has proved to be: its emotive heart.

So what divides ANC Classic and ANC Lite?

It may be easier to begin with what does not. Neither group is committed to the founding principles of the South African constitution. ANC Lite, despite its protestations, has waged continuous overt or covert war against the principles of an independent and professional public service, judiciary, prosecutorial arm, parliament and media. ANC Classic, to the extent that it has any coherent programme at all, promises to continue the struggle on all these fronts, just more so.

Mbeki closed down the Heath Commission, a highly successful independent anti-corruption unit, and ANC Classic voted to close down the Directorate of Special Operations (DSO), the Scorpions, the investigative arm of the National Prosecuting Authority (NPA), and enfold it in the South African Police Service (SAPS). As the former had a conviction rate of 85 per cent against the latter's 6 per cent, and with the incumbent commissioner of police facing corruption charges, it is not too hard to divine a political motive for the proposed undoing of the Scorpions.

If one charged Mbeki with ignoring the constitutional precepts for an independent and professional public service, the same charge would have to be levelled against ANC Classic. Hardly had the dust settled on Polokwane than ANC Lite appointees in the public service were being rooted out in favour of ANC Classic loyalists. Patronage is mobile and malleable: it flees from point of power to point of power at the drop of a conference vote. Both ANC Classic and ANC Lite believe fervently that the party is the government, which is the state. The only major point of dispute is not *whether* the ANC is the state, but *which* ANC is the state.

Both ANC Lite and ANC Classic believe in big government. The Mbeki administration devoted 50 per cent of the national budget to welfare; quadrupled the number of welfare beneficiaries in four years; in some respects sponsored a new middle class of two million black people through affirmative action interventions; sustained a labour relations regime so anti-employer as to be restrictive; consistently increased state expenditure at a rate double that of growth in gross domestic product (GDP); and presided over socially rather than economically driven inflationary wage increases for a decade. It has provided up to fifty kilowatt volts of free electricity per month and water up to six thousand litres per household. The administration built 2.4 million new houses between 1996 and 2007, installed 4.7 million fixed telephone lines, many to poor homes, and electrified 3 million homes by 2000, again most of them poor. Hospital treatment and education below a certain income level is free. When ANC Classic says it does not intend to change the economic principles of ANC Lite, it is probably being truthful. What *more* could a populist government do than Mbeki has already done?

Neither can one argue a moral differentiation. For every person with a criminal record, dubious past, dismissal under a cloud of suspicion or pending criminal charges serving in the new ANC Classic executive, there is an equal number in ANC Lite who have prospered under the protection of Mbeki's administration: the health minister allegedly expelled from Botswana for stealing patients' effects; the police commissioner who retained his post for twelve months after the president was repeatedly told of his alleged connections with crime syndicates; the clutch of ANC parliamentary fraudsters who got away with a slap on the wrists after fiddling travel allowances, to name but a few. At most, one can argue an equivalence of amorality between Classic and Lite.

Lastly, both ANC Classic and Lite have failed to grasp the essential dilemma of post-liberation South Africa. It is not ideology or ideas or money that is in short supply (although the latter may soon become a constraint). It is the failure of the society as a whole to transform itself to a new level of modernity. This transformation, the real one as opposed to the diversionary one represented by racial head counting, requires a set of new skills, disciplines, ethics, attitudes, focus and commitment across the board. The shift from Lite back to Classic does not presage this but rather the reverse: it simply means more money pumped into increasingly under-delivering state entities, more funding for the growing dependency society. The only outcome will be ever more ludicrous comparisons with our peers in terms of per capita investment versus per capita social output. ANC Lite under Mbeki did not advance South Africa's path to modernism – it diverted it. ANC Classic under Zuma in its present conformation threatens to reverse it.

If one wants to find differences between Classic and Lite, one looks to only two things: the *style* of leadership and the *mechanism* for expropriating and transferring wealth from the historic wealth-owning classes to the wealth-seeking classes.

Mbeki's aloof and querulous style failed to unite his country and even less his party. That is the simple fact. His tenure ends with a more divided society – racially, ethnically and class-based – than it began with. Even if one accepts the argument that social revolution demands forceful leadership, he has failed to keep a unity of purpose, even within his party, let alone the country. Mbeki's sin, then, was not merely the failure of his own leadership, but the even more serious one of failure to facilitate a successful leadership after his departure.

It is this failing, intensely personal, that opened the gap for a deeply flawed but serviceable individual such as Zuma to make his play in concert with what has perceptively been called the Coalition of the Walking Wounded. Zuma does not bring visible principle, ideas or vision to the issue. He is not even particularly respected by his peers. If anything, he is a default choice of all those arrayed against the Mbeki bid for a life presidency. But Zuma does bring personality, simplicity, approachability and a neat turn in campaign songs to a nation tired of angst, lectures, opacity, ineffectuality and aloofness. It will do for the short term, possibly the very short term.

Subsequent to the Polokwane conference there has been a noble effort by the country's professional optimists to see the bright side. Polokwane, the line goes, showed the inherent strength of the democratic instinct in South Africa. A despot was in the making. He was stopped by the force of democratic resistance. It is a warming theory and quite untrue. Apart from the fact that the deformities of the constitution ensured that less than 0.008 per cent of the population actually got to vote directly for the next potential president, democratic process can only have value if it has democratic outcomes.

The truth is that Polokwane did not represent a fundamental, generational step-change of the ruling party from its struggle past and its incompetent, corrupt and patronage-soaked present into the era of modern governance. To borrow a phrase from the *Rocky Horror Picture Show*, it merely took a jump to the left. ANC Classic assures that South Africans should expect to look forward to more of the same. South Africans should believe this.

It would be wrong to elevate economic differences between Classic and Lite to the level of principle, but it does have resonance for those black people seeking the best and most efficient way to access wealth and opportunity. ANC Lite favours a combination of state redistribution of resources through taxation, together with a redistribution of wealth, sponsored by the private sector, to the favoured elites. This resulted in rent taking at all levels by the privileged elites and hugely increased the income gap between rich and poor black people. ANC Classic, befitting its name, favours an emphasis on reallocation of resources through traditional instruments of the central fiscus: taxation and semi-nationalisation of public entities. It is really a question of degree, and the fact that as many 'careerists' sit in the new ANC Classic executive (indeed, some of the most egregious examples of all) as once sat in the ANC Lite executive means that anybody looking for a quantum shift to *ethical* government is likely to be disappointed.

In his introduction to the Human Sciences Research Council's *State of the Nation 2007* anthology, Roger Southall perceptively notes that the consequence of Mbeki's policies has been 'the increasing domination of the highest organs of party by a state, technocratic and empowerment elite which, appropriating the badge of racial entitlement, is engaged in a project of blatant accumulation, if divided about which champion to follow.'[2]

There is a last issue. If Classic and Lite may be divided by personalities and constituencies but not by policies or principles, there is one dark thread that binds them together. It is what has been generically called the 'arms scandal'. In the early years of ANC rule, certain very highly placed individuals became involved in a set of corrupt relations with arms dealers for the purchase of an array of sophisticated weapons the country neither needed nor could afford.

In an instant, this 1998 deal transformed the new South Africa, with all its promise and hope, into a very old cliché. It was all there: the newly liberated country, the corrupt politicians, the middlemen, the shady arms merchants, the cover-up, the subversion of the checks and balances of the infant constitution. It was tiresome and shaming beyond description. It was, in every imaginable sense, the most grievous betrayal of everything for which the liberation movement had stood. This transaction also remained the ANC's greatest burden in power. To coin an appropriate simile, it became like the unexploded Exocet missile still lodged in the hull of the ANC many years later. The deal and its aftermath claimed reputations and careers, including Mbeki's. It is not finished. It may not even have begun. It remains an uncomfortable secret between ANC Classic and ANC Lite: a shared past indiscretion between two now bitter adversaries, neither daring to detonate the charge for fear of what might happen. It runs as a subtext to everything that follows.

*   *   *

The ANC, an old and venerable institution in opposition, assumed power in South Africa on 10 May 1994 as the senior partner in a government of national unity, much to its own surprise. It had waged a resistance campaign against white rule in South Africa for eighty-two years when it came to office. Thirty-four of those years involved armed resistance.

The call, when it came, arrived quickly. With the transfer of political leadership in the ruling National Party from PW Botha's old regime to a born-again reformer, FW de Klerk, in January 1989, the stage was set for a radical change of plan. The key drivers of reform in the old elites – the military, Afrikaner intellectuals, progressive business and the public-service technocrats – were merely waiting for their chance.

This reformist instinct, all but ignored in the shallow, apocalyptic reporting of the era, was irresistible. The tip-over point, if one wanted to find it, was somewhere in the mid-1980s, when white Afrikaners became the community with the biggest average per capita income of any population group. Here, at last, was the matured result of the Afrikaners' march to modernity: a wealthy, educated, cosmopolitan and flexible community with the capacity for compromise. It was this group which, on behalf of its people, had finally realised the compelling absurdity of a handful of whites attempting to guide the destiny of a country in which the majority of citizens were black. Rather turn the burdens of government over to others better equipped, so as to better concentrate on the pursuit of wealth and lifestyle, they argued. 'Stand by for the biggest outsourcing exercise in this country's history,' a senior Afrikaans business leader once cynically remarked to me.

The missing catalyst for change, however, was a sense of security among the white community so that it could contemplate the surrender of state control. The external requirement for security was met when the Soviet Union retired from regional conflicts in the late 1980s and early 1990s, at which point the white minority could engage with the legitimate representatives of the black South African majority, without fear of annihilation. Had that not been possible, white South Africans would simply not have negotiated. The outcome, if one wants historical parallels, would have been a Middle East or Balkans scenario – a violent and destructive equilibrium of impotence.

The internal requirement was met with the almost total destruction of the ANC's capacity to prosecute an armed struggle. Infiltration of the ANC cadres and the efficacy of brutally repressive measures by the regime persuaded the ANC of the importance of at least exploring the prospect of a negotiated settlement. The white elite, wisely, did not insist on an *a priori* cessation of armed struggle before negotiation. Both parties accepted the risks of negotiating in conditions of an undeclared truce. Superb leadership on both sides pulled it through – albeit only just.

With external and internal security largely assured, the South African government withdrew a decade-long and virtually unimpeded military presence from Angola, participated in a settlement in Namibia sponsored by the United Nations (UN) and immediately began a negotiated revolution at home with the most legitimate opposition. In little under four years, the same South African military helicopters deployed in southern Angola against Cuban and Angolan government forces were trailing the new South African flag over the Union Buildings at the inauguration of President Nelson Mandela, the country's first leader who was both black and popularly elected. It was a stunning example of the right leadership in the right place at the right time, with the right mindset.

The details of the constitutional negotiations and the very many challenges along the way – some of them violent – need not detain us here. The main point is that the settlement reached was quite rightly lauded internationally for three main reasons: it was led by mandated leaders of integrity on both sides (two-thirds of the white minority had voted in a referendum to surrender political power to the black majority – one of the few times in history that an economically and militarily dominant minority chose to do so); it was transparent (tediously so); and it was home-grown. There was no smiling foreign head of state standing paternalistically between Mandela and De Klerk as they shook hands.

This has critical importance for the future of South Africa. No party can claim that a negotiated settlement or the constitution was foisted on the citizens or that they were not party to its outcomes. There can be no quitters. This high degree of consensus thus gives the South African constitution a compelling authority, equalled probably only by that of the United States. Its defence, viability and integrity is not an adjunct to the new order in South Africa: it *is* the order.

The general elections in 1994 were predictable in their outcome: the ANC won a massive majority but not enough to change the constitution, while the major opposition groups had just enough of a stake in the regions to make matters work. It was a generally well-run election (apart from a localised wildcat strike by some of the electoral commission staff, who wanted more pay before their liberation could commence) and infused with the deepest emotional resonance across the country. I chose to spend election day in Thokoza, one of the most violent Johannesburg townships in the years leading to the transition. It was a moment of inexpressible satisfaction to witness this triumph of the will, the mind and the spirit against the extremist forces that had come so close at times to derailing democracy in South Africa.

A few weeks later, President Mandela was taking the oath of office before a generally tearful country and indeed world. And that, really, is when the ANC began its long and unfinished walk to becoming a political party in the government of a modern state, as opposed to a resistance movement in exile. The Mandela years, rather forlornly remembered by many as the era of hope and by others as the time of naïveté, were to end with an impeccable transfer of power to a successor.

Mandela's personal choice as his successor – if not then, certainly later – was Cyril Ramaphosa: former unionist, chief negotiator at the constitutional talks and a consummate diplomat. But the party's vote went to Mbeki, the chief speech-writer for the iconic ANC leader in exile, Oliver Tambo. Ramaphosa subsequently became a very rich man and ducked a return to the political fray in 2007 when the party was faced with a choice between an impossible incumbent and an unthinkable successor. He later went – unsuccessfully – to help Kenya find peace. Mbeki went on to become the president of South Africa.

In its early years in power the ANC was remarkable for the way in which it kept its unity and its purpose, despite all the distractions and temptations of power. For those of us in the media it was in many senses an inspirational era. Here was a new government, fully aware of the burden of history and the future placed on its shoulders, doing everything possible to address the concerns and challenges of the times. It was a season of promise that infused everything, and even though there was confusion and spontaneous disruption, it was within the context of creating the groundwork for what all believed must be a more noble future. It was a Prague Spring.

It was also the time for reflection and reconciliation. The Truth and Reconciliation Commission, flawed in many ways, still helped move the country forward. Had it been introduced fifteen years later, when memories should have cooled and prejudices waned, it would most likely have blown apart what is left of the country's fragile consensus. Such has been the contribution of the Mbeki era to a common appreciation of what it means to be a modern South African.

The ANC inherited by Mbeki was the standard cliché: a 'broad church'. The relentless levelling effect of apartheid forced a false unity of viewpoint on black South Africans. Yet, even while the oppression was at its highest, when thousands languished in detention, the deals were being cut, the fortunes being made, the social striation of the black community taking shape. When the ANC took power in 1994 it brought three traditions to the fore.

The first was the embedded black resistance to white dominance that had expressed itself in a thousand ways through the decades. This was the tradition of black humanistic and liberal opposition; the traditionalist rural opposition to both white rule and modernism; a pan-Africanist strain of anti-imperialist defiance against racialism and capitalism; youth revolt and resistance by a small but growing black middle class outraged by the insult of racial exclusivism. This rich mix of resistance traditions was a constantly moving feast. It cropped up here in certain circumstances and there in others. It was the equivalent of the Afrikaner commando: elusive, penetrating, irritating, ever present, irrepressible, incapable of being ignored. Many of the courageous exponents of these traditions were to find themselves in South Africa's prison system. When they emerged many years later, they brought with them a remarkable degree of insight and leadership; in many ways, it was an indispensable element of the cock-tail that was to become the transition.

The second tradition was that of systematic internal resistance, which first began in its modern idiom in 1973 with the surge of strike action by disempowered black workers, and continued with the growth of internal resistance from the civic movements through the late 1970s and into the 1980s, fuelled by the 1976 student uprising in Soweto and culminating with the birth of the UDF in Cape Town in 1983.

This was the internal resistance, the real resistance, in all earnest. It challenged the system at all points and face to face: in wage talks, campus confrontations, rent and service boycotts, street marches, strikes and 'mass mobilisation' campaigns. On a daily basis it looked into the eyes of the opponent and learnt through two states of emergency and limitless strikes and civil protests both the efficacy and the limits of the power of repression. From the crucible emerged a rough and very ready understanding between the dispossessed on the one hand, and business and state power on the other. This engagement was the father of the social and political movements among both black and white that eventually created contemporary South Africa.

To a very large extent it operated independently of the ANC. Expedience, time and poor communications made it impossible to create a national surge of resistance: interaction between an ANC in exile and the resistance traditions internally were of necessity tenuous. The deep-seated sense of personal deprivation, particularly among young black South Africans, and not ANC organisational genius eventually contributed most to the quiet revolution.

The third tradition was that of the exiled ANC. This influence resided in two areas. The first was its engagement with the supportive governments and academics of both communist and non-communist countries, through which it was able to influence the imposition of international measures of ostracism on South Africa. The other element of the ANC in exile was the sharp end of the resistance: the military. This component of ANC power was in some instances both brave and resourceful. In others it was divided, incompetent and infiltrated. In any event, it was not *successful*.

During one of my visits to the ANC in exile I was wryly assured by a very senior commander in the armed wing that I should not worry unduly about an armed revolution. 'If one started we would probably be the last to get there,' he admitted.

Indeed, the armed struggle was so unsuccessful that to a large extent it hampered rather than expedited an earlier political settlement. The crushing defeats inflicted on it by the South African security forces and the paucity of visible successes merely increased white complacency and played into the hands of the regressive elements of the security forces. Mercifully, the white leadership recognised the opportunity created by the collapse of the Soviet Union and the black majority leadership conceded that the armed struggle was failing. The struggle was quietly retired with all appropriate honour.

This outcome was positive in that it accelerated the search for a political solution, but was also negative in that both sides were left with an uneasy feeling of unfinished business, rather like Germany in 1918. This was not a crushing defeat of one side by the other. It was a truce in which *post facto* glorification would weave its rich tapestry. There is nothing wrong with this, as long as it takes place within a settled environment, based on a common vision of the future. If not, it becomes the source not of reminiscence, but the fuel for a further round of triumphalism and idle boasting.

The point is that when Mbeki came to power in South Africa, he instinctively chose to rely on those with whom he had most affinity: the exiles. His support base was primarily among those who had operated in the rarefied atmosphere of academia and the international resistance circuit.

This will remain one of the enduring mysteries of the triumph of Mbeki. He represented a faction of the ANC that had contributed little to the resistance struggle and had a marginal or at least limited impact on the progress to the negotiated surrender of white political power.

In his book *Shades of Difference: Mac Maharaj and the Struggle for South Africa*, Padraig O'Malley paints a convincing picture of the fatal delusion whereby the ANC in exile concentrated almost entirely on the armed struggle, at the expense of the other major social and economic points of challenge to the regime.[3]

Thus, when the Soweto uprising occurred in 1976, the ANC in exile was oblivious to the moment and its import. It had caught up to some extent by 1983, when the UDF established itself in Cape Town. Two years later, the ANC branded the strategy 'ungovernability', although all sorts of people had been calling it that for a long time.

According to Maharaj, 'The masses were ahead of the ANC, but that did not mean the ANC had no strategy or that our strategy was wrong. Sometimes things on the ground ran ahead: sometimes Lusaka ran ahead. People on the ground fleshed it out in their own way, sometimes so fast you didn't know how to catch up with them.'[4]

In an attempt to bridge the gap between its external element and the internal dynamics, then ANC president Oliver Tambo sanctioned Operation Vula in the late 1980s, a programme to set up functioning internal ANC leadership within South Africa. Its foremost operator was the courageous if maverick Maharaj, but his frustrations were only beginning. Put simply, there were not too many in the ANC leadership willing to forsake their safe havens abroad to infiltrate what to a considerable number was by then a foreign and dangerous country. Maharaj did, and when the movement was legitimised and peace negotiations began in 1990, he was one of the few ANC military operatives illegally and clandestinely in South Africa. He was arrested on 25 July 1990 by the South African security police, which had just uncovered Operation Vula.

The early days of the negotiated transfer of power were a time of extraordinary delicateness. The De Klerk government was convinced the South African Communist Party was attempting to hijack the process from the African nationalists and convert it into an armed coup. The ANC was equally sure that the De Klerk government was arming Zulu nationalist groups to wage war on ANC supporters within the country.

Maharaj's arrest coincided with this moment. The ANC moved quickly to distance itself from the Vula operation. In fairness, many of the senior members probably were not aware of it, given the obvious need for total secrecy. However, no bail was put up for the defendants and a number of senior ANC members in the negotiating teams put it out that Vula was an unmandated operation launched by Maharaj.

The importance of all this is to illustrate the simple point that, at the moment of greatest political opportunity in the life of the ANC in exile, its cadres were wrong-footed, divided, uninformed and hesitant. Why then did they end up playing such a major part in the future of the country? How did this 'Bolshevik' element (in terms of its size and not necessarily its ideology) occupy the high ground or, in the words of one commentator, seize victory from the jaws of the internal movements? The answer is complex, but necessary to understand Mbeki's subsequent actions.

The initial point of contact between the regime and the ANC had in fact been with Mandela in prison. This had caused huge concern to the ANC in exile and the internal parties, but as the progress of these contacts accelerated, all parties were subsequently drawn into the loop in some way or other. It was in this flurry of activity that some emerged winners – Ramaphosa made a stellar rise in the movement, nudging out the diplomats like Mbeki and the soldiers like Maharaj. Thus it was Ramaphosa who ended up holding the megaphone when Mandela made his first public speech in Cape Town after his release from prison on 11 February 1990.

Still, over the long haul, it was the exiles' victory. Why?

First, the South African security establishment, steeped in conspiracy theories, clearly thought the ANC in exile had more of an influence on events than history reveals. It would therefore make sense for the white minority to engage this group most closely in negotiation rather than the internal resistance groups. There was also a brutally pragmatic reason: the exiles still held the threat – if not quite the reality – of renewed armed insurrection and should therefore be engaged and neutralised as soon as possible.

Second, the ANC in exile, largely under Mbeki's suasion, had begun a major marketing campaign directed at the white elites from the mid-1980s onwards. It had worked. Top businessmen were enthused by the old-worldliness of Oliver Tambo and the pipe-smoking affability of Thabo Mbeki. I well remember the almost schoolboy braggadocio accompanying the early foreign forays by the private sector to Lusaka, Dakar and London.

Finally, steeped in revolutionary traditions and having learnt at the knee of the old Eastern European communist security services, the ANC in exile was a past master at all the black arts of subterfuge, deceit and propaganda. This experience did not go amiss as the Mbeki Ascendancy, the tight group of ideologues and executors who banded around Mbeki, began building its power base.

When Mbeki eventually assumed the mantle of authority, he was intensely aware that he came from a tradition far removed from the experiences, world view and insights of the internal resistance, and, indeed, much of the South African populace. He and his closest advisors were the outsiders. This was to influence much of his thinking and underlie his first and most immediate task: taking control of the organisation.

In the eyes of Mbeki's supporters, the necessity for this action was self-evident. The ANC, it was frequently put to me by his supporters in the early days, was an organisation capable of demonstrable discipline and resolution when required. But it was also fatally prone to self-doubt and division.

It was, however, a mark of the peculiar paranoia of the Mbeki Ascendancy that such divisions could not come as a result of its members following their own volition, genuine differences of opinion or the weaknesses of the organisation itself, but had to be incited.

Thus a range of enemies was conjured to account for factionalism within the movement: the white minority, media, leftists, capital, non-governmental organisations (NGOs), foreign governments, the US, dissident factions, AIDS zealots, the CIA, rivals for office and so on. In my dealings with President Mbeki while editor of the largest newspaper in the country, I could never but be impressed by the surpassing creativity with which he sought conspiracy in every adversity, agendas in each criticism, malice in every disagreement.

The tragedy was that it was all so unnecessary. Media monitoring agencies at the time gave consistently high ratings to positive news carried in the media about the government. Mbeki may not have enjoyed as high a personal profile and enthusiasm as Mandela, but in the early years of his tenure he was well respected, and in many instances supported by a broad range of media, black and white.

It was only later, after much wasted witch-hunting, that the leadership identified the real problem in the ANC: the irresistible opportunities for self-enrichment created for the party rank and file through the networks of privilege established by patronage, 'empowerment' and the appropriation of the state institutions by the party. Typically, Mbeki and the ANC leadership would bewail the spirit of 'careerism', corruption, self-enrichment and entitlement eroding their once proud movement, but would not acknowledge their part in creating the culture and the structures that made it all possible.

That the ANC was indeed a potentially fractious host is indisputable. The incentive for disloyalty and self-enrichment was enormous, and Mbeki must often have been struck by the irony whereby his predecessors had been able to keep order in a time of powerlessness, while he had to manage only disorder in a time of power. Tight discipline and effective action were always going to be essential in transforming this group from its resistance traditions and polyglot political cultures into an effective political party operating in a modern state.

He had two options. He could establish a clearly defined code of expect-ation and ethics and act promptly, ruthlessly, transparently and consistently against offenders. Alternatively, he could act on an ad hoc basis against certain individuals, do it surreptitiously within the confines of the organ-isation and then, when challenged, smother all debate. The former is the style of successful modern political parties. The latter is that of authoritarian states. The Mbeki Ascendancy, tragically and misguidedly, chose the latter. Thus he and his lieutenants – in particular his ferocious janissary and former revolutionary bed-sit mate, Essop Pahad – spent the time running themselves ragged trying to root out subversion and revolt wherever it was suspected, while failing to build a common platform of trust and understanding within the organisation and its allies.

In his majestic biography of Mbeki, Mark Gevisser draws the distinction between Mandela's utter confidence that he had the good wishes of both friend and foe when he went into office, and Mbeki's deep sense of insecurity: 'He carried that anxiety, that heaviness with him into power – a hunched, sceptical counterweight to the inspirational "free at last" optimism of Mandela – and would never be able to release it.'[5]

Mbeki's plan of control was to be realised through three simple devices. The first was to establish control over all political appointments. The second was to run any potential contenders for succession off the ranch. The third was to create a culture that would discourage dissidence or even debate.

The defining moment in regard to the first device was in August 1998, when the party's national executive committee (NEC) agreed that premiers of the country's nine provinces should be appointed by the president. This was later extended to the mayors of the biggest cities and other key appointments. The step had been made almost inevitable by the roiling series of bitter, personal and often violent conflicts that had erupted at provincial and local level between ANC claimants for office and patronage. Part II of this book looks at the impact this had on the quality of service delivery to ordinary South Africans, but it is necessary to note that had the ANC leadership *not* acted, there is every likelihood that the entire second and third tiers of civil administration, apart from the major centres where there was a sufficient countervailing force of professionalism and modernism, would have collapsed.

The problem, as always, was a lack of consistency by the Mbeki Ascendancy in dealing with culprits and the manner in which such action was communicated. Increasingly, the willingness of the Ascendancy to deal with corruption by some people and not others, those within the inner circle, led to a growing credibility gap that culminated in the ultimate crisis for the party in December 2007.

The *communication* of reasons for such actions was also enormously deficient. This was due to a simple fact, which became more evident as time went on. The ANC, precipitated into being the ruling party of a comparatively modern state, was, to put it baldly, an organisational mess for the duration of the Mbeki tenure. It had seen a significant escalation in members from 416 846 in 2002 to 621 237 in 2007 – largely the result of the scramble for patronage among the rank and file. Its investments had also grown to R1.75 billion by 2007 – a not inconsiderable amount for a political party. Yet it was still not *capable*, except in very rare circumstances, of hosting debates about key ideological and ethical issues among the grassroots membership, let alone 'the masses', and least of all able to deliberate sensibly on the reasons for actions against this or that individual.

In 2005, ANC secretary general Kgalema Motlanthe delivered a scathing report on the state of the ANC to the organisation's national general council. A few quotes suffice: 'In many of our branches there are no sustainable political programmes and community campaigns'; 'conflict ridden and unstable and fraught with fights over leadership positions, selections and deployment'; 'the problems rest primarily on the preoccupation on the part of the public representatives with securing access to and control of public resources'.[6]

This was the Achilles heel in the Mbeki dream of creating a unified, compliant, obedient and respectful organisation. When the final count was made at Polokwane and Mbeki was reduced to the definitive lame duck, he would confide that all his woes began when the party structures failed to explain properly the reasons why he had fired Jacob Zuma, his deputy, in June 2005. There is a simple and universal rule for successful authoritarianism: it has to run deep and it has to run tight. The chaos in the ANC structures could guarantee neither for the Mbeki Ascendancy, and thus Mbeki fell victim to the most dangerous of all authoritarian delusions: the belief that the command fosters the fact. This was as true for his remit within the party as it was as president of the country in relation to the public service, as we shall see later.

If Mbeki was to an extent a victim of circumstances in regard to the inability to impose authority on the ANC, he was entirely culpable in regard to the consequences of his actions when it came to securing continuity of credible leadership within the movement to which he professed such devotion. This went to the heart of his determination to leave no rivals standing.

In April 2001, then minister of safety and security, Steve Tshwete, made the astonishing public claim that a triumvirate of the old ANC stalwarts – Cyril Ramaphosa, Mathews Phosa and Tokyo Sexwale – were planning a 'coup' against President Mbeki and that he was in some sort of personal danger. It still remains difficult to get to the bottom of the claim. Was this Gang of Three involved in subversion? Treason? Just a little party politics? If the latter, why on earth were the police involved? Tshwete, a fierce Mbeki loyalist, was afflicted by many disadvantages and was, to use the English euphemism, often 'tired and emotional' in the exercise of his public duties. This clearly did not disqualify him from senior service in Mbeki's cabinet and neither, obviously, did it prevent him from making these astonishing claims.

Subsequently it was discovered that the allegations arose from a discredited member of the party facing criminal investigation for corruption in regard to a public office he had held. The source was therefore disreputable and the messenger largely insensate. Who, then, the author? We will probably never know who within the Mbeki Ascendancy thought this was a good idea, but the reality was that it backfired in spectacular fashion.

The response from the public, ANC formations, trade unions and civil society was of such a nature that Tshwete, instructed by his patrons and seizing a rare moment of lucidity, apologised and backtracked. However, the source of the decision to reveal the 'plot' remained unidentified and the ANC, fearful of the ramifications, covered it all up. In so doing, the ANC made a fateful error, and one that was to characterise its rule for the decade. It postponed the tough call. It papered over the cracks.

The intention of the statement, one must surmise, was to fire a warning shot across the bow of the most visible, popular and credible likely opponents to Mbeki for his second term of office, which was then still three years away. It may have done so in the short term, but the long-term results were incalculable. Two of the senior members of the ANC's NEC instructing Mbeki post-Polokwane on the conduct of state affairs are ... Sexwale and Phosa.

A senior ANC member once told me privately that the handling of the 'plot' was the beginning of the parting of the ways between the conscience of the ANC and its president. It was not merely the crassness of the attempt to neutralise putative opponents. It was the use of state power to do so that aroused so much concern. This was in 2001. Much water was yet to pass under the bridge, but in its usual timeless way on this continent, the response would come, and it would be certain.

Having been rebuffed in this attempt to wipe out the pool of potential rivals through innuendo, the Mbeki Ascendancy began a more nuanced and longer-term project to make it almost impossible for possible successors to compete. This relied on exploiting a very important protocol within the movement. Like all clandestine organisations, not least one that had operated underground for thirty years and more, unity of purpose and internal cohesion were paramount. This led to a practice, call it an article of faith, that competition for office should be conducted in very precise and formalised ways.

Open competition was branded 'careerist' and the overambitious culprit would risk discounting him- or herself from ever holding senior office. Feeding into this were elements of traditional African respect for age, seniority and position. It was to a large extent this manner of internal election by anointment that maintained the remarkable ANC cohesion for all those long years in opposition and into the party's second term in power. In modern politics, the concept that open competition for office should be discouraged is the very antithesis of democracy – the system in which ideas and track records can compete so that informed choices can be made.

It was this protocol that was seized on by the Mbeki Ascendancy and deliberately distorted to imply there should be *no* discussion of succession at all, except within the highly controlled parameters set by the Ascendancy itself. A better recipe for the unfair advantaging of incumbents can scarcely be imagined.

It was because of this that the competition for leadership of the ANC, and in fact the proxy leadership of the country, degenerated into confusion, illuminated only occasionally by farce. While all competitors faithfully insisted they were *not* running for office, they in fact were. Policies became submerged in rumour and rational debate took backstage to increasingly vitriolic personality politicking between ostensibly non-competing rivals. The vast South African public, watching this with a mixture of incomprehension, exasperation and contempt, not surprisingly called down a plague on all their houses and marked the institution of party democracy one notch down.

The only person who openly challenged the process was Sexwale, who publicly declared that he would run against Mbeki in the 2007 leadership contest and actually went out on what would amount to the only modern hustings campaign in the entire 2007 leadership battle. He was one of the very few who could give the finger to the Ascendancy. A former military commander who had been one of the minority actually involved in armed activities against the security forces inside South Africa, he had been captured and imprisoned. Later he had served with distinction as the premier of South Africa's wealthiest province, Gauteng, and then moved into business, where he rapidly became a multimillionaire.

He was thus untouchable and it is probably because of this that he was to endure an almost ceaseless stream of smears, leaks and innuendo from the Ascendancy, alleging criminal activity in his past. It did not work. He ended up on the newly constituted NEC, while the authors of the campaign against him found themselves without jobs.

Meanwhile, the hounding of any potential candidate for high office that did not meet the approval of Mbeki and his associates created a pressure-cooker atmosphere within the movement and caused some of its leading lights, mostly from the UDF tradition, to leave in disgust, while the balance sharded into innumerable conspiring, leaking, trouble-making factions. Eventually, they coalesced under the battle flag of Jacob Zuma and threw out Mbeki.

In this endeavour they were enormously helped by powerful allies in the form of the communists and the unions. Both had their own interests. The communists had always regarded themselves as the vanguard of the struggle and deeply resented their relegation to praise singers for the ANC leadership. The unions, likewise, believed they had greatly contributed to the building of the internal resistance, only to be cold-shouldered at the moment of crowning achievement. This injury was made worse by the fact that union membership had been declining through the decade, with only the public-service unions showing any growth.

Overlaying this authoritarian approach to dissent within the party was the extension of a blanket of intellectual intolerance, which for a period smothered open debate, not only within the party but also within academia and the media and even the broader society.

The premise was simple. If one was black and a member of the Mbeki Ascendancy, one was entitled to an opinion; all others were not. The binding core of this sole orthodoxy was markedly different from the rich intellectual and cultural traditions of earlier black resistance.

The intellectual orthodoxy which the Mbeki Ascendancy assiduously cultivated as an instrument for its seizure of power and influence at all levels of society was a grim and foreboding place for the mind to be. It was a world inhabited by conspiracy and clanking chains and iron ceilings. It held an ever-present fear of what others had done in the past, were doing or would do. It starts from an assumption of weakness and proceeds in a cloud of negativity, hatred and suspicion. It purports to arm the soul and mind of black people with the guidance necessary to find their place in the world. In effect it does not do that at all. It makes them eternal slaves to the machinations of others (whites, imperialists, neo-colonists) and, if anything, simply perpetuates the very intellectual dependency it presumes to dispel. It is not the way modern people approach the world.

It does another thing: it creates a wall behind which all forms of iniquity, sloppy thinking, depravity, sloth and criminality can flourish. It creates sectors of society that are royal game – never to be challenged, inquired after, restrained or chastised. By the compelling logic of *reductio ad absurdum*, those who attempt to do so are either racist or the tools of racists. Along that road, as we know, lie book burnings and death camps.

When historians look back on this period of South African history, they will no doubt marvel at how such a pre-modern way of thinking could have been elevated to almost a state religion in what was supposed to be Africa's pre-eminent modern state. They will ask, as some did of the apartheid era during the Truth and Reconciliation Commission, what was the society *doing* to allow such a manifestly deforming intellectual orthodoxy to come to fruition under Mbeki?

The obvious aside, it is a difficult question to answer. After liberation, South Africans were so busy trying to put new things in place, fix old ones, get to know each other, make money, preserve wealth, enjoy new experiences, have a good time, be nice, get one up on the other guy, that they failed to notice this insidious menace creeping up like a mist out of the valleys.

The origin of this peril cannot track to any one individual. Mbeki must take some responsibility. The orthodoxy underlined much of his speechifying, albeit at a very sophisticated level. His chief lieutenant, Essop Pahad, was a key proponent and implementer who lacked the sophistication. My earliest experience of him was when I was requested, as political editor of the *Sunday Times*, to have our Moscow correspondent research some newly released Kremlin archives on developing-world countries.

Our interest, obviously, was the connection between the old communist regime and current South African personalities. The request mysteriously ended up in Pahad's hands and then as the lead story in the South African Communist Party newspaper, naturally redolent with warnings about police agents and subversive plots. It was my first lesson in the double standards of historical inquiry. It was plainly acceptable to investigate the past of some people through the Truth and Reconciliation Commission, but not that of others through archival research. The entire incident did not bother me in the slightest, but it was an early introduction to the Mbeki Ascendancy's intolerance of the wrong sort of inquiry.

Clearly, it served the interests of a great many in the liberated South Africa to adopt this limiting dogma. It protected failing public servants, corrupt politicians, avaricious beneficiaries of Mbeki's style of affirmative action, among others. But by the time the society had woken up it had embedded itself as a universal way of thinking, and only a few very courageous people were prepared to take it on.

One of those who did was Xolela Mangcu, one of the foremost black intellectuals in the country and a constant critic of what he calls the 'racial nativism' of the Mbeki ideology. In his book *To the Brink: The State of Democracy in South Africa*, he argues that it was this nativism which brought intellectual traditions to a crisis point.[7]

Perhaps the most chilling example recounted in his book was Mbeki's

35

attacks on the integrity of Professor Malegapuru Makgoba, the scientist who headed up the Medicines Control Council, the statutory body set up to oversee the testing and quality of medication in South Africa. The attack, bizarrely, was an attempt to force Makgoba to agree with a group of discredited HIV/AIDS sceptics and to allow distribution of a so-called AIDS cure that was subsequently found to contain industrial solvent. To his credit, the doctor refused to be browbeaten, but the incident had a most uncomfortable similarity with Stalin's irrational and catastrophic support for genetic quackery in the 1930s.

In retrospect, it is a wonder that such an astute politician as Mbeki believed he could hold the line indefinitely by means of intolerance and the suppression of debate. The only basis for the miscalculation was what affected his judgement on all governance: an arrogant assumption that his views were not only right but *must* prevail, and to the extent that they needed to be conveyed at all (most were not) that this would be done through a competently functioning party structure. In this he completely misread his constituency and overestimated the capacity of his organisation. It was neither silent, informed nor acquiescent, and although it took a long time to arouse itself – after all, it had elected Mbeki back into office for a second term, although by then it was fully aware of his failings – when it was roused, it acted. Mbeki would pay the ultimate political price.

CHAPTER 2

The deployees' playpen

In my country, as in yours, public men are proud to be servants
of the state and would be ashamed to be its masters.
— WINSTON CHURCHILL[1]

'DEPLOYMENT' IS A TERM USED WITH GREAT AFFECTION BY the African National Congress. It refers to the assignment of loyal supporters to areas of key influence: parliament, the public service, business, scientific bodies, sporting associations, NGOs and so on. It has a comforting sound of order, planning and discipline. It suggests structure and expectation and outcomes. In fact, it is none of these things.

Early deployees rapidly created a life of their own, and, as the headlong race for entitlement and enrichment speeded up under the Mbeki administration, the notion that the ANC could retain control of these far-flung emissaries became laughable, as it must in any modern, fast-evolving society. Public servants became more interested in their personal emoluments and bonuses than in slavish support of the ANC's policy direction. Businessmen became rich and drifted reluctantly back into the fold only when it was time to show a face. Party luminaries were rapidly snapped up for boards and senior jobs in the private sector, where their interests ran more to the next golf day and the annual results than to the plight of the unemployed poor. At local government level, the main interface with the populace, the deployees leapt at each other's throats in competition for office from the moment the starter's gun was fired.

Deployment is an old-world, statist view of the way that modern societies function, but on its back the principles of an independent and professional South African public service were effectively crippled. It was not transformation, but deformation.

This process is often confused with the parallel one of affirmative action or empowerment. They need to be separated. The ANC government's affirmative action programme, particularly under Thabo Mbeki, involved the replacement of white public servants with black ones at all levels of the structure. The increasing representation of black people in the administration was both necessary and indeed essential for the building of legitimacy for state institutions. The manner of achieving it, however, was destructive.

It became an open-ended, numbers-driven scramble for position and patronage in both public and private life. It became appropriated by beneficiaries and racial ideologues and developed a momentum that was divorced from economic reality: the capacity of the state to accommodate it or the skills requirements of a growing economy. It was, at least at the level of implementation, as misdirected as the implementation of Grand Apartheid half a century before. Purely on the basis of race, it sought to deny the country the opportunity to maximally utilise its most scarce resource, namely human talent, both apparent and latent. The effect of this on South Africa's infrastructural and institutional capacity is dealt with in depth in Part II.

The political and cultural transformation of the state was something altogether more profound than the affirmative action component alone. It entailed the reshaping of the bureaucracy to expand the remit of the public service from serving a privileged white elite to serving all members of the population. It required a change of culture, focus, resource and imagination. Above all, it required the highest level of skills, adaptability and experience. It was without a doubt the most important process in post-liberation South Africa, and on its success rested the hope for progress to a successful modern state.

By 2004, the ruling party's programme of appropriating the state bureaucracy was all but complete. At national, provincial and local levels, ANC-appointed public servants were in office, if clearly not in charge. When Mbeki spoke of the state, he actually meant the ANC. And when he referred to the government, he was talking about the ANC. With a 70 per cent majority in parliament, control of the public service, political control of the parastatals, presence in a range of sporting and cultural bodies and an increasing network of cronyistic appointments into the heart of the private sector, he could be well satisfied with having created what amounted to a *de facto* one-party state in a very short space of time.

But hardly had the edifice been crafted than it began to crack, as it inevitably would. The reasons were simple. The ANC did not have the skills base to control its own party efficiently, let alone the nation. Secondly, the deployment of inexperienced party figures into public-service offices led to a diminution of the offices themselves. This was particularly true at local government level.

The involvement of the ANC itself in the acquisition of state contracts, much of it managed through front companies, created its own tensions as opportunity and conspicuous wealth went the way of the insiders in the Mbeki Ascendancy. It was not by chance that one of the first things ANC Classic did when it got back into the driving seat was to launch an 'asset assessment' of ANC investment holdings. The more cynical saw it as a chance for those denied access to the trough in the first round to get their crack in the second.

The failure of party deployees in their public-service roles quickly mounted. The instinctive response of the Mbeki administration was simply to deny that any problem existed. Various directors-general were fired or reassigned, some big-city administrators were moved on, but the principle of deployment did not cease for a moment. If anything, it speeded up, and the appointments sections of newspapers grew fat year after year as the state endlessly kept searching for affirmative action alternatives for the staff that had to be replaced.

It was only when the results of the policy became apparent in systemic failures in the delivery of services to the public, roughly coinciding with Mbeki's second term of office, that the administration began to wake up to the fact that it had a crisis on its hands. By then it was to all intents and purposes too late, at least for Mbeki. The public outrage triggered by the failures swept him away and replaced him with the coalition of ANC Classic. The latter's view on the question of deployment is unlikely to change, for the obvious reason that a number of their senior executives are living testimony to the personal benefits to be derived from the practice.

But the most serious effects of deployment were to be found when the one party in the one-party state fractured in the run-up to the 2007 leadership elections. As the bureaucracy turned to counting who was pro-Mbeki and who pro-Zuma, the already weakened professionalism of the public service took another nosedive. As directors-general hedged their bets by avoiding action on divisive policy issues, the very function of public service became imperilled.

This tension was most acute in the security services, as one would expect. Here the battle revolved around a highly professional corps of investigators, the Directorate of Special Operations, under the auspices of the National Prosecuting Authority. The group, popularly known as the Scorpions, had been involved in all the high-level investigations into corruption and crime syndicates. Their work had targeted a number of prominent ANC politicians and public servants, and by early 2008 two were in the process of being prosecuted. One was the leader of ANC Classic, Jacob Zuma, and the other was Jackie Selebi, head of the South African Police Service, a senior ANC personality and the first chairman in the history of Interpol to have been forced to resign over allegations of criminal activities.

The political contours of the subsequent fight are simply traversed. Mbeki clearly had an interest in seeing Zuma in jail rather than in the presidency. Zuma, contrarily, wanted to see the Scorpions out of business and the charges against him dropped: he in any case always maintained the whole thing was politically inspired by Mbeki to keep him out of contention. Logically, then, after its victory in Polokwane, ANC Classic pushed vigorously for the Scorpions to be closed down, while Mbeki fought to retain its function in some form or another.

The case involving Selebi was more confused. The Scorpions had been gathering evidence for some time that the police commissioner was consorting with international criminals and was, in fact, aiding a number of illegal enterprises. Their efforts to have him arrested, however, were thwarted by Mbeki on several occasions, culminating in the remarkable suspension – though it was effectively a firing – of Vusi Pikoli, head of the prosecutorial service, in late 2007. The reasons for Mbeki's dilatoriness on the Selebi issue are uncertain, other than his instinctive dislike of having to fire incompetent people who are black (firstly), in his faction (secondly) and while under pressure (thirdly).

An alternative conclusion is alarming: that Mbeki needed to protect Selebi for some nefarious reason and therefore not only kept him in office but also misled the country when he claimed nobody had brought him evidence of Selebi's wrongdoing. The claim was rebutted in an eighty-one-page sworn affidavit by the acting head of the NPA, Mokotedi Mpshe, who pointed out exactly when Mbeki had been informed and of what. It was yet one more blow to an already shattered presidential credibility.

Selebi did eventually end up in the dock, but before this could happen a cabal within the police, supported by members of the intelligence services, launched a bizarre attempt to have the lead Scorpions investigator arrested on trumped-up corruption charges – which were summarily dismissed. Selebi also went to the High Court to apply for an order halting the investigation against him and preventing the Scorpions from arresting him without first giving him a chance to consider the evidence – surely one of the few times in the history of jurisprudence that a suspect asks a court to prevent the legal process. His bid failed.

Were not the fate of a floundering democracy at stake, it would all be hugely entertaining and rank among the best of crime thrillers. Leaving aside for the moment the question of guilt or otherwise, the saga illuminated some vital issues around the state of Mbeki's Political Kingdom.

Firstly, it illustrated the ease with which state machinery could be manipulated to serve the interests of one or other party. Mbeki used his executive office to fire the country's chief prosecutor and Selebi used his men to arrest the chief investigator into his alleged crimes. The consequences of such actions are incalculable. The Mbeki administration will forever be held to have abused state power in pursuit of political foes. This is less important for what it does to the reputation of one flawed politician than it is for the implications for the institutions themselves.

Secondly, the saga of the Scorpions revealed how ineffectual Mbeki had become in controlling his own *de facto* one-party state. His efforts at intercession ranged from the diversionary to the malicious. In the absence of any firm leadership on the issue, the problem bounced unhappily between courts, individuals, party congresses and parliamentary committees, each telling of the tale revealing new twists and gobsmacking allegations.

Thirdly, it showed the extent to which the system of patronage had developed within the Mbeki state. Were it not for the determination of the Scorpions and relentless media coverage, it is entirely likely that Selebi would still be nestling warmly in the bosom of the Mbeki state and that of his suspect friends – he confirmed, incidentally, his personal friendship with the kingpin of an alleged drug-smuggling ring.

Fourthly, it illuminated the grim legacy of the Mbeki state. The ANC majority in parliament forced safety and security minister Charles Nqakula to announce the disbanding of the Scorpions by June 2008. Mbeki launched a last-ditch attempt to have elements of the DSO incorporated into a new super-investigatory body, but, as this would fall under the inefficient and often corrupt SAPS, it was hardly an encouraging proposal. The mere fact that such an important organ of state with a demonstrable record of success could be made the football of whim, expedience and prejudice was an indication of the fragility of state institutions fourteen years into ANC rule. And it is to these institutions we now turn.

CHAPTER 3

Unchecked and unbalanced

All modern revolutions have ended in a reinforcement of the power of the State. — ALBERT CAMUS[1]

IT DOES NOT TAKE A POLITICAL SCIENCE 101 LECTURE TO KNOW that out-of-control executives in constitutional states are kept in check by four things only: an informed and vigilant polity supported by a competent press, a strong and incorruptible bureaucracy (especially the security forces), an independent parliament and a fearless judiciary with integrity.

Together with Part II, this section of the book deals with the erosion of integrity in two of these institutions during the Mbeki era. Parliament retreated under his suasion and the public service became an adjunct to his party, a diminishingly competent one, but an adjunct nevertheless. The third aspect, an informed public, probably qualifies as a half-won contest. The judiciary, the last pillar of the democratic state, has become the new front line in the assault by demodernising elements of society.

In the nation's founding constitution, South Africa's parliament was conceived as a citadel of power. Although composed of representatives drawn from various political parties, its role and primary function in both intent and early practice were to act as a check and balance on executive power.

A central element of this power was to be exercised through the range of parliamentary committees set up to maintain oversight of state functions and legislation. In ideological terms, the constitution had all the right elements. It suffered, however, from some fatal defects.

The most problematic was that the electoral system of the country, agreed to by all parties, was a pure proportional representation model. This affords every party contesting the elections a chance of being represented in parliament. This was crucially important at the outset to ensure that the country did not have a winner-takes-all approach, which would inevitably have favoured the ANC. Through the proportional representation system, the first post-apartheid parliament was able to represent effectively the balance of the electorate's voting intent.

The weakness of the system, however, is that it means no parliamentarian is accountable to a particular constituency. Members of parliament are simply ranked on a party list and, depending on the apportionment of seats after each election, are either called to higher service or relegated to some or other sinecure job. This process places enormous power in the hands of the party bureaucrats and – inevitably – immeasurably strengthens the hand of a political leadership intent on consolidating its personal power. In other words, it exacerbates factionalism and cultism within the ruling party.

The first weakness of the South African parliament, then, is that it is simply not accountable to the electorate that put it in place. This has led to a widening gap between legislators and the public, and heightened already existing tensions between an aloof executive, an absent representation and a seething following.

The gap between the two grew over time. This lack of accountability was aggravated by the blatantly undemocratic principle of 'floor crossing'. This mechanism, whereby a member of parliament can periodically choose to switch allegiance to another party without losing the seat, was initially agreed to by all. Subsequently, when it was seen to be the cynical device for buying parliamentarians that it is, attempts were made to change the system. This was rejected by the ANC, and for good reason. By enticing parliamentarians with offers of secure seats and government posts, the party was able to swell its considerable majority. The minorities were weakened and the ruling party hardly strengthened by the sort of mercenaries who joined this migration of the political wildebeest. In total, it diminished the accountability of representatives and the aura of the institution.

The second problem about parliament was a universal one: skills. In his *Anatomy of South Africa*, Richard Calland of the Institute for a Democratic South Africa tracks the consequences experienced by the legislative heart of South Africa from the constant 'deployment' of competent parliamentarians into other 'untransformed' areas of society.[2] By 2003, 186 of the 252 strong crop of 1994 parliamentarians had been deployed elsewhere. This had only one effect: it took quality people who were doing a reasonable job of keeping an eye on the executive and put them into positions where they replaced often competent people who were of the wrong colour. It also reduced institutional memory in the legislature. Of the thirty-five members who had served in parliament's crucial Standing Committee on Public Accounts (SCOPA) – the institution's watchdog over the state's finance and probity – only nine returned for the second term.[3] The net effect was a weakening of parliament and little gain for the 'untransformed' sectors of government, other than finance and revenue, which scored some very fine talents.

'From 1997,' Calland observes, 'parliament entered a new phase, which one might, perhaps harshly, describe as the period of degradation, in the sense of "downgrading" rather than ruin.'[4]

This weakening of parliament led to a slow but inevitable decline in its capacity to exercise oversight. Under the withering and continuous fire of a rampant Mbeki Ascendancy, the legislature became less and less of a check and certainly nothing of a balance. By the end of Mbeki's tenure as ANC leader, parliament had so diminished itself as to be drawing from public polls the lowest integrity ratings of any institution in the country. Part of this, no doubt, was due to exposure of a material number of the ruling party's members as having been involved in a scheme to defraud parliament through manipulation of the travel voucher system.

Frene Ginwala was the ANC's first Speaker, until she was sidelined in 2004. Although a feisty personality, she failed to protect the integrity and independence of parliament to the required level, particularly in regard to the seminal arms deal inquiry, which will be dealt with later. Interestingly, she remained intensely aware of the dangers of irrelevancy courted by the institution during the latter Mbeki years. Increasingly, the legislature was subjected to acts of gratuitous insult from the executive in, for example, failing to answer members' questions or not arriving for committee sessions. Rather than being a process that Mbeki sought to control, the reverse was true. Neither was his disdainful treatment reserved for parliament. Increasingly, the ANC caucus within parliament was marginalised from consultation on vital policy issues that it was expected to defend in the chamber.

This juniorisation of a key institution was, however, to exact a heavy toll on the Mbeki administration. In the bitter contest for leadership of the ANC and potentially the state in 2007, the caucus became a crucible of power. When Mbeki lost his bid for a third term as ANC president to Jacob Zuma, all eyes turned to the parliamentary caucus. Would they remain loyal to the executive or would they support the party?

The answer was quick in coming. In the first weeks of its 2008 session, parliament and its committees launched scathing attacks on under-performing ministries and public servants. For a moment the earlier, headier days of non-partisan oversight of failing state departments had returned. Whether it would be a sign of a sustainable renaissance of this key institution or just another Prague Spring remains to be seen.

Meanwhile, it was enjoyable to see both ruling and opposition party members – as well as the media – climbing into subdued ministers, including the less than effective minister of health, Manto Tshabalala-Msimang, and Dali Mpofu, the imperious head of the South African Broadcasting Corporation (SABC).

While parliament enjoyed a resurgence of authority and influence in the interregnum, the media pursued its somewhat uneven trajectory during the Mbeki years, at times magnificent and at others guilty of the shallowest forms of pack journalism. Three features are relevant here. The first was a generalised blandness and incompetence that often gave grist to the mill of the Mbeki camp when they complained they always received a bad press. This was all too often the result of inexperience, haste and indifference. Sadly, not even the Fourth Estate escaped the weaknesses of all South African institutions.

The second feature was the sustained attempt by various political and other agencies to divide the media along racial lines. One of the biggest personal disagreements I had with President Nelson Mandela was his claim that black journalists who wrote critical comments about the ANC were tools of some mysterious cabal of white editors and news editors. Where such insulting nonsense could arise is difficult to determine, but I have my suspicions.

Such deliberate attempts at racialising the business of reporting on society was faithfully followed by others. Some in the Mbeki camp made a practice of calling blacks-only briefings. The Human Rights Commission under Dr Barney Pityana undertook a hopelessly botched investigation into the alleged prevalence of racism in the media, which came within an inch of blowing apart the fragile consensus that had just been reached in the newly created non-racial editors' forum.

But the third feature of the media, which arose from the second, was wholly uplifting. This was the emergence of an echelon of very gifted, courageous and incisive editors and columnists, predominantly black, who challenged with increasing determination the growing political and ideological totalitarianism of Thabo Mbeki and the moral turpitude and incompetence of Jacob Zuma.

This contest reached its height just before Mbeki's rejection at Polokwane when my old newspaper, the century-old *Sunday Times*, ran articles exposing a series of prior criminal, personal and administrative failures surrounding the health minister.

The immediate consequences – whether all connected or not is hard to discern – were:

- a police investigation into the 'theft' of the minister's medical files from a private hospital, with a corresponding warning that the editor faced arrest;
- a 'protest' by a civic organisation with close ties to the Mbeki camp, demanding that the editor of the *Sunday Times* be charged for crimes allegedly committed while he was a member of an ANC resistance group during the apartheid era (the contradictions here boggle the mind); and
- a threat by the minister in the President's Office, Essop Pahad, to withdraw government advertising from the newspaper.

It didn't take rocket science to work out the range of measures the aggrieved parties were prepared to take through state agencies to respond to a story that was never once contested in regard to its veracity.

By the end of his term, the Mbeki ANC was talking about a media tribunal to assure 'quality' of reporting. Little imagination was needed to see that this was heading for exactly the same sort of institution that the old apartheid ministers had unsuccessfully attempted to impose over many decades. This was one of ANC Lite's proposals that *did* survive Polokwane and made its way onto the to-do list of ANC Classic.

What was the effect of all this vituperation, smear, insult and intimidation?

In the early days of the Mbeki administration, I would venture to say, it deadened to some extent the tenacity and exuberance of media reporting on governmental failings, rather as had apartheid-era security legislation and the Inkatha Freedom Party's propensity for resorting to the courts at the drop of a hat.

But there was a broader dilemma than government merely being huffy. Whites did not want to be seen as unreasonably critical, for fear of being branded racist, and blacks did not want to be seen as traitors to the cause of solidarity. It is a mark of the maturity of the profession that these restraints have mostly been resolved and the media, on the whole, is a faithful if not always meticulous analyst and recorder of facts. The evident failure of the Mbeki Kingdom compelled that.

This is not to say that the South African media is harmoniously unified on all issues – God forbid. In early 2008 there was another attempt, almost anachronistic, to restart a forum for black journalists only. The bid probably says more about those who have fallen out of the mainstream of modern, non-racial journalism than it does about the media profession in itself.

The one major exception to this march to democratic modernity remained the state public broadcaster. After experimenting with various liberal and independent news managers, the SABC settled for a managing band of executives safely pro-Mbeki and not averse to using the institution to serve his interests. The issue came to a high point when it was revealed that the organisation had a blacklist of personalities that its staff could not approach for comment, because they were regarded as too critical of Mbeki and his administration. The repeated denials were confounded when one of the corporation's broadcasters refuted his own bosses live on air during one of his programmes.

The SABC also became a site of fierce contest for the appointment of a new board: one that had to be approved by the president. Despite the deepest misgivings by a whole range of parties, the presidency pushed for the appointment of Christine Qunta, arguably the most extreme exponent of Mbeki's strain of Africanist exclusivism or what academic Xolela Mangcu calls racial nativism. Her appointment became the centre of a struggle between the Mbeki camp and ANC Classic, particularly the unions, and she was eventually appointed as the deputy chair of the SABC board. Later the corporation would descend into a farcical round of firings and rehirings as top officials and board members fell prey to the ANC's internal wars.

But perhaps the most important and as yet unresolved struggle to emerge during the Mbeki era involved the South African judiciary, whose independence is entrenched in the constitution.

The judiciary could not escape the need for change in the new society and nor should it have expected to do so. At a functional level it was enormously strengthened by a Constitutional Court with wide powers of adjudication on issues relating to constitutional interpretation.

Like all South African institutions, the judiciary underwent a rapid process of affirmative action. In twelve years the proportion of white males decreased from 97 per cent to 47 per cent. In some cases, inevitably, the sheer pace of this process led to inappropriate appointments. In one instance in 2007, there was also a disturbing decision by the Judicial Services Commission, which appoints and monitors the conduct of judges, that effectively exonerated a black High Court judge president guilty of hearing a case after previously taking undeclared payments from one of the litigants. The commission declined to proceed to a full inquiry on the basis that there was insufficient evidence, although it was an outcome that divided this crucial body along racial lines.

But these setbacks were comparatively limited, and in general the judiciary, apart from some of its administrative offices, escaped the systemic weaknesses experienced by other elements of the judicial chain – police, prosecution and prisons – and, indeed, the failure of the state apparatus on a wide front.

It was thus all the more surprising when the Mbeki administration sought to push through the Superior Courts Bill and the fourteenth constitutional amendment in 2005, which many believed would effectively reduce the powers of the judiciary and make it more accountable to the minister of justice, in this case an utterly ineffectual person.

The ostensible reason was a desire by the state to have a greater role in tightening up and making more efficient the judicial process, but it gave enhanced powers to the minister to make rules and to the president to appoint acting High and Constitutional Court judges. The measures were rejected by the former chief justice and a battery of the country's most senior jurists – many of them committed members of the liberation struggle.

Given the demonstrable inability of the ANC government to manage state functions effectively, it was a somewhat suspect argument. The cynically minded pointed to a more likely reason: the Mbeki administration had repeatedly expressed its unhappiness about the lack of 'transformation' in the judiciary. Roughly translated, this meant irritation with independent judges, including those of the Constitutional Court who handed down rulings and orders against the government, of which there were many as the Mbeki state began unwinding. The judge who acquitted Zuma on a highly suspect rape charge would no doubt have qualified in the eyes of the Mbeki camp as 'untransformed'.

Fiddling with judicial independence is a two-edged sword, as Mbeki rapidly found out. Having constantly harped on about the untransformed nature of the judiciary since 2002, he was hardly in a position to mount a moral offensive against his arch-rival, ANC Classic, when it too began complaining about a judiciary not responsive to the will of society.

In this case, however, they meant a judiciary that had the undemocratic habit of convicting – and in some cases sending to jail – members of ANC

Classic's elites and unionised members of the working class. Worse, it was the same judiciary that would be trying their leader on corruption charges in 2008. It was thus not surprising that before and after Mbeki's political demise, union and youth elements of ANC Classic mounted full-scale attacks against the institution and in some cases the personalities of the judiciary – attacks that were (again, correctly) condemned by some of the country's most respected and senior jurists.

The political attack against the Constitutional Court worsened in mid-2008 when ANC Classic supported a judge president accused of attempting to influence the court in a matter relating to Zuma's corruption trial. The judge president, already once before the Judicial Services Commission on charges of failing to disclose an interest in a matter before him, branded the Constitutional Court judges 'liars'. ANC secretary general Gwede Mantashe reportedly called the judges 'counter-revolutionaries'. He subsequently denied this but his clarification was even more ominous than the initial statement.

The point is obvious. A decade of sniping, obstruction and in some cases subtle intimidation of the judicial arm by ANC Lite had opened the way for an even more virulent and dangerous campaign by ANC Classic to undermine arguably the last remaining uncontaminated bastion of constitutional power. Mbeki was the Trojan Horse by which this was achieved.

CHAPTER 4

Arms and the man

*There is no art which one government sooner learns of another
than that of draining money from the pockets of people.*

— ADAM SMITH[1]

T HE REASON I HAVE CHOSEN TO DEVOTE A CHAPTER TO THE
arms deal is simple. In essence, it represents everything that was
wrong about the Mbeki Ascendancy and the consequent damage caused
to the institutions of South Africa in pursuit of the narrowest and basest
political advantage.

It is also instructive in another way. The arms deal was a catalyst that
divided the ANC, terminated Mbeki's pretensions of further power, exposed
the fragility of the constitutional institutions and revealed the darkest side
of a political movement once rightly lauded as an icon of modern reform-
ism on the African continent. Its legacy will live on after Mbeki and will be
one of the first challenges faced by his successor.

Admittedly, the story is still only partly known. Powerful vested interests
prefer it that way. I did have an early insight when the tendering was still
in progress for this R29 billion (subsequently R43 billion) project for new
sea and air defence platforms. A friend who had once been in the US
government had been retained by one of the international tenderers as
a consultant. He and I met socially on a number of occasions while he
was in South Africa and then, one evening over dinner, he told me his
consortium was pulling out of the bidding. I asked why. Professionally
diplomatic to the last, he would only say 'something is going wrong here
and we cannot afford to be part of it'. That was the beginning.

The arms deal itself is a chimera. A defence review carried out soon after
the ANC came to power reached the conclusion that the military should be
revamped to focus more on internal and border security as well as peacekeeping missions in Africa. There was no mention of massive investment
in costly naval and aerial weapons systems.

Less than two years later, and with minimal debate, this position was overturned and South Africa was suddenly in the market for corvettes and fighter jets. While the military may well have rejoiced at the opportunity to refurbish its tired arsenal, the broader ANC was perplexed. Surely it was an agreed strategy to wind down defence expenditure in favour of social spending? Had not the defence establishment itself accepted that it did not need a capital acquisition budget of more than R8 billion in 1997? Why, then, a sudden budget for fighter planes and corvettes in the order of R29.8 billion which, with interest, would total about R43 billion at 2000 values?

In fact, they need not have worried. The government still kept defence spending a comparatively small component of overall state expenditure, by the simple expedient of subsidising its expensive and unnecessary arms acquisitions through degradation of the conventional armed forces to a point where they were barely able to sustain fourteen infantry battalions and had endless trouble keeping their peacekeepers equipped and fed.

Why, then, this expense?

The ANC has consistently defended the arms deal on the basis that it was necessary and would attract up to R110 billion in offset investments that would create 64 000 jobs. This system of offsets is a common and much abused system, whereby a defence contract with one country is accompanied by a series of complementary investments in the buying country. A mountain of evidence from past arms deals around the world shows that these deals rarely survive the arms-sale signing ceremony and invariably fall far short of the promise.

It was not that the government was unaware of the issues. An independent study commissioned by the government itself raised concerns about the affordability and desirability of the deal. The offset trade agreements were also evaluated and questioned. Yet it went ahead.

The charge against the ANC administration is that the deal was a means to enrich certain key people in the ANC hierarchy and the party itself. The chief culprit was alleged to be the late Joe Modise, a former head of the ANC's military wing in exile and South Africa's first post-liberation defence minister. He later retired from public life and accepted a position in the private sector involved in … the arms industry.

The most insightful story yet written on the issue comes from Andrew Feinstein, the former ANC senior representative on SCOPA and a prime mover for investigations into the deal. He was forced out of the ANC as a result and committed the tale to paper.[2] It is an extraordinary, fascinating resource and one of a crop of books by dissident voices from within the ANC ranks disillusioned with the Mbeki Ascendancy.

The central charges were that:

- Modise received between R10 million and R35 million in cash from a variety of the bidders;
- other key government players received millions in bribes; and
- the ANC may have received many millions more in campaign funds for the 1999 election.

The allegations first surfaced in parliament when Patricia de Lille, later leader of the Independent Democrats, a small opposition party, used the privilege of the house to make a number of allegations against various people. The matter was referred to the auditor-general, who duly tabled a report. It was, to use the cliché, a bombshell. The report (intriguingly since removed from the auditor-general's website) made the following points:

- potential conflict of interest between the head of the arms procurement process, Chippy Shaik, and his brother Schabir;
- irregularities in the process of approving the tenders;
- inadequate offset guarantees (the system whereby selling countries undertake to provide collateral investment to the benefit of the buying country);
- material deviations from standard procurement policies;
- an extraordinary decision to ignore pricing as a factor in accepting a contract for fighter aircraft, with the result that the country paid twice as much as it would have cost to buy the aircraft favoured by the military; and
- the acceptance of a foreign tender for a naval combat suite that far exceeded the price of a local vendor with the capacity to supply it.

A report of this kind from the auditor-general in any modern state would have hit every alarm bell in the country and demanded the fullest attention and commitment of government to resolve.

In South Africa, the reverse happened. To leap ahead of the story: attempts to investigate this astonishing tale of malfeasance so early in the life of the democracy (the arms deal went down virtually before any other major commitment of state resources by the new government) resulted in a cover-up of epic proportions that drove the small band of pursuers of the truth from public office and, in some cases, into exile.

Having received the auditor-general's report, the ANC study group within SCOPA resolved that this was a matter of both party and national integrity and that it had to be handled with the utmost transparency.

The group proposed the creation of a Joint Investigating Team (JIT) to pursue this looming challenge to the integrity of both the ANC and its leadership. In very short order Feinstein and the chairman of SCOPA, Gavin Woods, a member of the opposition Zulu-based Inkatha Freedom Party, had arrived at a non-partisan approach among the parties in SCOPA.

They also proposed that the key investigatory elements of this issue should be:

- SCOPA, a committee of the new parliament;
- the auditor-general, the ultimate defender of public probity in public accounts;
- the Special Investigative Unit (the Heath Commission) set up during the period of transition to investigate corruption in government and headed by a crusty white judge;
- the Public Protector, an office established by the constitution to investigate corruption in public office; and
- the DSO (Scorpions), the investigative arm of the NPA and specialists in high-level corruption inquiries (called in at a later stage).

To those who had stood with tears in their eyes at the birth of this democracy, this could have been its finest moment: the fearless investigation of corruption and the bringing of the culprits to justice through all the relevant organs of state. The Mbeki Ascendancy obliterated both the moment and the opportunity, and this will probably stand as one of the blackest marks against his presidency.

In quick succession, the ANC study group was instructed to terminate its non-partisan approach; the Health Commission was excluded from the scope of the inquiry and subsequently closed down; Feinstein was called into a meeting with Essop Pahad, where, according to Feinstein, he was famously asked, 'Who the fuck do you think you are?'; and all the forces of the Mbeki Ascendancy were mobilised to crush the investigation.

The Speaker of parliament, Frene Ginwala, withdrew her support for the project; Mbeki trotted out four of his most credible ministers to deny there had been any corruption involving the main contractors (nobody was prepared to vouch for the subcontractors); the Public Protector resigned under mysterious circumstances, to be replaced by a party loyalist who proved his worth by exonerating the ANC in a major party-funding scandal; and only the Scorpions managed to survive – for a while.

At the end of the day, a much watered-down report was produced by the JIT. A parliamentary committee hearing was held at which the ANC majority ran through a resolution accepting the key finding of the report, which read:

> The Committee accepts the findings and recommendations of the report of the JIT, in particular the finding that 'no evidence was found of any improper conduct by the government'. The irregularities and improprieties referred to in the findings as contained in the report, point to the conduct of certain officials of the government departments involved and cannot, in our view, be ascribed to the President or Ministers involved in their capacities as members of the Ministers' Committee or cabinet. There is [sic] therefore no grounds to suggest that the government's contracting position is flawed.

This extract from the executive summary of the JIT report was in such blatant contradiction to the numerous other findings of tendering malpractice that it immediately sparked a public outcry. An outraged tenderer was granted a court order forcing the government to disclose some of its documents, which revealed that the presidency had been involved in some form of editing the report and had insisted on the exculpatory clause cited above. The auditor-general vigorously denied that he had been pressured by the politicians to change his findings, and another round of legal action ensued between the auditor-general and the disappointed arms contractor.

But the proverbial cat was out of the bag. The issue moved into the courts, where this apparently flawless arms deal resulted in:

- conviction of the chief whip of the ANC, Tony Yengeni, for defrauding parliament by not declaring the benefit he derived from one of the contractors in the form of a discount price on his vehicle;
- the conviction and sentence of Schabir Shaik, the brother of the senior arms procurer, for a corrupt relationship with the deputy president (Jacob Zuma) relating to bribes from a French defence contractor; and
- arraignment of the by now former deputy president himself on charges of having accepted bribes from a principal arms dealer to cover up the initial crime.

The extraordinary thing about this whole saga was that the person ultimately in charge of the entire arms procurement programme on the government side signally failed to feature. In a puff of smoke, he largely disappeared, ensuring that a cast of thousands was left to answer the charges, deal with the inquiries, fend off the challenges, do prison time and go on television to defend their integrity. Who was this person?

Jacob Zuma was kind enough to reintroduce the maestro in the run-up to his court appearances. He was asked to comment on a letter he had sent to Gavin Woods, head of SCOPA at the time, containing a full-blown attack on the committee and a ringing defence of the probity and ethical standards of the arms industry. The former deputy president readily admitted he had signed the letter, but suggested questions should be addressed to its author. That person? Thabo Mbeki.

And thus Mbeki re-entered centre stage. It was he, the nation suddenly reminded itself, who had chaired the ministers' committee that had signed off on the deal and taken the final decision to go with the expensive British 'no cost' fighter option, compared to a cheaper Italian model favoured by the military. Although he claimed he could not remember meeting any of the representatives of the arms suppliers, subsequent evidence challenged this lapse of memory. The then ambassador to France, Barbara Masakela, later confirmed that Mbeki had met the French arms company's representative, and other evidence suggested he might have done so on three occasions. It is thus Mbeki who should answer both to the party and to the country for the whole mess.

But why this evasion of his responsibility, even to the point of writing a letter to a parliamentary committee under some other person's name? Why the reticence about admitting he had met the principals from one of the arms companies? Why, indeed, this massive attempt to cover up the scandal over so many years?

The charitable view is that the Mbeki administration, terrified at the damage this would do to the reputation of the young government, closed ranks and tried to keep it quiet. In other words, it was a misguided but still noble attempt (at least from the party's point of view) to salvage the reputations of the organisation and some of its old stalwarts. The less benign view was that it was done to protect wrongdoers up to the highest levels from having to pay for their criminality.

But perhaps another option presents itself. Feinstein recounts that a senior member of the NEC once confided to him that the ANC had to cover up the scandal for the simple reason that the arms suppliers had paid for the party's election campaign in 1999. Intriguingly, the ANC treasurer, Mendi Msimang, confirmed at the 2007 Polokwane conference that after the legendary fund-raising capacity of the Mandela era, the party went through 'the most difficult period in its financial life' around 1999. Certainly the ANC does not derive the money to build its R1.7 billion asset base from its rank-and-file subscriptions. Members' failure to pay dues is an endless plaint of successive secretaries general. The bulk of the ANC's income is from corporate donors, and increasingly there is evidence of ANC front companies with major government contracts. Is it possible that somewhere around 1999 the lure of easy money became compelling for a desperately cash-strapped organisation?

Certainly, the ANC and its organs have consistently proved willing to accept donations from less than salubrious sources. It is still resisting a demand by the liquidators of the Brett Kebble estate to repay millions of rands given to the party by the crooked businessman from his embezzled funds. The ANC did, however, confirm in 2007 that R11 million in election fund donations had been paid back to a donor when it was discovered the money came indirectly from a state agency. The deeply unsettling question was left hanging, however, as to whether the ANC was in principle opposed to accepting tainted money or whether this applied only when it was exposed as having done so. It has consistently refused to open its books for inspection, opposes tighter control on campaign funding in parliament, and in August 2008 again rejected calls for a judicial inquiry. Indeed, so opaque are the ANC's financial dealings through its front investment company, Chancellor House, that even its senior members know little about them. The new ANC executive has called for a full inquiry into its operations. The ghost of the Russian oligarchs thus hangs heavily over the Mbeki legacy.

If money was indeed accepted from the arms traders, it would account for the near panic in party ranks when the story first broke. If true, it would expose all the protestations of the ANC about honest and open government as a monstrous lie. It would also explain why there is such an extraordinary egg dance on the issue. Is it possible that neither Classic nor Lite can afford to tell the truth? Could it be that to do so would reveal that the resources they use to run their party to this day are built partly on criminal proceeds?

It is difficult to know where this story will go. Barring the subversion of the South African legal process, which is not impossible, Zuma will go to court. What he might say has the nation and ANC Lite on the edge of its seat. Meanwhile, investigations into the actions of the British fighter supplier have confirmed that, despite the lack of assistance from the South Africans, authorities in the United Kingdom are convinced that bribes and kickbacks did, in fact, pass to South African politicians, and that an as yet unnamed 'Mr Big' pocketed up to R25 million. German investigators have meanwhile closed their probe into the corvette deal, partly because of 'lack of cooperation' from South Africa.

In the fallout after Polokwane, the ANC ordered another inquiry into the arms deal. The proposal was immediately met with heated resistance from some members of the Mbeki Ascendancy who had scuppered the inquiry in the first place. It is tailor-made for the most horrendous internal party disputes. ANC Classic will no doubt seek to prove that Zuma was set up and is innocent or, alternatively, merely a loyal soldier trying to cover up this mess in the interests of party prestige.

ANC Lite will try to kill the process at what is really only the latest barricade before the advancing tide that first swamped Yengeni (out of prison after serving only four months of a four-year sentence, despite demonstrable parole violations, and promoted to ANC Classic's executive), then Schabir Shaik, doing a fifteen-year stretch while desperately trying to spend as much time as possible out of his cell and in private hospitals, and of course Zuma, the alleged ineffectual cleaner, who began the first of his new round of court appearances in August 2008.

Zuma has consistently cried foul while doing everything in his power to avoid his day in court – launching endless delaying legal actions and then complaining that the delays in bringing him to court are prejudicing his case. In early 2008 he travelled to Mauritius to urge the government and courts there not to release certain possibly incriminating evidence to South African prosecutors. Zuma's counsel has denied that this was the purpose of the visit, but, if it was, this benighted arms deal would have given South Africa yet one more cliché: the leader of the ruling party – and possibly future president – begging a foreign government not to assist his own country's prosecutors in their pursuit of a criminal case.

Nobody is under any illusions as to the damage this entails. It may explain why ANC Classic wants urgently to close down the Scorpions and perhaps, just perhaps, account for why ANC Lite wanted another term in office to deal with unfinished business – what *Business Day* editor Peter Bruce memorably called 'painting the house out before the next tenant'. The unavoidable result of all this was twofold. The current and putative leadership of the ANC destroyed its right to claim the respect of the nation. The institutions of state, judiciary excepted, are still painfully susceptible to political manipulation. This is a terrible legacy to bequeath to the nation.

The ultimate absurdity of the situation is perhaps encapsulated in two recent revelations.

The offset trade that was an integral part of the arms deal has failed to materialise at anything near the promise – as usually happens. The biggest victim has been the Coega Industrial Development Zone in the Eastern Cape, which has seen the delay or collapse of a number of offset projects. Power shortages now impose further constraints on those projects which were bought with such huge state largesse and have survived.

And the outgoing chief of the Air Force told a parliamentary committee in 2006 that the investment in the fighter aircraft was basically pointless. There were insufficient qualified engineers to maintain them or pilots to fly them at optimum operational efficiency. And so the cliché lives on.

CHAPTER 5

The denouement

I claim not to have controlled events, but confess plainly that events have controlled me. — ABRAHAM LINCOLN[1]

THE PRECEDING CHAPTERS HAVE SOUGHT TO SET THE CONTEXT within which the debacle of the Polokwane conference was to occur. The events leading up to it were a long time in the making, and the usurping of Thabo Mbeki's Political Kingdom was not something that happened by whim or passion.

In tracing the underlying causes it is necessary to distinguish between three powerfully running streams. One was rank-and-file unhappiness over failure of the administration to deliver on agreed policies. The second was damaging disputes about policy in three key areas: HIV/AIDS, Zimbabwe and economic policy, although this skirmish was waged more in the realm of perception than reality. And the third was the personality and style of the Mbeki Ascendancy.

It is arguable that had Mbeki the charm of a Jacob Zuma, had he stayed on the right side of the HIV/AIDS and Zimbabwe issues, properly explained economic policy and run a skilled administration, his Political Kingdom would have stretched happily into a third authoritarian term, with Mbeki as both party leader and constitutional president. Authoritarianism *per se* does not worry most people in developing states. Failure to deliver and injustice do, fundamentally.

Mbeki could offer none of the aura of a Mandela, but he could and did hold out the promise of technical and administrative excellence. If he could not charm his constituency and the country into liking him, he could wow them with his efficiency. He failed to do so, despite all the breathless enthusiasm of an initially beguiled media and business sector.

The reason: he attempted to be the technocratic leader while simultaneously obliterating his technical base through affirmative action and ideological overreach. The result was systemic failure through wide swathes of the administration. These failures most affected the broad support base of ANC Classic: it was, after all, the poor who suffered most from bad public education, failing hospitals and collapsed state attempts to encourage job growth. Crime affected all communities, the minorities more than others, but the poor were also intensely affected by the scourge.

However, the poor were also burdened much more than the rich by something else: corruption. This grassroots corruption was, to my mind, one of the great unwritten stories of the Mbeki era and, above all else, could eventually turn large numbers of the normally quiescent black working class against the ANC as a whole – whether Classic or Lite. The pervasive nature of this graft was exposed in a Public Service Commission report released in February 2008, which found that incidents of corruption had doubled and its cost increased by 186 per cent year on year. More worrying, only 18 per cent of perpetrators were ever fired.[2]

Nobody who lives and works in South Africa can but be aware of the burden, often anecdotally conveyed, that this pickpocketing form of corruption in the public service places on poor people.

When young men and women are working over weekends to raise money not to pay for a house, but to pay for the bribe to get onto the housing list, there is concern. When a young black entrepreneur making cardigans for security companies refuses to do business with state departments because of corruption, there is a problem. When poor squatter families are deprived by corruption of the money given to them via private-sector developers to relocate, there is danger. When a student is prevented from completing his studies because his grant has disappeared, there is threat. When hundreds of thousands of welfare grantees are regularly deprived of their entitlement because of corruption or its evil sister, incompetence, there is mortal peril. Taken as a whole, there is an incalculable burden of anger and cynicism building here, and because it is distant from the lives of the rich and the indifferent, it hardly gets a mention. Yet if not dealt with, it may become the greatest motive force for revolution – real revolution – in this country's history, which would sweep away ANC Lite with all its pretensions, ANC Classic with all its posturing, and indeed the South African state.

I have seen the inevitable consequence of this pervasive corruption in the many African countries in which I have worked. It is a deeply antagonistic, disempowered, angry and cynical electorate prepared to believe the worst of their leaders and their public service – usually with justification – and a propensity to resort to violence whenever it offers itself as a viable alternative. Kenya remains the living contemporary example of what happens when the elites survey the ship from the deck and not the hold.

The unhappiness with Mbeki's management of his mandate was therefore not about policy: he was as socialistic, welfarist and redistributionist as the next person, as succeeding chapters in Part II of this book will prove. The resistance raised by the alliance partners – the unions and communists – about the 'business' bias of Mbeki was thus a red herring. It could easily have been finessed away had the presidency been more accommodating. Finance minister Trevor Manuel's ill-considered comment when introducing the government's Growth, Employment and Redistribution (GEAR) programme – namely, that its principles were non-negotiable – would come back to haunt him. No serious attempt was made to bring the unions on board, and this is where the problem started. There was a second critical failure. The Mbeki Ascendancy simply did not deliver – at least not on the scale it recklessly kept promising.

The resolutions arising from the Polokwane conference when all the dust from the leadership fight began settling were interesting for how little they differed from existing Mbeki policy. In short, they called for:

- an extension of free basic education;
- an expanded mass-based literacy campaign;
- renewed efforts at promoting sexual health policies to combat AIDS;
- improved housing delivery and ownership;
- speeded-up conclusion to the land-reform process; and
- the disbandment of the Scorpions.

None of this was a ringing call to profound revolution. Indeed, the conference remained intriguingly quiet on issues like black economic empowerment (BEE), the cornerstone of Mbeki's racial re-engineering of the economy. While the conference was redolent with calls for greater 'participation' in decision-making and governance (a clear rebuttal of Mbeki's top-down approach), there was little discussion about the crux of the problem: the absence of the technical support base to drive limited, let alone extended, ambitions through.

There was an irony in all of this. One of the greatest impediments to implementation of Mbeki's grand social visions was the low quality of public service, itself largely a function of the deadening effect the relevant unions had on attempts to introduce discipline, professionalism and performance standards in the public service. Mbeki was thus hoist not by his own petard, but by one created by the unions – who then blamed him for lack of delivery.

But if Mbeki was caught in a conundrum not entirely of his making in regard to delivery, he was entirely responsible for misreading the key issues that concerned his constituency.

The first was the question of HIV/AIDS. The impact this had on health care is dealt with in Part II, but it is necessary to note here that the *political* effect of his failure to take control of the issue was devastating in regard to his personal popularity. AIDS was not an academic construct, as Mbeki continually made it. Nor was it something distant from the lives of millions, as Mbeki suggested when he said he did not know anybody who had died from AIDS. This denialism, defined as a persistent refusal to acknowledge mounting empirical evidence, led to a number of the original romantics and idealists of the early ANC deserting the party, while others joined the growing wave of anti-Mbeki populism.

The dissatisfaction focused on his choice of Manto Tshabalala-Msimang as his minister of health. A colleague of old and a fierce loyalist, she was also a desperately flawed personality with an attitude to the disease that verged on voodoo. She was deeply disliked by her department, the health profession, the medical industry, the pharmaceutical companies, the hapless patients in her hospitals and the AIDS activists. In fact, her ability to unite the entire sector against her was nothing short of inspirational.

Suspicion about her capabilities was not allayed when it was reported that she had once been convicted in a Botswana court of stealing patients' effects while they were under her care, and had been deported. It was also claimed that she had received a liver transplant while still an unreformed alcoholic, in contravention of public health policy, and had been a less than accommodating patient in hospital. These allegations could have given Mbeki the opportunity to remove and replace her with a competent minister. He did not do so. On the contrary, he again went to bat for a horribly flawed colleague, thus deepening popular resistance.

These errors were compounded when he fired his minister's deputy, a person much admired by the anti-AIDS lobby and health professionals, on the flimsy grounds that she had abused the cabinet travel policies by going to an overseas conference without permission. The real reasons were not hard to find. She had bucked the Mbeki–Tshabalala-Msimang orthodoxy on HIV/AIDS and had exposed the ministry to embarrassment when she expressed outrage at the number of infant deaths occurring in an

Eastern Cape hospital, due to gross dereliction of nursing duty. For the heresy of admitting error in the Mbeki administration, Nozizwe Madlala-Routledge was fired in August 2007.

Mbeki's second major misjudgement was in his approach to President Robert Mugabe of Zimbabwe. Mbeki's remorseless opposite number effectively reduced a once prosperous country to chaos and economic devastation over just fifteen years of concentrated ideological madness. During his entire term of office, Mbeki repeatedly refused to publicly condemn Mugabe's actions and held out the promise of some form of negotiated settlement in the neighbouring state – so often did he hint that settlement was around the corner that it became a standing joke in local and international quarters. Settlement prospects rose in mid-2008 but Mbeki had by then dented his image through serial rebuffs by Mugabe. The March 2008 elections descended into a violent farce when Mugabe refused to go. Mbeki sought to entice him with the offer of a power-sharing deal. The Zimbabwe crisis showed Mbeki at his most indecisive and ineffectual.

The Zimbabwe factor was initially sidetracked in South Africa, as the focus was on Mugabe's unlawful seizure of white-owned farmland. This action deeply agitated white South Africans and the international community, but would have had little impact on the broad ANC constituency: opinion polls showed a material number believed it was all a rather good idea.

Where Mbeki erred was when Mugabe's actions started veering into a terrain sensitive to ANC Classic. When he began arresting and suppressing trade unionists, deported a visiting South African trade union delegation and ordered the demolition of urban shacks housing the poor because they were considered politically hostile, the image resonating with most ANC supporters was apartheid. It was not merely the *fact* of the actions that disturbed them. It was that Mbeki refused to condemn them. If he could condone steps like this in Zimbabwe, what might he do at home, they asked.

The fears were, of course, overdrawn. If anything, Mbeki's manner of dealing with Mugabe stemmed from his ill-judged aversion to supporting any criticism of a fellow African head of state, for fear of being seen to side with 'racist' Western viewpoints. It was the sort of blind and conscienceless toleration of iniquity through a misplaced sense of racial solidarity that risks keeping Africa forever marginalised.

It also led Mbeki and his administration into a series of other mis-judgements in international affairs, which left even South Africa's staunch-est friends bewildered. A 2007 report by UN Watch, an NGO watchdog on voting trends by countries within the UN, ranked South Africa the 'chief villain' among democratic countries when it came to voting on human rights issues in the forums of the world body.

The report listed South Africa as having supported repressive regimes in Sudan, Zimbabwe, Belarus, Cuba and Myanmar. The claims drew a furious denial from the South African Department of Foreign Affairs, which alleged that many of the resolutions were imperfectly worded or addressed to the wrong forum – a legal nicety that had never bothered the ANC when the organisation was considering anti-apartheid resolutions.

Certainly, the deeply held view in the developed world was that South Africa was voting not on principle, but with anybody and anything that was against the United States. This was not the basis for a credible foreign policy, and patience with South Africa through a whole range of multi-lateral organisations was wearing extremely thin by 2007.

It is almost certain that these issues of foreign relations played no part whatsoever in the minds of the delegates at Polokwane. Why should they? Such matters were distant, arcane and immaterial to their everyday experience. But Zimbabwe was just across the border. Mbeki's failure to deal with the issue had seen waves of desperate refugees crossing the border into South Africa, giving rise to tension, xenophobia and competition for scarce resources. It had also brought crime. Whatever Mbeki's motives were in regard to Zimbabwe, the consequence did nothing to feed his popularity among ANC Classic.

But, in fact, all these issues of delivery and policy differences merely masked the true precipitating factor for the denouement at Polokwane in December 2007.

That factor arose in June 2005 when Mbeki summarily dismissed Jacob Zuma as deputy president of South Africa. The ostensible reason was that he would be facing charges for corruption in regard to the ill-fated arms deal. The action was in the best interests of good governance and was hailed as such locally and internationally. Such acclaim was premature.

Mbeki's public explanation for Zuma's dismissal immediately rang hollow for many in the ANC – the insiders who knew the trademark of the Mbeki Ascendancy – and it became increasingly threadbare as time went on. By 2007, leading up to the Polokwane conference, the reasons were so worn as to be hanging by a thread.

First, the dismissal of Zuma was a remarkable action by a president who had done more than anyone else to attempt to subvert the inquiry into the very scandal for which Zuma was now being hung out to dry.

Second, it subsequently became apparent that the president had done everything possible to impede the Scorpions' investigation into other players in the scandal. Why was Zuma not afforded the same protection?

Third, this prompt action against his deputy stood in stark contrast to Mbeki's later refusal to act against the police commissioner on the basis of far more compelling evidence of corruption.

The reason for Zuma's dismissal, then, became ineluctably linked to Mbeki's own political interests. Zuma, his supporters firmly believed, was fired not because he was corrupt, but because he was beginning to threaten Mbeki's plans for an extended presidency. He was a menace to ANC Lite. He was the barbarian at the gate.

Whether this view is totally correct, partially correct or even untrue is unimportant. It was firmly believed by large numbers of a by now utterly disenchanted ANC membership and became the rallying cry for the Polokwane conference.

Mustering rapidly behind this *casus belli* came the unionists – smarting from marginalisation and insult – the communists – forced into humiliating retractions of allegations about Mbeki's Zanufication of the movement – the poor – despairing of ever getting decent service – the unemployed – tired of waiting for jobs – the wounded high and mighty – excluded from office and patronage – and the usual band of carpetbaggers and political *condottieri*.

It was this unlikely front that took to the field in the months preceding Polokwane and, despite widespread allegations of bribery, impropriety and intimidation on both sides, it won the day in a rowdy, disrespectful and disturbing conference. Mbeki, not quite realising the scale of the disaffection, was advised not to make the run for a third term, but did so nevertheless. The bad counsel he had consistently received from his kitchen cabinet during his whole term triumphed, and he went forward to the greatest humiliation ever of an ANC leader. His 1 500 supporters were outvoted two to one.

Justice Malala, a South African columnist, observed with particular acuteness in the *Financial Mail* the real reason why Mbeki lost at Polokwane. While ANC Classic was marshalling its khaki-clad legions in the conference centre to vote out Mbeki, ANC Lite was thronging the corporate

hospitality venue, the so-called lizard lounge, working on the next empowerment deal with big business, which was footing the bill for the conference.

Always fond of the literary allusion, Mbeki might have considered
a variation on Tennyson's famous 'Charge of the Light Brigade' as he
mounted the stage at Polokwane in assumed bonhomie with his arch-
rival, Jacob Zuma, to surrender the mantle of power.

> Half a league, half a league,
> Half a league onward,
> All in the valley of Death
> Rode the fifteen hundred.
> 'Forward, the Lite Brigade!
> Charge for the guns!' he said.
> Into the valley of Death
> Rode the fifteen hundred.
>
> 'Forward, the Lite Brigade!'
> Was there a man dismay'd?
> Not tho' the delegates knew
> Someone had blunder'd.
> Theirs not to make reply,
> Theirs not to reason why,
> Theirs but to do and die.
> Into the valley of Death
> Rode the fifteen hundred.

PART II

The Economic
Kingdom

CHAPTER 6

Getting into GEAR

*Ask five economists and you'll get five different answers – six if
one went to Harvard.* — EDGAR R FIEDLER[1]

ON 14 JUNE 1996, THE ANC UNVEILED ITS CORNERSTONE
economic policy. Optimistically named the Growth, Employment
and Redistribution programme – GEAR – it sought to put economic growth
before redistribution of wealth. Its base was a free but responsible market
economy. Gone was the rhetoric about nationalisation and the people
shall rule. The policy was very much Deputy President Thabo Mbeki's
brainchild, the result of months of intensive work, research and discussion.
Typically, Mbeki's objective was broader than just South Africa. He hoped
he could dispel for all time the stereotypical view that African leadership
was inherently incapable of managing successful modern states.

The elements of GEAR were revealed by finance minister Trevor
Manuel during his budget speech. Controversially, he implied the policy
was not open to amendment. The outraged unionists and communists
would never forget it. Contemporary South Africa is an embodiment of
negotiated outcomes. Nothing is beyond compromise, often good, sometimes bad.

Preceding the announcement of GEAR lay years of fragmentary consultation between the ruling party and the business community, some of it
pre-dating the legalisation of the ANC in 1990. Led by some foremost business moguls, the private sector had engaged the government at a number
of levels and through a variety of forums. President Nelson Mandela had
relied on a group of senior South African business leaders, called the
Brenthurst Group, for informal advice and input. When Thabo Mbeki
came to power, he chose instead a more formalised panel of international
business leaders as a sounding board for ANC economic policy. There can
be no clearer example of the difference between Mandela and Mbeki: the
one informal and home-based, the other formal and internationalist. A
Big Business Working Group was also later set up, but it did not have the

same level of influence as the Brenthurst Group. Later still, Mbeki would work with a group of senior executives banded together under the banner of Business Leadership South Africa.

Preparatory work for the unveiling of GEAR had been done by the finance ministry, the media and opinion makers, flagging Manuel's speech as the ANC's definitive response to persistent demands for the organisation to table its proposals for an effective and sustainable economic policy for South Africa.

After the speech, relays of journalists, businessmen and trade unionists were invited to meet Mbeki – at the time still deputy president – to discuss the policy. He is variously reported to have said, 'Call me Thatcher' and 'Is it Thatcherite enough?' but my recollection is that at our meeting he said, 'It is not Thatcherite enough.' No matter.

It was very apparent that the deputy president was in his element: confident, knowledgeable and loquacious. Little did any of us know at that stage what a divisive instrument the policy was to become and how its promise would subsequently be soured by acrimony, diversion and misunderstanding.

The story of the Mbeki administration's Economic Kingdom is a mixture of success and terrifying misjudgement. It would be reassuring to believe that this kingdom arose as part of a grand and seamless project conceived with clarity, prosecuted with determination and concluded with long-term success. It was not quite that way. In fact, contrary to popular opinion, it was a constantly moving feast in which external perception and internal public pressure played major roles.

The initial economic project, the Reconstruction and Development Programme (RDP), commenced under Mandela as part of the ANC's election manifesto for 1994, was Keynesian and focused on the demand side. It was supposed to bring growth and jobs through big government spend. It did neither, at least not quickly enough.

When he became president, Mbeki replaced the project with his lodestone GEAR, firmly based on the Washington Consensus, the ten-point package of economic policy prescriptions drawn up by John Williamson in 1989 to assist countries in economic trouble. The consensus relied heavily on a growing role for the private sector and a lesser one for the state. The package, adopted by major multilateral financial institutions, has been the subject of fierce dispute between its supporters – who claim it has largely worked – and its detractors, mainly left wing, who argue it is nothing more than a device for the entry of multinational companies to developing countries. From the South African perspective, it was relied upon to bring jobs and growth. Again, it did neither, at least in the short term.

And so the administration once again resurrected the 'developmental state', a reversion to Keynesian economics with some quick-fix ways to address the burning issues of unemployment and poverty.

This constantly adapting policy, accompanied by propitious international economic circumstances, was nevertheless bringing the desired results by 2006. Unemployment was high but stable; growth was improving; inflation was under control; and government deficits had not only been reduced but were moving into positive territory. Whether these outcomes were all the result of planning and implementation or simply large doses of luck will keep the economic historians debating for years to come.

As Mbeki approached the end of his second term as president of the ANC, there were two incontrovertible realities. He and his economic managers had brought unprecedented macro-economic stability to the country, and millions of citizens were enjoying better living standards than they had ever done before, although high levels of poverty remained an intractable feature of the landscape. Tragically, he was never to have the full recognition he deserved for these achievements.

By 2007, the boom years were ebbing. The sense of well-being created by the good times was being eroded as the economic indicators turned negative before the government could fully consolidate its gains. The country was waking up to not only divisive political battles within the ruling party and a changed international economic environment, but also to the unintended consequences of many of the policies adopted and implemented during Mbeki's first eight years in office.

These unintended consequences were twofold.

First, South Africa had become a perilously dependent society. Nearly half of the two million people in a newly created black middle class believed, correctly or incorrectly, that their successes were the result of the government's affirmative action interventions and fully expected them to continue indefinitely. Meanwhile, almost unnoticed, one-third of the country's households, the poorest, had become dependent on state grants for survival. Only a very high growth rate could underwrite the continuation of these policies.

Perversely, the second unintended consequence of both Mbeki's political and economic kingdoms was erosion of the country's capacity to sustain the sort of growth rates needed to ensure the continuation of these dependency programmes.

Ideological overreach weakened the institutional ability to support the dynamic changes taking place in society and government. The reinvention of the developmental state, Mbeki's last big idea before being dispatched as leader of the ANC by his exasperated colleagues, simply exacerbated the problem, although in reality it was an old policy, picked up by default.

To understand the nature of these complex and often contradictory themes, it is necessary first to grasp the flow of ANC economic policy and its impact on key economic and social indicators. Thereafter, it is easier to understand the institutional challenges confronting the South African state as it grapples with both an acute and largely self-induced skills crisis on the one hand and contradictory policy formulations in a whole range of governmental functions on the other. The short-fire impact of both these forces has been a serious weakening of the state's capacity to provide adequate human and physical infrastructure. In particular, this relates to the provision of hard services such as energy and communications and the soft services such as education, skills, public health, justice and food security – in sum, the key drivers of any successful modern state.

When the ANC took power – if not exactly charge – in 1994, it inherited an economy battered by the final years of apartheid. Growth had been minimal or negative for a number of quarters; the national debt was at a record high with interest payments accounting for R34.4 billion in a budget of R173 billion in the first year of ANC government; inflation had at times run away; the currency was volatile; and interest rates oscillated wildly, at one point reaching a ruinous 25 per cent.

Economic sanctions had begun to bite and the cost of maintaining the military machine had grown prohibitive in financial and human terms. Investment had shrunk, capital had fled and employment was stagnant. The conventional wisdom was that the region was pencilled in for a racial Armageddon some time in the mid-1990s. Wise people gave the country a wide berth.

In the last years of apartheid, the regime's attention turned almost entirely to the protection of minority political power in some form of new dispensation and, secondarily, to the entrenchment of white pension and employment rights. It was small wonder that attention to infrastructure and forward planning was minimal. Expedience seized the white elite.

Despite this, the *ancien régime* did leave some things of value: an effective power and communications network; a bedrock of technical, financial and managerial skills; networks within the international financial community; and functioning, if not highly effective, policing, courts, public health and state educational systems. Indeed, spending by the state on education as a percentage of GDP had soared in the last years of National Party rule to a point where it rivalled that of Japan.

An ANC educational publication for its cadres in 1997 correctly identified the smorgasbord of challenges confronting the fledgling government. Key among these were unequal development caused by unbalanced state spending during the apartheid years, the internal and external debt left by the departing apartheid government and the fiscal deficit.[2]

Also of concern were the size of the civil service, which in 1996 comprised 1.3 million people; declining local manufacturing capacity; currency weakness; lack of domestic and foreign investment; slow or no job growth; adverse balance of payments; minimal research investment; low productivity levels; the lack of a skilled workforce; and small production runs, leading to price inflation.

Yet not all was lost. The ANC identified six major opportunities. These were the international goodwill South Africa enjoyed after its emergence from a repressive racial regime; significant state assets capable of leverage; a huge informal sector which could become a major engine of employment growth; raw materials in abundance; a well-developed services and communications sector; good transport networks; and sufficient electricity and water resources to create a platform for growth.

The challenge faced by the ANC was daunting. It had to move quickly to reassure the investment and minority communities that the economy was in safe hands. But at the same time it needed to ensure that a liberation dividend would be quickly passed through to its supporters.

The first step was to appoint a white minister of finance, Derek Keys, and then a conservative banker, Chris Liebenberg, who was in turn later replaced by the competent and highly successful Trevor Manuel, the country's first black finance minister. It was a calculated risk: the ANC needed to show it had its hands on the levers of economic power. In the event, the markets showed some jitters and then settled. Today, it is impossible to find an investor or South African business leader who is not full of praise for Manuel's stellar performance.

Next, the government set about devising economic policies that would meet the twin objectives of growth and redistribution. From the mountain of policy documents drawn up by the ANC's theoreticians – each document either elaborating or refuting in part or in totality the preceding one – four tracts and one concept are germane.

The first policy was the RDP, which was, in all honesty, a sort of quick fix. It aimed at social and infrastructural 'delivery' to the poor and was a cornerstone of the Mandela era. GEAR was nominally the centrepiece of the ANC's strategic macro-economic plan. Ostensibly it was to remain the Bible of the Mbeki administration, although in fact key elements were to be amended, morphed and in some cases dumped as time went on. In 2002, a Micro-Economic Reform Strategy was introduced, aimed specifically at addressing poverty and creating jobs – by then of pressing concern to the government.

When these initiatives still failed to produce the requisite growth, a fourth was implemented in 2006: the Accelerated and Shared Growth Initiative for South Africa (AsgiSA).

But already an old yet still compelling concept was beginning to dominate government thinking: that of the developmental state. Each initiative needs to be investigated in a little more detail to be able eventually to measure the promise against the reality.

The RDP was launched in April 1994 as part of the ANC election manifesto. It had all the hallmarks of a populist exercise aimed at assuring the newly enfranchised poor that something was on the way. The ANC sold the programme as a 'socio-economic' policy framework and made clear that it was aimed more at the demand side of the ledger than the growth side, although it conceded they were closely interlinked.

An early ANC document identified some basic elements of the RDP: an integrated and sustainable policy; people-driven or participative; peace and security; nation building; links between reconstruction and development. In the words of the first draft of the RDP report:

> The RDP integrates growth, development, reconstruction and redistribution into a unified programme. The key to this link is an infrastructural programme that will provide access to modern and effective services like electricity, water, telecommunications, transport, health, education and training for all our people.
>
> The programme will meet basic needs and open up previously suppressed economic and human potential in urban and rural areas. In turn this will lead to an increased output in all sectors of the economy and by modernising our infrastructure and human resource development, we will also enhance export capacity.[3]

The policy was fundamentally Keynesian, with redistribution and re-construction driving development and growth. In the eyes of the planners, significant spend on infrastructure programmes was important, not only for improvement of the infrastructure, but also for providing access to goods, services and jobs in order to meet the basic needs of the poor.

Stripped of the poetry, the project was really a national campaign to provide poor people with basic services and utilities, while creating as many jobs as possible along the way. It all seemed alluringly simple. The programme would coordinate existing funds, with additional injections for more effective ends. Former unionist Jay Naidoo was appointed minister of the project.

A better recipe for catastrophe would be hard to imagine. Naidoo soon found he had responsibility but no authority, a cruel place for an executive to be. Coordination between the various central, provincial and local authorities was all but impossible. These authorities were themselves in a state of profound turbulence, with only recently consolidated provincial and municipal boundaries, new leadership and a white skills exodus.

In the end, the RDP claimed success in some hard service areas, but it is demonstrable that these projects could have been managed through line functions without the existence of the RDP office. When he became president, Mbeki quietly closed the office and retired the project. Retro-spectively, confirmed presidential economic advisor Alan Hirsch,[4] the programme foundered on the twin rocks of a lack of revenue and skills. It is best remembered now for the RDP house, the generic term still given to the millions of small, formal dwellings built by the state during Mbeki's tenure. Neither growth nor jobs had been created. It had been a pretty fruitless exercise, but most South Africans were prepared to write it off as school fees. The ANC should be allowed at least one mistake was the prevalent view.

Tolerance of failure was to wear a lot thinner as time went on. It was probably because of this that Mbeki put so much thought and effort into his next major policy pronouncement. It was important that *this* one should succeed.

The heart of GEAR fell under three headings: fiscal reform to contain costs and reduce the deficit, monetary reform to create an enabling environ-ment for investment, and trade policies aimed at pushing exports and the growth of a robust non-mining sector.

Other policies were aimed at the expansion of physical infrastructure and human skills development. It was pretty much a 'Mom and apple pie' policy and its careful wording tried to avoid tripping early landmines. The word *privatisation* was banned so as not to alert the unions (*restructuring* was the weasel word, but it did not fool the unions for a moment) and the phrase *structured flexibility in the labour market* sounded so much less threatening than *social contracts* to the bosses (they were not fooled either).

In essence, then, GEAR constituted a major shift away from Keynesian theories. The fat government chequebook was withdrawn and the hope of the economic planners within the ANC was that good trade policies and plenty of investment would drive growth and jobs.

Optimistically, the targets for 2000, then only four years away, were:
* a 6 per cent growth rate per year;
* 400 000 new jobs to be created every year;
* fiscal deficit at 3 per cent;
* stability of the currency (the foreign exchange rate at the time was R4.5 to the US dollar); and
* a core inflation rate of between 3 per cent and 6 per cent.

The document identified the strategic outcomes as being:
* a competitive and fast-growing economy (6 per cent per annum) which created enough jobs for all work seekers;
* a redistribution of income and opportunities in favour of the poor;
* a society in which sound health, education and other services were available to all; and
* an environment in which homes were secure and places of work productive.

There it was: the ANC's economic contract with South Africa, Mbeki's Economic Kingdom. It was to be the yardstick by which the Mbeki administration would be measured; the constant reference point of both business and trade unions in assessing the success or failure of the government's policy in the years to come.

Given the broadly socialistic nature of his constituency, why did Mbeki embrace such a high-risk policy?

There are two schools of thought. One is that with his background in economic studies and firm grasp of the issues, Mbeki realised that in the context of the mid-1990s it was important, above all else, that the domestic and international investment communities be kept happy. GEAR was a rational and thoughtful response to this imperative.

The other view is that the new ANC administration, overwhelmed by the responsibility of government and spooked by the negative response to its RDP, hastened into a policy direction that it knew would create warm and fuzzy feelings in all the right quarters, not least among international investors and South African business. And it did. During this period, five major South African corporations were given permission to seek primary listings offshore. Billions of rands left the country. It was a huge leap of faith on the part of the new administration.

This view of having been railroaded into a 'pro-business' position has been roundly rejected by Mbeki. A senior business leader concurs: 'As soon as Mbeki came into office, it was abundantly clear that he was going to do things his way. The informal but quite intense relations we had with Mandela on economic issues simply melted away.'

But, six years after GEAR was introduced, investment flows and employment growth remained worryingly weak. The government turned more fiercely to issues of poverty reduction. The micro-economic reform strategy was heralded in the presidential State of the Nation address in 2001 and implemented the following year.

It was not a departure from GEAR, but an elaboration. It correctly identified a disjuncture between the formal economic sector and the informal, and thus signalled a shift from a concentration on macro-issues to the real economy – to all the factors that were hampering micro-economic performance. It also signalled an intention by the government to become more directly involved in job creation than had been presumed under GEAR.

Yet again, various challenges were identified as limiting the objectives of job-generative growth, among them infrastructure, human resource weakness, deficiencies in the public utilities and access to finance. Five sectors were highlighted for special programmes aimed at employment creation, value addition, export, small-business development and black empowerment. These sectors were agriculture, tourism, information and communications technology, cultural industry and export. Growth and development talks, colloquially known as the Jobs Summit, were held in June 2003 between government, business and the unions.

But by 2004 it was abundantly clear to the ANC government that the objectives set out so confidently in the GEAR document eight years before

– particularly the growth and employment targets – were worryingly off course. Growth had averaged 3 per cent, half the targeted objective, and unemployment was continuing to rise alarmingly. Those living in poverty – defined as having less than one US dollar a day to spend – had doubled since 1996. The ANC was beginning to confront challenges on all fronts, not least its restive alliance partners in the unions and the South African Communist Party, who were smarting from the summary dumping of the RDP in favour of GEAR.

This did not stop the government from committing itself yet again to ambitious and unattainable targets. In its 2004 election manifesto, the government pledged to halve unemployment and poverty by 2014. The manifesto was heavily influenced by the UN Millennium Development Goals and particularly its emphasis on poverty reduction and restructuring of the international trading order. Yet the manifesto prudently scaled down some of the earlier, headier assumptions about growth. Now a 6 per cent growth rate was to be achieved only in 2010 and not 2000, as earlier ANC policy documents had forecast.

To achieve this more modest objective, the government undertook a thorough review of all constraining factors in the growth of the economy. Thus was born AsgiSA, unveiled in February 2006.

It was to be a set of targeted interventions to loosen the fetters on the GEAR objectives. In the words of the 2006 AsgiSA report, it was 'a national initiative supported by key groups in the economy'. If GEAR was the motor of government economic policy, AsgiSA was to be the turbocharger. The key constraints identified were:

- the relative volatility of the currency;
- the cost, efficiency and capacity of the national logistics system;
- shortage of suitably skilled labour and the impact of past apartheid policies on low-skilled labour costs;
- barriers to entry, constraints on competition and limited new investment opportunities;
- the regulatory environment and the burden on small and medium enterprises; and
- deficiencies in state organisation, capacity and leadership.

A raft of corrective actions were proposed, ranging from macro-economic issues and infrastructure to education and skills, industrial-sector strategies, 'second'-economy initiatives and governance questions. The overall

objectives were summarised in the ANC publication *Umrabulo*[5] as the reduction of infrastructure backlogs, reduction in the cost of doing business
in core export industries and an increase in the stock of 'social capital'
or skills and human resources. The cost would be high. The medium-
term expenditure framework anticipated infrastructure expenditure of
R409.7 billion between 2005/6 and 2009/10.

If this latest government initiative was notable for anything, it was
repetition of the self-evident. It was as if frequent intonation about
'strategic constraints' and 'capacity problems' would in itself solve the
problems. This had by now become a defining feature of the Mbeki administration. Policies, strategies, protocols, documents and white, yellow and
green papers flowed with the rapidity of the continent's great rivers, yet
little else followed in their wake. Increasingly the document, the policy
framework, became the excuse for avoiding its diligent implementation.
As the failures of state policy mounted and the skills crisis went critical,
the consequences were to be found in all state functions, as we shall see.

Mbeki's ninth year as leader of the ANC in 2007 also marked his eighth
year as president of South Africa and the thirteenth year of ANC rule. It was
time to take stock of what had been achieved in creating the Economic
Kingdom and assess the extent to which Mbeki had met the economic
objectives enshrined in his 1996 policy debut.

Of the five key financial objectives he had set himself, he had succeeded
in reducing the deficit in state spending (helped by increased tax receipts
and reduced debt-financing costs) and in stabilising the currency (with a
little help from the international environment). Government consumption
was 18.1 per cent of GDP and inflation at 6 per cent was on target. He
had failed in his growth targets and job creation. Overall, he had greatly
improved macro-economic stability, but he was seven years behind in his
key promises. Critically, private investment had lagged for a variety of
reasons. It was this that would cost him dearly in December 2007.

He had failed epically in three of the strategic objectives set for GEAR.
The economy was not competitive (in fact it was sliding back down the
world competitiveness ratings at an alarming tempo). His health, education
and other services were in a parlous state. To talk of security in the home
was gallows humour in the year in which South Africa's violent crime
rate became a near world-beater. And productivity in the workplace was
slipping.

In one area, however, Mbeki had succeeded. He had presided over a significant reallocation of national wealth, opportunity and income, both private and state, to black South Africans: the rich, the super rich, the middle classes, the poor and the very poor. Here, ultimately, lay his enduring legacy.

It is possible to get into a chicken-and-egg argument as to why the Mbeki administration succeeded so well at the macro-economic level and did so badly at just about everything else.

Did South African business and foreign investors sell out on the basic elements of the GEAR contract? Did they fully embrace a new economic citizenship and did they work diligently to expand markets, deepen investment and support the ANC in getting to grips with the complexity of government, and – finally – did they create jobs? It was certainly the ANC's view that they had been sold down the river, and to the end of his tenure Mbeki nursed a bitter grievance against the business community for not, in his eyes, reciprocating his good faith.

Not surprisingly, the business community held a different view, arguing that there are long lead times for any investments and that what is critical is track record. Before this could be established, goes the argument, the Mbeki administration terminated the sort of informal discussions that had occurred under Mandela in favour of a Big Business Working Group; imposed an inflexible labour regime (perhaps to placate the unions angered by GEAR); rammed through an aggressive affirmative action policy; presided over systemic failures in the state bureaucracies; changed the regulatory environment, often confusedly and contradictorily; and introduced a harsh, abrasive style of race-based discourse which was both divisive and offensive.

There were elements of truth on both sides. South African business, dominated by white executives, remained sceptical of the new government's ability to meet its promises. With exceptions, they remained aloof, hesitant, one foot dangling in the wind as if preparing to take off.

But, outside its macro-economic management, there was certainly much about the Mbeki administration that was of justifiable concern, pre-eminently its inability to control corrosive crime, maintain an efficient public service and combat AIDS. Mbeki's inability to take a principled position on human rights abuses in Zimbabwe much exercised the broad white minority, but counted less in business computations, other than the possible impact a collapsed Zimbabwean state would have on South African services and on investment views of the subcontinent.

In this debate about who was right and who was wrong, there is a clue to where the answer might be found in the host of global competitive indexes that keep a fierce eye on country performances in a range of spheres from economic performance to lifestyle. By 2007, South Africa was incontrovertibly slipping badly in the ratings.

The 2007 Global Competitiveness Survey of the World Economic Forum saw South Africa slide from thirty-sixth to forty-fourth place behind Saudi Arabia, Puerto Rico, Oman, Bahrain, the Slovak Republic, Portugal, Slovenia, Kuwait and Lithuania.

Out of 131 surveyed countries, South Africa came in at 126 in terms of crime, 128 for the quality of its science and maths education and 117 in general education. It also scored badly in the efficiency of the bureaucracies and health. All these areas were squarely within the remit of the state. South Africa did well in areas such as financial market sophistication and efficiency (twenty-fifth), business sophistication (thirty-third) and innovation (thirty-sixth). The country also scored in terms of sophistication of commercial operations and strategy (twenty-eighth) and its boardroom efficiency came in at a remarkable fourth position. These were within the ambit of the private sector. The legal framework and protection of property and copyright, functions of both public and private efficiency, also scored highly.

Meanwhile, the International Institute for Management Development's *World Competitiveness Yearbook*, measuring 323 criteria for competitiveness, pushed South Africa back from thirty-eighth to fiftieth place in 2006. By 2007, South Africa was in fifty-third place, along with Ukraine and Venezuela. Another shove and it will be off the ratings altogether.

A more telling indicator can be found in the UN human development index (HDI) – the measure by which a society is judged on life expectancy, GDP per capita, adult literacy and school enrolment rates. While South Africa had maintained its global position in terms of GDP at roughly the same level (fifty-five out of 180) it had slid down the HDI index since liberation in 1994. In 2001 it was in ninety-fourth position. By 2006 it was at slot 121 out of the 177 countries polled.

In 2007, South Africa underwent a novel form of assessment and league tabling – one that Mbeki had been instrumental in creating through the New Partnership for African Development (NEPAD). Part of this project was a peer-review mechanism whereby African countries rated each other on their performance and reported publicly on the outcome. The peer review of South Africa identified fourteen areas of weakness, including race relations, minority fears on educational and cultural issues, the enrichment of a few through black empowerment, poor education, HIV/AIDS, xenophobia and skills shortages. Not unexpectedly, the South African government shirtily objected to a number of the findings.

There is a last index that is relevant. The Global Entrepreneurship Monitor tracks the level of entrepreneurial activity across a number of countries. One of its key indexes is that of early-stage entrepreneurial activity, which gives a pointer as to how much new business is being developed in a particular country. As one would imagine, highly developed countries exhibit a lower index than emergent states where economies are preparing to take off. The 2006 report found South Africa at a ranking of 5.3, which is among the developed economies scale. South Africa's peer emerging-market countries were streets ahead. Argentina was at 10.2, Brazil at 11.7, China at 16.2, Colombia at 22.5, India at 10.4, Indonesia at 19.3, Jamaica at 20.3, Malaysia at 11.1, Peru at 40.2, the Philippines at 20.4 and Thailand at 15.2.

What do these tested and trusted indexes tell us?

First, until 2008, South Africa was still pulling its weight in terms of its capacity to produce wealth, but had plummeted in its ability to distribute it in such a way as to make a meaningful difference to the lives of the majority of its citizens.

Even making concessions for the impact of AIDS (its incidence itself a manifestation of state failure to implement an effective public health approach), this correlates roughly to the private sector's skill in generating wealth being among the best in the world, and the public sector's ability to use it for the benefit of the society among the worst.

Secondly, the country's ability to spark entrepreneurial activity is weakening relative to its peers and has declined in recent times. In short, South Africa is running out of steam. For a purportedly young and emerging country, we are firmly in the old-world camp in terms of entrepreneurial resource, despite our vast reserves of commodities, space, population and the benefits of fourteen years of political stability and the best economic growth rate in decades.

Not surprisingly, outsiders perceive the country to be working best in those areas run by the private sector, and least well in those areas that are in the hands of the public sector. As the private sector is still largely run by whites and the public sector predominantly by blacks, the issue cannot but become infused with the deep racial tensions that run through South African society. It thus contributes to both the cynicism of whites and the defensiveness of blacks. Neither attitude is helpful.

Still, the undoubted consequence of this disagreement between private sector and government as to who should bear the 'blame' for the lack of progress in dealing with jobs and poverty was a pull-back by business and investors that led to a classic downward spiral of expectation. Business accused the administration of failing to create an enabling environment; government accused business of refusing to commit itself.

The outcome was a response by the government that saw the effective sidelining of the programme of privatisation of state entities and the resurgence of a central role for government in the 'developmental state'. This in turn sparked a reciprocal round of business negativity as it was excluded from key investment opportunities and watched with foreboding the prospect of an already ineffectual state trying to shoulder even more of the load.

On the other flank, as we have seen in Part I of this book, Mbeki faced a restless and increasingly angry reaction from the trade union movements, communists and civil organisations. They repeatedly dismissed the policy as 'pro-business' and took exception to the way in which it was imposed by fiat. Their opposition was fuelled by an unfortunate lateral consequence of the government's affirmative action policies: the emergence of a some-times crassly consumerist elite who, by their very ostentation, seemed to mock the plight of the working people.

Had Mbeki been of a different character and had the administration been of a different order, it is just possible that this antagonism could have been contained, mediated and channelled into more positive directions. But the administration, hamstrung by an almost liturgical lack of trust by its nominal alliance partners and seemingly always stumbling from one crisis of confidence to another, appeared unable to engage the left in any way beyond insults and threats. Its defeat at the ANC conference in December 2007 by its leftist opponents was a foregone conclusion.

Nevertheless, from the think-tanks of both government and the left emerged a consensus that the markedly pro-market policies of the ANC needed revision.

The notable failure of some international cases of privatisation, not least the wholesale and disastrous sell-off of state assets in the former Soviet Union, strengthened the hand of those counselling caution in disposing of state resources, particularly those that could be used as engines for job growth. One of the victims of this process was public–private initiatives for the generation of power. The country would later pay dearly for this.

The phrase *developmental state* had come into vogue. In June 2005 the ANC's national general council observed: 'The developmental state ... is a state with a programme around which it is able to mobilise society at large. It is also a state with the capacity to intervene in order to restructure the economy, including through public investment.'

The only problem, as we shall see, is that the South African state does not have the capacity to intervene in such a large-scale mobilisation and direction of resources, and to believe that it does is reckless in the extreme. The point was driven home at a high-level government seminar in November 2007, where the bald assessment of nearly all present, including senior ANC strategists, was that the public service was simply not ready for such a major role.

Nevertheless, the intent was clear and the rhetoric of the ANC's newly elected left-leaning national executive committee is likely to be more, rather than less, in favour of interventionist policies. The state will thus be called upon to play a more aggressive role in the economic affairs of the country and will intervene actively in areas in which it believes it can advance its stated objectives of reducing poverty and enhancing job growth. Having given the markets and the private sector the space to do the job, ANC Classic believes they have largely failed. Now it is time for the state, ill-equipped as it is, to take a firmer hand. Thus has South Africa moved from Thatcher to the developmental state, via the Washington Consensus, in a decade.

CHAPTER 7

Noise and haste

Obstacles are those frightful things you see when you take your eye off your goal.
— HENRY FORD[1]

FINANCE MINISTER TREVOR MANUEL IS MEASURED AND CAU-tious in his statements. It was typical, then, that he should observe in his February 2006 budget speech that 'in the noise and haste of economic policy debate, we forget too easily that there are long lead times in the practical implementation of policy. Our present economic performance reflects the choices we made a decade ago and the economic reforms now in progress will yield their returns five and ten years from now.'

What has been the economic performance of Team Finance South Africa? How have Manuel, Reserve Bank governor Tito Mboweni and commissioner of revenue services Pravin Gordhan performed?

On the macro-economic front, the team could claim a wealth of significant achievements by 2006. National debt had been massively reduced. Inflation had been pegged in the 2006/7 year to a target between 3 per cent and 6 per cent. Interest rates had remained at historic lows for most of the period from 2004 to 2007.

The deficit on the budget was within target and huge strides had been made in improving budgeting and reporting procedures through the introduction of instruments such as the medium-term expenditure framework. For the first time in South Africa's history, tax collection exceeded estimates in 2006/7 by 0.6 per cent and turned a greater surplus in 2007/8. In all, it was a performance of unparalleled virtuosity.

Currency volatility, identified as a major problem in both the GEAR and AsgiSA programmes, had not initially been as accommodating. The rand had gyrated wildly in the early 2000s due to a number of hostile international influences, driving the currency's value at one stage to more than R12 to the US dollar – nearly three times weaker than when the ANC first took power.

The fluctuations had so concerned the government that, with untypical macro-economic naïveté, it instituted a commission of inquiry into the rand's performance, in search of the conspiracy that Thabo Mbeki congenitally believed lay behind every misfortune. Not surprisingly, the commission could find no real culprits, and when the rand rebounded spectacularly afterwards to become the best-performing currency in the world in that year, there was no repeat commission to investigate why the currency was performing so well.

By 2007, the rand had stabilised in the R7 to R7.60 band against the US dollar and South African reserves had grown from $8 billion in 2004 to $35 billion by the end of the year, thereby giving much greater predictability and confidence to investors. The rand, as Manuel said, was no longer a one-way bet. Yet by the end of 2007 it was still worth 38 per cent less than when the ANC took power.

Reserve Bank reports showed that gross fixed capital formation (GFCF), a measure of the net new investment in the domestic economy in fixed capital assets, grew at an annualised rate of 21.75 per cent in the first quarter of 2007 – the highest since 1989. As a percentage of GDP (the total market value of all final goods and services produced within South Africa in one year), GFCF rose to 21 per cent. This was the best in twenty-two years. All sectors boasted improvements in capital formation.

The second quarter of 2007 showed foreign direct investment – made to acquire lasting interest in enterprises operating outside of the economy of the investor – at R11.98 billion, three times what it had been a year before. Portfolio investments – passive holdings of securities such as foreign stocks, bonds or other financial assets, none of which entail active management or control – amounted to R42.02 billion. In short, the former is a bricks-and-mortar investment that is not going to take flight at the drop of a hat, while the latter is a paper commodity that can up and off whenever things turn sour. To use the old truism about the difference between the bacon and the egg: in the former, investors – like the pig – are committed; in the latter, investors – like the chicken – are interested.

The numbers showed that for every R1 put in as bacon into South Africa during the period concerned, R3.50 came in as egg. Yet again, this illustrated the willingness of foreign investors to enter South Africa in the short term, but a reluctance to engage in the longer term. The popularity of private equity investment during this period compounded the problem. Such investors come in for a limited period and have their eyes firmly on the exit date. The long haul is not on the agenda. This lack of fixed investment was a problem that dogged the whole of Mbeki's tenure and led to deep frustration.

Growth in GDP had staged a comeback by 2005 but was still falling short of the government's targets. In the 1960s the average annual GDP growth was 6 per cent. By the 1970s it was just over 3 per cent. In the 1980s it was 1 per cent lower, and in the 1990s it reached its nadir at a little over 1 per cent, dropping in some years to a negative level. The full cost of the National Party's financial stewardship can be counted in this doleful record.

But from 2000 to 2008, the initial growth forecast was more than 4 per cent. In 2005 it was 5.1 per cent and in 2006 it was 5 per cent. Consensus forecasts had put growth for 2007 to 2010 at between 5 and 5.5 per cent before the power crisis of early 2008 called off all bets. By the third quarter of 2007, the country had enjoyed thirty-six quarters of uninterrupted growth – again a South African record.

What helped this improvement, apart from the obvious benefits of a liberated economy after the end of apartheid?

To answer this, one has to look at the international economic environment. Rarely has the government of a developing country been so blessed with propitious financial circumstances as was South Africa in the first five years of the twenty-first century.

The US dollar had weakened against the rand. While this did not help exports, it did improve the balance of payments and allowed the country's financial administrators more room to manoeuvre. The Chinese commodity scramble also helped. South Africa's raw minerals were swallowed up by the voracious Far Eastern markets. Finally, the Mbeki administration had the good luck to be sitting amid the greatest global investment liquidity in the history of the world. Of the trillions of dollars of investment sloshing around the globe looking for a home, *some* had to come South Africa's way.

Government policy also unlocked internal flows. The reallocation of income and wealth from the traditional wealth-holding classes to the new black elite helped trigger a massive credit-led consumer boom. The retail, hospitality, manufacturing and processing sectors soared as South Africans took to restaurants, resorts, car showrooms and boutiques to enjoy what was widely seen as the liberation dividend. The creation of a vast welfare class also helped drive consumption, albeit in a very different sector. Finally, the announcement in 2004 of an infrastructural development programme worth R407 billion over three years (subsequently rising to R563 billion) buoyed a construction industry that had already been given a whiff of smelling salts by the major housing programmes undertaken by the state. Everywhere, except among the very poorest, was a sense of movement and confidence and well-being.

And yet, below the surface of this boom and the undoubted successes of the Mbeki presidency in managing the economy, glided sharks. By 2007, they were mustering.

The first predator was South Africa's trade and industries policies – or lack of them. These policies had remained in a state of constant flux and permutation during virtually the entire period of the Mbeki presidency, compounded by endless 'restructurings' of the Department of Trade and Industry (DTI).

By the eighth year of Mbeki's presidency, a low-intensity war was being waged between a highly protectionist DTI and a liberalist Department of Finance, precisely because the government had failed to consolidate a coherent view on this most crucial of economic-development pillars – one which had been identified *eleven years* earlier as fundamental to the success of GEAR.

In 2007, the DTI produced its national industrial policy framework. It entailed a heavy reliance on direct support for South African manufacturing – the country had already spent billions on developing a motor manufacturing capacity. On the protectionist side, the government introduced an ill-advised trade ban on cheap Chinese linen, clothing and shoe imports. Apart from the bilateral trade tensions this created, it failed to achieve its objectives and was quietly wound down.

Minister of trade and industry Mandisi Mpahlwa was at pains to point out that in reality South Africa had little room to move on tariffs. In the early 1990s South Africa's average tariff was about 23 per cent on imports. By 2007 it was 8.2 per cent. Of import lines, 54 per cent were zero rated and the number of tariff lines themselves had been reduced from 13 609 to 6 420. By 2012, 94.9 per cent of the country's exports to the United Kingdom would be duty free and 86.3 per cent of European Union exports would be duty free. How much more can we be expected to do, he asked?[2]

The row between the industrial focus of the DTI and the trade liberalisation views of Finance came to a head with the introduction of the government's 2007 mid-term budget review, in which Manuel called for South Africa to embark on a policy of unilateral liberalisation. This was met by a counter-charge from his ministerial colleague that such action would worsen the short- to medium-term current account deficit, with little guarantee of long-term competitiveness.

Manuel's case was helped by a shock report from the South African Institute of International Affairs in late 2007, showing that the South African economy could be sacrificing as much as R32 billion a year, 2 per cent of GDP, due to non-tariff barriers – the cost of physical transport of goods through customs, toll roads, weighbridges and harbours. Together with the World Bank findings that South Africa was trailing way behind its peers in cross-border competitiveness, the report showed how dilatory the government had been in addressing a key constraint to economic growth.[3]

The situation worsened in December 2007 when South African intransigence on new-generation issues like telecommunications and financial services in the European Union's Economic Partnership Agreements (EPAs) split the Southern African Development Community (SADC) and left South Africa isolated. The dispute led to much finger-pointing, with accusations that South Africa was being unreasonable, isolationist and protectionist in its determination to hang on to its hard services role in the region and counter-charges that the EU was attempting to railroad unfavourable terms for the region.

The finer points of the very drawn-out international trade negotiations need not detain us here. Suffice it to say that, eight years into the Mbeki presidency, there was still no unanimity on a crucial piece of economic and industrial strategy – not between industry sectors, industry and government, government and trading partners or even within government. The impact on the country's export sector, a vital component of all the ANC's economic recovery plans, was serious and costly. The sector was already battling with a strong rand for much of the early twenty-first century and capacity restraints caused by skills shortages. This policy indecision merely compounded the problem. Inevitably, it affected the economic growth rate.

The second shark was debt – both private and public. Household debt was the direct consequence of the consumer boom of the first half-decade of the early twenty-first century, induced by lower taxes, cheaper money and the growth of the new black middle class. It rose to historic highs. By 2007, household debt was 77 per cent of disposable income – while national savings declined to an all-time low of 17 per cent against a target of 25 per cent. By 2008, household debt stood at R1 trillion and had quadrupled in five and a half years. The implications were clear: liberated politically and with plastic in hand, South Africans were spending themselves into extinction.

Now while public debt looked very good at central government level, despite an average 9.4 per cent a year increase in state spending (government debt was a credible 16 per cent of GDP in 2007), it was horrible at local government level. The biggest debt factor at this level was the money owed by local authorities to the national electricity supplier for power consumed by newly electrified communities. These debts, some reaching back to the apartheid era, were a consequence of the inability or refusal of large numbers of poor urban communities to pay for the power consumed. Despite numerous amnesties by the local authorities and the introduction of free power and water quotas, the level of uncollected charges had reached a disturbing R35 billion in 2008 for the largest twenty-seven cities alone.

There was a bigger long-term problem. The presidency had been justifiably proud of delivering a surplus on its budget for the first time in South African history, yet there were few in the high reaches of government who did not realise that this was not the product of state parsimony but more the result of a dramatic improvement in the collection of taxes under the indefatigable Commissioner Gordhan. State spending had increased above 9 per cent for almost the whole of the ANC's tenure, but had been offset by the improved efficiency in tax collection and savings from debt financing. The commissioner had revamped the revenue collecting function, clamped down on evaders, closed the loopholes, prosecuted defaulters and brought back billions in illegal offshore investments through an amnesty.

But there was a limit to how much more could be done, short of increasing the direct personal and company tax rate or entering into a punitive collection regime. Neither option was attractive to the government. The reality, then, was that the budget surpluses were more a result of good collection than prudent spending. But it could not last – and before long the state would be faced with the dilemma of how to fund the growing burden of its dependency state on a limping growth rate.

This brings us to the third shark: inflation. Simple economics tells us that if the currency weakens, inflation increases. If inflation increases, competitiveness declines and one is in a vicious downward spiral. By late 2006, the conservative financial and central bank administrations were seriously worried. Inflation began running away from the government's target level of 3 per cent to 6 per cent from mid-2007 onwards. By early 2008 it had powered through the 9 per cent mark and was touching 10 per cent. High oil prices (more than $140 a barrel at times) and rising food prices were key exogenous drivers. Years of meticulous attempts at controlling inflation were being eroded.

The government's first concern was that private debt was getting out of hand. It had to be brought under control, not only to avoid a post-boom meltdown with serious political consequences, but also to create space for the massive cost of the state's capital-development programme. The objective, then, was to impose austerity on consumers in order to create an opportunity for the state to set its infrastructure right. To repair the infrastructure without completely blowing the balance of payments – and thus the currency – consumers would have to bear short-term pain. It was the sort of delayed gratification that post-war Japan used to great effect to build itself an economic empire. But, as Mbeki learnt on 19 December 2007, South Africa is not Japan.

The chosen instrument for this policy was inflation targeting. The central bank would set inflation targets and then use all means necessary to achieve this. The chief tool was higher interest rates to increase the cost of money and dampen demand for credit. The price would be high: it would be measured in mortgage foreclosures, repossessed 4×4s, failed businesses, struggling empowerment deals and miserly wage increases.

Between June 2006 and June 2008, the Reserve Bank raised its repo rate (the cost to institutions of buying currency from the central bank) ten times, pushing it from 7 per cent to 12 per cent – a 71 per cent increase. The consumer bank lending rate hit 15.5 per cent. Comparatively, South Africa's real interest rate was higher than that of Canada, the Eurozone, the US, Hungary, China, Japan, Russia and India.

Simultaneously, the government introduced tough new credit control laws that put the onus on the banks if they over-lent to consumers. There was irony in this. From hectoring the financial institutions to lend more to poor and specifically black people, the government was now penalising them for doing exactly that.

With the slow upward march of interest rates and a sudden acute credit crunch, it was not surprising that the usual ills became apparent. Liquidations and sales in execution of repossessed property jumped between 2006 and 2007. Company liquidations increased 113 per cent in September 2007 compared to the same month the year before.[4] Forced home sales surged by 75 per cent in January 2008 compared to a year earlier.[5] The sobering fact was that 60 per cent of home loans in existence in the third quarter of 2007 were taken out in less than four years. In 2008, one of the country's major motor financing houses reported that loans to black consumers had increased from 1 per cent of its book in 2003 to 45 per cent in 2007. With debt service as a percentage of monthly income standing at 9.7 per cent, it was apparent that a huge number of first entrants into the property market and new financed car buyers, mainly black, were under serious pressure from the rates increases.

Retailers reported jumps of 40 per cent in bad debt and debt collectors warned of a 'tsunami of bad debt'.[6] The most troubled part of the market was the middle – and particularly the new black elite. From all points came warnings that the Reserve Bank was over-correcting. A political flashback was unavoidable.

At roughly this time, a young black colleague told me that I should not pay heed to all the talk of mounting middle-class black debt. President Mbeki had gone to a great deal of effort to create the class and he was unlikely to let it be destroyed through the machinations of Mr Mboweni, said my associate. The comment aptly captured the sense of confidence of the mostly young black middle class that they would not, in their eyes, be betrayed just at the moment they were enjoying the fruits of a liberation wrought so painfully by their parents.

In December 2007, Mbeki was unceremoniously rejected for a third term as leader of the party by an alliance of the new black middle class and the workers. Their key concern, to be frank, was not economic policy, but rather a sense of alienation from their austere, autocratic and aloof leader. But if economics did play a part, it had to be inflation targeting, which they saw as threatening their gains under the black empowerment programme and their standard of living under a steadily rising real rate of black income.

There was to be no question of delayed gratification – rather, the reverse. There was to be a populist response. Whether there will actually be such extravagance under Mbeki's successor is a question time will answer. The fact is that the government's attempts at fiscal prudence have been challenged by his party and the very role of an independent central bank may be at stake in the future.

In the end, it may all be irrelevant. The simple fact is that the Mbeki government's programme of fiscal prudence and inflation targeting was doomed anyway, not just because of external forces – although they did not help – but because of internally generated inflationary forces *which were a direct consequence of the Mbeki presidency's policies in the first place.* To the extent that the new ANC leadership, which took power in December 2007, has said it does not intend changing Mbeki's economic policies, it means South Africa is condemned to a high-inflation, low-growth future, with all its attendant consequences.

Let us deal with these self-generated inflationary pressures in turn.

The first and most dangerous is the massive surge of capital investment which is due to occur in South Africa in the next three years – more than R563 billion, including an injudicious project to host the 2010 Football World Cup and another R700 billion in private-sector spend. There are material doubts whether this level of spending can ever be achieved, due to the simple fact that between apartheid, affirmative action and a bad educational system, the technical skills base of the country has been critically reduced.

It is important to understand the charge against the Mbeki presidency. It is not the fact that the administration embarked on a capital investment programme. For a decade before the old regime exited and until 2006, there had been virtually no investment in major capital projects – and a quarter century without that sort of development is a long time in a growing economy. By 2007, the economy was using about 86 per cent of its capacity to satisfy current demand. The investments, or at least some of them, had to be made.

The error, a grievous one, is that these investments were not made earlier and in a more sequenced way, on a schedule that would soften the impact and escalate the costs in a manageable way, without putting at risk the economy. No such programme was adopted. In his penultimate State of the Nation address, Mbeki conceded that errors in planning had been made. This acknowledgement will live as one of the great understatements of his career. The capital-development project has all been done too late and too fast for it not to have serious inflationary effects.

The first of these effects came through in 2007, when the national electricity generator posted a 14.35 per cent increase in tariffs and warned that tariffs would have to double in two years and double-digit increases would be needed indefinitely, going forward, to fund the utility's capital expansion. This level of charge, and higher, will continue as the government belatedly tries to catch up with the acute shortage of power supply in a country that once had massive surplus generating capacity and some of the lowest electricity charges in the world. These administered costs had long been recognised as a threat by Reserve Bank governor Tito Mboweni in his antiinflationary strategy. It has now come to pass.

Control of wage inflation is traditionally the first method of managing inflation targeting. It is directly within the power of the state and employers to control and has again been repeatedly singled out by Mboweni as a critical area of restraint if inflation targeting is to succeed.

But wage settlements have pushed the limits of prudence and undercut a key element of the GEAR policy, which declared it imperative that productivity remain above wage inflation. In this regard, government policy was itself the biggest driver of private-sector wage inflation. Legislation such as the Basic Conditions of Employment Act of 1997 and the Employment Equity Act of 1998 pushed up the cost of labour dramatically as a raft of more employee-friendly conditions was introduced. Minimum wage legislation contributed to further inflation and, finally, the black empowerment project, imposed on a situation of dire skills shortages, saw a premium being paid for scarce black skills. It is hard to conceive of a better example of the unintended consequence. Short of a drastic revision of the whole programme, there is no way that BEE, broad-based or not, will not continue to be a vigorous driver of national inflation.

In July 2007 the government reached a settlement with its unions on an inflationary 7.5 per cent increase after a month-long strike. This had an immediate knock-on effect in the private sector, where salaries followed the international pattern of being higher than those of the public service. Average wage settlements of 9 per cent to 9.5 per cent followed in the coal- and gold-mining industries, while metal and engineering industries settled at 8.5 per cent. The cement industry settled at 7.5 per cent, chemicals at 8.5 per cent and the parastatal electricity supply entity gave 8 per cent.

The Monetary Policy Committee of the Reserve Bank, justifying yet another hike in the repo rate, reported that in the first half of 2007 wage settlements averaged 6.8 per cent, but later settlements were all pushing the 8 per cent range, compared to 6.5 per cent for the same period of the previous year. Similar and indeed higher demands were anticipated in 2008 – claims in excess of 15 per cent were tabled – and business was warned by the respective industry bodies to gird for a rough year.

More disturbing, Mboweni pointed out that in the first quarter of 2007 labour productivity increased by only 2.2 per cent, compared with 5.3 per cent in the fourth quarter of the previous year. His concerns about productivity were justified. A September 2007 report by the International Labour Organisation showed that between 1980 and 2005 the average employed South African added value of 0.7 units compared with 5.7 units in China and 1.7 by workers in the US. In fact, South Africa was beaten in value add by Moroccans, Ethiopians, Kenyans, Ugandans and Zambians.[7]

Wage inflation is also due for a major new boost if the government proceeds with a plan to introduce a national pension scheme that could add very material charges to the wage bills. Should such a system be implemented as demanded by the unions, the outcome could go only one of two ways: a drop in the take-home pay of workers, which precipitates high-skills exit and low-skills strikes, or – the more likely outcome – it becomes enrolled as part of the total cost to company and is passed on to the consumer of goods and services. Either way, inflation wins.

Another shark is to be found not at national but local level. The Municipal Property Rates Act, passed in 2006, was beginning to be implemented in late 2007 and was expected to roll forward over three years. In every instance, the local authorities seized the moment to revalue property and then adjust rates in order to deal with their yawning deficits. The impact was a massive increase in property taxes and charges on agricultural land, thus effectively rolling back the benefits that ordinary citizens had enjoyed from the successive personal and business tax cuts introduced by the minister of finance over a number of years. The *objective* of the legislation was to give local authorities the resources to deal with their crippling debts and administrative collapse (dealt with more fully elsewhere). The *effect* could only be to give another push to inflation.

The Great White Shark, however, was the deficit on the balance of payments account. South Africans were importing more than they were exporting. A host of reasons contributed to the latter, not least of them confused state policy, and there were even more reasons for the former.

Prime among these, however, was a ballooning deficit on the balance of payment account that was expected to result from the public sector's huge capital-development programme. The economists in the government knew that this growing deficit – the measure of the difference between all the payments and liabilities *to* foreigners versus all payments and obligations received *from* foreigners – was scheduled to reach a sixty-year high of 7.8 per cent of GDP by 2010, when South Africa hosts the football world at play. This would have a disastrous effect on the currency if foreign investment for any reason slowed down, and it was for this reason that South Africa had to do everything possible to ensure those flows kept coming.

But would it?

The first tremors of concern were felt when statistics for the 2007 calendar year started coming through in early 2008. The deficit on the current account looked as if it was going to be even worse than anticipated. Estimates for the deficit in 2007 ranged from 7.5 per cent to 7.8 per cent of GDP – well beyond the official forecast of 6.7 per cent for the year. In fact, warned some economists, the deficit in 2008 at 8.4 per cent was likely to already exceed the worst-case deficit anticipated by the government for 2010, although a serious fall in the currency had boosted exports and helped narrow the gap slightly.

Foreign capital inflows had declined since the previous year from R100 billion to R81 billion – a 20 per cent drop. There was no immediate concern, because foreign exchange reserves stood at $35 billion and most economists were confident that capital inflows would cover the deficit. But it would be tight: an international credit squeeze and injudicious internal policies or events could spark that most feared of developing-world scenarios – capital flight.

It was at this inauspicious moment that South Africa acknowledged its energy crisis – an emergency that might well mark the point at which the country began to retreat from its high water mark of post-liberation growth. The event – correctly declared a national emergency – dampened investor confidence in the country as a long-haul destination for funds. In four days of trading in January 2008, more than R8 billion in local bonds and equities were sold by foreign investors – most from the power-plagued gold and platinum sector. By the end of February 2008 disinvestment stood at R17 billion.

This emergency capped a series of issues that had led to investor frustration and slowly diminishing confidence in the country. These included:

- It took a long time for the government to issue 'new order' rights to mining operations. The intention was to enhance black ownership in the mining industry and establish the primacy of the state as the owner of mineral wealth – objectives more consistent with the ANC's Freedom Charter of 1955 than with GEAR. The process began in 2003 and only culminated in 2008 with the awarding to the major mining houses of their new rights – just as the mines were shutting down operations for lack of power. The confusion surrounding this exercise and the government's lack of urgency on the matter led to material amounts of potential fixed investment sidestepping South Africa for more predictable destinations such as Chile, Canada and Australia.
- Delays in announcing revised motor subsidy schemes discouraged further investment in the industry.
- The failure of the government to move ahead in seeking private investor support for its power generation programme discouraged investment. The net outcome was not only a loss of the investment itself but also the discouragement of other high-energy industries.

- The drawn-out land-reform programme of the government cast a pall over both local and foreign investment in agriculture, precisely at a time when international food prices reached historic highs.

The combination of all these factors could not but have an effect on the three key areas set out by the ANC as crucial to their programme of social and economic rectification: economic growth, job growth and the reduction of poverty. None was achieved on a significant enough scale to alter the big picture. The personal consequences for Mbeki were severe, and for his legacy, even more so.

Even at the most optimistic, the growth rate for South Africa until 2010 will not exceed 4 per cent – significantly short of the benchmark 6 per cent growth rate needed to accommodate the expectations of the old elites, the new elites and the numerous members of the welfare classes. Indeed, in early 2008, the national electricity supply authority was begging the government to delay any further major investments until 2013 because of the self-induced national energy crisis. In other words, the country was to close for new business for four years. The impact on growth can scarcely be imagined, but some brave economists did. They put it at 2 per cent off the national growth rate, which would bring it back to 3.5 per cent.

Comparatively, the growth rate for 2007 at 4.5 per cent and even the most optimistic projections of 5 per cent looked unimpressive against competitor countries with no discernible greater advantage (indeed, many with less): China at 11.5 per cent, Poland at 6.5 per cent, Russia at 7.8 per cent, India at 9.3 per cent, Indonesia at 6.3 per cent, Pakistan at 7 per cent, Singapore at 9.4 per cent, Argentina at 8.7 per cent, Colombia at 6.9 per cent, Venezuela at 8.9 per cent and Egypt at 7.4 per cent. More careful analysis of the elements of GDP growth also flagged concerns: stripped of the contribution by finance, real estate and business services (all the beneficiaries rather than the drivers of growth), one ended up with a growth rate of 2.2 per cent.

Unemployment remained stubbornly high through the entire tenure of the Mbeki administration. The RDP had suggested jobs first and then growth. Neither came. GEAR had focused on private-sector jobs as the panacea for the problem. They did not materialise. By 2007, the government had come very much full circle, now accepting a major role in job creation through infrastructure and public-works projects.

The absolute number of unemployed South Africans in an economically active population of 17.1 million increased from 3 163 000 in the year Mbeki took office to 4 391 000 in 2006 (strict definition) or 7 958 000 (if one used the expanded definition that includes those who have not looked for work in the previous four weeks). By March 2007 it was 4.34 million, using the strict definition. Percentagewise, the biggest increase in unemployment was among whites, a clear indication of the impact of affirmative action. But in real terms the numbers were still negligible. The black component carried the heaviest burden, with a 31 per cent increase in unemployment in that period.

If one looks at the unemployment rate, however, a different picture emerges. Unemployment as a percentage of the workforce increased from 25.2 per cent in 1998 to a high of 31.2 per cent in 2003 (strict definition) and 42.1 per cent (expanded definition). Thereafter it began falling. By 2006 it had reached 25.6 per cent in terms of the strict definition. In the second quarter of 2007 it fell to 25.5 per cent and then again to 23 per cent in early 2008. In its Labour Force Survey in September 2007, Statistics South Africa reported that between September 2001 and September 2007 just over two million jobs were created. One and a half million of these were created in the period from September 2004 to September 2007. Much of this positive trend could be attributed to the growth in employment in the construction, financial and retail sectors as the economic boom times led by the credit boom and state consumption spending set in.

Yet analysts warned that it would take double the growth in employment to reach the millennium target of halving unemployment by 2014. By 2007 it was clear to everybody that yet another promise of the Mbeki state would not be met. Inflation and a slowing economy meant fewer new jobs in the formal sector until at least the middle of 2009. The informal sector was failing to generate jobs, and although domestic and agricultural employment had picked up in the period between 2006 and 2008, it was still inadequate. And a massive skills crisis constrained job growth at all levels.

This was the Achilles heel of the Mbeki project: the inability to lift the job absorption levels in the economy on a sustainable basis and ensure a reasonable spread of the benefits of economic growth.

To a large extent, the problem of unemployment was of such a nature that not even the most luminary government could have solved it. The reality was that large numbers of the unemployed were effectively un-employable – uneducated and unskilled. Apartheid education eroded mass-based public education and what was left was further damaged by the policies of the ANC when it came to power. The rate of job creation was further bedevilled by a labour system hostile to employers, which benefited employers who got by on short-term casual labour and penalised those who entered into formal and permanent labour relations. By 2008, half of South Africa's workforce was in casual or temporary jobs – a terrifying indication of the unwillingness of employers to enter formal employment relations under existing legislation. This was a source of enduring irritation to the Mbeki administration: whatever it attempted to do to liberalise the labour regime to push job creation was stymied by the unions protecting their members – in effect the working aristocracy. And then the unions had the temerity to blame them for a lack of long-term jobs!

A key element for the growth of jobs, the small-business or informal sector, simply did not feature. The government's own efforts at enterprise and job creation on a sustainable basis were derisory. As part of its campaign to encourage small-scale business, the government set up four agencies: the National Small Business Council, the Khula Enterprise Finance Corporation, Ntsika Enterprise Promotion Agency and the DTI's Centre for Small Business Promotion. The plethora of bureaucracies alone should have been a warning of what was to come.

The National Small Business Council, set up to encourage this sector in 2003, collapsed three years later in a welter of maladministration and corruption. It is too early to know whether its successor, the Small Business Advisory Council, will fare any better. The other agencies have had a dismal record of job creation, as they failed to support small business.

Between September 2001 and September 2007, employment in the non-agricultural informal sector had grown from 1 967 000 to 2 1222 000 souls – a princely 7 per cent – while its share of total employment had fallen in the same period from 17.6 per cent to 16 per cent, according to Statistics South Africa's 2007 Labour Force Survey. Agricultural employment had stagnated during the same period, despite the huge investments the state had made in its land-reform programme with all its supposed work multiplier effects. The point is that both target sectors in which the ANC had staked reputation, money and ideology to grow jobs had failed miserably. It had been private formal-sector employment and government jobs that had grown.

An endless series of reasons were adduced for the failure of small and predominantly black businesses. Some were hard factors – failure by government to pay its suppliers on time due to the implosion of these departments; the red tape for even small businesses and the glacially slow decision-making in the state agencies. Ivor Blumenthal, chief executive of one the largest Sectoral Training Authorities, claimed in *Business Day* on 5 February 2008 that state tardiness in financing small business had led to the loss of a million business opportunities – an astonishing proposition if true.

Alan Hirsch, former presidential economic advisor, remarks that the lesson of these failed initiatives was that it was easier to succeed if one built on existing institutions rather than erect new ones.[8] The lesson, an obvious one, was true for nearly all state ventures during the Mbeki administration as it heedlessly pursued its ideological and legislative overreach by destroying as much that was good as was bad, then failing to replace it with anything that functioned to expectation.

Less explored in all this, however, was the issue of business culture. In many cases, the black small-business operator was an entrepreneur forced into the mould of a proxy corporate executive, in order to qualify for support and funding. It was a naïve hope.

From personal experiences in setting up small-scale enterprises as part of an industry-led project to advance black media entrepreneurs, I believe the missing element in almost every case was an understanding on the part of the entrepreneur of the concept of finite resource. In most cases, loans and capital investment were regarded as something to be used for immediate advantage; profit was there for instant consumption; a business plan was only useful to the extent that it could secure the funding; and the long term stretched only from breakfast to dinner.

This was such a universal phenomenon that it would be naïve to suggest that it is not part of a prevailing informal business culture. It is something that, if not changed, must inevitably result in greater consumption of wealth than its creation.

With inadequate growth rates and sluggish job growth, poverty remained as intractably embedded as ever. The exact extent of this poverty was difficult to gauge. My personal view is that it is overstated, for the simple reason that at least one-third of the households in the country and 22 per cent of its inhabitants, recipients of state handouts, can be guaranteed to lie about their other sources of income. It is like that the world over. Ironically, the more the ANC expands the welfare state, the higher will be the reported poverty levels.

Nevertheless, the stats showed that the number of South Africans living on less than one US dollar a day doubled during the Mbeki era, but decreased as a proportion of the population. The creation of Mbeki's ambitious dependency state had by 2006 pegged back the rise in poverty and forced a marginal reduction, but nobody was fooled. This was not a reduction in poverty primarily through the creation of sustainable jobs. It was Band-Aid.

In October 2007, finance minister Trevor Manuel all but read the eulogy for the post-liberation boom times. In his mid-term budget he warned that contrary to government forecasts, growth rates would not exceed 5 per cent until 2010; the state would have to prune its expenditure significantly; South Africa had to improve its productivity and export performance; and the deficit on the current account was projected to climb to 7.8 per cent in 2010, the highest in sixty years, as imports fed the voracious costs of the government's infrastructural investment programme. By the end of 2007, the South African Chamber of Commerce Business Confidence Index had sunk to its lowest level in four years, and audit firm Grant Thornton's *International Business Report* for 2008 recorded the third successive year of a drop in optimism levels. Growth in retail sales in November of 2007 had yielded their slowest rate of increase in five years.

These sombre notes from the internal market were matched by negative signals arising from the global markets. Fears of recession in the United States sent the Johannesburg Securities Exchange tumbling in the opening months of 2008 – down 12 per cent (R700 billion) of its value. The tumble challenged the wisdom that the developing world could be uncoupled from the major markets. Rather, the signal sent was that hostile international indexes were being compounded by internal concerns relating to the quality of governance in the country.

Thirteen years into ANC rule and well into the seventh year of Mbeki's tenure, the government had achieved remarkable macro-economic stability and, with propitious international circumstances, had maintained it over a long period. It had ensured that very large numbers of its voters were living better, more prosperous lives. A wealthy new middle class had emerged and millions of South Africans were keeping the wolf from the door through state grants and subsidies.

And yet the Mbeki administration had failed to meet its economic growth target and had met less than half its job creation objectives. Inflation control was slipping away and poverty remained intractable. The credit-linked consumer boom had spluttered to a close, cost of living was on the march, public services were parlous and power was intermittent.

Money had become expensive, house prices had stagnated, stocks tumbled and a slew of expensive new government social programmes was on the table.

Why should this be so? Why should a second-tier country which began in 1994 with international credibility, good infrastructure, deep capital markets, a bedrock of high-level skills, limitless commodities amid an unprecedented international commodity scramble, investment allure amid the greatest global investment liquidity in history and an impeccable record of macro-economic management under its new leadership – a veritable economic paragon – suffer comparatively pedestrian growth rates, stagnant employment and falling international competitiveness?

The answer, central to understanding the Mbeki legacy, lies in a number of interlinked factors that will be explored in succeeding chapters. Some of these were exogenous, some inherited. But many were the result of self-defeating actions by the administration, which resulted in it being trapped by the logic of the unintended consequence.

The first of these actions was the high cost incurred by the country in competitive terms because of the government's single-minded focus on inappropriate rectification, redistribution and often retributive economic policies. The second, tied to the first, was failure to nurse the institutions of state through the challenges of growth. The third lies in the administration's contradictory regulatory policies and its failure to reduce red tape, while the fourth, linked to all the others, was the government's failure to shore up expeditiously the country's ailing infrastructure. Historically this will be the central charge against Mbeki and his stewardship: that ideology overwhelmed pragmatism; vision supplanted action; the desirable outflanked the doable; and, finally, delusion usurped reality.

CHAPTER 8

Neither civil nor serving

Good government only happens when the people working in it
do their jobs, and do them well. — MATTHEW LESKO[1]

T HE BUREAUCRACY INHERITED BY A LIBERATED SOUTH AFRICA
in 1994 was still largely the misshapen creature of the apartheid years.
It fell into three broad categories. The first was a reasonably sophisticated
and efficient public or civil service, geared to looking after the interests
of the racial minorities to a developed-world standard. The second was a
clutch of horrendously incompetent and corrupt bureaucracies, serving
the homeland administrations created by the apartheid state as a substitute
for a national franchise for black people. The third was a range of parastatal
organisations in the hard services: research, strategic industries and public
financial sectors. Some were good, some excellent and some weak.

Cross-cutting all levels of government was thus a divide between a
public service catering to the Californian lifestyles and expectations of a
minority and, on the other side, the endless round of poor service, bribery
and insult that the majority of black South Africans encountered daily. No
greater challenge was set the new government than turning this bureaucracy around so as to serve all the citizens in terms of the constitutional
demands for transparency, fairness and efficiency.

The task, let it immediately be said, was impossible within the time-
frames set by the new government. Only revolution would achieve that.
Reorienting a deeply entrenched bureaucracy towards new ways of thinking
and doing things is a lengthy and arduous process. Mountains of management theory exist on the topic. But this task was immeasurably complicated
in South Africa by a series of other factors, some self-induced and others
exogenous.

First, the state reorganised its architecture. The previous four provinces
and several homelands were consolidated into nine provinces. Cities and
towns were swept into single mega-cities. Resolving the consequent chaos
absorbed at least the first four years of the ANC's tenure in government,

and even as Mbeki approached the end of his last term as president, there were still sometimes violent disputes over provincial boundaries. Not content with this shambles, the government indicated in 2007 that it intended creating a unified 'super civil service' – thus guaranteeing yet more years of turmoil.

Second, the sheer volume of additional services was overwhelming. While the ANC massively extended its educational, welfare and health systems, at least quantitatively if not qualitatively, the bureaucracy battled to keep up. In most sectors the demand for services doubled; in others it trebled; and in many, quadrupled.

Third, the inevitable consequence of the heavily rights-based society at the heart of the ANC philosophy was a corresponding increase in the level of demand from the citizenry. And so the administration found itself caught in the classic vice: increasing expectation of service was met by a falling capacity to meet that expectation. In the last years of Mbeki's tenure, the incidents of public protests against 'service delivery' in the poorer areas reached levels not seen during the height of the anti-apartheid struggle (although mercifully not nearly as violent, largely due to more civilised policing methods). There was a huge injustice to Mbeki here. The reality was that hard services *had* improved, but not to the expected levels of its more demanding electorate. This was particularly so in the sphere of the services such as security, health and education, where, as we shall see, a massive misdirection of state resources, coupled with the ANC's obsessive pursuit of numbers, ensured greater access to these services, but at a materially degraded quality.

But it is the last compounding factor that played the most corrosive role in the weakening of the state system. This was the view that the South African state – and indeed society – had been somehow decimated by the apartheid system and that only its complete reconstruction in both principle and personnel would suffice. The comparison assiduously cultivated was with Germany or Japan in 1945. This was of course untrue, and a canard that would cost the ANC heavily.

The reality is that while apartheid policies had undoubtedly taken their toll on the society through legislative measures, most of the social and economic segregation laws were off the statute books a full ten years before the ANC came to power. By the time Mbeki assumed office, they were nearly fifteen years gone. And by the end of Mbeki's rule, it will be a quarter of a century since the first apartheid laws were repealed.

Additionally, from the early 1980s onwards, the state had invested massively in education to levels equal to Japan as percentage of GDP. Much of this investment was directed towards black schools but was in the end pointless, as these schools had become sites of political struggle from which they never recovered. Increasingly, even under the apartheid system, large numbers of white civil servants had been forced to address the growing new black middle class and its demands for better services.

The public service, with its strong layer of existing expertise, was arguably both willing and capable of reorienting to the new demands. The political liberation of the country in 1994 had invoked a very powerful national sense of *zeitgeist*, of mission and of hope which, if not exactly enthusing the existing servants (enthusiastic public servants are in any case a contradiction in terms), did not demoralise them. In all my discussions with senior old-era administrators at this crucial juncture in the country's history, all without exception said they were willing to continue, but had little illusion that they would be allowed to do so. They were just waiting for the tap on the shoulder.

Here at least was the base upon which to build. But the loyalty or otherwise of this old-guard bureaucracy was never to be tested. The watchwords on the lips of virtually every cabinet minister I met at that time were 'major restructuring' and 'bringing in our own people'. The ANC was disarmingly honest about its intentions. Members of the party were to be deployed to the public service, and immediately. The bureaucracy was to become an arm of the party as quickly as possible. I recall one newly installed minister asking me what I thought would be the greatest error the ANC could make at this early stage of its tenure. I responded unhesitatingly: 'Squandering our scarce human resource.'

The aggressive new affirmative action policies of the government – greatly increased under Mbeki and often with a distinctly cronyistic flavour – simply swept the old guard away with generous handshakes and many slaps on the back. Those that hung on were marginalised. Those that still held high office were often subjected to endless conspiracies by their new staff, usually alleging racism and sexism. Most simply left for a quieter life. In 1993, whites comprised 38.5 per cent of public servants at national level. By 2003, according to Roger Southall,[2] it was 23.6 per cent, where it more or less stabilised. The attrition was highest at the senior level. The point to emphasise here was not that it was *white* public servants that were leaving, but that it was *experienced* ones who were going. Institutional memory was being lost at a terrifying rate.

The combination of all these factors left the public-service platform weakened precisely at the time it was most needed to drive through the government's ambitious reform proposals. The turnover in high-level black managerial staff was disturbing as incumbents came and went because of reassignment, illness, incompetence, corruption or, increasingly, into the ranks of the private sector where they swelled the equity numbers. In the rank and file, vacancies mushroomed: there were few whites prepared to take service under the conditions offered (most advertisements in any case stated preference would be given to black applicants), yet there were simply not enough qualified black candidates. By 2008 the public-service databases showed 330 987 vacant posts.

Newly employed staff found themselves in sections under heads of department who were themselves new to the job. Section heads found themselves endlessly transferred from one post to another to fill vacancies. As soon as an iota of skill was acquired, the official was promoted and the section lost the expertise.

Competent heads of department, black or white, who attempted to impose discipline and a work ethic were all too often targeted for smear attacks, subversion and back-channel complaints to the political leadership. Protective measures in the labour laws militated against quick and speedy finalisation of disciplinary actions against miscreants, while the rapid unionisation of the public service by the ANC's alliance partners ensured in too many instances the entrenchment and defence of mediocrity as the yardstick of performance.

The greatest victims of this, ironically, were the new black incumbents who had to endure the accusation by the racial minorities that they were incompetent, and the charge by the majority that they were 'sell-outs' if they tried to do anything about it. It was a grossly unfair position in which to place people, and it is a lasting tribute to the many dedicated and competent black administrators that the situation was not even worse.

The cumbersome nature of public-service disciplinary processes is best illustrated by the case of one Hamilton Ntshangase. In 1999, while employed by the Department of Arts, Culture and Tourism in KwaZulu-Natal, he was suspended for financial irregularities involving R1.2 million of public money. Three years later and still suspended on full pay, an internal inquiry gave him a reprimand and reinstated him. The matter was taken on appeal by the then minister of culture, and in late 2007 a labour appeal court ruled the penalty was 'grossly unreasonable' in the light of the facts and ordered him fired forthwith.[3] It had taken *eight years* to reach the decision, during which time Mr Ntshangase had drawn a salary every month. This incident, one of thousands, characterised the inability of the public service to discipline its employees effectively and expeditiously.

If that were not enough, the departments themselves were in an endless process of 'restructuring' – the oldest refuge of the desperate manager who has run out of ideas.

This erosion of the core competence to actually get things *done* was greatly compounded by what I would call ideological overreach – the imposition of strategies that were inappropriate, in some cases catastrophically so. Five particular areas are important here: the decision to focus on preventative policing at the expense of crime detection, the emphasis on preventative as opposed to curative public medicine, the imposition of elaborate pedagogical regimes that would tax the educational systems of even developed countries, inappropriate land-reform measures and, finally, developed-world answers to developing-world housing problems.

The reasons for this overreach are varied, but overwhelmingly it was the ANC's reliance in its early years on irrelevant international theory, and all too often on consultants infused with the idea of using this fragile new society as the laboratory for every outdated and clichéd theory tried and largely rejected by the developed world. The exiles and their ideological allies, having spent many long years languishing in distant parts or the more disconnected regions of academia, dreaming about what they would do if they were in power, now had their chance. Retrospectively, we now realise how out of touch they were with the country and the society they had been summoned to govern, none more so than the president himself. The cost for the country has been high.

In nearly all cases these early strategies failed. Late in the Mbeki administration's tenure, the ANC made attempts to scrabble back, but by then it was too late. Damage had been done to the cause of internal cohesion and the nation-building project had been set back by a decade or longer. In many cases, however, critical lessons remained unlearnt and new waves of legislation promised nothing but more of the same – wasted costs and misspent time.

Into this strategic and ideological malaise was injected an endless flow of new policies and legislation, generated by a legislature maddened with the delight of law-making and often in contempt of its practicality or consequence. Ideological overreach was compounded by legislative overreach.

To top it all, the bitter political struggle for succession to the presidency within the party inevitably replicated itself throughout the ANC-led bureaucracy. The most obvious example of this was internal wars between various security forces supporting different candidates.

Not surprisingly, the creaking bureaucracies staggered, cracked and slowly began to disintegrate, leading to the emergence of what I have called the proxy state, to be discussed in a later chapter.

The most immediate example of a declining quality of public administration was a rapid deterioration in the quality of public financial management. To be fair, part of this was the result of another piece of ideological overreach by the ANC government: onerous financial accounting standards encapsulated in legislation. Between this and the exodus of skilled white staff, public finances fell into a parlous condition.

In late 2007, auditor-general Terence Nombembe reported that only three out of thirty-four national departments had clean audit reports and only ten of 108 provincial departments were clean. More than one-third of the national departments and 40 per cent of those in the provinces received qualified reports. His warning was stark: unless the situation improved there would be serious consequences within two to three years. The reports indicated that there had been little improvement over the previous two years.[4]

By 2008 the stage had been reached where the office of the auditor-general was itself at risk from financial collapse, due to late payments by municipalities for its auditing services and the high costs of appointing private external auditors to help the overwhelmed internal staff. A report by parliament's standing committee on the auditor-general observed that it was extremely concerned about the deficits in funding.

This weakness in internal operating procedures by the public departments was compounded by a rolling drama of tender irregularities in both the state and parastatal departments that kept the media, judiciary and investigators busy during the Mbeki presidency. In one case alone, a R1.3 billion suit was brought against the post office for a revoked contract. In another, the national lottery was suspended for eight months due to a bungled tender process.

The *political* response to this by the Mbeki administration was typical: denial followed by attack. The *technical* response was threefold: thousands of 'consultants' to get things back on track, information technology (IT) systems (state IT spend was due to rise to R8 billion by 2011) and mountains of new documents and plans. All are poor crutches for a culturally and technically bankrupt bureaucracy. Consultants have a vested interest in perpetuating chaos. IT vendors have an interest in selling complicated systems to unskilled people so they can benefit from onerous post-installation maintenance agreements. Both responses translated into tens of millions of wasted rands and even more precious time. By the end of 2007, the minister of finance was warning that state departments should cut back on their 'temporary' (many retrenched and white) officials and consultants. The total bill for all public departments for these services was estimated to be approaching R1 billion a year by 2008. Sadly, when attempts were made in early 2008 to follow the minister's instruction, such chaos occurred in a number of departments, including justice, that the decision had to be reversed and the 'temporaries' rehired. For some it was the third time they were being called back into public service after being retrenched.

As the manifold failings of the departments became more apparent, directors-general and ministers fell into the ageless trap best summarised by the old adage attributed to an erstwhile chief executive at General Electric: 'All faces to the boss and arses to the customer.' The South African public service at national, provincial and local level became fatally introspective, demoralised and defensive. Any casual reading of the various annual reports of the departments of state will immediately show that an inordinate amount of time, energy and money is devoted to the internal organisation, theory, development and training of the bureaucracy as opposed to the efficacy of policy.

These are not state departments at work: they are giant planning workshops and in-house training projects. Further, the performance criteria commendably set for each department as reported to parliament each year are redolent with objectives for the completion of plans, reviews, strategy documents and programmes. What they lack, in some cases entirely, are performance targets on the *outcomes*, the material impact on the public they serve. It is, to use the cliché, analysis paralysis and it goes to the heart of the problem: the proliferation of planners and marketers in the new public service and the aching absence of implementers.

The problem proved to be particularly acute at local government level, the interface with most ordinary citizens. The political context that contributed to this – lack of accountability by councillors and internal ANC politics – has been dealt with in Part I of this book. Here we will look at the impact the skills crisis had on the local authorities.

By 2007, 136 out of 284 municipalities were determined by the government to be unable to fulfil their basic functions and had to be helped by external interventions. Put simply, little more than a decade of ANC rule had reduced very nearly half of South Africa's local authorities and millions of citizens to a situation of semi-administered rule, not so very distant in principle (though very different in style) from the way black townships had been administered in the apartheid era.

Across the country these institutions had collapsed, one after the other, in a surge of underfunding, corruption, destructive internal politicking involving party factions, incompetence, nepotism and indifference. Delivery of services had been affected.

A paper prepared in 2007 by the official opposition, the Democratic Alliance, on the basis of government documents and answers to questions in parliament, painted the gloomy picture.[5] It pointed out that for the 2005 financial year, 46 per cent of local authorities had not submitted their annual financial statements on time or at all.

Nearly 80 per cent of the municipalities had difficulty recovering enough in revenue to pay for basic services. This non-payment factor was a direct result of the 'rent boycotts' of the apartheid era against the administrators of the black townships. Like much else in the ANC, this struggle culture survived the transformation to a liberated South Africa. The auditor-general observed: 'Overall an alarming trend was discovered, namely the debt management and the basis of income generation might not provide sufficient funds for delivering the services expected of municipalities. This means that sustainability of service provision by local government has to be called into question.'[6]

By 2007, total municipal debt stood at R40 billion and debt in the major cities of South Africa had increased by more than 20 per cent since the previous year. The auditor-general cited the lack of skilled personnel as one reason for the failure to recover debt – one municipality had creditors' days, the average period of outstanding debt, of 489. The DA report also disclosed that whereas only 30 per cent of municipal revenue should be spent on wages, in South African municipalities the salary bill *exceeded* the cost of services by R10 billion. Yet, according to government statistics, 36 per cent of municipal managers had only matric and a diploma qualification or less. The South African ratepayer was clearly not getting bang for the buck.

The public had responded initially by petition and representation, but as these failed to bring about results, protest began to escalate to street level and even violence.

In 2004/5 there were 881 illegal demonstrations against 'service delivery' and 5 085 legal protests across 90 per cent of the country's municipalities. By 2007, the incidence was estimated in the region of 10 000 – a far higher occurrence of public disturbance than at the height of the anti-apartheid struggle, although infinitely less violent.[7]

The government argued that a number of these protests were incited by political factions within the towns seeking to advance their own programmes of self-enrichment. This was undoubtedly true, even if they were factions within the local ANC, but this could still not camouflage the fact that a growing wave of public anger was afoot.

The government response was to embark on an aggressive programme of intervention called 'Siyenza Manje' which was part of the broader Project Consolidate. More than R741 million was allocated over three years to assist the municipalities. The Development Bank of Southern Africa received R45 million to assist with the completion of projects and to deploy 118 experts in the municipalities to assist in the key areas of financial management and engineering. Many of these were ... retired white former local government administrators.

In most cases, new local government financing regulations greatly increased the rates burden on property owners and businesses, with a potentially negative impact on inflation. The government also passed draconian new regulations penalising councils that did not collect outstanding debt from consumers. It is doubtful whether this will succeed – every prior effort has failed through a lack of political will and it is hard to believe a populist government under a new president will have any better luck.

In April 2007, the Centre for Development and Enterprise published a report that found the following in regard to national issues inflaming the situation:

> Among these issues are shortage of skills, an absence of leadership and accountability over a wide range of governance functions, and a yawning gap between the formulation of ambitious policies and the availability of management resources and expertise on the ground to make them a reality. To these might be added a tendency to underestimate the strains and pressures of the restructuring and transformation of local government.[8]

Specific contributory issues at local level were:
- an inability to spend funds, even where available, because of lack of skills;
- personality rows between administrators and elected officials;
- incompetence and indifference of councillors;
- corruption in awarding of tenders;
- infrastructural collapse;
- empty promises;
- lack of high-level skills;
- unionised and unproductive workers;
- lack of internal financial controls;
- no maintenance of plant and equipment; and
- indifference to the protests of the public.

Encouragingly, into this void had stepped local agencies, in many cases NGOs and white-led business, church and social groups, to work with the poor neighbourhoods in redressing the failures of state policy to the benefit of the whole town. This was to largely replicate a phenomenon in the agricultural sector, which will be discussed later. The intriguing effect, as the report observes, is that the protests in a particular town could be characterised as a coalition of the previously advantaged and the currently disadvantaged against an incompetent and indifferent new elite.

A last point about this report is worth making. The senior officials and elected members of these towns were virtually to a man (or woman) ANC members, beneficiaries of the policy of the same 'deployment' of cadres as had occurred at national level. Public response to this deployment is worth reporting in full:

> As interviewees and focus groups in both areas amply confirmed, it leads to profound cynicism about all public appointments, and encourages conspiracy theories about all political governance issues. Responses in both areas were marked by cynicism, conspiracy theories and anger fuelled by a sense of betrayal.[9]

The response to the report by Sydney Mufamadi, minister of provincial and local government, is worth considering in its totality, for no other reason than that it was almost a template for ministerial response to most criticism during the Mbeki era. He began by impugning the motives of the researchers, blamed apartheid, claimed the protests were an indication of ANC success in that communities which had not yet benefited from the improvements seen by others were impatient, and ended by hinting at some conspiracy by the protestors and 'instigators' to embarrass the government.[10]

Finally, Mufamadi alluded – quite correctly as it turned out – to the huge improvements that had been made in providing basic services to the poorer communities. By 2007, 75 per cent of residents had access to electricity and 85 per cent to potable water. It was also true that under the Mbeki administration, 2 355 913 houses were built by the government between 1994 and 2007 – an astonishing achievement – although the back-log of the unhoused never seemed to decrease, due to corruption in the administration of the scheme, fraud and the influx of illegal immigrants.

He might also have pointed out that central government expenditure on local authorities had increased from R63.1 billion in 2001/2 to R114.4 billion five years later – a material escalation of 16 per cent a year. By 2008/9 it is expected to pass the R160 billion mark, although part of this will be spent on infrastructure for the 2010 Football World Cup.

The statistics, however, were small comfort to those who had neither home nor water or electricity, and meant not much more to those who did – not when rolling power outages due to the lack of generation kept them in the dark, unemployment meant they could not pay the bills or rates, children went uneducated, safety was at risk and the local hospital acted more as a hospice than a place of recuperation.

In the end, what the minister thought was irrelevant. Mufamadi paid the ultimate price of the politician who does not listen early enough. In the purge of Mbeki's men from the ANC's NEC on 7 January 2008, he received his marching orders from his party, if not yet his president.

It is to an examination of the impact of institutional failure, arrested state formation, that we now turn, beginning with the critical areas of enforcement, justice, education and health, moving to the hard services, housing and infrastructure, dealing with food security and concluding with a discussion of the proxy state that has emerged and is one of the legacies of the Mbeki era.

CHAPTER 9

Crime and punishment

Crime is a fact of the human species, a fact of that species alone,
but it is above all the secret aspect, impenetrable and hidden.
Crime hides, and by far the most terrifying things are those
which elude us. — GEORGES BATAILLE[1]

PERHAPS NO AREA OF GOVERNMENT EXPOSES THE MBEKI state's failure to get to grips with the challenges of modernity as much as that of security and justice.

The scale of the problem needs to be stated baldly. In the year from April 2006 to April 2007, 19 202 South Africans were murdered. Another 20 142 people escaped murder attempts. Slightly more than 126 000 experienced robbery with aggravating circumstances and 52 617 people were raped. In general, one-quarter of the South African population is subjected to at least one instance of crime every year.[2]

The sheer scale of this assault by the criminal formations on the citizenry is terrifying. Compared internationally it is even scarier. The murder rate per 100 000 in South Africa is 40.5, compared to 1.43 in the United Kingdom and 5.62 in the United States. Overall, a resident in South Africa is eight times more likely to be murdered than the average of all other countries in the world, and three times more likely to be robbed.

It is, however, immediately necessary to raise a caveat. Police statistics show that 81 per cent of the people murdered in South Africa are killed by somebody they know – a spouse, partner, relative, fellow gang member or friend. The social milieu within which this can happen will be discussed later, but suffice it to say here that if one strips out such domestic violence, the rate of slaughter by an unrelated party in South Africa becomes more manageable on a comparative basis, and brings us to the category of only 'very' as opposed to 'insanely' violent societies. But this is semantics and statistics. The reality is that in South Africa, both strangers and acquaintances are killed at a terrifying rate.

The international context within which this occurs was captured best by the Mo Ibrahim Foundation's annual award for good governance in African countries, which gave South Africa a ranking of forty-six out of forty-eight countries for safety and security, slipping from eighth from the bottom when Mbeki took office. Only the Sudan, convulsed with civil war warranting the intervention of the African Union (AU) and the UN, and Burundi, trapped in the continuing turbulence of the Great Lakes region, were worse than South Africa. Even Nigeria, the quintessentially lawless country of South African imagination, did better.[3]

The irony is that while the government *has* committed resources to the problem, and even though violent crime levels *have* generally dropped over the decade, the public perception remains intractably guided by the view that things are getting worse and that the crime rate is uncontrollable. One reason for this belief is the most obvious: the crime rate *is* appallingly and unacceptably high. Another is that Mbeki failed to convince his citizens that he was either concerned about the issue or capable of dealing with it. The worst suspicions of the public were confirmed with the release of the 2006/7 crime statistics, which showed a significant rise in nearly all categories of crime. Whether this was due to unique circumstances or is part of a new trend remains to be seen, as the new half-yearly statistics, conveniently released just in time for the ANC national conference in 2007, showed some roll-back in the worst contact crimes. The insouciance of the commissioner of police, Jackie Selebi, and his senior staff to the bad news at the public release of the numbers was less than reassuring.

The crime trends in the first twelve years of the ANC government's tenure were generally positive in regard to murder and attempted murder. The number of murders decreased from 25 965 to 18 528 – 26 per cent – during this time, although one must bear in mind the numbers in 1996 still contained many politically related killings at the tail-end of the political transition. Most of the improvement took place during Mbeki's tenure. Attempted murders decreased by a similar rate. Robbery with aggravating circumstances, however, increased by 49.3 per cent and rape climbed by 17.6 per cent, although the latter figure needs to be treated with some caution.[4] The greater openness about the issue and the sterling work of anti-rape groups have tended to improve reporting of this crime. The high point of violence was 2002/3; thereafter, significant improvement was shown in the serious and 'contact' categories, although the total incidence of crime increased from 2 022 899 in 1994/5 to 2 125 227 in 2006/7. The bottom line was that although the criminals were murdering and attempting to murder fewer people, they were robbing them (often brutally) and raping them at an increasing tempo.

The 2006/7 statistics showed murder rates on the climb again compared to the previous year, with murder up 3.6 per cent and attempted murder up by 2.1 per cent. Aggravated robbery was up 5.7 per cent and rape increased by 4.2 per cent over the previous year. Digging deeper, residential burglaries increased by 25.4 per cent, car hijackings blossomed, business burglaries were up by 52.2 per cent, bank robberies by 118 per cent and cash-in-transit robberies by 21.9 per cent. As many of the business burglaries were in shopping malls and cash-in-transit heists on the main roads, the public sense of vulnerability to crime in their homes, streets, restaurants, banks, cars and public spaces was enormously strengthened.[5]

Even these figures, horrific as they are, might be understated. A 2003 survey estimated an 18 per cent under-reporting by the police in the category of housebreaking, merely because large numbers of the public did not bother to report intrusions because they had no confidence anything would be done about them. Again, the authorities introduced a requirement in 2004 that the police reduce the incidence of serious crime categories by between 7 per cent and 10 per cent a year. While admirable, anecdotal reports indicate that this has had the effect of the police seeking to redesignate crimes or even avoid accepting complaints. This obviously affects statistics.

Some short-term explanations were proffered for the surge in crime between 2005/6 and 2006/7. The state had cleared large numbers of short-term prisoners from the prison system because of space problems. It was also a year during which there had been a prolonged and bloody strike by security guards. More than fifty people were murdered during that strike, most allegedly by security guards, and the police argued that the criminal fraternity made hay. A more sinister possibility, not canvassed by the police, is that a number of the striking workers may have found common cause with the criminals, and that such relationships may be continuing. If so, the likelihood of business or residential crime declining in the near future is minimal, as was borne out by the release of the April to September 2007 crime statistics, which saw yet another hike in the levels of robbery at residential (7 per cent) and commercial premises (29 per cent), precisely the sites most vulnerable to renegade security guards. The rise in business robberies between 2006 and 2007 in provinces outside Gauteng (where hugely active policing had begun to force such crime down and out) was terrifying: 169 per cent in the Western Cape, 191 per cent in the Free State and Limpopo, 150 per cent in the Northern Cape, 112 per cent in the Eastern Cape, 71 per cent in KwaZulu-Natal and 48 per cent in the North West.[6] The surge in crime could thus be a trend driven by new dynamics and not an aberration: an alliance between the private militia (part of the proxy state) and the criminal formations. More about this later.

Whichever way the government sought to gild this wilting lily, the reality was that crime still constituted a devastating injury to the lives of the citizenry and to the business of the country. It demanded at the very least an elevation of the problem to the level of a national crisis and the fullest, unswerving attention of the president and his administration. No such thing.

Part of the denialist ideology of the Mbeki administration as it relates to crime is to scapegoat its victims. Perhaps the most insidious charge is that those who complain are exhibiting a latent racist sentiment. Crime thus becomes a preoccupation of the wealthy minorities – captured infamously by the minister of safety and security, who suggested that people who whinge about crime should leave the country. Black people, the argument runs, have endured crime in poor areas for generations.

The research is against this fondly held ANC prejudice in two ways.

A survey of public perceptions of crime undertaken in 2003 showed a significant and generalised increase in both the perception and experience of crime across all income and race groups, although the white and Indian minorities had a heightened perception.[7]

Comparisons between a 1998 survey and a 2003 one show a decline across the board in people's levels of perception about security in their homes and on the streets. A 2007 survey, meanwhile, showed that fully two-thirds of the population believed crime had increased, again with the strongest negativity in the Indian and white communities. A third survey, carried out in Johannesburg in September 2007, showed that the percentage of households that felt unsafe in Alexandra, Sandton and Johannesburg had risen from 27 per cent in 2006 to 41 per cent a year later.[8]

The impact of crime has also changed lifestyles for most South Africans. In the 2003 survey, one-third of the respondents said they did not let their children play on the streets, while slightly less said they did not walk, play or rest in public places. One in five rural dwellers did not walk to collect firewood for fear of crime and one in ten said they did not walk to fetch water.[9] If one looks at the urban statistics on a racial basis, it is clear that the

Indian and white minorities are most affected by these changed lifestyle patterns in the cities. These results, if anything, are probably worse today.

But the results do raise the intriguing question of whether the white and Indian minorities, the wealthiest, are affected by an irrational negativity in regard to the crime issue or have legitimate reasons for their fears. The answer was given in a May 2007 research project, which showed that while roughly one in every ten black and coloured people had been a victim of crime in the six months prior to the survey, double that proportion of whites and Indians had been victims (20 per cent and 22 per cent respectively) in the same period. Ironically, it was also the white and Indian minorities who showed in the same survey the greatest willingness to assist the state by joining neighbourhood watch groups and the police reservists.[10]

The research thus challenged the conventional wisdom that black people endure the heaviest burden of crime, although it is undoubtedly true that black and coloured communities experience the highest rate of murder, 81 per cent of it domestic or peer related. The research also rebutted the view that the racial minorities, particularly the whites, simply complain. The reverse is true: whites are the most proactive in supporting the state policing agencies, whether through joining the reserves or by taking part in community anti-crime activities.

This crime premium carried by the minorities, proportionately twice as heavy as that carried by the majority, coupled with the dismissive attitude of the Mbeki administration, was one of the major reasons the president's already limited support among these minorities all but evaporated during his tenure.

Crime played out in other areas as well. Dr Susan Steinman, an author and expert in workplace violence, observed the way generalised violence had found its way into the workplace, with a steady rise of incidents during strikes.[11]

The levels of crime also had a significant impact on business. The country's major retailers estimated that shrinkage and theft added another 3 per cent to their costs. In 2007, the total cost to business of shoplifting, fraud and theft was estimated to be R3.5 billion. As this was inevitably passed on to the consumer, the effect was inflationary. A report by the consulting firm Grant Thornton came to the conclusion that the direct cost of crime on sales was 1.1 per cent and 5 per cent on labour costs. The SAPS report for the first semester of 2007 observed ominously that the heaviest burden of the runaway business robbery category was on small to medium factories and shops. Given the government's attempts to build this sector of the economy, the broader political implications of this statistic are obvious.

The PricewaterhouseCoopers global survey published in 2007 showed that South Africa had the highest number of companies in the world affected by crime. These criminal activities include money laundering, bribery and fraud with an estimated R600 million lost to economic crimes (excluding direct robbery and theft) between 2005 and 2007. More than 70 per cent of South African companies doing business in the country had fallen prey to fraud, compared to 43 per cent on a global scale. South African companies, as distinct from global ones operating in the country, reported an average of twenty-three incidents of economic crime each during the period, which was about 200 per cent higher than the global average and 110 per cent up compared to 2005.[12]

The effect of crime on business was compounded in another way – criminal sabotage of infrastructure. As the capacity for enforcement declined and the appetite for crime rose, the incidence of theft of cabling from electrical and telephone systems became endemic. Long before crippling power outages became a feature of daily life due to under-provision by the responsible authorities, large residential areas were periodically left without power or landlines because of the depredations of cable thieves. The costs were estimated by the Non-Ferrous Metal Anti-Theft Association to be about R500 million in a single year, with a potential economic effect ten times greater.[13] Telkom's reported direct loss from cable theft between 1 April 2007 and 31 January 2008 was R863 million – a destruction of the country's telecommunications infrastructure comparable to a low-intensity war of sabotage.

Ineffectual as they were, the guardians of law and order also found themselves victims of this new lawlessness. A South African Institute of Race Relations survey released in 2007 showed that 64 per cent more policemen had been killed in the line of duty in the eleven years since liberation than in the corresponding period immediately prior to 1994. The numbers were a sobering reflection of the increased violence and firepower applied by the criminals and the weakening levels of discipline among the police.

Why this mayhem? The long-term explanations for the high levels of crime in South Africa are variously, furiously and sometimes vacuously argued by statisticians, academics, police, politicians and social workers.

The structural argument, dear to the heart of the Mbeki administration, remains that crime is a consequence of poverty and an unequal society. This may be partly true, but it fails to explain why societies with far greater poverty – and even greater inequality – experience less crime, particularly the violent variety. Nigeria is a case in point and here I need to digress slightly. One of my enduring memories of time spent working in Nigeria was receiving a cellphone text message (SMS) from my wife in South Africa, telling me she had narrowly missed being killed in a shootout during a bandit raid against a jewellery store in a northern Johannesburg shopping mall.

The SMS arrived in the middle of a business meeting in Lagos with a group of Nigerian businessmen, every one of whom had visited, worked or lived in South Africa. Not surprisingly, my electronic missive caused a fairly dramatic interruption to proceedings. Having once established from home that everybody was safe, the conversation around the table immediately turned to crime in South Africa. My colleagues recalled with genuine horror the crime and the police indifference they had personally encountered while down south – so different from their experiences in Nigeria, where crime and criminals (the white-collar variety excepted) are dealt with expeditiously and robustly, as I have witnessed first hand.

The discussion was advanced further when I returned home and a senior Nigerian embassy official told me how humiliated he felt by having to take responsibility for the Nigerian criminals who come to South Africa, precisely because it is so much easier to do business here than in their own country, due to the incompetence, corruption and indifference of the immigration and security services. Demanded my host: Who lets them in? Who makes it possible for them to thrive?

The point is that poverty cannot be a sole or even sufficient reason for explaining South Africa's astronomical crime rates. The police profile of perpetrators involved in violent crime against persons and property does not, in fact, include poverty at all. Most of these criminals, I was once told by a senior police statistician at a government scenario-planning exercise in which I was involved, are from what could be termed the lower middle class. The same policeman observed that as long as a young man has more chance of going bankrupt by starting his own small business than being caught for a violent crime, crime is a rational career choice.

In any event, the 'needs'-based argument so frequently advanced by the Mbeki administration to explain the high levels of crime is roundly rejected by a broad swathe of South Africans. A 2003 survey of perceptions on crime showed that less than 20 per cent of black people supported this explanation for violent crime and only 30 per cent accepted it in regard to property crimes. Most correctly assessed it for what it is: simple greed.[14]

The cultural explanation maintains that South African crime levels are an indication of the sickness of the society. There may well be truth in this. The corrosive effect of apartheid and the absence of strong, inspiring and moral political leadership since Mandela have merely compounded the problem. A chilling police statistic is that 89 per cent of people assaulted in South Africa are the victims of somebody they know. More than 81 per cent of those murdered are killed by someone known to them. The figure for rape by someone known to the victim is 76 per cent.

These numbers suggest a dreadfully suppressed tumult of anger, violence and indiscipline just waiting to boil over – often when inflamed by excessive alcohol or drug usage. HIV/AIDS could also be an aggravating factor. Research in 2006 involving Baltimore's Johns Hopkins University indicated that up to eight million people in sub-Saharan Africa could be suffering from AIDS-related dementia. By extrapolation, as many as one million would be in South Africa and it is possible this could be contributing to increased crime levels.

The fact that so much of this crime occurs in what the police call a social fabric environment makes it even more difficult to combat. What policeman stands outside a person's house waiting for an occupant to attempt to kill their partner, child or friend?

There is also a socio-political dimension to the debate. The underlying philosophy of the ANC in power has been a programme of redistribution and entitlement. The reckless manner in which this has been propagated by some political leaders can only have the impact of inciting a generalised view among young people that appropriation by crime is affirmative action by other means. Indeed, theft from the white minority during apartheid was widely and tolerantly described in some black quarters as 'redistribution' or 'liberation'. It is not too far a stretch to suggest that the violent attacks on foreigners in May 2008 were merely a very extreme expression of this culture of enrichment by expropriation.

Then there are demographics. An element of specialised crime is committed by immigrants: Nigerians in the financial and drug area and Zimbabweans and Mozambicans in the armed crime sphere (some have proved to be former soldiers). Finally, there is also instrumentality: the availability of weapons from the southern African region's past conflicts.

This rich and lethal mix of the *causes* of crime does not, however, answer the question of why the state has failed so epically to combat it. Between 2000 and 2008, the complement of the police service increased by 40 000 members, while the budget rose from R17 billion to R43.3 billion – a 254 per cent leap in eight years. A target strength of 192 000 will be reached by 2010. The ratio of police to members of the public is 1:370, higher than during the apartheid era, and better than the UN benchmark of one police officer to four hundred members of the public. If force strengths and finances are not the issues, what then accounts for the intractably high level of crime? The answers to the state's failure are fourfold:

- During its fourteen years in power, not once has the problem been politically elevated to that of a national crisis.
- A primarily preventative policy has not been complemented with an effective detection policy.
- The raw material with which the police service works is currently institutionally incapable of carrying out the task of combating crime.
- After fourteen years in power, the ANC government has still not effectively coordinated the justice process from handcuffs to prison door.

It is important to understand each element of this mosaic of failure that will be so much a part of the Mbeki legacy.

The failure of political leadership on the crime issue underlies the whole of Mbeki's tenure. In one scenario-scoping meeting comprising a wide range of experts, a senior ANC government official turned to me during a very intense debate about violence and crime in South Africa and observed, 'Don't you find it so depressing talking about crime?'

This probably captures the essence of the Mbeki administration's response. The crime crisis, like the collapse of the education and health systems, was an inconvenience, an embarrassment to be avoided, diverted, minimised and ultimately denied. The increase in police numbers and budget could be alluded to if necessary. A succession of quite pointless new strategic documents and service restructuring would be launched. Mandatory sentences could be applied. There could be constant reference to poverty being the driving force of crime, an almost subliminal message that until poverty was eradicated, crime would have to wait. Under no circumstances should the presidency admit there was a crisis.

The closest that Mbeki came to admitting the problem was to acknowledge what he called a 'perception' of crime among the public. This 'perception' was no doubt more strongly felt by the families of the people involved, 2 125 227 of whom were victims of crime in the year that he spoke.

The second element in the failure of the state's anti-crime campaign must lie squarely with the philosophy adopted by the government at the outset. Intensely aware of their vulnerability among a recently liberated constituency, it was very wary about using the heavy hand. The constitution in any case significantly shifted the society away from a tradition of reverse onus to positive onus. Successive judgments and regulations pertaining to police activities and a mounting pile of civil claims against the commissioner (R6 billion by 2007) limited police action and introduced a culture of extreme caution and even avoidance of aggressive policing. Unsurprisingly, the criminals flourished under these circumstances.

Anthony Altbeker, a criminologist, has written extensively on this subject. He was one of the civilian advisors to the minister of safety and security in the early days of ANC rule, and his insightful book, *A Country at War with Itself*, makes two revealing points.

The first is that the political decision by the new administration to concentrate on preventative policing through a naïve reliance on community policing instruments led to the winding down of conventional police detection capacity. In short, the old detective force was marginalised in favour of the uniformed branch. The net result of that was a precipitate plunge in the state's capacity to actually lock the baddies up.

Altbeker's second point is that with so many criminals at large, the effect was to draw in more and more people who might not have been criminals in the first place. Crime, in short, begets crime.

'The decision to focus criminal justice attention on the prevention of crime rather than on the arrest, prosecution and incarceration of offenders has itself helped to shape the way the crime wave has developed in post-liberation South Africa,' Altbeker notes. 'In this regard, it is worth asking if the failure to incarcerate sufficiently large numbers of people involved in violent crime is itself a factor in explaining the prevalence of violent crime in South Africa.'[15]

The third element in the state's inability to combat crime was the fatal frailty of the police service's human resources. This was partly due to a general programme of affirmative action that saw swathes of the old experienced policing elements, particularly the detective branch, disappear. By 2007, 83 per cent of the SAPS was black, a material number holding positions for which they had neither the technical expertise nor experience. Huge gaps existed in the technical and specialist departments in which whites had once played a major role. Part of the problem was also due to inept restructuring – Altbeker, who was in the safety and security ministry at the time, describes this process as 'massively destabilising' – which saw the detective branch constrained in resources, subject to the uniform branch, stripped of their specialist investigative elements and generally declared poor cousins. Detective caseloads soared to unmanageable levels amid a massive exodus of basic skills.

By 2007, a special business working group on crime was advocating an immediate increase in the number of detectives from 22 000 to 52 000. The SAPS was also confirming critical skill shortages in the fields of scientific analysis, facial reconstruction, ballistics and facial identification experts – all vital for effective detective work. Also on the shortlist, despite an abundance of available manpower and funds, was the Task Force, the specialist weapons reaction unit. The majority of the core members of this highly efficient unit had long since departed in the first waves of affirmative action. Many ended up in private military companies operating in Iraq, much to the chagrin of the government that had driven them out in the first place.

Yet, remarkably, this police service is capable of spectacular success. In incidents of high-profile murder it has reacted with lightning speed and positive results. When called upon to protect visitors and delegates for big international events, it works flawlessly. Thus the benefit of complete focus. But nothing short of a revolution in management practice and morale will change its endemic underperformance; certainly not the billions of rands that the state, private sector and NGOs have thus far poured ineptly and inefficiently into improving the system.

The core problem is that having destroyed an effective detective service, the SAPS uniform branch is also failing. This failure has many fathers, but probably the most important is the collapse of, or conversely the failure to inculcate, a high level of professionalism in the police service during the Mbeki era.

This was not for a lack of trying. In the 2006/7 police year, 52 173 police officers underwent medium- to long-term training. Thousands attended one of thirty-five development courses on offer and thousands more attended various employee assistance service courses to deal with stress, anger, trauma, moral regeneration and other confidence-building exercises. Tens of thousands attended adult basic education courses to address functional illiteracy levels that once stood at a quarter of all serving members in the SAPS and were unlikely to improve with the quality of public educational output.[16]

While admirable as a signal of the government's intention to upgrade the force, the numbers show the extraordinary investment in time and money that has to be made to deal with the largely self-induced critical skills crisis within the police. When one further considers the downtime caused by generous sick, study and long leave provisions in the force, one arrives at a depressingly low effective police strength on any one day. This high level of absenteeism, albeit curbed in recent years, is a major contributor to police inefficiency.

Without the inherent professional core and given the diminishing quality of output from the state educational facilities, the chances of a short-term upgrade of police competence is illusory. Even were this possible, the police managers are still faced with the constant obstruction of the unions to performance criteria and the enormously cumbersome disciplinary processes required to deal with infractions.

The image of professionalism has not been helped by the flawed qualities of the politically appointed leadership of the police service. The political aspects of police commissioner Jackie Selebi's forced exit from office in the face of charges of conspiring with criminal elements to expedite a host of illegal activities, and the protection extended to him by Mbeki, were dealt with in the first part of this book. Suffice it to say here that a commissioner spending his time fighting a summons for alleged participation in criminal endeavours is not exactly the ideal person to lead moral regeneration within the force. Nor were things much better with the head of the local police in the country's largest municipality. Robert McBride, a former imprisoned bomber, was suspended from his post as Ekurhuleni metro police chief, the most powerful local-level police service in the country, only after months of incidents including allegedly pointing firearms at members of the public, insulting his officers, alleged drunk driving and street protests against him by his own officers. The litany of his infractions was finally topped when he lost control of and rolled his vehicle after an official year-end party. Having summoned some of his cohorts to his aid, the incident culminated in a massive public face-off at a filling station between the Metro cops, McBride, a few hapless SAPS officers and some members of the public, which allegedly included much pointing of firearms, swearing and threats.

The ensuing alleged cover-up involved some of his subordinates and a crooked medical certificate. However, the cops who helped McBride eventually fell out with their boss, fingered him and were suspended amid claims that he had threatened to rape their wives and kill their children and even family pets unless they stuck to the story that he had been under the influence not of alcohol but of medication for diabetes at the time of the accident. This proved too much for even the supine mayor of Ekurhuleni and clearly stretched the bounds of the generous political protection and patronage that had been extended by the ANC to McBride through the years. He was eventually suspended pending prosecution on charges of driving under the influence of alcohol and attempting to escape the law. The courts must decide on the truth of these claims, but the incident further affected public confidence in policing standards.

Not surprisingly, an assessment of the SAPS in 2006 by the Centre for the Study of Violence and Reconciliation (CSVR) rated it well on its capacity to police democratic political life – which meant it did not kill protesting citizens – but very badly in what it called 'proper policing conduct'. This, essentially, was everything to do with policing as understood and experienced by the public.

In his analysis of the report's findings, David Bruce of the CSVR observes: 'The South African Police has a good statement of values, but commitment to these values is not consistently carried through in its organisational practice. There is evidence of a pervasive problem of corruption and anti-corruption measures are weak.'[17] Remarkably, his views were entirely shared by the police service itself, in which 96 per cent of serving officers surveyed in 2007 by the Institute for Security Studies ranked corruption as a problem in the force.

The Selebi indictment merely capped what was a growing public disillusionment with its police force. When a local television station ran a poll the day after it was announced that he would be charged, asking viewers whether they thought the Selebi situation had damaged the SAPS, 95 per cent answered in the affirmative.

This combination of factors had its inevitable impact on police discipline. The 2007 *Police Report* indicated a ratio of successful civil claims against every serving member of the police at 1:152 in that year.[18] If one considers that the average police officer will serve for twenty years, this means that one in 7.6 officers will have a successful civil case brought against him or her at some point. That is a rate of malfeasance higher than that of the population that the force is supposed to police. The US State Department's *Country Report on Human Rights* for 2007 observed that there had been 698 deaths in police custody in the year under review. That represented a trebling of the number of custody deaths since Mbeki's accession to office.

The impact on public perceptions began to tell. Although the average South African's access to police services had improved – nearly two-thirds are within half an hour of a police station, using their normal mode of transport – their confidence has fallen. Again, the issue is not funding or physical infrastructure: it is lack of skills and the culture of policing.

A May 2007 survey found that only one-third of South Africans felt that the government was handling the issue of crime fighting well, the lowest level since 2003, which saw the height of the crime wave.[19] Topping the list of concerns was the long response time, despite a massive increase in state investment in vehicles (most of which were to be found outside police stations or ferrying senior officers on private sorties) and corruption.

Part of the debate about the crime problem in South Africa has been misdirected. The police, being the interface with the public at its most vulnerable and stressed, have been saddled with the brunt of responsibility for the failure of the anti-crime war. Also at fault are the justice system, which fails to effectively prosecute, and the prisons, which are desperately overcrowded and prone to corruption.

Central to this problem are the gaping holes in crime intelligence. Thus courts continually grant bail to criminals who are already out on bail for other crimes. The control of dockets in the courts has also become a huge challenge for the criminal justice system, with the sale and 'disappearance' of dockets through bribery reaching epic proportions. The rate of criminal conviction for those brought to court has also fallen, often due to bad preparation, deficient documentation, inept prosecution or simply the absence of the correct witnesses.

The consequence of all these factors is a plunging conviction rate (ironic, given the swelling prison population) and a growing sense of impunity among the criminal classes. The SAPS annual report for 2006/7 gives the warming news that the detection rate in priority crimes (such as violent or sexual assaults) increased to 42 per cent. However, since the majority of perpetrators in these categories of crime knew their attackers, this detection statistic is less impressive, particularly if one considers that victims' surviving family members probably also knew the culprit. More to the point, the same report confirms that 68 per cent of crimes investigated by the police do not even make it to court. So what happens between the opening of a dossier and appearance in the dock?

The answer is chaos: lost files, bungled forensics (60 per cent of crime-scene evidence is unusable), lack of witnesses, illegible statements and endless postponements until outraged magistrates throw the case out altogether. Even those who do go to court have small chance of success, due to incompetent prosecution. Less than 6 per cent of the violent crimes committed in South Africa end in conviction. A seminal study by the South African Law Commission of 15 000 violent crimes in eight police districts in 1997/98 found that in four categories conviction rates totalled 6 per cent – 75 per cent did not even get to court. The breakdown in conviction rates per category was as follows: rape (adult), 5 per cent; rape (under eighteen), 9 per cent; robbery, 3 per cent; fraud, 5 per cent; murder, 11 per cent. Not surprisingly, the report concludes that '[c]rime pays. South African criminals, even violent criminals, tend to get away with their crimes.'[20] There is little to suggest things have much improved in the decade since.

By 2007, South Africa had one of the lowest prisoner-per-murder rates in the world, despite having the highest homicide rate. Despite this appallingly low rate of detection and conviction, South Africa's prison population increased from 116 846 in 1995 to 183 036 in 2004, but dropped back in 2007 to 160 198 convicted and awaiting-trial prisoners – a *decrease* amid a crime explosion. The prisons were built to hold only 113 000 inmates and so by 2007 had a 40 per cent overcrowding ratio, leading to violence, escapes and physical deterioration of facilities. The nature of this population also substantially changed. Driven largely by public outrage, the government introduced amendments in 1997 and 1998 to the Criminal Law Amendment Act to introduce mandatory sentences for a range of serious sexual and violent crimes. This was a classic case of political posturing, especially towards the gender lobbies. The issue was never the severity of sentences; it was the low rate of convictions.

The amended law eventually saw a change in the profile of the prison population. In 1995, 74 per cent of prisoners in South Africa were serving less than seven-year sentences. By 2005, the figure had been reduced to 48 per cent. The pressure on accommodation saw an acute crisis as the average prisoner's internment was lengthened, thus affecting churn rate.

The authorities responded not by building more prisons, but by reducing the number of awaiting-trial prisoners for minor offences, which meant easier bail conditions, complemented by sentence remissions such as one in 2005, to reduce the short-term prison population. The net effect was a tremendous effusion of petty and middleweight offenders back onto the streets, which undoubtedly contributed to the 2006/7 spike in criminal activity. South Africa has an extraordinarily high rate of recidivism. Various researchers put it at between 85 per cent and 94 per cent,[21] which means that virtually every prisoner released is likely to offend again. These releases, then, could lead at the very best to only a continuance of high levels of crime, and at the very worst to another surge, which seems to have been the case.

The cracks in the criminal justice system were brutally brought to light in December 2007, when eleven robbers were shot dead by police in a foiled cash heist. The action brought immediate public acclaim: a local television poll that night showed that 98 per cent of viewers fully endorsed the police action. When the police got around to patching together the profiles of the gangsters, they discovered that two were already wanted men, while another five were awaiting trial for earlier offences. One had no less than four different trials pending – for murder, attempted murder, child theft and illegal possession of firearms. Another was awaiting trial in five separate cases of armed robbery.[22]

The police were unable to confirm whether the slain gangsters had escaped from custody, been released on bail, paroled, let out as part of an amnesty or simply walked out of prison. The incident again revealed the utterly porous nature of the judicial process and the consequent sense of impunity in the criminal fraternity. It also gave a powerful impetus to the public argument for reinstatement of the deterrent effect of the death sentence: once executed for the first murder, there is a reasonable assumption that a killer will not commit a second, as all too often happens in South Africa.

The continuing crisis in the justice chain was highlighted dramatically in April 2008 when Susan Shabangu, the deputy minister of safety and security, memorably charged police to shoot to kill and not ask questions. The instruction raised an uproar among human rights lobbies but was widely applauded by the general public. It had finally come to this: realising that it was quite unable to offer a modern policing service, the state was advocating unlimited warfare by its enforcement agencies against criminals. I could almost imagine the wry comments from my West African colleagues in Nigeria.

The bitter legacy of the Mbeki presidency with its denial, indifference and scapegoating, interspersed with brief flurries of punitive activity, has deeply eroded public confidence in policing. South Africa's violent crime rate is among the highest in the world and continues to climb. Offenders are being sent to jail for longer periods, but fewer of them are being convicted. In order to make space for them in the existing prisons, ever more petty criminals, who are almost certain to reoffend, are being released or granted bail. Crime is thus encouraged and this, in turn, acts as an inducement to others to become criminals – the Altbeker thesis. White-collar crime in South Africa is a world-beater, the police are demoralised and ineffectual despite being almost permanently in training, and the courts creak under the burden of an inefficient and at times corrupt system. And, worst of all, the government's attitude veers from dismissing crime as an issue to seeing it as a tool for racist enemies to embarrass and humiliate the president and his party. This is hardly a recipe for a stable criminal justice system.

As always, it is the citizens who take on board the responsibility of protecting themselves. This has two dimensions. In the wealthier suburbs it led to a profusion of 'gated complexes' and an explosion in private security. In the poorer areas it led to a growth of vigilantism as a substitute for a failed state of policing. Of the two, the latter has proved more effective.

The growth of the private security industry as a response to the state's failure to protect persons and property will be dealt with at more length later. Here it is necessary simply to observe that the number of private security guards in South Africa trebled in the first ten years of ANC rule and by 2006 was at 300 000. Put in perspective, more people are privately employed to fulfil the first responsibility of the state, the protection of person and property, than the entire police and military service combined.

The growth of this sector of the services industry and the proliferation of protected enclaves in wealthier communities has, unsurprisingly, drawn the ire of the government, which sees it as a living reproach to its own ability to protect its citizens. Its response, predictably, has been further regulation and limitations on the functioning of this service.

The growth of the vigilante movement is also to be dealt with at more length elsewhere in this book. Here it is worth recording the findings of a 2003 survey which indicated that one-third of South Africans had seen a non-governmental agency apprehending a criminal suspect and one-fifth had seen such groups administering punishment, largely in black residential areas.[23] The number of people killed by vigilante action is difficult to establish but authoritative sources indicate it is material and on the rise.

It may also account for the incidence of crime in black residential areas being half that of predominantly white and Indian suburbs, according to the surveys.

This raises the sensitive question of the death penalty. If suspected criminals are being apprehended and killed on a regular basis by citizens, what should these be called but executions? Granted, they are not administered by the state, but they are executions nevertheless. The government under President Mbeki has steadfastly refused to reintroduce the death sentence, even when he had the parliamentary majority to amend the constitution. The government's stance has been defended by reference to existing studies that indicate that the death sentence does not have a deterrent effect. Reliance on these studies by the government is strange given its stated suspicion of foreign imposed models. The studies are overwhelmingly the result of research in developed countries with high levels of both compliance and probability in the identification, apprehension, prosecution, conviction and incarceration of offenders. Under those circumstances it is not surprising that death sentences have little discernible effect on the reduction of murder. What is missing, however, is a study of the impact of judicial executions in states with weak executive and judicial arms, a considerable lack of internal cohesion and a high recidivism rate – places like South Africa.

Nevertheless, public support for the return of the death sentence has grown enormously during the ANC's tenure, particularly among the black community. A 2006 poll indicates that 72 per cent of the country now supports a return of the death penalty.[24]

The growth of the private security force and vigilantism are two faces of the same coin: the failure of the state to effectively defend its citizens against a violent criminal class within the country. It reflects the failure of the SAPS to convince citizens that it is on their side.

In a fine piece of journalism, Jonny Steinberg wrote about a murder in an informal settlement in Johannesburg and the refusal of the witnesses to talk to the investigators, because they were afraid they might be reported to the perpetrators by corrupt policemen.

'Suffice it here to define the problem – we are talking of a failure of post-apartheid state formation,' writes Steinberg. 'A murder was committed in a shack settlement and still, 13 years into the new order, the state did not arrive on the scene.'[25]

In November 2007, South African business proposed to the cabinet a permanent justice system operations team comprising an A-level collection of detectives, forensic experts and senior prosecutors, working in a co-ordinated way to target priority crimes. If this sounded depressingly familiar, it was because this was the concept behind the special crimes units and, ultimately, the Scorpions, two instruments that became blunted and eventually destroyed either through lack of personnel or politically when they started nailing the powerful and connected.

CHAPTER 10

Hey, teacher ...

Much education today is monumentally ineffective. All too often we are giving young people cut flowers when we should be teaching them to grow their plants.

— JOHN W GARDNER[1]

IF THE MBEKI ADMINISTRATION'S FAILURE IN THE ARENA OF crime fighting is serious, its management of the educational and skills requirements of a modernising South Africa has been disastrous. Because the consequences will be manifest in the long-term destruction of the national human capacity rather than the violent obliteration of the citizenry, education and training has enjoyed less passionate public attention than crime. But the problem is every bit as insidious. It is more intractable. It has an effect that, like crime, will last many years into the future.

The cause, as always, was not a shortage of ideas, ideological enthusiasm or finance. It was simply that the policies were too ambitious and the resources too fragile. It was the old story of the Mbeki administration: ideological overreach meets capacity under-reach.

The number of school-going children in South Africa increased from 11 764 918 in 1998 to 11 808 377 in 2006 – a marginal 0.35 per cent, probably due to the ravages of the HIV/AIDS pandemic and the exodus abroad of families from the racial minorities.[2] But the number of those progressing to higher levels of schooling improved dramatically as a proportion of total school-going population. Larger numbers of children also qualified for free schooling.

By 2007, the government was devoting 5.4 per cent of GDP to education – among the highest in the developing world and equal to many developed states. For seven consecutive years the state had devoted nearly a fifth of its national budget to education. Between 1998 and 2005, the number of South Africans with no education had been reduced from 14.1 per cent of the population to 10.3 per cent. Those with primary, secondary and tertiary education had all increased appreciably as a percentage of the population.

While primary enrolment had held reasonably constant, secondary education numbers had greatly improved. The number of schools had remained
constant and teacher-to-pupil ratios had dropped from 34:1 in 2004 to 32:1
in 2006.[3] While matriculation passes were at 58 per cent when the ANC
took over, they had risen to 67 per cent in 2006. All of this was in line with
the ANC's commitment to improve access to public education, and should
have been acknowledged as a triumph of the administration.

But it was not, and for a simple reason. While education improved
quantitatively, it did not do so qualitatively, either in absolute terms or
in comparison with other developing countries that continued to course
ahead. This was particularly so in the critical areas of primary school literacy
and science and maths education, cornerstones for the development of
modern economies.

The Global Campaign for Education's 2007 annual report put its finger
on the problem. It gave Mbeki high marks for expanding access to education, but marked him down for what it diplomatically called 'quality issues'.
South Africa ranked fiftieth out of 156 countries – in the same category
as Grenada, Jamaica, the Philippines, St Kitts and Nevis, and Vietnam.
Written in the form of a school report, it finds that 'not only has he [Mbeki]
fared very badly on the sub-regional examination scores, but he is now
faced with a negative trend in primary enrolment'.[4]

By 2007, only 30 per cent of South African adults had finished high
school, against the average of 41 per cent in emerging markets and nearly
70 per cent in developed countries. In South Africa, the growth rate of the
number of people finishing school between 1995 and 2006 was 2.1 per cent,
and the growth rate for those with exemptions or endorsements (those
who had subject passes of a high enough grade to progress to tertiary
education) was 1 per cent. The number of students with university pass
grades had declined from 18 per cent in 2006 to 15 per cent in 2007. That
an educational system could increase its school-going population by only
0.35 per cent in a decade and grow its spend by more than 10 per cent a
year for a decade, yet still fail to produce enough graduates in the key
disciplines necessary to build a modern economy, points to a massive
disjunction between physical and financial resource and output.

Why?

The reasons are many: weak school management systems, inappropriate curriculum changes, a 'wholly under-performing' teachers' corps,
progressive lowering of academic standards and requirements and a

collapse of basic discipline in the schools, fed by an inappropriate and Western-based philosophy of classroom management.

The core pedagogical problem, however, lies with the implementation of a process called outcomes-based education (OBE), which in South Africa is called a 'statement', on a fatally deficient educational platform. The country has yet to feel the full impact of the problem, but in 2008 the first products of this process will leave school.

The theory of OBE is that all education must be geared towards equipping pupils with the sort of skills needed to survive in a modern and technologically evolving world. Understanding and flexibility are more important than content; the process of learning is more relevant than what is learnt. Gone is rote learning and traditional testing. It was experiential education driven by its chief convert, education director-general Chabani Manganyi, introduced in 1996. The model chosen for South Africa was one of the most dauntingly complex in the world: a mixture of 'transformational' and 'transitional' OBE. It relied on very high levels of sophistication and experience among the teaching staff.

The cabinet's champion of the system was Professor Kader Asmal, an ANC stalwart and long-time exile. He was minister of education from 1999 to 2004. The system was implemented with little regard for the capacity of the already shattered South African educational system to absorb it and it fell to his successor to try to pick up the pieces.

One of the keys to a successful education system is the quality of teachers. It is a truism, but the comparison between countries that recruit their best graduates to teach and those that recruit the worst is startling. That is why Scandinavian countries score so well in tests while the US, despite huge investment and comparatively low teacher–pupil ratios, fares so badly.

South Africa's public education system has long since ceased recruiting the best, other than in a few instances such as the former Model C schools, where additional funding by parents helps to attract a better level of staff. And once employed, attempts to upgrade teachers have invariably failed. South Africa devotes a much higher proportion of its budget to training of teachers than virtually any other developing country. Yet this has no significant impact, for two reasons. A material number of teachers are untrainable because of history, background or disposition. The extent of this problem is hard to gauge. A very senior educationist once confided that as many as one-third of teachers might fall into this category. They remain on the staff of schools largely because of their union protection, he said.

Second, attempts to create a performance basis for teachers have repeatedly been stymied by the South African Democratic Teachers' Union. Only in early 2008 did the government and the teaching unions reach agreement on a settlement that had a component of performance pay. This move, while welcome and a tribute to Minister Naledi Pandor and the unions, has still to be bedded down. The fear, a not unnatural one given history, is that these performance considerations will simply become embedded as part of routine remuneration. In early 2008 the government announced that school inspectors would be deployed to evaluate teaching performance. Riots during the apartheid years and union resistance during the ANC era had kept them out of the classrooms for an incredible twenty-four years. The point, however, is that it was fourteen years into ANC rule and in the midst of a crisis that the major stakeholders finally shook themselves free of the rhetoric and posturing to agree to a practical and doable remuneration system with a component of performance risk, and even then the details still had to be worked out.

The tests that have been done to date on teacher proficiency in the state schools show an extremely long road is ahead. In one rural school that escaped the union's strictures and was assessed, teachers tested on Grade 6 level material failed the literacy test, while the mathematics average was 66 per cent.[5]

More terrifying is the fact that according to surveys, while middle-class suburban schools spend more than six hours on instruction daily, the figure for township schools is only three and a half hours a day. One survey showed that teachers in poor schools, who were supposed to devote 85 per cent of their time to teaching, in fact spent only 40 per cent. Where did the wasted time go?[6]

The answer lies in endless form filling (a Human Sciences Research Council investigation in 2005 found this took up 28 per cent of teachers' time), absenteeism, disorganisation, failure to enrol students in time, logistical problems in the delivery of books, lack of discipline among pupils, external interruptions and sheer sloth. The inevitable consequence has been a flight of black pupils from township schools to the former Model C schools (interracial institutions set up during the apartheid era) in search of professional teaching. This flood, sadly, merely compounds the problem, as the existing teaching cadre, weakened by large-scale emigration of former white teachers, is simply unable to cope. The result is a widening circle of failure.

It was onto this fragile platform that OBE was injected. The result was predictable. Teachers who could themselves barely read or write lapsed into teaching a mix of traditional rote learning and the easiest aspects of OBE. Educational standards plummeted and functional illiteracy and innumeracy soared. The warning signs of the coming deluge were apparent early. A prescient academic work for a doctoral thesis in 2000 by educationist Sigamoney Naicker highlighted the teaching profession's lack of preparedness for the introduction of the foundation phases of OBE in Western Cape schools.[7] As this province is comparatively well resourced in its education departments and consistently turns out the highest matric pass rate, it beggars imagination that this complex system, requiring the highest levels of judgement, discernment and discretion from its teachers, could be applied in, say, an Eastern Cape village school. In September 2001, a Grade 3 national assessment study was carried out by the government. It found low achievement levels in numeracy and literacy and that 'learners performed better on tasks that required them to identify and select a correct response than on tasks that required them to produce their own response'. Not only was the OBE statement failing to produce literate and numerate pupils, it was failing even to get them to think, which was the object of the exercise in the first place.

The national survey of performance in 2001 for Grade 3 pupils (the class of 2010) showed that one-third failed in the targets for numeracy and half failed in literacy. When the class of 2011 was tested in 2005 as Grade 6 pupils, those failing at the numeracy levels had increased to 70 per cent, while 60 per cent failed the literacy tests. In other words, things were rolling back rather than forward.[8] These early warnings were ignored and the system followed its relentless implausibility until its young victims were to graduate from the formal schooling system in 2008.

This inappropriateness of content was matched by a sudden decline in the number of teachers. In 2002, the government embarked on a major programme of consolidating tertiary institutions by joining former technical and teacher training colleges to universities. The intention was to raise the level of teaching and wind down the inherited apartheid-era system of producing tens of thousands of under-qualified teachers from numerous sub-standard institutions. But the remedy proved worse than the disease. The number of teaching graduates dropped from 70 000 a year in 1994 to less than 6 000 in 2006.

The full impact of the catastrophe is yet to be counted. Only now are the products of OBE from the poorer schools reaching the higher levels of schooling. Soon many will be in the job market and joining the ranks of the unemployable in the country. A generation has very largely been wasted.

By 2006 the precarious situation in national education was becoming widely reported on and debated, despite the insistent mantra of the educational authorities that graduates of the new OBE system would be better equipped in cognitive skills to take advantage of work opportunities. In that year the results of the government's Grade 6 assessment were released. They pointed to 'relatively low levels of performance in all three learning areas, with a relatively small percentage of pupils functioning at the appropriate level for Grade 6'.[9]

If that was the assessment at home, the views from abroad were damning. The Progress in International Reading Literacy Study, conducted in 2005 and reported in 2007, revealed the disturbing result that 78 per cent of South African Grade 4 pupils could not read. The score was the lowest among thirty-nine countries tested, including many with far fewer resources and higher incidences of poverty. The international average was 6 per cent. Other tests in the same year in the Western Cape showed that only 5 per cent of township children could read at an appropriate level and only 2 per cent could do mathematics at the required level. These are not products of the old pedagogical system. They are the children of OBE – and they are among the worst educated when measured against South Africa's peers.

The second alarming statistic emerged from the Trends in International Mathematics and Science Study in 2003, which again showed South Africa at the bottom of the pile of forty-six participating countries. Again, these results were the product of seven years of OBE. At a score of 264, South Africa was beaten by Ghana, Saudi Arabia, Botswana, the Philippines, Chile, the Palestinian National Authority, Bahrain, Egypt and a host of other countries. Tired of being bottom and perhaps also wearied by the humiliation of being beaten by the battered and endlessly divided Palestinians, South Africa withdrew from the survey.

An investigation by the Centre for Development and Enterprise showed in 2007 that far from doubling the number of science and maths matriculants as required by the government, the number had actually slipped backwards since 2005.[10] Half of South Africa's secondary schools failed to achieve a single higher-grade pass. In 2004, 467 985 pupils wrote the senior certificate examination, with 39 939 writing higher-grade maths. Only

5.1 per cent passed higher-grade maths, and of those only 1.5 per cent were black. Let us again put that in context: ten years into ANC rule and after the investment of billions of rands on education, only 7 236 black pupils out of a total population of forty-eight million managed to pass maths at a level sufficient to get them to university. Of these, only 2 406 achieved a C grade or higher. Looked at more closely, 70 per cent of these were yielded by the 11 per cent of schools that were previously interracial Model C institutions.

The 2007 matric results reinforced the picture of more but certainly not better. Although the number of matriculants increased by 16 000, for the fourth year in a row the pass rate dropped: from 66.5 per cent to 65.2 per cent. The rate of university passes, now called 'endorsements' but previously known as university exemptions, also continued to decline in both absolute terms and as a percentage. By 2007 it was 15.1 per cent, representing 85 454 pupils – 376 less than the previous year.

This deeply troubling picture of the state of public education was offset, as usual, by extraordinary results in the Independent Examination Board exams written by 7 362 candidates from private and some Model C schools. They scored a 99 per cent pass rate and a 78 per cent university exemption rate. The results again starkly illustrated the dangerously widening gap between a failed state education system and a privately driven one, with all its implications for continuing inequality and resentment.

Put simply, despite all the inflated rhetoric, resources and grand schemes, after fourteen years the impact of state policy on improvements in poor and predominantly black schools is, to all intents and purposes, precisely ... *nil*. This is not an academic failure in state educational policy; it is a catastrophic collapse with far-reaching implications for the future of South Africa.

The conclusion of a range of assessments of South African public education is captured in the following excerpt from a report by educationist Anil Kanjee in 2007:

> The provision of quality education in South Africa has been the stated goal of the new government since its installation in 1994 and has been the primary focus of all education stakeholders in the country over the last decade. The results from the three national assessments conducted provide a gloomy picture – marked as they are by low levels of learner achievement across the learning area assessed. Despite the large number of interventions in the last decade, there has been little

improvement in achievement levels. The specific reasons for this are unclear and there is little consensus on the exact nature of the problem and the likely solution.[11]

Mary Metcalfe, a former ANC provincial minister of education in Gauteng, laid much of the blame at the door of weak leadership, bad planning, lack of focus on core issues like numeracy and literacy, lack of teacher support and the exodus of black children from poor residential areas to the suburbs in search of better education: 'The research is unequivocal: the conceptual knowledge of our teachers is low; teachers have a poor grasp of the subjects they teach; there is a high level of teacher error in the content and concepts presented in lessons; and teachers have low expectations of learners, who then achieve to these low expectations.'[12]

The message is clear. Not only is the content and process beyond the grasp of many teachers, but the mere imposition of the system leads to severe confidence problems with the teachers' corps and a spiralling decline in expectation and thus performance. Even as the 2008 school year began, there were grumbles from matric teachers that they were not fully equipped to teach the new curriculum to that year's crop of matriculants – this *twelve years* after introduction of the new curriculum.

It is not surprising that, thirteen years into the rule of the ANC, a fierce debate had erupted over the reasons for the failed educational system and a wasted generation of young people's hopes. Professor Asmal belatedly admitted in September 2007 that OBE was imposed on inadequately trained teachers and blamed his advisors. But, he told the South African Society of History Teachers, there was no alternative to OBE other than rote, 'which does not do anything for the intellect'.[13] Rob Sieborger, deputy director of the School of Education in Cape Town, said that the system might have survived the introduction of OBE, but 'what made it worse was that a whole lot of policies were implemented at the same time that were not properly thought through and we did not have the proper resources for implementation'.[14]

David Balt, president of the National Professional Teachers' Organisation, summed up the reasons for the declining standards of national education at the time of the 2007 matric results: 'Unrealistic teacher-pupil ratios, inefficient departmental officials, poor resourcing, inadequate teacher support by subject advisors, inadequate monitoring of performance in lower grades and lack of ongoing support for school managers ...' He could well have added a collapse of professionalism and commitment among large swathes of the teaching corps.

Equally concerning was the mounting evidence of an embedded culture of indiscipline – and in some cases violence – among pupils. Research in 2007 showed that 77 per cent of children in South African schools did not feel personally safe in the classroom – a chilling indication of the inability of teaching staff to keep order, and an indication of serious social pathology among young people. This, it should be noted, when the ANC was attempting to pioneer yet more 'best in the west' legislation through parliament that would make it even more difficult for teachers, and indeed parents, to discipline their children.

This obviously had its knock-on effects. One of the more concerning aspects to arise from all the assessments during more than five years was the lack of support in the home environment for schoolchildren. This should, and did, instantly raise warning signs. If there was no culture of learning at home, what was happening? A consistent element of black public education during the early apartheid years had been the extraordinary support given by black parents to their children in pursuing the very best education they could afford, often amid the most appallingly adverse conditions. But the physical environment at home had improved dramatically during the Mbeki era. Surely the home nurturing of education should have grown commensurately? The fact that it did not gives a potentially frightening insight into another possibility. The lack of a culture of education in the poor black home may be yet another victim of the Mbeki administration's dependent society.

The government's ponderous response to this long-developing crisis was to announce the launch of what was grandly called the Foundation for Learning Programme in 2007, when the full horror of this man-made catastrophe became apparent. As early as 2001 the education authorities had begun a programme to improve science and maths, called Dinaledi, which began promisingly by focusing on a few schools and then expanded to 529 schools. The results were not encouraging. Most of the improvements in higher-grade maths and science were achieved by a small proportion of schools (not surprisingly the former Model C schools) while those outside showed marginal improvement or actually regressed. In 2006, nearly 40 per cent of these schools into which so much resource and effort had been invested had actually produced fewer higher-grade science and maths matriculants than the previous year. Only 30 per cent of the schools that had enjoyed the full attention of this scheme managed to produce more than ten higher-grade maths and science graduates.[15] Despite all this effort, the state system managed to produce precisely *198* more maths higher-grade pupils in 2007 than the year before, but science passes declined by 1 659. At 24 415 higher-grade maths matriculants and 28 122 higher-grade science matriculants, the ratio to the total number of 564 775 matriculants was 4.3 and 4.9 respectively. A much smaller percentage was black. Of even more concern was the huge shift in the number of pupils taking ordinary-grade matric science and maths, as opposed to the higher-grade subjects that would qualify one for tertiary education. Minister Naledi Pandor, admitting she was a worried woman, raised the unthinkable: that teachers were actually encouraging pupils to take lower-level subjects so as to make it easier for them to teach.

The target of doubling the number of science and maths graduates to 50 000 in each subject by 2008, set as an absolute minimum for the requirements of the growing state, is thus unattainable.

A further feature of the state educational system was the high number of pupils who persevered right through the educational process – sometimes taking up to fifteen years – and then dropped out in the final year. By 2007 this number was breaching 15 per cent of all final-year pupils. Research by the Human Sciences Research Council released in early 2008 indicated one of the main reasons for early drop-outs was the need to repeat years and the low levels of remedial teaching available. Other factors included financial constraints, frustration with the low quality of teaching, lack of parental support and fears for personal safety. The implications were serious. Huge investments were being made by the state to keep children in school to at least the minimum legal age, but large numbers were dropping out thereafter.

In May 2007, with the crisis in national education beyond the deniability of even a minister in the Mbeki cabinet, Pandor commissioned a study of the eighteen state schools in poor communities that had miraculously achieved more than 80 per cent success rates in the senior certificate examinations. The winning formula, the report found, was an intense focus on the central task of teaching, learning and management, supported by a work ethic, achievement and recognised success. One should not belittle such statements of the blindingly obvious. The mere decision by the department to focus on the driving factors for success in the demonstrably successful schools was a quantum philosophical step forward from its historic focus on attempting to redress the wide and irreversible malaise of the system as a whole.

From the results of the 2007 matriculation exams came, of course, a fair crop of extraordinary success stories by poor schools, all of them the result of strong leadership and committed teaching. One of the most remarkable achievements was that of the 173 matric pupils at Badirile Secondary School in Khutsong. Plagued by teacher absences, civil disturbances, collapsing infrastructure and weak leadership, the class of 2007 was heading for annihilation. Instead, the Department of Education sent them to an empty school 300 kilometres away, together with the pupils from two other schools. Isolated from outside influences, in an intensive learning experience with committed teachers under strong leadership, the matriculants scored a 73 per cent pass rate. This iconic story vividly illustrates the benefits of focus.[16]

But the opportunity of extending such focus to all schools, and thus turning the situation around, is limited. The very success factors of these achiever schools – professionalism, a work ethic, organisation – are exactly the elements lacking in the rest of the system. And they cannot be conjured up by magic wand.

Whatever the *post facto* justifications were for this failure, the knock-on effects on skills creation in South Africa were enormous. And just as OBE might have survived if not swamped with other elements of ideological overreach, so too was the workplace skills crisis infinitely compounded by arguably the worst administrative decision of the Mbeki presidency: the imposition of a costly, ideological, corrupt, bureaucratic and ineffectual skills-development structure on South African industry.

The Sector Education Training Authorities (SETAs) were established in 1998 and then, as the Department of Labour coyly put it, 're-established' on 3 March 2005. The need for re-establishment was created by the implosion of the first wave of the scheme under the weight of its own implausibility. The SETAs were based on the assumption that state institutions were in the best position to judge the training needs of the companies whose very profits depend on ensuring a flow of appropriately skilled people. The thirty-three Industry Training Boards were therefore replaced with thirty-three SETAs, which were to be funded by a 1 per cent levy on national payrolls and would reimburse companies for creating compliantly qualified skills within a national qualification framework. The principles, as always, were impeccable ... for highly developed states. In South Africa, they have proved a disaster.

The skills base of the SETAs has proved unable to manage the process. The accumulated funds have either not been spent (at one time turning the SETAs into the largest small-sized banks in the country) or spent so badly and corruptly as to have had no effect. The 'learnerships' that purport to be the channel to skills acquisition resemble the old-style 'intern' system, whereby young people ended up manning the photocopying machines and running errands. Unscrupulous businesses have turned to 'learnership' farming to profit from the system. Worst of all, most major private-sector companies have simply discounted the SETA levy as another tax and gone back to doing their own internal training. As budgets for training are usually a percentage of payroll and hard won by the human resource elements of business against the boards of directors at budget time, the cost for the SETA is excluded, and what is left is put towards internal apprenticeship training. The result, inevitably, is less money and a lower standard of training.

By 2006 there were seventy-seven standard-generating bodies, 645 general qualifications, 7 804 provider-based qualifications, 8 425 unit standards, 640 qualifications used in learnerships and thirty-one education and training quality-assurance bodies. The introduction to the National Skills Development Strategy Implementation Report, covering the period from 1 April 2006 to 31 March 2007, has a list of no less than forty-six acronyms to explain the various entities involved in the programme. One section of the text reads: 'The success indicator is supported through the NSF's Workplace Skills Development Support Programme (WSDSP) which is part of the Industry Support Programme Funding Window. The WSDSP is linked to the SMEDP Investment Incentive Programme of the Department of Trade and Industry. In addition, the Department of Labour initiated a Social Plan Programme that is implemented by the NPI.'

This impressive example of interdepartmental cooperation was marred by only one thing: the output in terms of successful candidates in this particular 'success' indicator had *declined* by 20 per cent in five years.

The state's skills-development programme in the Mbeki era had thus moved from confusion to farce. Activity supplanted action and the national skills shortage grew and grew and grew, as the following examples show:

- The Department of Labour set itself an ambitious target of decreasing the level of illiteracy among 700 000 workers by March 2010. In the first two years of the programme the department had achieved only 11 per cent of its entry targets and 2 *per cent* of its completion targets.

- Training of workers who were being redeployed from distressed businesses declined by 20 per cent between 2002/3 and 2006/7.
- Only half of the budget for the training of unemployed or underemployed was used during the year under review, due to capacity constraints and lack of take-up.
- An ABET (Adult Basic Education and Training) programme to train 20 000 unemployed people at a cost of nearly R2 000 per person in 2006/7 failed to get off on time. The success or otherwise of the scheme is awaited.
- A skills-development programme for unemployed people achieved a completion target of only 29 per cent.
- A special skills-development programme targeted at unemployed young people achieved a 19 per cent completion rate.[17]

But perhaps the most ominous statistics of all lay in analysis of the types of skills training that lead to qualifications being offered. In 2005/6, learnerships, bursaries, apprenticeships, internships and skills programmes were awarded to a total of 70 362 recipients. In 2007 this had declined to 58 462 – 17 per cent less at a time of acute skills demand. This in itself would not have been so bad if the decline had been restricted to the worthless skills-training and internship programmes offered. In effect, it hit the most important skills-qualification path hardest. Apprenticeships – the artisan sinews of a modern state – declined from a total of 8 247 in 2005/6 to 3 230 the following year. This amounted to a 60 per cent decline in one year.

The Institute for the National Development of Learners, Employment Skills and Labour Assessment, which is responsible for the assessment of artisans, gives a clue to the problem. It reported it had arranged for 9 387 assessments for apprentices of which only 34 per cent passed. The rest failed, withdrew or did not even pitch. That year, in short, a skills-hungry South Africa was fed precisely 3 192 approved apprentices – less than 10 per cent of the number that had been approved a decade earlier, when even then it was widely recognised as deficient.

The crisis in key skills was simple enough to sum up. In the place of the traditional, tried, tested and successful apprenticeship system, the skills-development authorities had focused on creation of a plethora of sub-skilled learnerships, internships and skills-growth opportunities. The impact on the industry was predictable.

Research regarding the SETAs conducted among business leaders in

2007 by the Centre for Development and Enterprise found an almost universal condemnation of the system as wasteful, inefficient, corrupt, hideously bureaucratic and contributing to no discernible improvement whatsoever in productivity.[18] A report by the Construction Industry Development Board in 2007 observed that most SETA trainees were in basic levels of training that made no significant contribution to the specialised skills required by industry.

By 2007, 88 410 people were in learnerships of dubious value. The SETAs themselves had been prone to endless incidents of corruption and a number had been placed under administration. At one stage, one of the SETAs reported that it suspected 40 per cent of its claims were fraudulent, while another uncovered a R150 million fraud.

In order to generate the standards of training required for the various sectors of the country, a hideously complex network of bodies was created. Oceans of paper had gone into creating the SETA system, along with countless millions of hours and tens of millions of rands. The only beneficiaries so far have been the clerks, lawyers, educationists, unionists and academics. It has been a massive over-elaboration of systems, a waste of valuable time and resources. If one considers that the total cost of this structure to South African industry runs at approximately R5 billion a year and will rise to R9 billion by 2010/11 (of which 10 per cent is regularly unspent because of the incompetence of the SETA), one can argue that rarely in the history of private enterprise has so much been spent on producing so little for so few.

Nor were things that rosy at the postgraduate level. In 2002, the government consolidated the country's thirty-six institutions of higher learning, both academic and technical, into twenty-three. Of these, four made it into the 500 top universities of the world as ranked by the Academic Ranking of World Universities. All four were previously white-dominated institutions that had benefited from state funding, effective management and an embedded ethos of learning under the old apartheid system.

If the amalgamation of these institutions was intended to improve the quality of output, it did not. With a postgraduate student population of nearly one million, the drop-out rate continued to increase, despite mounting state investment. By 2006, only 15 per cent of those entering institutions of higher learning were graduating, against a government target of 25 per cent. Stung by the charge that many poor black students could not afford to study, the government introduced a national student financial aid scheme that was revamped in 2004. By 2005, it was providing some 110 000 students, almost exclusively black, with loans to complete their education. At the same time, the government began a massive programme of capital investment in the formerly black universities to improve facilities, tighten financial management (which had historically been a mess) and upgrade teaching capacity. By 2007, there was no appreciable improvement in pass rates and Minister Naledi Pandor was still expressing her concern at falling graduation rates in early 2008.

There were two problems. One was the continuing poor quality of entrants emerging from the weakened state educational system; the second, which internal investigations began detecting, was 'take-up', which, put simply, means the willingness of young people to commit to a rigorous study programme. Was this yet another example of the baleful impact of the dependent society?

A study by Higher Education South Africa in 2007 involving interviews with one hundred companies revealed high levels of dissatisfaction among employers regarding the products of the institutions in reference to written skills, ability to find and use information, the skill of finding information to resolve problems and a lack of understanding of economic and business realities.[19]

By 2008, the country's tertiary institutions were due to start implementing a programme of better screening and pre-admission support in order to weed out the most likely failures, and thereby reduce the drop-out rate, with all its attendant costs. The intervention, necessary as it may be, can only have one effect. Graduates of former Model C and private schools will be the first in line. The poor public schools will be far behind. The differential between advantaged and disadvantaged can only grow and will continue to do so until such time as the state is able to properly acquit itself of its responsibility to provide an even halfway decent standard of graduate from its poorer communities.

The chain of failure from primary through tertiary education has had its inevitable effect on the job market and, through that, on wage differentials. In a speech to the United Association of South Africa in 2007, economist Mike Schussler said that those with higher than a high-school qualification earned 461 per cent more than the average wage earner: a direct result of the small number of graduates emerging from the country's shattered educational system. Comparatively, the numbers were even more terrifying. The salary differential between degreed and non-degreed workers in developed countries was 64 per cent. In South Africa, it was 1 110 per cent.[20]

Research among forty top South African companies in 2007 revealed some deeply disturbing outcomes and are worth quoting in full:

> The skills shortage is not getting better: in fact it is getting worse because of the emigration of skilled people, the ageing of skilled staff, the movement to more senior positions, and the interventions by the government itself. The government's growing emphasis on employment equity is making the skills market far tighter because the most skilled people – whites – are no longer freely employable. Perhaps most significant of all is the fact that private sector employers have grave reservations about the overall quality of our education system at all levels.
>
> The implications for productivity, growth and profits are far-reaching. In responding to scenarios in which skills would be more freely available, the firms made it abundantly clear that the skills issue was not merely a matter of ease of management or operational performance, but was intimately related to core issues of productivity, prospects for expansion, growth and profits.

The summary of the research is also worth recording:

- The failure of the educational system to deliver quality outputs had reached crisis proportions.
- The unintended consequence of transformation policies had increased pressure on already limited pools of skills.
- Human capital was being lost to global markets.
- The immigration system was flawed in concept and its capacity to deliver.[21]

What is to be made of all this? The simple answer is that educational and skills policy in South Africa crashed and burned like so many others because the ANC's ideological imperatives outstripped the capacity of the country to deliver. Professor Asmal may have declared there was no alternative to rote learning other than OBE, but by 2007 the country's employers would have given their annual bonus just to have employees who could read, write and add to some limited extent.

In its desire to push for numbers rather than quality of education, in its pursuit of fashionable foreign pedagogical formulas, the government failed in its first duty – namely, to equip its young citizens to earn a living and, in doing so, keep the economy growing for the benefit of all. Rather than focusing critically limited resources on areas of key need in the short term, it embarked on a quixotic mission to uplift the entire educational system in the shortest time possible. Fearful of accusations of being elitist, the government failed to deliver either high-quality candidates in sufficient numbers or a mass of rudimentarily educated individuals. It also fell victim to the common misperception that education alone is the ticket to a full and productive engagement in the employment field. It is not. At least as important, often more so, is what one institute has identified as the range of skills in language, analysis and research, as well as life or work readiness. Over and over the country was to experience the damage wrought by highly educated people appointed to positions without the requisite disposition for success. Inevitably, this subject, too, became fraught with racial over-tones and was all too often politely ignored or dismissed under the phrase 'mismatch'.

Ironically, the hope of the country eventually came to lie not in the products of a revamped public education system for the masses, but in the reviled and constrained elitist private and former Model C schools – the same schools to which the ANC elite sent their children in increasing numbers to save them from the disaster that the public schooling system had become. Increasingly, black parents in the poorer areas sent their children long distances to suburban schools, emptying township schools and filling to capacity those in suburbia. It was an illusory quest. Many of the core teaching skills that had once served these institutions had been lost to the profession or even the country. The disciplines that had made those schools what they were began to weaken, splintering except in a few quite exceptional cases.

Still, it was this thin line of graduates who were to provide the last vestiges of hope for supporting the growth of the black middle class and achievement of the ANC's empowerment programme. Once again it was to be the private institutions and the multiracial schools of the late apart-heid era that would come to the rescue of the country in the face of the wasteland that was state public education.

But none of this did much to serve the cause of internal social cohesion. Indeed, the reverse occurred. Rich young black children went to rich people's schools. Middle-class black children went to the interracial schools crafted by the old apartheid system. Poor black children went to schools where they could expect three and a half hours of tuition a day – if they were lucky – delivered by indifferent, under-skilled and often absent teachers, answering in the first instance to their union and only after that to their profession or their charges.

Mbeki's failure to address the substance of educational transition as opposed to the rhetoric was to cost him dearly. Members of the educated and sophisticated black middle class, which would have voted for him in numbers within the ANC youth structures, were not there when he needed them. His administration had helped destroy them before they had ever been.

Compounding this failure of the educational system was conceivably one of the most ineffective and bureaucratic skills-development programmes imposed on a modern state.

The cumulative effect of this chain of failure was to leave South Africa desperately under-supplied in critical skills. This was exacerbated by the pull effect of an international skills crisis, which saw large numbers of educated and equipped young South Africans move abroad. The exact number is difficult to gauge and the country is awash with anecdotal tales about London and Perth being swamped by people with flat vowels.

Although official statistics show that the white population of South Africa remained relatively constant between 1996 and 2007 at the 4.3 million to 4.4 million mark, the South African Institute of Race Relations estimates that between 1995 and 2005 the white population declined by 861 000. Anecdotal evidence would suggest the latter number is the more plausible. As this segment of the population never exceeded five million, the statistics indicate that one in five of the educated and skilled minority left for foreign shores during the period of greatest need of their skills. British census figures, meanwhile, indicate that the earnings of employed South Africans in the United Kingdom fall into the top 10 per cent of immigrant earnings, illustrating again the skills levels of the lost compatriots.[22] Fifty-six per cent of South Africans resident in the United States have bachelor's degrees and higher, versus 24 per cent in the general population.

The cost of emigration was high. A 2001 survey by a postgraduate University of South Africa student indicated that between 1994 and 1997 alone, South Africa lost intellectual capital to the value of R285 billion through emigration. The main reasons for the exodus were crime and affirmative action. A year later, the minister of labour was conceding that whereas before 1994 only 2 per cent of companies polled in a state survey had rated emigration as a serious problem, the number had crept to a third by 2001. An 11 per cent drop in the rate of emigration between 2001 and 2002 gave some temporary relief, until it was discovered that the official South African figures were under-reporting emigration by some 40 per cent.

It is reasonable to assume that these numbers have not improved since that time.

The crisis spurred the government to launch yet another programme with a catchy name – the Joint Initiative on Priority Skills Acquisition (JIPSA), a sister to AsgiSA, discussed earlier. One of its key recommendations was that the importation of foreign skills should be made easier – an acknowledgement of desperate pleas from the private sector over more than a decade.

The view of the administration, deeply ideological, was that the skills gap could and should be filled by South Africans in general and black South Africans in particular. It took *ten years* to pass the bill easing immigration restrictions after numerous amendments, delayed negotiations, changes of promoters, political wrangles (the Inkatha Freedom Party at one point held the home affairs portfolio), changes of mind and general dilly-dallying. The amendments to the immigration laws merely bureaucratised the process and complicated an already challenging task of bringing skills to a country which was known for high crime levels and institutionalised discrimination against employees who were not black. Ironically, the most hostile attitudes were reserved for fellow Africans, whom the authorities seemed to regard as a direct affront to local black people (conversely, other Africans often seemed offended by the assignment of black South African expatriates to their countries). The stories that Nigerians and Kenyans have told me about the contortions they had to go through to get work permits in South Africa are illuminating, but would be time-consuming to recount. It was not surprising, then, that of the 35 200 'quota' jobs available to immigrants with key skills, only 1 123 had been taken up by 2007. Employers and potential employees had simply run out of energy or interest by that stage.

The impact of the skills crisis in the engineering field was widely felt and created a major challenge to the government's infrastructure investment programme. In a paper delivered in December 2007, the executive director of the South African Federation of Civil Engineering Contractors, Henk Langenhoven, estimated that the sector was haemorrhaging up to R6 billion a year in lost construction, due to a lack of skilled personnel. The blame was to be laid equally at the door of the government and the industry, which had failed to take its own steps to anticipate the skills crisis, he said. In the first quarter of 2008, First National Bank's civil construction confidence index revealed that 98 per cent of construction companies were experiencing skilled labour shortages.

Predictably, South Africa has neither created nor attracted the skills it needs, thereby directly undercutting the Mbeki administration's capacity to deliver on its promised service infrastructure. In 2007, vacancies in public-service departments amounted to the following proportions of available posts:[23]

- Home affairs: 29 per cent.
- Trade and industry: 30 per cent.
- Science and technology: 23 per cent.
- Education: 20 per cent.
- National Treasury: 31 per cent.
- Justice: 20 per cent.
- Health: 20 per cent.
- Land affairs: 24 per cent.

This high level of vacant posts, many of them held open for long periods so as not to damage the affirmative action quotas, was particularly critical at local government level. There was little more damaging to realisation of the Mbeki dream than the failure of his administration to urgently confront and rectify the errors of earlier educational and skills policy formulation. It was hara-kiri on a national scale.

But an even more concerning issue runs like a dark thread through the reports of the National Skills Development Strategy: the low take-up of educational and training opportunities offered to the poor and the unemployed. This indicates a much broader problem: the capacity or indeed willingness of large parts of the population to improve their skills and thus their lifestyles. If this is true, if the problem is neither financial resources nor access to training, if the problem is one of a culture arising from the dependent society, then there is very little any government or any leader can do to change it in the short term. This will remain one of the biggest challenges for Mbeki's successor.

CHAPTER 11

Health check

Those who have given themselves the most concern about
the happiness of peoples have made their neighbours very
miserable.   — ANATOLE FRANCE[1]

THE NEWLY ELECTED ANC GOVERNMENT CONFRONTED A
functioning but bifurcated public health system in 1994. It bore little
resemblance to the real needs of South Africa, public spending having
been skewed towards the white minority and the urban communities.

The ANC correctly and commendably identified the major areas of concern and moved promptly to address them. In order, these problems were:
- a profusion of authorities responsible for health care, with more than
  fourteen different state agencies involved;
- an over-heavy focus on curative as opposed to preventative medicine;
- major investments in urban hospitals and less on rural clinics able to
  offer preventative medical care;
- a growing divide in health-care spend between private health provision
  and public health services; and
- an unconscionably high cost for medicines.

Most of the policy directives set by the state after the accession of the ANC
were both necessary and appropriate. The problem, as always, was implementation – the moment when the rubber hits the road. Thus it was
that, despite world-class theory and programmes, the quality of health
care followed the route of justice, policing and education – backwards.

In 2000, the World Health Organisation (WHO) rated South Africa
175th out of 191 member countries in terms of the health-care system's
overall performance. South Africa was beaten by Niger (170), Equatorial
Guinea (171), Rwanda (172), Afghanistan (173) and Cambodia (174) but
licked Guinea-Bissau (176), Swaziland (177), Chad (178) and Somalia (179).
This was the sombre picture of health performance found by President
Thabo Mbeki one year after taking office.

A comparative WHO statistic six years later might have given an indication as to how the health situation had improved in South Africa, relative to other countries. Sadly, those direct comparisons are not available due to new key health-measurement indices and reporting. What we do know, however, is that state expenditure on health increased by an average of 13.3 per cent a year from then until 2007, when approximately R60.3 billion – or 11 per cent of the budget and 8.4 per cent of GDP – was devoted to the sector. By 2008/9 this had risen to R75 billion. This is very respectable, measured by international standards.

We also have an interesting per capita comparative statistic from the 2006 WHO report regarding spend relative to output, measured against the most basic national health indicators. Tonga is the only archipelago in the Pacific Ocean never to have been colonised. It has 112 000 inhabitants with a per capita GDP of $7 984, compared to South Africa's $10 070. In 2006, its government spent almost exactly the same as South Africa per head of population on health care – $255, against South Africa's $258. How do the comparative key health indicators stack up?

In 2006, life expectancy at birth in Tonga was seventy-one for males and seventy-two for females. In South Africa, the figures were fifty and fifty-three respectively – a decline from 56.2 years in 2000 to 50.7 in 2006. If one wanted to be utterly mischievous, this could be interpreted as meaning that for every year of Mbeki's tenure, South Africans have sacrificed nine months of their life expectancy. Infant mortality under the age of five was thirty-two per one thousand births for males and seventeen for females in Tonga. In South Africa, the numbers were seventy-two for males and sixty-two for females. In Tonga, the mortality rate for members of the population between the ages of fifteen and sixty was 140 per 1 000 for males and 194 for females. In South Africa, it was 667 for males and 669 for females.

There is another statistic. The Tongan government was able to cover 85 per cent of the country's total health-care expenditure with its $255 per person. The South African government could manage to pay for only 38 per cent of total health care with its $258 – the rest came from the pockets of private citizens.

It is thus hard to avoid the conclusion that during Mbeki's tenure, public health outcomes as a function of spend hardly improved. Indeed, there is research to indicate that it has regressed. Again, why should this be? South Africa's expenditure on health as a percentage of GDP was 8.4 – in the same league as Hungary, Italy, New Zealand, Slovenia and Sweden. Why should a well-resourced country with plenty of good ideas and enthusiastic people do worse than Tonga in the key health indicators, even though the latter is a much smaller, poorer country?

Part of the answer has to be the high mortality rate caused by HIV/AIDS. But the intractably high incidence of HIV is itself a feature of inefficient health policy and public indifference to safe sex. Another factor is the high mortality rate from violent crime. Both hugely affect the indicators, but that is only part of it. The rest is a failing public health system that is the product, yet again, of ideological overreach.

The ANC government did an exceptional job of combining the fragmented health departments into nine provincial departments and creating a further fifty-three districts to provide preventative medical care. It also embarked on an ambitious building programme, erecting more than 1 345 new clinics and upgrading 263. By 2007, there were 4 100 clinics and 400 hospitals. Free hospital visits increased from 67 000 in 2000 to 128 000 in 2006, and from 1996 all pregnant women and children received free treatment.[2] Investment in health remained at above-average annual growth of all government spending and in fact nearly doubled between 2003 and 2008. And yet the quality of care did not materially improve for those trapped in the public health system.

There were three major reasons: the system did not have the requisite number of skilled personnel to maintain itself; the organisation and management lagged behind the infrastructural roll-out; and, finally, the investment in hospitals simply fell away, leading to a material deterioration in these major health-care providers. As conditions in the clinics worsened, patients fled in greater numbers to the crumbling hospitals. In between a preventative health-care system that never took off properly and a national hospital grid that was collapsing, compounded by virulent epidemics, the citizens without access to private medical aid schemes paid the price, sometimes with their lives.

First, let us deal with the shortage of skilled personnel. The government's initial response to the shortage of health-care professionals was to import 450 foreign doctors, mainly from Cuba. This was a romantic project, given that then health minister Dr Nkosazana Dlamini Zuma had been exiled in those islands as a young medical practitioner. The import programme did not work out that well, least of all for the patients, and the Cubans went home. The next project was the imposition of a year's national service on graduate doctors, rather as the apartheid era had deployed doctors conscripted for military service to rural areas. The ANC's plan failed to deliver the yield: indeed, it simply hastened the exodus of young doctors to other countries. Thereafter, the government recruited 258 Tunisian doctors and drafted them, along with 2 000 nurses, into rural areas to bolster the failing primary health-care sectors. The outcome is awaited.

In 2006, there were 29 912 doctors registered with the Health Professions Council of South Africa in both private and public health – an increase of exactly 124 doctors on the 2000 register. By 2005, South Africa had a vacancy rate in the health professional ranks of 27.1 per cent and the numbers of health-care workers had been on the decline continuously since the ANC had taken office – 235 000 in 1996 versus 225 000 in 2006. A report commissioned by the Human Sciences Research Council in 2007 attributed the decline to fewer professionals being provided by the tertiary institutions (as with education, the government's grand consolidation programmes had reduced output of professionals). The same survey indicated that 70 per cent of medical students indicated they intended emigrating once their studies were complete.[3]

In 1996, the country produced 2 629 professional nurses. In 2004 the number fell to 1 716. As nurses are the bedrock of the health-care system, one can appreciate the impact on service of such a decline, particularly with the additional huge burden of the HIV/AIDS pandemic. By 2008, efforts were being made to provide a greater volume of nurses, but as secondary-school education had considerably weakened, the quality of output was less than could have been expected – not least by the patients.

Successive research projects found that a second contributory feature of the decline was a deep loss of morale, with one survey indicating that half of the country's nursing staff saw themselves working overseas if the opportunity arose. The reasons for this low morale? Surveys pointed to over-work, poor pay, lack of support, weak management, inadequate equipment, personal security concerns and crumbling physical infrastructure.

The 2007 report for the Gauteng Health Department, the most active in the country, showed a 20 per cent vacancy rate for doctors and 24 per cent for nurses.[4]

A national audit commissioned by the Critical Care Society of South Africa, representing high-level medical practitioners and published by the *South African Medical Journal* in 2008, reported that an acute shortage of intensive-care unit (ICU) staff was posing threats to patients' lives and driving up costs.[5]

The researchers found that 75 per cent of ICU managers were properly trained, but only 25 per cent of the nurses under them were adequately qualified. Only 3.8 per cent of them were trained as neonatal ICU nurses. The ICU nurse deficit was estimated at 8 000.

'Our nurses are tired, often not healthy, and plagued by discontent and low morale,' the report said. 'The quality of the training and continuing medical education is dubious [and] there are no effective recruitment and retention strategies.'

Even making allowances for special pleading, this is a disturbing indictment.

The government policy of supporting community district health care at the expense of the major hospitals was beginning to take its toll by 2005. The number of hospital beds per 1 000 of the population had slid from 5.5 per thousand – well above the international norm of 4.2 – in 1996 to 3.7 per thousand in 2005.

The quality of care had also declined as the government pumped money into its underperforming and under-equipped district clinics. A seminal report in 2006 by members of the National Labour and Economic Development Institute (NALEDI), a labour-oriented institution, observed the following about the public hospital system:

> The rapidity of this restructuring in the health sector may well have had a negative impact on quality at all levels. The state-funded Hospital Strategy Project whose recommendations on hospital reform have informed government policy since it reported in 1996, warned against a too hasty reallocation of funding to primary health care, and warned also that district and regional hospitals should be strengthened before attempting to reduce services at central hospital level to avoid undermining an already precarious system.[6]

This was not done. Ideological overreach did not allow for caution, prudence or even deliberation.

The second major problem was to be found at the level of hospital management. The government followed a policy of a high degree of centralised decision-making, in most cases marginalising the hospital leadership on the ground. Compounding the problem was a lack of internal coordination between various functions – a classic silo effect – in which the medical profession reported through one chain, the nursing staff through another and the support and cleaning staff through a third. This system led to a very high degree of dysfunction and plunging morale, not helped by an aggressive unionism that militated against performance standards and a functioning disciplinary process.

The NALEDI investigation recorded a truly depressing tale of management dysfunction, lack of communication, weakness in function, staff shortages and failing outcomes in the major state hospitals it reviewed. The only hope it could find was in innovative and imaginative managers who bent or broke the rules in order to get things done.

In its conclusion, it diagnosed high levels of institutional stress brought about by:

- managerial paralysis and disempowerment that follows from the lack of a clear locus of managerial responsibility; and
- work overload, physical and psychological stress, inefficiency and clinical failure caused by understaffing.

'If this situation is allowed to continue,' warned the report, 'a long-term erosion of the public health sector is likely, as the older generation of public-service professionals retire and the younger generation is so overwhelmed by workloads that it opts for the private sector.'

As in the security sphere, the status of the leader element was also a challenge. In this case, the minister of health, Dr Manto Tshabalala-Msimang, was exposed in a national newspaper as being an unreformed alcoholic, recipient of an undeserved liver transplant, a fractious patient and, to cap it all, a convicted thief who had been expelled from Botswana for stealing items from patients in her care. The political impact of Mbeki's protection of this person was dealt with in Part I. Here, it suffices to observe that a health minister exposed, in the immortal words of the newspaper headline, as 'A Drunk and a Thief' hardly encourages public confidence or professionalism in the organisation.

So what was the effect of this paralysis of public health capacity on health deliverables – whether preventative or curative?

Inevitably, negative. The results were found in the exorbitant levels of HIV/AIDS, tuberculosis, an increasing incidence of septicaemia in hospitals and mounting infant deaths.

The HIV/AIDS issue is worthy of a book in itself (in fact it has been the source of countless publications) but warrants mention here in one key aspect: the thwarting of public and private efforts to combat the disease and its malevolent co-rider, tuberculosis, through the insidious and unintended effects of the dependent culture fostered by the Mbeki legacy.

The political dimensions of this issue are dealt with elsewhere and relate entirely to the world views of a president confronting arguably the country's equivalent of the Black Death of the Middle Ages. The issue in South Africa became massively confused with an instinctive suspicion by the president of the major pharmaceutical companies and a distrust of the agenda of the AIDS industry – a huge and very vibrant enterprise with enormous budgets and a vested interest in overstating the problem at every turn.

The fact remains, however, that the South African government did not begin effectively addressing the AIDS pandemic until late in Mbeki's tenure, when HIV-infection rates were peaking at 10.8 per cent of all persons over the age of two years, according to the South African National HIV Survey of 2006. South Africa was fifth in the world for the incidence of TB, which had doubled since 1998. When the government did respond, it presented a world-class programme to combat HIV/AIDS, with huge state resources behind it. The only problem was by that time many people had been needlessly infected or had died, and attempts by the Department of Health to counteract the disease and TB (up to 60 per cent of adult TB sufferers are HIV-positive) were nullified by the unintended consequence of other state policies that had led to the dependent society.

Let me be clear on the argument. The failure of Mbeki and his top team to embrace the AIDS issue as one of the great crises of this continent and to emblazon his own leadership in confronting the challenge will always be marked against his name. There is no excuse for the hoops through which the country jumped for years as the presidency and the health ministry cast about, with charlatans offering industrial solvents and health diets as a way to combat the disease.

The full absurdity of the intellectual basis of the government's position on AIDS is captured in a 2007 report by fifteen scientists from the Academy of Science of South Africa: 'Recent public debate about the value of certain foodstuffs and supplements in the management of HIV and AIDS as well as claims of benefit arising from unproven diets and therapies have caused confusion within communities and among health care workers.'[7]

But in fact there was nothing that Mbeki or his team could have done to avoid an extremely high and continuing level of infection and mortality from AIDS through preventative or curative methods. At most they could have saved several hundreds of thousands of lives. The fact that they did not is eternally to their discredit, but should not sway us from the wider issue.

The reality is that both public and private anti-HIV/AIDS programmes and the associated TB initiatives were crippled by three things: an embedded culture of public irresponsibility, which virtually nullified AIDS educational campaigns; a systemic refusal by a number of AIDS and TB sufferers to take medication, so as to prolong state welfare grants; and the incapacity of an uncaring bureaucracy to implement the programme. All, to some extent or the other, were the consequences of the Mbeki dependent society that traded personal accountability at a discount and treated consequence as irrelevant.

Let us explore the theme in more depth, starting with a possibly appropriate anecdote. When I was a senior newspaper executive in the mid-1990s, I was involved in a very active AIDS education programme aimed at sexual health lifestyles of young people. The project, supported by a major international health NGO, took the form of newspaper supplements on a monthly basis. A year after the project was launched, the sponsors commissioned an audit to determine outcomes. The result was deeply disturbing. Although more than 90 per cent of young people were aware of the connection between unprotected sex and the possibility of HIV/AIDS infection, only 14 per cent cared. For the rest, it was business as usual. Later, I was to learn that there also existed a strong resistance among many adult males to using condoms: it was regarded as unmanly.

This was my introduction to the enormous challenge of changing lifestyles in an environment where there was little to impel such a change, a challenge that was brought home even more forcefully a decade later, when the ANC elected as its president a man who had unprotected sex with a young woman who he knew was HIV-positive, and showered afterwards to minimise the consequence. This person, incredibly, had once headed the South African government's anti-AIDS alliance. He was, of course, Jacob Zuma.

In early 2007, the *South African Medical Journal* reported on a study of the prevalence of HIV/AIDS among South Africa's nursing professionals. The results indicated an incidence of 13.8 per cent among student nurses and 13.7 per cent among those who were already qualified. The overall incidence was 11.5 per cent.[8] The results give pause for thought. If this is the incidence among educated young women in the nursing profession, exposed to all the knowledge in the world, what could one expect in terms of personal responsibility from millions of other young people in the country?

The refusal of some AIDS and TB sufferers to take medication so as to prolong access to state grants is not an urban myth. In a survey of possible perverse incentives introduced by the state welfare system, researchers found clear evidence of such a trend. This was confirmed in a 2007 report by the Institute for Security Studies. Health minister Manto Tshabalala-Msimang referred in 2004 to the fact that the government's TB campaign was being nullified by patients who refused to complete their course of treatment. In a February 2008 report, a major pharmaceutical company, Aspen, noted that one in six people enrolled for free anti-retrovirals was not taking them. The scale and durability of this tendency is debatable, but not its incidence or the fact that it is a consequence of a culture that puts access to state subsidies above life itself.

The third issue relates to the capacity of the state to implement an effective policy. Between March 2006 and March 2007, more than R5 billion was spent on AIDS programmes in South Africa – R3.5 billion by the state and R1.5 billion by private donors. But a report from the Institute for Security Studies in 2007 warned that such levels of funding were creating fertile ground for corruption through a lack of effective accountability.[9] Reports from a number of NGOs also indicated that although funds and processes for the roll-out of anti-retroviral drugs had been secured, there was an extremely low rate of implementation.

Research at fifteen hospitals in South Africa in 2007 showed that only 3 per cent of the children who died were on anti-retroviral medication, although half were clinically indicated for the medicine. The report, titled *Saving Children 2005*, was compiled by the Child Problem Identification Programme and the Medical Research Council. It indicated that half the dead children had never been tested for HIV and only 7 per cent of their mothers were known to have been given anti-retroviral medication to prevent mother-to-child transmission.[10]

The reality was that political obstructionism had now morphed into bureaucratic inefficiency. Either way, the state's anti-AIDS programme suffered.

It is small wonder, then, that a USAID publication on infectious diseases reported in 2006 that 'despite South Africa's investment in TB control, progress towards reaching program objectives has been slow. Treatment success remains low compared with other African countries with high HIV/AIDS prevalence and considerably fewer resources.'[11]

The answer to the puzzle, of course, was that the other African countries had not created a dependent society and an utterly unaccountable public health service.

The weakness of the public health system had another effect that unchained its own set of unintended consequences. With a generally weakening public health system, the demands for private health care increased – not just for the wealthy, but also for a section of the formally employed. Whereas once a lower-level employee might have considered entrusting personal and family care to the public health system, this was no longer possible. The demand for employers to provide private health care for workers became clamorous, and thus membership of the country's medical aid schemes rose to 7 127 000 by 2006 – roughly correlating to the combined population of the expanded definition of the new black middle class and the racial minorities. This number, interestingly, had remained fairly constant for a decade, but had dropped as a percentage of the population from 17 per cent in 1992 to 14.8 per cent in 2005, due to the higher population numbers. The reason for this static number is most likely to be found in the fact that employment levels remained largely constant during the period, although there was probably a churn in the profile of this private health group as whites emigrated and blacks moved into more senior positions in the corporate world.

There were two consequences to this growth in the private sector. The first was a widening of the disparity between the poor and the non-poor in terms of social benefit. This had political repercussions, which culminated – along with many other issues – in the outcome of the ANC presidential ballot at Polokwane in December 2007.

The second was financial. Those in the private health net were subjected to the rising cost of medical treatment for the higher standards of care. Medical cost inflation thus became one of the major concerns of earners at all levels and ensured an increasing imbalance in the proportion of national health spend between public and private patients – roughly 40 per cent versus 60 per cent. The key driver of private medical aid costs was not so much medicine and over-prescription (a huge problem in itself) but the cost of acquiring high-level skills in a situation where the state was failing to produce any, and where those that existed were being poached left, right and centre.

A report by the Health Systems Trust, an independent NGO, showed that per capita spend of private schemes was five times more than public expenditure in 1998, but had widened to 6.6 times more by 2005. It further warned that private health care was in danger of becoming unaffordable for many already in the net.[12]

The cost impact on the private schemes could be seen in the report of the Council for Medical Schemes in 2006. Of the R51.3 billion spent by medical schemes in that year, R10.9 billion went to specialists (a 17.1 per cent increase over the previous year) and R17.7 billion to private hospitals (13.6 per cent), while payment for medicine dispensed outside hospitals rose to R8.7 billion (8.8 per cent). But even these increases were inadequate, argued the health-care funders. In order to stay profitable (some would argue excessively so) they began tightening admission criteria even further, reducing benefits and pushing generic medication.

It all came to a head in early 2008 with another major clash between the minister and the industry, when private hospitals indicated that they were going to pass on inflationary increases for ward care and some specialist services such as anaesthesia. Both the minister and the council warned they would go to court to stop the increases, which they claimed were not within the compliance agreements and were therefore illegal. It was yet another round in a bruising engagement, waged amid a slowly withering public health system.

A classic egg-and-chicken argument has developed.

The state argues that the reason it is unable to fund its public health mandate is that too much national health spend is going into private health systems. The private medical-care sector argues that the state's incapacity to train and retain staff, its failure to maintain its public hospitals because of inefficiency and misdirection, and the fact that its spend on health has remained almost constant in real terms for a decade has forced members of the public into private care, where they obviously encounter the higher cost of quality treatment. The state is therefore the architect of its own misfortune and is the key driver of the imbalance in both health-care spending and outcomes, and it is not for private health-care providers to shoulder the responsibility for improving access to the mass market, particularly as the state disposes of 78 per cent of hospital beds.

The argument is circular, but it is perhaps worth making the point that if tiny Tonga can deliver much better health care than South Africa with the same amount of money per head, the problem points not to the quantum spent on public versus private health, but rather to how effectively the state money is spent *within* the public health system. The challenge, therefore, is not how much more money can the state prise out of private pockets to pump into a manifestly ailing system, but what it can do to improve the system.

By 2006, the government was in retreat on a number of its health-care policies in a desperate effort to deal with the unintended consequences while still actively pursuing others. Among its responses and its challenges are:

1. 'Revitalisation' of the hospitals – weasel-speak for refurbishing institutions that should never have been allowed to deteriorate in the first place.

2. An ambitious human resources expansion programme to grow its health-care professional pool – a campaign obviously hampered by the poor quality of output from the state educational institutions and the general exodus of existing skills.

3. Decentralisation of control to hospital administrations and attempts to eliminate silos – commendable but subject to the availability of managerial skills in sufficient numbers and level, a doubtful prospect for the reasons enumerated in (2).

4. Introduction of a national health insurance scheme to which the private sector would be expected to contribute – again, appropriate but not likely to succeed if a static pool of individuals (the famous seven million) is called on to sacrifice expensive but efficient private health care to subsidise inefficient and wasteful state health systems that they might never use.

5. Creating a risk-equalisation fund within private medical aid schemes to ensure that the younger and employed support the older and sicker – admirable but questionable if the current slow augmentation of the high-level employed continues, due to the reasons adumbrated in (2) and (3).

6. Continuing attempts to reduce the cost of medicines. This initiative had it origins during the first days of ANC rule and was initially driven by the relentless first minister of health, Dr Nkosazana Dlamini Zuma. Her premise was absolutely correct: medication costs in South Africa were unacceptably high and the local industry had run riot for too long.

With a liturgical suspicion of the multinational pharmaceutical companies brought to the table, however, it was inevitable that the engagement between the minister and the sector would be long and bloody. The battlefield ranged over the price of dispensing medicines, the role of generic drugs, margins on drugs, wholesale pricing practices and, inevitably, intellectual property rights. The battle was fought in the media, parliament, the courts and the journals, and at the end of it all the government could rightly claim it had marginally reduced the price of medicine. A report by the Health Systems Trust in 2006 indicated that changes to bulk discounts and rebates, uniformity of sale prices to customers, irrespective of volume, and the move to generic drugs had materially reduced the proportion of money spent by the medical schemes on medicines. It did observe, however, that not much of the benefit had been passed on to the consumers.

The minister's opponents, meanwhile, could complain that the initiatives had imperilled the small pharmacists, alienated the medical profession, undercut the viability of private health-care providers and administrators and thoroughly angered the multinational pharmaceutical companies to the point of withdrawing from South Africa. Five thousand jobs were lost in the sector between 2000 and 2007 as multinationals closed their doors and left.

A secondary set of skirmishes raged between the Council for Medical Schemes, a statutory body charged with overseeing the schemes, and the major health-care insurers. The central battles here were around the scale of charges of the administrators' and brokers' fees.

As Mbeki's tenure drew to its confused and divisive conclusion, his legacy in public health remained ambivalent. He had extended the access of health care to ordinary people and made it cheaper in some cases and free in others. But he had not presided over an improvement in either the quality of health care or its deliverables. Instead, South Africans were destined to die at a younger age after his tenure than before, and children under five years of age were still dying at a rate out of all proportion to the level of spend when compared with other countries.

A study in 2008 which synthesised three previous reports on child mortality concluded that no progress had been made in achieving the Millennium Goals of reducing child deaths by two-thirds by 2015. South Africa's infants, according to WHO statistics, were dying at a rate comparable to Bangladesh, North Korea, Eritrea, Guyana, Kyrgyzstan, the Marshall Islands and Nepal.[13] If that was a league in which the ANC government was uncomfortable to be playing, it certainly did nothing during Mbeki's term of office to move into a higher sphere. Indeed, a 2008 report titled 'Countdown to 2015: Maternal and Child Survival Report for 2008', published in the *Lancet* medical journal, rated South Africa among the worst ten of sixty-eight countries in reducing infant mortality.

In the central challenge of his tenure – building his pool of health-care professionals and the efficacy of his hospitals – he had also failed. More, he had not risen to the call for inspired leadership to confront one of the great health crises in the continent's history. Instead, he had obfuscated, prevaricated and ultimately retreated into a sort of grumbling sulk. But perhaps his greatest disappointment must have been the realisation that failure is truly indivisible. Precisely as the country embarked on a visionary and world-class anti-AIDS campaign, all the other unintended consequences of his ideological overreach and the dependent state came crowding in to destroy even that hope. There was the inability of the educational system to provide quality nursing candidates in numbers; the weakening of professional standards; the irresponsibility of the dependent society; the perverse incentives of the grant system; the prevalence of violence in society … it went on and on.

CHAPTER 12

Lights out

*If we continue to develop our technology without wisdom or
prudence, our servant may prove to be our executioner.*

— OMAR N BRADLEY[1]

I F THE EARLY ANC ERA IS REMEMBERED FOR ONE THING, IT WILL
be the towering resolve with which both Nelson Mandela and Thabo
Mbeki rolled out physical infrastructure for the poor. By 2007, 2.4 million
new houses had been built and another 400 000 municipal houses converted to private ownership, three million homes electrified and more
than 4.7 million private fixed-line telephones installed. Countless hundreds
of thousands of toilets had been erected, football pitches levelled, roads
tarred, sidewalks built, community centres erected and fresh-water points
provided.

In the early years of the ANC's administration, it was a remarkable
indication of the country's capacity to undertake such vast projects, either
as the state or through the commercialised utility companies. It is debatable
whether such expansion would be possible in 2008.

Mbeki and the ANC could be justifiably proud of this achievement,
and indeed, right to the last, with everything else falling around his ears,
the president was still quoting the dry statistics of this bricks-and-mortar
campaign.

But there was one problem. The *easy* part was creation of the physical
product. The cash, the political will and the resources — both private and
public — were available in those days. Unleashed, the awesome capacity of
the administrative machine left behind by the apartheid era was able to
meet even these extraordinary targets. The *tough* part was maintaining
what the ANC had created.

It was not simply a question of whether all beneficiaries of this roll-out
were able to afford it. They were not, and many of the electricity and telephone landlines were later disconnected, leaving a legacy of very low returns
on capital employed for many years to come. The question was whether the

public authorities had the capacity to administer such a hugely expanded network on a sustainable basis. Again, they did not and could not, and as the years marched on, the gap between the legacy and its sustainability grew and grew.

Housing was one of the victims. As fast as the state built houses, the backlogs inexplicably increased. Here follows an exercise in statistical imaginings.

In 1994 the ANC government presented its white paper on a new housing policy and strategy in South Africa. It was a carefully researched document which concluded that by 1995 the country would have a short-fall of 1.5 million housing units. This could fairly be called the apartheid legacy. This shortfall, it estimated, would increase by 178 000 units a year if not addressed. In short, by 2007, the country could expect a deficiency of 3.6 million units.

This number was in itself suspect. In 1996 the population census showed there were 40.6 million people living in South Africa. The 2007 mid-year census put the number at 47.9 million – a growth of 7.6 million souls. At a census occupancy rate of 4.8 persons per unit, the state would have to build 1.6 million units if one made the absurd assumption that all additional people who required houses during that eleven-year period were provided with them by the state.

If one is more conservative, one would argue that only the one-third of households that were dependent on state grants for survival should qualify. Let us be generous and push that to 50 per cent.

Purely on the basis of statistics, this meant that the state should have provided 1.5 million units to make up the shortfall as at 1994 and an addi-tional 800 000 to cater for the poorest 50 per cent of the population to accommodate the additional citizens to 2007 – a total of 2.3 million units. From the outset, then, the government's estimates were at material variance with the census numbers.

Between 1994 and 2007 the state in fact built 2.4 million units. In theory, then, the country should by that year have been experiencing a shortfall of 1.2 million units in terms of the 1994 white paper, and would have a credit of 100 000 units on the basis of Statistics South Africa's census numbers and an estimate of the qualifying poor.

Yet in 2008 the government was insisting there was still a shortfall of 2.2 million units – *one million more than its own extended 1994 projections and 2.3 million more than the national census indicates were required.* What on earth was going on? Was it housing for displaced agricultural workers affected by a weakening sector? Between 2002 and 2007, 400 000 workers lost their jobs. If half were rehoused by the state, it meant another 200 000 units would be needed. Serious but not material.

Was it illegal immigration? Were the hordes of desperate economic refugees from misgovernment in the rest of Africa, and particularly from Zimbabwe as a result of Mbeki's failed 'quiet diplomacy', being given houses at South African government expense? The Department of Housing was adamant that they were not. By 2007, the Department of Home Affairs would admit to only 100 000 registered refugees. In terms of South African occupancy rates, that would mean about 19 230 units.

The number of illegal immigrants in South Africa ranges from two million to eight million. More realistic estimates put it at approximately five million due to the collapse of Zimbabwe and South Africa's porous borders. Again using South Africa's occupancy rates (generous for immigrants who statistically have a higher occupation density), that means 1 041 666 units would be required to house all South Africa's illegal immigrants as of 2007.

Let us restate the puzzle. Official government housing-backlog statistics as of 2007, if met by the South African taxpayer, would mean it would be able to meet all the housing requirements set by the ANC in 1994, *plus house every illegal immigrant in the country as of 2007*. If one takes the more authoritative Statistics South Africa numbers, the state, if it met the current estimated backlog, *would have cleared the apartheid legacy, matched population growth since 1994, housed all illegal immigrants, rehoused all dispossessed agricultural families and still have 800 000 units to spare*. Something is clearly wrong.

International development experts argue that the ANC government's insistence on providing formal housing units is slowing down delivery and therefore compounding the backlogs. This is true. Cumbersome planning processes are adding 20 per cent to house costs and hugely delaying roll-outs. In yet another case of ideological overreach, the state is ignoring the proven capacity of informal settlements to develop substantial housing platforms on their own initiative and with targeted state support. But this is more a question of *timing*, not *quantum*.

Arguments that the increased demand is due to lower occupation densities is belied by the statistics. South African housing density had moved from 4.8 persons per unit in the 2002 census to 5.2 in 2007 – probably because poorer households are either taking in AIDS orphans or are caring for more children under child-care grants. Higher densities means fewer homes.

There are two points to be made from this analysis. First, the fatal inaccuracy of government projections, which confirms Mbeki's 2008 State of the Nation admission that there had been mistakes in state planning. Second, the chilling prospect that material numbers of state-built houses have been, or are about to be, 'lost' through systemic misgovernment in the Housing Department and local authorities.

The scope of this fraud is difficult to gauge, and if the South African media for a moment lost its interest in who among the elites was scoring political points off whom, it might consider properly investigating this story, which could ultimately prove more explosive than even the arms scandal.

Anecdotal evidence indicates there has been wide-scale abuse of the housing programme by virtually all parties involved. A number of investigations are under way or have been concluded into scams committed by developers with the connivance of state officials. Overstatement of units delivered is the most common fraud.

State officials themselves have not been slow to see the advantage. In March 2008, more than 1 000 public servants in KwaZulu-Natal alone were hauled before the courts to explain how they received homes meant for the poor. A senior housing official confided that this is 'not the tip of the iceberg, but the tip of the tip'.

There is also material evidence of bribe-taking in the allocation of houses and abuse of the informal rehousing programmes whereby informal dwellers claim state homes and then immediately send members of the family to new informal settlements to claim rehousing rights again, and so endlessly on. One of the aspects under investigation is the possibility that public officials have themselves become major landlords of state-owned houses and are living off the rental proceeds. Again, allocation of houses to illegal immigrants with fraudulent home affairs documents is common.

ANC Classic appears pleased by the progress of the housing programme – raw numbers have always impressed the ANC leadership. It has retained the minister of housing on the NEC in deference to the number of units built. This is understandable, because the construction of 2.4 million homes is by any definition an achievement. But the best interests of any new administration might be to look long and hard at what, exactly, has been bought by this massive state investment; what price this miracle.

Research into the huge numbers of civic protests in the country in recent years has identified one burning issue in the minds of poor people: the feeling that they are being shafted by corrupt officials in the allocation of homes. The ANC would ignore this at its peril.

The issue of sustainability arose even more dramatically in the two main drivers of modernity: power and telecommunications. The primary driving force for the economic growth of twenty-first-century Africa, apart from rising commodity prices, has been technology. The advent of reliable power sources, the mobile telephone and the internet brought the impossible into the realm of the attainable. It opened up communities and space and opportunity. Nobody who has worked on the African continent can but be aware of the revolutionary change that communications and power have made to business, society and politics.

At the dawn of its liberation, South Africa stood arrayed with the sort of physical infrastructure that other African countries could only dream about. Not only was the country massively equipped with an electricity grid and spare generating capacity, it also had an effective and affordable telecommunications platform capable of scaling as required.

The distribution of both power and telecommunications was, as always in developing countries, skewed in three ways: in favour of the rich rather than the poor, urban rather than rural, and industrial rather than agricultural. This did not, however, detract from the fact that the systems were resourced, efficient and cost-effective.

A survey in 2001 found that the price of electricity in South Africa was the lowest in the world, while the reliability and quality were excellent. The average energy available from Eskom power stations had increased from 76 per cent in 1991 to 92 per cent in 2000. Generation load factors had improved from 50 per cent to 55 per cent over the same period.[2]

Seven years later, the country could still boast among the lowest energy costs in the world, but it had entered a period of the most devastating rolling power outages, caused by lack of generation capacity and the crumbling of existing infrastructure. So bad had it become that by 2008 the government was forced to declare a virtual state of emergency and Eskom, the electricity supply authority, was begging the government to dissuade further capital investment in major power-intensive new projects until at least 2013, on the grounds that it could simply no longer market itself as a low-cost energy source.

How had this happened, and in such a comparatively short period of time?

The answer: the gravest misdirection of national resources towards purely ideological projects, weak-leader group management and prevarication on key policy decisions. Compounding all of this, as elsewhere, was the racially engineered loss of institutional capacity and the growth of a voracious bureaucratic elite which, as elsewhere in Africa, began to regard these public utilities as their private domain for personal enrichment.

Failure of the major parastatal agencies to meet their primary obligations to the society and the economy, coupled with the absence of a strategic urgency on the issue by the state, will stand as one of the most enduring reproaches to the Mbeki presidency in the decade to come.

Eskom supplies 96 per cent of the power in South Africa. Of this, 60 per cent is sold in bulk directly to about 400 major clients and the rest is distributed through 172 local authorities. The local authorities buy in bulk and on-sell to consumers. It is the failure to recover the costs of a material part of this supply because of weak systems at local government level that has led to the huge deficits in municipal accounts, as we have already seen.

The country is a hungry electricity consumer. About one-third goes to industry, a quarter to transport, 20 per cent to domestic consumers and the balance to mining, commerce and agriculture. The apartheid government, a heavy investor in national infrastructure, had seriously oversupplied generation capacity in the 1970s and 1980s in anticipation of higher growth rates that never materialised. The result was the mothballing of a number of coal-firing generators.[3]

By 2007, South Africa had thirteen coal-fired power stations, one nuclear station at Koeberg near Cape Town and two pumped storage stations, one in the Drakensberg and the other in the Western Cape. There were also a clutch of smaller gas turbine and hydroelectric operations. The power was distributed through 26 461 kilometres of transmission lines which ranged in size from 132 kilovolts to 765 kilovolts. Within the distribution network there were 267 864 kilometres of line and 6 463 kilometres of underground supply cables. The whole constituted the largest and most expensive electricity generation, transmission and distribution operation on the continent.

Eskom remains a financially strong entity. Year after year it showed a strengthening balance sheet, increased revenues and better profits. Its debt-to-equity ratio declined and productivity per employee increased as staff numbers were reduced from 39 000 to 32 000 in ten years. This rosy picture, however, hid a grim reality. Eskom was spending too little on capital development and was creaming the profits from a captive market and a growing economy.[4]

In 1998, Eskom's equity was deemed to vest in the state and fell within the ambit of the Department of Minerals and Energy. The utility was restructured as a limited liability company in 2000. The regulating body for the electricity industry is the National Energy Regulator of South Africa (NERSA), which determines tariffs and the deployment of resources. Responsibility for strategic planning had also been taken out of Eskom's hands in 2001 and given to central government. It was a fatal error.

Although South Africa was well set up for growth, the systems were patently not ready for the type of national economic expansion projected by the ANC government when it took office. Its first projections, remember, were for 6 per cent growth rates by 2000. It never reached that objective, but average growth rates of 3.5 per cent from 1999 through to 2005, peaking near 5 per cent in 2006 and then falling back, created their own immediate and urgent challenges for new-generation power facilities and a review of the distribution systems.

Both issues were critical, and Eskom planners and the private sector repeatedly warned the government that this would become a strategic constraint unless addressed early in the life of the new administration. Indeed, while the administration banged on about annual GDP growth rates of 6 per cent plus, Eskom was consistent in warning that the existing power network could underwrite only a 4.8 per cent growth rate – tops. In 1998, an Eskom strategic document to the then minister of mineral and energy affairs, Phumzile Mlambo-Ngcuka, prophesied that unless urgent capital investments were made immediately, the country would face an energy crisis by 2007. The minister chose to ignore the warning. She went on to become Mbeki's deputy after he shunted Jacob Zuma in mid-2005. The country went on to an energy crisis.

The government, to its credit, did begin a wholesale review of the sector and in its energy policy white paper in 1998 proposed private-sector involvement in the generation side of the business and the establishment of regional electricity distributors to take away the distribution function from local authorities – a proposal hotly contested by some municipalities.

But the reality was that the Mbeki administration and the national power utility, instead of concentrating on the urgency of maintaining and increasing generation, became massively diverted into three ideological projects that ramped up the long-term cost of the system and plunged large swathes of the country into darkness.

The ideological component of the government's power spend was driven by the deeply socialistic views of the ANC. Almost the first major programme was the roll-out of a very ambitious and enormously expensive plan to electrify as many homes as possible. From 1994 to 2000, 2 006 773 homes were electrified. By 2002 this had risen to three million. This was an astonishing achievement by any token. The only problem, a big one, was that many of these connections were in poor communities and recipients could not or would not pay. The result was 40 per cent less take-up of supply than had been anticipated, which massively reduced the supplier's chances of recovering its investment, and huge debts for local authorities. By 2007, Eskom was providing R1.5 billion a year for bad debts. Recovery rates in Soweto, for example, were showing declines through most of the period from 2000 to 2004 rather than improvements, despite the massive publicity campaign intended to get residents to pay up.[5]

Infrastructure, naturally, began deteriorating and illegal connections into the grid became a huge problem for both local authorities and Eskom. The administration had made the fatal error of priming demand before ensuring sustainable supply. When the demand did come, as it inevitably would, it then cut supply.

But the ideological overreach did not stop there. Having connected millions of poor households in South Africa and then encountering difficulty in recovering the costs, the ANC encouraged NERSA to consistently gazette deflationary increases in power pricing, then added to the woes of the generator by providing free electricity to a swathe of poor households. The numbers did not, could not, add up and yet, in the pursuit of its populist vision, the government, the regulator and a reluctant Eskom perpetuated the myth of perennially cheap electricity until it could no longer be supported and came tumbling down, with disastrous consequences for the public and the national economy.

The other ideological element of state power policy was tied to Mbeki's grand Africa vision, entrenched in NEPAD. Material investments were made on behalf of African countries to assist with generation and distribution capacity. The return on capital, as even Eskom was willing to concede, was disturbingly low. By 2008, South Africa was drawing 2 000 megawatts of power from neighbouring grids but exporting 3 000 megawatts – the output of an entire power station. Much of this was going to a bankrupt Zimbabwe, which was in any case unable to pay for the power, its economy having long since collapsed.

None of these populist and ideological forays would have been in themselves an insuperable problem in the short term, were it not for the fact that the capacity of Eskom to meet its objectives was allowed to deteriorate.

An alarming report by Eskom in 2007 revealed that of the power stations in operation, only two were reaching optimum levels of output. The degradation of the system in five short years had thus reduced power supply even before the additional requirements were taken into account.

In regard to the additional requirements, there was nothing but prevarication and delay. It was always the government's intention that there be a high level of private-sector involvement in power generation – its white paper proposals were 70 per cent state and 30 per cent private sector. But the private sector was scared off by the deflationary increases in tariffs passed year after year by NERSA and the endless delays caused by the government as both the concept and the content of the initiative were pushed back and forth. Part of this was undoubtedly due to internal disputes between the favoured classes as to who was to benefit from the empowerment component of privatisation.

Instead of pushing ahead, as prudence dictated, the government went into paralysis. The delays in bringing a comprehensive plan to the table meant that commencement of construction of the new generation of coal-fired generators in the short term, and nuclear-powered reactors in the long term, let alone alternative energy generation sources, did not commence. Indeed, fourteen years into the life of the ANC government, planning and funding had not even been completed.

The initial R95 billion capital cost grew to R150 billion for the five-year projection and then ballooned to R244.5 billion and then again to R300 billion by 2008 – six and a half times more than had been spent in the previous five years. Of this amount, 50 per cent would have to be borrowed so as not to compromise the utility's balance sheet. To fund the exercise, warned Eskom, the utility would have to levy tariff increases of about 20 per cent a year for five years.

In the event, once top-management changes had been made and an experienced and mandated team had been able to access Fortress Eskom, the true horror of the situation became apparent. Not only was Eskom way behind in its recapitalisation programme and its maintenance regime, but it had reduced its coal stock to virtually nothing in a misguided attempt to introduce a 'just in time' principle for its key production input. Financially, the initiative had the benefit of hugely improving the bottom line of the utility in the short term, thereby making management look good, but it failed catastrophically on two grounds. Soaring commodity prices in 2008 meant the utility was unable to restock to safe reserve margins without huge expense. Secondly, in a noble but misguided attempt to empower its supplier networks, it had created tumult and erratic deliveries. In short, it would be hard to find a better example of the price of ideological over-reach and the destruction of institutional memory and experience in one entity. Typically, not a single person was called to account. The net effect, however, was a doubling of electricity tariffs in two years and a 10 per cent reduction in power supply to the country for an indefinite period.

What then became crucial was the extent of state commitment to the project. Yet even in the midst of the energy crisis anticipated by Eskom *nine years previously*, the government was still equivocating in early 2008 about its funding of the expansion programme. With the escalation of costs and the lack of clarity from government on how to fund the project, the inevitable happened. In early 2008, the major rating agencies in the world whose job it is to assess the viability of both countries and companies were beginning to waver on this once priceless national asset. Standard & Poor's, one of the foremost agencies, reduced Eskom to a negative rating, thus en-suring its bids to raise capital would be more difficult and more expensive.

If the delays in generation of power were costly, the delays in settling on a new system of power distribution were even more so. The initial govern-ment plan for creating regional electricity distributors to take over the role of the municipalities was originally proposed in the 1998 white paper. Nine years later, there had still been no finality. Even then, a huge question mark hung over the project. Given the public sector's track record, the only certainties were that the project would lead to further disruption, cost more, create another layer of incompetent bureaucrats, give the ANC elites more opportunities to enrich themselves and further bedevil the lives of con-sumers. Meanwhile, a senior official in the Public Electricity Distribution Industry Holdings warned that distribution problems due to delayed in-frastructure would outweigh those of generation unless urgently addressed.

The serious nature of the oversight can be gauged by the fact that in late 2007 Mbeki publicly apologised for the failure in power supply: 'We said, not now, later. We were wrong. Eskom was right.'[6] It was one of the very few times in his tenure that he apologised for anything.

A report under the banner of NERSA circulated in 2007 identified the problems:

- significant management and technical shortfalls at all levels of the electricity supply chain: generation, transmission and distribution;
- inadequate planning and introduction of new plants;
- inadequate generation capacity;
- crime, vandalism and illegal connections to networks; and
- inadequate redundancy.[7]

Skills often topped the agendas and the impact of the government's failed governance in all the cross-cutting effects on the electricity industry was apparent. In particular, these were:

- A skills exodus (whether by resignation or affirmative action) and the inability to replace people with the products of the secondary schooling system and the sectoral training authority had led to an acute crisis which would take years to resolve. In 2008 the energy SETA was placed under administration after managerial 'irregularities'.
- Fragility of local authority billing and collections systems led to cash-flow problems.
- The state was unable to protect installations from criminal elements and vandals – the National Non-Ferrous Metal Theft Combating Committee reported in 2007 the loss of underground cable from the major parastatals due to theft amounted to R500 million a year in replacement costs and the direct financial impact was in the order of R5 billion.[8]

The priority risks were identified as maintenance backlogs, crime, limited generation capacity, primary energy shortages (such as the coal price) and transmission bottlenecks.

The challenge facing South Africa is indeed daunting. South Africa's energy requirements had increased by more than 50 per cent since the ANC had taken office. By 2008, South Africa's peak demand was reaching 36 500 megawatts, while Eskom's supply, including feeds from other southern African states, was in the order of 40 000 megawatts (38 000 megawatts without its partners). It did not take a genius to know that South Africa's reserve capacity (or margin) was running perilously low. With the progressive deterioration of the system, meanwhile, the margin for error became even more uncomfortable. From a target of 15 per cent reserve capacity versus an international standard of 25 per cent, Eskom was running its operations at less than 5 per cent for most of 2007, and by 2008 it had dropped in some cases to zero per cent. As existing stations had to be taken down for repair, the only possible way to manage the reserve was to cut off supply.

In a February 2007 release, the Department of Public Enterprises, under which Eskom falls, confirmed 'concerns about the adequacy of the trans-mission system to deliver power to all regions in the country'. It also announced Eskom's determination to focus on 'demand side management' by which it meant reducing consumption of the very resource it was supposed to be providing. Its aim, it said, was to reduce demand by 153 megawatts every year for twenty years. It also said it was planning more ambitious savings of 3000 megawatts between 2007 and 2012 (about 1.25 per cent of national peak demand at 2007 rates). What the department did not mention was that these reductions were to be made by the subtle device of allowing Eskom officials to switch off the power arbitrarily to selected areas as they pleased.[9]

Consider the absurdity of the situation. Having electrified millions of domestic residences in poor communities and having anticipated annual GDP growth rates of 6 per cent from at least 2000, with all its attendant huge energy requirements, Eskom announces that its strategic objective is to *cut* supply. Not only that; it also declares that this is an *ambitious* reduction in output – surely one of the first times an enterprise has boasted about its success in reducing supply at a time of high demand. It is small wonder that serious people in South Africa and abroad began at this point to wonder about the authority's grasp on reality.

Nevertheless, the long-term intention of the government, for what it is worth, is to grow capacity to 80000 megawatts within twenty years – in other words, a doubling of capacity. The additional capacity would come from clean-burning coal-fired generators, nuclear generators and open-cycle gas turbines in the south-western Cape. In the short term, the objective is to recommission some of the mothballed generators. Three are being refurbished at a cost of R20 billion each and will furnish an addi-tional 3600 megawatts – about 4.5 per cent of the required total output.

Even here there are major problems. Because of the state's refusal to address the energy crisis at the appropriate stage, it clearly did not give consideration to environmental issues affecting energy generation. The recommissioned plants will be major carbon dioxide generators and will fall foul of many of the government's existing agreements to reduce green-house gas. Again, a big dilemma faces the state: bring on desperately needed power or keep to the international agreements. This conundrum need never have arisen had the state paused long enough a decade earlier to draft an effective programme of clean-burning coal generators, augmented by an array of alternative energy sources. Such a debate never took place, for the simple reason that the ANC government was too busy following its vote-catching roll-out of electrified houses and rock-bottom power prices, and arm-wrestling over which of the chosen would be beneficiaries of the privatised generation operations (the victor ended up being a company with very close links to the ANC). Eskom, for its part, had no interest in surrendering its monopoly and its unconscionable profits.

'We are paying the price, as business and as a country, for bad policy decisions made ten years ago,' said Business Unity South Africa's Jerry Vilakazi sombrely in 2008.[10]

A major new generator at Medupi, in the province of Limpopo, which would deal with the immediate crisis, was due to come on stream in 2010, but this was postponed by two years due to a delay in delivering the generators, though any executive who understands the shorthand knows this actually means a delay in ordering them. Much further down the line are nuclear reactors and alternative energy sources.

What was the effect of these power outages at this very fragile state of national confidence? The simple answer is: serious.

The economic cost is impossible to quantify other than to observe that it will clearly affect both the government's job creation and growth targets. Through that, of course, there will be an impact on poverty reduction. The nearest assessment of the economic impact was offered by Fanie Joubert of the Efficient Group, who estimated that a three-hour outage cost the economy about R2 billion in lost production or 22 per cent of output. If sustained, he warned, the outages would cut GDP by 2.2 per cent. More immediately at risk were a R22 billion aluminium smelter and a number of mining operations – all funded from abroad.

The public and business response was instantaneous and furious, not so much at the reality that there was an energy crisis (the more knowledge-able had accepted that it had to happen, given the track record of the state) but in the manner in which it was effected. Without any notification, some official jerked a switch and … chaos ensued.

Central business districts seized up as traffic lights went out; cows in milking lots stood awaiting reconnection; a big pressed-board manufacturer drawing 60 per cent of the power in its area spent nine hours chipping out the solidified pulp after the lights went off without so much as a call from

Eskom; Table Mountain's two cable cars came to a halt in mid-air, causing the emergency evacuation – for the first time in history – of 500 tourists; police stations were plunged into darkness; hospitals, including some where surgery was in progress, were forced to rely on dilapidated generators; piles of fresh produce rotted on the way to market.

South Africans reacted with customary resilience. Sales of generators, battery power packs, gas stoves, lamps and camping equipment soared. Hugely less advantaged than Nigeria, where households and factories have their own generators, South Africa battled on through the blackouts. Housewives cooked when power came on, children did homework when light was available or by lamp, barbers learnt to cut hair in stages and from all sides to avoid a customer emerging half shorn (this is not fabricated – my own barber was among them) and houses coming onto the market with their own generators commanded a premium. Subsequently, Eskom and the local authorities settled at approximately six-hour outages per week. Schedules were released and people began to build their lives around them.

The culture shifted. Lack of power – euphemistically dubbed 'load shedding' by the authorities – became the stock excuse for people arriving late at work or not completing an assignment. Tradesmen excused their tardiness on the basis that parts had not arrived because of the blackouts. South Africans had come to the point that was most problematic in doing business on the rest of the continent: the insidious attraction of blaming all delays and failure on external intervention. Before long, people hardly even mentioned power cuts in conversation and adjusted their activities to revolve around guessing when the next outage would occur. The quick and the canny and the advantaged were those who had the prescience not to rely on the authorities for their needs, but arranged their own alternative power sources. In a single step, South African society had become what Mbeki had always wanted: it was one with its continent where, according to the World Bank, thirty-three countries suffer acute power and energy crises.

But the South African spirit, not unlike that of the British during the Blitz in World War II, was in for a rude shock. By the third week of the crisis, thirty-one South African mines had closed down. Total losses were estimated at R1.8 billion in the first three weeks.

The state response was interesting. The power outages occurred in the interregnum, the period when nobody knew whether political power lay with the ANC in office or the ANC in opposition, with ANC Classic or ANC Lite, and so the responses were different. The president broke tradition by admitting culpability and for once acted with celerity in the face of a crisis. The new ANC NEC, behaving as if it was not part of the party that had elected Mbeki through two terms, demanded an instant response from the presidency as to what he was going to do.

Eskom hovered between being apologetic, blaming consumers for using too much power and appealing for the nation to pull together without recriminations. This last was a bit like the driver of a car who, despite all the appeals, warnings and instructions from his passengers, drives the car off the cliff and as everybody hurtles towards their doom says, 'Now is not the time for finger-pointing, we are all in this together.'

In more concrete mode, the state declared what amounted to a national state of emergency on 25 January 2008 – as if the problem was the result of divine intervention like a flood or a foreign invasion rather than nine years of the grossest, indeed treasonous, dereliction of responsibility by the utility, the state and the ruling party.

Announcing a raft of new incentives and penalties to be introduced under the Electricity Regulations Act, the government asked industry and domestic consumers to cut consumption by 10 per cent each; agriculture by 5 per cent; commercial business and the public service by 15 per cent each; and tourist, retail and conference facilities by 20 per cent. The problem was that the significant residential consuming pool that refused to pay for its power or illegally tapped into the mains supply was hardly likely to be persuaded to cut back. Suburban residents would most likely pitch in following such an appeal – they always did – but the savings would be marginal. Industry, mining and agriculture, already acutely aware of power costs, could cut back only at the expense of reducing output and, by implication, jobs. It was another classic example of the silencing logic of the unintended consequence.

The other major infrastructural state service – telecommunications – was also to be plagued during the Mbeki era with problems relating to the volume and affordability of its service. The advent of the mobile phone and its rapid adoption in South Africa by all levels of society reduced the burden on the monopoly provider. The problems here were of a different order: regulatory flip-flops that discouraged investment in fixed-line competitors and, on occasion, massively devalued the worth of mobile phone stocks on the one hand and an extortionately high cost of service on the other.

It was this latter fact and failure of the monopoly to assist with the rapid expansion of broadband that ensured South Africa had one of the highest costs for broadband by 2008. The impact on both business and the growth of small business was immeasurable. Compounding the problem was a huge surge in the roll-out of connectivity to poor households. Ideologically driven, as had been Eskom, it had the same effect: massive disconnections for non-payment, huge amounts of redundant distribution capacity and lowered return on capital.

The state telecommunications fixed-line monopoly in South Africa is Telkom. It is listed on both the JSE Securities Exchange and the New York Stock Exchange. The government has a stake of 38 per cent and the Public Investment Commission has 15.7 per cent; the rest is held by a few minor consortiums and a 36 per cent free float. One of Telkom's more profitable acquisitions is a 50 per cent holding in Vodacom, the South African joint venture with Vodafone in the United Kingdom. In alignment with its promise to liberalise the economy, the South African government has allowed the entry of a second fixed-line operator called Neotel, with more than 30 per cent state equity and then a variety of consortiums, some with close connection to the ANC. The conclusion of this deal took almost eight years. Telkom's shares, meanwhile, have not enjoyed huge success, largely due to investor wariness about regulatory changes, leadership and negative earnings before interest, taxation and depreciation. This was perhaps not surprising when one considers the findings of the seminal fourth South African Telecommunications Sector Performance Review by the Learning Information Networking and Knowledge Centre (LINK). This prestigious body reported that the government's management of the state telecommunications network's liberalisation programme had been so badly handled that the gap between South Africa and the world was growing.

The central point was that while other countries were seeing a reduction in state intervention in telecommunications, South Africa had experienced the reverse. The research pointed to a 'dismal' performance of the state monopoly in providing broadband access and affordable service. Its fixed-line monopoly, meanwhile, offered extremely high costs of service, particularly leased lines, which were indispensable to business. Neither did what the research called the duopoly of the major cellular providers help much. Their rates were also extraordinarily high.

The research confirmed what had been almost a decade of extraordinary confusion and imprecision in the telecom regulatory framework within South Africa. The problems revolved not simply around the content of policy, but about the appropriate authority to administer it, with the Independent Communications Authority of South Africa (ICASA) and the Department of Communications in an almost uninterrupted see-saw battle over responsibilities and power since the formation of the body.

In 2006, in an attempt to clarify the situation, the government introduced its Electronic Communications Amendment Act. In effect, the LINK research pointed out, ICASA would have to draft 230 regulations to give it effect and go through a complicated process for the regimenting of operators. All of this, meanwhile, was in stark contrast to the extraordinary success that Nigeria had achieved in rolling out a successful and very competitive mobile phone sector, while introducing affordable broadband. The secret was simplicity of regulations and flexibility of regulators. Yet again, it appeared, South Africa was guilty of over-elaboration of systems at the cost of efficiency.

'The idea that South Africa's ICASA was the most sophisticated regulator on the continent was widely rebuffed: regulatory environment is not the challenge in Africa. In fact it's the opposite: it is a challenge in South Africa,' the survey quoted a Johannesburg mobile equipment manufacturer as stating.[11]

Accessibility to broadband was a problem. South Africa was served by the Southern African Telecommunications Cable (SAT-3) which was owned by existing telecom operators in each of the countries in which it landed – including Telkom. The costs, however, were high and a persistent refrain from both government and NGOs was that this monopoly service was extracting rent from its position at the cost of cheaper broadband by both charging high fees and refusing to sell its wholesale capacities to other parties. In this, they were almost certainly correct.

Concerns over the behaviour of SAT-3 and its West African equivalent, the West Africa Submarine Cable, led to a serious confrontation between the parties when it came time to address opening better access to African nations, and East Africa in particular. On the one hand was a deep suspicion by some African countries of the power that private-sector interests would wield in new cable services. On the other hand was the view by major sponsors, including the World Bank, that private-sector interests could be the only lead partner able to guarantee success of either installation or operation. This last was clearly informed by many, many experiences of partnerships with African governments.

The issue culminated in 2007 when the South African government took a decision not to allow any underwater broadband cables to land in the country without South African majority ownership of the local company. While in line with much developed-world thinking about strategic resources, the position immediately put in question whether South Africa would benefit from Seacom's Sea Cable, an ambitious privately led project to link India, South Africa and Europe through a cable along the East African coast. The project had the support of the World Bank and nearly all other African countries, but had been stymied by the South African position. A senior official working on the project once told me that South Africa would have to stop being greedy.

A second cable, promoted by NEPAD and the World Bank, would encircle the whole continent and link Africa, Europe and the Americas. The project, however, has run into ideological tensions between NEPAD and the World Bank, as well as between member states, over the extent to which governments should be involved. NEPAD is pushing for significant government involvement while the World Bank, cognisant of the deep distrust global players have for doing business with African governments, insists it should be largely driven by the private sector.

The issue here is not the dispute about ownership of the systems: that was inevitable. It was the *time* taken by key parties to resolve the issue and move forward. It was this delay that contributed to South Africa's constantly deteriorating position in e-readiness in comparison to its peer countries.

But if problems were being encountered in the development of cable infrastructure, a similar measure of confusion surrounded the deployment of funds collected by the state from national and private telecommunications companies to a programme that would allow cheaper public access to telephony and broadband.

The Universal Service and Access Agency of South Africa was set up in 1999 as a statutorily recognised body with the laudable objective of improving telecommunications penetration in poorer communities. The operators paid 0.2 per cent of their annual revenue to the Department of Communications. By 2007, this had reached an amount of R456 million, of which only R195 million had been paid out to the agency, leaving a balance of R261 million lolling in state coffers and 20 000 schools earmarked for internet connectivity – only one of the planned projects – still in isolation.[12]

The failure of yet another well-intentioned project to get off the ground

was characterised by the usual round of finger-pointing. The agency accused the Treasury of tardiness in handing over the money. The Treasury
responded that the agency consistently failed to provide proper budgets or
account for the money spent. This was probably largely true, as the agency
had earlier in its life fallen into the hands of a group of idealistic young
'media activists' who had never seen a balance sheet in their lives, let alone
read one. Nine years into the existence of this organisation, it had an abys-
mal delivery record, and even where it did manage to provide computer
and internet facilities, material amounts of funds were misappropriated,
equipment was purloined or staff were unavailable to run the facilities. Once
again, the country suffered from the government's failure to effectively staff
and operate a semi-state operation relying on public and private money.

As state regulatory confusion, over-elaborate policies, weak administration and power politics bedevilled the country's telecom industry, so
the toll was felt in the country's international competitiveness. In its fourth
performance review of South African information and communications
technology (ICT), LINK prefaced its report thus:

> Despite the continual overall growth of the telecommunications sector
> in South Africa, the full potential of ICT to contribute to the growth
> and development of the country is not being realised. The descent
> by the country down international scales for competitiveness and
> e-readiness raises serious questions about the failure of the policy and
> regulatory strategies which aim to propel South Africa into the global
> knowledge economy through the development of a participatory in-
> formation society. South Africa now lags behind many of its traditional
> competitors on key indicators of access and affordability and is rapidly
> being overtaken in a number of areas by African states which historic-
> ally it has dominated.[13]

In 2004/5, South Africa was ranked thirty-fourth in the World Economic
Forum's Network Readiness Index, a measure of the country's telecom
policy and regulation. Three years later, South Africa had dropped to forty-
seventh position. It was the difference between being compared with
Slovenia or Kuwait.[14]

This weakening capacity to project an effective internet platform was
echoed in the more mundane but still vital arena of physical infrastructure
– the roads, bridges, dams, ports and airports that support the modern
state. A report by the South African Institution of Civil Engineers in

February 2007 gave the country a D+ mark. Although some infrastructure was good, observed the report, much of it was unsatisfactory – particularly in regard to maintenance and renewal.

'In terms of its mandate, the government is continuing to invest at a rapid pace in infrastructure for previously disadvantaged communities,' the report observed. 'However, once the infrastructure is built and commissioned, it needs to be looked after. After it has been built, people and governments appear to take notice of infrastructure only when it fails.'[15]

And here was the heart of the problem. Even if the government of South Africa was not called upon to build a single new house, electrify a single dwelling, put in one more sewer line, construct another road or lay another fibre-optic cable, the reality was that it did not have the resources to maintain *even what it already had*. Here, then, was the gap between Mbeki's screeds of data on new physical infrastructure and the 10 000 civil protests a year – it was what the Nigerians wryly call 'the maintenance culture' or, in both Nigeria and increasingly South Africa, the lack of it.

The report noted the absence of the technical skills needed to maintain the infrastructure. Of the 231 local municipalities in South Africa in 2007, seventy-nine had no civil engineers, technologists or technicians. There were more than 1 000 vacancies in these skills alone. Most countries have more engineers as a ratio to population than doctors. South Africa, by contrast, had one engineer for every 3 166 people and one doctor for every 1 493 people. Competitively, South Africa was at between a ten- to twenty-fold disadvantage compared with Western Europe, North America, India and China, where there are between 130 and 450 people for every engineer, noted the report.[16] A further report by the same institute estimated a shortfall of about 1 800 vacancies in roads engineers. The Municipal Demarcation Board's *National Report on Local Government Capacity* of November 2006 reported an 'exceedingly high' number of municipal managers appointed without the necessary experience and qualification and found 48 per cent of all local authorities were performing at less than 50 per cent capacity. Thus the wages of 'deployment'.

The message of the reports is unmistakable. Even discounting major public projects like the 2010 Football World Cup, the Gautrain rapid transport system, and port and road expansion, the country cannot support the current infrastructure, both pre-apartheid and that created in the headlong ideological rush from 1996 to 2004.

The great power blackouts of early 2008 and continuing failure to provide affordable telecommunications services marked a significant turning point in the delicate equilibrium of public confidence. Rampant crime and violence had been the first warning signs. The power outages were the second. Each event defining what separated hope from reality eroded public confidence and precipitated further flight of skills, capital and confidence, not necessarily immediately, but in the long term. What was to come? Another shock undoubtedly awaits at the end of 2008, when the first generation of undereducated young people are released from the state educational system onto the job market. A fourth will be when the full cost of restoring the country's failing physical infrastructure is brought fully to book in terms of roads (approximately R200 billion according to the South African Institution of Civil Engineers) and water distribution systems (the government insists this is under control; experts say that demand already exceeds supply in 80 per cent of South Africa's catchment areas). And the last looming but not yet manifest challenge is whether South Africa will be able to fulfil its most basic responsibility: the ability to feed its own population.

CHAPTER 13

The land question

The government solution to a problem is usually as bad as the problem.
— MILTON FRIEDMAN[1]

ONE OF THE MOST EMOTIONAL DEVELOPMENTAL ISSUES CONfronted by the ANC when it took power in 1994 was land distribution. In South African history, land has played a particularly significant role in defining political positions. For whites, ownership of land was the inviolate affirmation of their presence on these distant and often dangerous shores. For blacks, it was a continuous and haunting reminder of what they had lost. Any political party, no matter its history or future hope, would have to manage the question of restitution and redistribution with sensitivity.

It is a tribute to the ANC that for most of its first decade in office it proceeded with great caution on this road and only later, as the programme risked foundering entirely, did it begin to propose constitutional amendments that would change the willing seller, willing buyer principle. That it could hold the line so long against insistent and clamorous demands for instant and massive land transfers from voluble vested interests is something of a mystery.

Yet, despite this sensitivity, the reality is that the land-reform programme in South Africa has been slow, inefficient, confused, inadequate and ideological. It has caused and will continue to cause damage to the interests of agriculture in South Africa and the long-term security of food in the region, unless dramatically reshaped. This failure was not because of a lack of good ideas or a missionary zeal from the top. It was not even due to a lack of cooperation by white farmers. It was hampered because it was too ambitious, it misunderstood the real nature of 'transformation' and the platform called upon to manage it was too fragile.

South African agriculture has historically been divided into a highly successful commercial farming sector, dominated by whites, and an inefficient subsistence sector, managed often on a communal basis by black farmers. This very broad division has changed in recent years as a number of black entrepreneurial farmers have moved into commercial farming, and an increasing number of farms were transferred to black syndicates under the government's land-reform process.

South Africa has about 100 million hectares of farmland. Of this, about 82 per cent is in the hands of white commercial farmers or agribusinesses. There are approximately 40 000 commercial farmers in South Africa – half as many as there were at the end of the 1980s. Some 100 000 black small farmers own about 5 per cent of the commercial farming land, mainly in very small holdings. Although substantial amounts of high-quality agricultural land can be found in the rural areas that once comprised the homelands (or bantustans) created under apartheid, this land is mostly underutilised due to inefficient ownership and production methods.

When the ANC came to power, its agricultural rural reform programme comprised four or five major economic and social strands. The first was the restitution of land to black people evicted under apartheid legislation. The augmentation of agricultural land held by black people was another, as was the reform of existing tenure systems to give farm workers rights of occupation. On the more technical side lay a raft of legislation introducing minimum wages for farm workers, restricting water rights to farmers, levying new rating systems on agricultural land and imposing BEE obligations on farming enterprises above a certain size.

For the commercial farmers, this new flow of regulation was difficult. South Africa had moved dramatically from its highly protected and single-channel marketing past under the old administration. Progressive liberalisation of markets had opened the country to fiercely competitive imports. In a presentation to the parliamentary agriculture and land affairs portfolio committee in October 2007, the National Agricultural Marketing Council claimed that South Africa had the third-lowest level of agricultural subsidy in the world. The only countries worse off were New Zealand and Australia, but this was offset by huge government investments in infrastructure and research in those countries. In South Africa, conversely, the investments were going to emergent rather than commercial farmers.

The council reported that those carrying the heaviest burden were medium and small farmers, who were going out of business at the rate of one thousand a year, and farm workers, 400 000 of whom had lost their jobs through casualisation and job shedding in the previous decade.

Confronting a very liberalised market, volatile input costs and market prices, periodic drought, personal security risks (more than fifteen hundred commercial farmers had been murdered in a fifteen-year period up to 2008) and the withdrawal of the previously generous financing deals offered by the old Land Bank, the number of farmers and farming units began to diminish as the small operators sold up and agribusiness moved in. By 2006 the imbalance was marked: the Statistics South Africa Survey of Large-Scale Agriculture showed that the top 11 per cent of farmers employed 78 per cent of the labour, produced 65 per cent of total production by value and earned 47 per cent of total net farm income.[2] Another disturbing feature was the massive conversion of agricultural land to game farming and eco-tourism – high hard-currency earners with none of the problems of conventional farming operations.[3]

Theoretically, the land becoming available should have been accessible to the new generation of black farmers. In this way, the dual strategy of increasing black holdings while maintaining food security would have been met. It has not worked out that way.

The primary problem was that the new government confused its own emotional rhetoric with reality. The government's position on reform consistently harked back to a naïve and romantic vision of large numbers of dispossessed black peasants returning to some sort of bucolic bliss on the land, thereby adding enormously to job multipliers, incomes, self-sufficiency, exports and all those other good things.

It did not happen and nor could it, for the simple reason that the vast majority of black South Africans had little interest in returning to the back-breaking drudgery of running small farms when other and better opportunities may have been available. So while the government was obsessed with the land issue – hinting darkly at a Zimbabwe-style outcome unless white landowners cooperated – its constituency thought differently.

Research into the key concerns of black South Africans in 2001 indicated that only 9 per cent of respondents had any interest in farming. On a scale of national priorities, only 2 per cent of respondents marked land reform as their number-one issue. By far the greatest concerns were jobs, housing and urban-related services, which is not surprising when one considers that 60 per cent of the population lives in urban areas.[4]

This did not stop the ANC from elevating land reform to a major objective or from raising expectations in this regard. It is a dangerous and populist ploy that presents a sword of the kind upon which Mbeki fell in December 2007, and one that will no doubt claim many more ANC politicians in the future, unless an element of reality is reintroduced to the debate.

The hope that a hugely expanded black small-farming sector is going to greatly assist in growth of the South African economy in the twenty-first century is stretched. Agriculture, from contributing nearly a quarter of South Africa's GDP in 1920, had declined by 2007 to just over 3 per cent. Whatever was to be done in terms of land reform would therefore have more of a social than an economic impact.

Having misplaced the order of importance on the national agenda, the government then compounded the fault by misunderstanding the nature of the transaction. Defining it as racial transfer of land in terms of a policy of restitution undercut what the policy really should have been: a rational and modern land-reform programme based on sound economics, properly resourced and realistically targeted. By overreaching on targets and under-providing in terms of support, the government had already written the script for failure of the first wave of projects by 2000.

Why was this so?

The first challenge was the oldest one in the book: human resources. The land-reform programme envisaged by the government was a hugely complex one, requiring the highest levels of knowledge, commitment and discretion on the part of officials. The easiest part of the process was in fact the identification of, and negotiation for, suitable target land. The toughest was the legions of competing claimants to the land. The range of bureaucratic skills was simply not available and the consequence was repeated failure by the government to meet its self-imposed objectives.

The government's stated aim as of 1996 was the redistribution of 30 per cent of South Africa's land to black people by 1999 – a mark of naïveté on the complexities of the process. This date was later shifted to 2014. By 31 March 2007, the government claimed 93.4 per cent of claims in terms of the restitution programme had been settled,[5] but many more had piled up when the commission extended its cut-off date, and, in reality, huge tracts of productive land were under claim, with legions of angry farmers and restive claimants waiting for some clarity. In practice, however, only 1.7 million hectares of land had been delivered for restitution – about 2 per cent of commercial agricultural land. In total, taking all elements of the reform programme, about 3.5 million hectares – some 4.3 per cent of commercial land – had been transferred and experts were warning that delivery would have to be sped up fivefold to meet the 2014 target.

The time lag on this reform programme led to the usual round of denunciations. The government argued that resistance from the white commercial farming sector had delayed action and that 'unrealistic' price demands had stymied the project. Inevitably, there came calls for the scrapping of the constitutional provision for a willing buyer, willing seller basis for land redistribution.

The countercharge from the agricultural lobby was that the delays were caused by horrendous bureaucratic inefficiencies. They pointed out that only two out of 24 000 cases of restitution had been challenged on the basis of quantum of compensation. A comprehensive report by the Centre for Development and Enterprise supported them. Land price claims by white farmers, far from escalating, had shown a deflationary trend during the land-reform process. If the government invoked Zimbabwe as a dark harbinger of what would happen if farmers did not cooperate, the agricultural lobbies invoked the same country with a different argument. Land reform in Zimbabwe had collapsed, not because of a lack of resources or willingness of farmers to sell, but because of monstrous corruption and incompetence. The same would happen in South Africa, they warned.

Whatever the merits of the argument, the reality was that land redistribution began to fall far behind targets. Worse, the result of the transfers began increasingly to challenge the efficacy of the whole project. The efficient 'take-up' of land by the beneficiaries of the transfer proved to be miserably inadequate. Fertile and well-run farming projects collapsed within months of being transferred. Farming cooperatives set up by the government to own the farms fell to squabbling between themselves. Efficient farming units were subdivided into subsistence plots. Shack farming grew.

State support in terms of extension services, facilitation of funding, channels to market and the host of other requirements to move farming from the romantic to the economic were absent. The Land Bank, traditional bedrock of the South African commercial farming sector and one of the main pillars of its international success, imploded. In 2002/3 it reported a R1.7 billion impairment of loans.[6] These defaults were largely from twenty major clients – most of them beneficiaries of the Land Bank's BEE programmes. In 2007, the entire board was fired and its senior executives suspended. It transpired that the bank – ostensibly charged with helping small-scale farming units get onto their feet – had been granting public money to property developers to build equestrian and golf estates for the super-rich. Not surprisingly, the allegation was that those same directors and officials had interests in the development companies. The state and its organs, clearly, were incapable of meeting the mandate.

Research in 2004 on farming operations deriving from the land-reform programme showed a 100 per cent failure rate among the thirty-four projects researched.[7] The subsequent book was damned at the time by the government as being racist, but there was no definitive rebuttal of its content. In 2008, meanwhile, land affairs director-general Thozi Gwanya conceded that the failure rate could be as high as 50 per cent – still an astonishing misadventure. It is impossible to record the various factors that drove this doleful outcome, but perhaps one example of the challenges of rural agricultural development will illustrate the problem, albeit one that was not involved in the restitution programme.

The Massive Food Programme was launched in a former homeland area of the Eastern Cape with a R50 million budget in 2003. The following year it received a once-off allocation of R150 million, and then, between 2005 and 2008, another R336 million was allocated to the programme.

Rather than provide poor people with food handouts, the programme extended a conditional grant scheme to encourage people to grow their own maize. Once farmers were producing, the subsidy would be phased out. Farmers could then lease their allotments to aspirant commercial farmers and be paid back by a share of the crop.

Grants were up to R2 300 per hectare to cover input costs, and up to 25 per cent of the amount was to be paid back in the year after reaping the crop. The balance was repayable at 25 per cent a year thereafter. Interest-free loans were extended to farmers or tractor contractors for machinery. Extension officers were appointed.

The intention of the programme was to build a secure source of food for the people, while also addressing infrastructural and human resource deficiencies in the region. It would help consolidate land ownership out of communal holdings, secure credit for farmers and improve farm infrastructure. The project was only to be rolled out on very high-value arable land.

The subsequent audit on this superbly conceptualised and appropriate project highlights its travails:

- The units were in most cases sited on low-yield land because of 'political' reasons – in other words, corruption.
- The yields were subsequently one ton per hectare – a third less than expected.

- Hardly any farmers paid back the input grants.
- Virtually all stakeholders – farmers, suppliers, commercial farmers and officials – colluded to defraud the scheme by signing off on orders never delivered.
- There were widespread technical errors in the production of the crops, despite extension advice.
- The tractor contractors were called 'profiteers with little concern for the well being of the farmers' who had formed 'units like taxi associations with enormous power to the detriment to the emergent farmers'.
- Corrupt Agriculture Department officials signed off on contractors' cards for a fee.

By 2005, the project was a failure and it was decided to write off the costs and start over again. This was done and the programme is now a success, for the following reasons:
- Ten commercial farmers were brought on board with salaries and performance bonuses.
- The grants were extended only after deposits were paid and defaulters were expelled from the project.

This particular project is recorded here only because it illuminates the difficulties encountered in rural agricultural development. The moral of this story was simple: effective management.[8]

By 2005, the implications of the legions of failed projects were beginning to come home to roost. If the programme was carried to term and the same rate of failure prevailed, the country would have lost nearly a third of its agricultural output. Such a reduction often occurs in wartime, but the thought that a government would pursue such an objective as *policy* was terrifying.

Fortunately, wiser counsel prevailed (most of the previous models had been based on foreign advice). In late 2007 Gwanya, then still the acting director-general of land affairs, was quoted as saying that the targets needed to be revisited and called for a land-reform process that was driven by quality and not merely targets. Objectives should be measured not simply by land transferred, but by jobs created and wealth created.[9]

The government, meanwhile, set itself two objectives: speeding up the rate of land acquisition to end the state of uncertainty in the sector, and ensuring that it was properly farmed. This marked a switch from the utopian to the pragmatic and was welcomed.

A new target was set of delivery of 3.1 million hectares of land per year. Of this, 2.5 million hectares would come from land redistribution and the rest from restitution. A proactive land acquisition strategy was put in place. More money was voted – R3 billion in 2006/7 – and the department began spending its full budget, which had been consistently underspent for years.

The government invited the private sector to assist and the take-up was impressive. A number of successful public–private partnerships began to start delivering on land transfer *and* development. The Land Bank, reconstituted after its collapse, indicated that it would look to the existing commercial farming cooperatives to assist with the deployment of know-how and investment to help support the beneficiaries of the land transfers. From taking a go-it-alone attitude, the state and its institutions had returned to the assistance that could be offered by the skilled, established and inter-nationally competitive commercial farming lobby. It was more than a decade late, but it had happened.

However, the ANC's land-reform programme still has its hurdles.

The extension of the deadline for the filing of restitution claims to the end of 2008 prompted a surge of new claims. By early January, some of the major operators in South Africa were warning about the effect of this uncertainty. Major timber companies had daunting claims against their land – 48 per cent for Mondi, 17.5 per cent for Sappi and 75 per cent for Komatiland Forests.[10] The sugar industry in KwaZulu-Natal had the same problem. A document prepared in 2007 said that regardless of the assertions made by the government in regard to the processing of claims, the situation of outstanding claims was bringing the sugar industry to the point of crisis.[11] Large amounts of valuable land were still subject to restitution claims and this had a deep dampening effect on investment in farming operations. Worse, land already allocated in terms of the reform programme to black owners was again subjected to claims by other black claimants, using the restitution terms of the Act. Who would want to in-vest in a new irrigation system if one's land was about to be expropriated?

Many of these land claims were vexatious and a number were simply fraudulent – aimed more at extorting settlement amounts from major corporations than acquiring land. Still, they all had to be evaluated and adjudicated. This took time.

Another problem had intruded. Between 2003 and 2006, land prices in South Africa saw a dramatic rise. The reasons were many: a natural correction after many years of depressed prices; the national credit boom; foreign investments (still less than 4 per cent of total land ownership); and investments flowing from the tax amnesty that allowed South Africans to bring back their illegal foreign funds. Agricultural land was not immune, although, as mentioned earlier, prices for land under claim rose less steeply than general land prices. The government rhetoric switched from accusing white farmers of being uncooperative to the issue of *affordability*.

Ominously, new regulations were introduced in 2008, moving the expropriation of farms from within the ambit of 'public purpose' to the much wider 'public interest', giving more power to the minister and restricting judicial review of the outcome. Organised agriculture in South Africa immediately warned that this was a step in the Zimbabwe direction and complained that there had been no consultation on what was a substantial change in both the intent of the constitution and the basis of cooperation between the commercial farming sector and the government. The valuations of agricultural land earmarked for appropriation suddenly plummeted – in some cases, valuations were carried out by 'experts' imported from other African countries. It was clear that the government might be bending in the direction of pragmatism in the matter of usage of land, but it was embarking on a dangerous new path in its acquisition thereof.

The third problem was that questions still hung over the capacity of the beneficiaries to farm effectively. Throughout the period of ANC government, large numbers of organisations representing commercial agriculture had extended material amounts of support to emergent farmers: mentoring, access to markets, extension services and even capital. The most successful of these had been the programme undertaken by the South African Sugar Association, which from mid-1970 to mid-2000 created 40 000 black small farmers on about one-third of total arable land. In fact, statistically the commercial farming community had effected more transfers of agricultural land to black farmers through market forces than had the government. Certainly, the farms acquired through private treaty had maintained their viability much better than those transferred through state intervention.

The government's attempts to invoke the support of the farming lobbies was less than optimal – not because of a lack of assistance, but because of inefficiency in deployment. One year after compiling a database of deployable mentors (all former and current commercial farmers), not one had been called to service, and this at a time when a senior government official confirmed that the restored farms were losing productivity.

Neither was black empowerment in the agricultural sector promising to be any easier than in other sectors. Rian Coetzee, head of the Industrial Development Corporation's food, beverage and agro-industries strategic business unit, listed the difficulties found in a 2006 survey:

> The main challenges are finding and retaining suitably qualified managers; finding equity partners who have or can obtain sufficient funding and who can add value to the business; procurement in terms of verifying the status of suppliers and finding quality of products or services that are also competitively priced; getting guidance from regulatory bodies in terms of Broad Based Economic Empowerment [BBEE]; and the implementation of schemes, including managing expectations.

Nevertheless, he urged commercial undertakings to engage in BBEE transactions only for economic as opposed to compliance reasons.[12]

The above quote has an almost Monty Pythonesque quality about it. With that list of challenges, why *would* or indeed *could* anybody in agriculture get into BBEE for economic reasons? The question was weighing heavily on the minds of many farming enterprises in early 2008, particularly as the rise in agricultural land prices had made the acquisition of equity by black partners even more difficult.

The net effect of this turbulent period of transformation in South Africa's agricultural sector was sadly not the enhancement of food security, but its diminution. The skilled farming base halved in numbers; small commercial farming enterprises went to the wall; and agribusinesses moved into the vacuum in areas where no land claims were involved.

Food prices began to move upwards from 2007 onwards. Part of this price movement was undoubtedly due to imported inflation from fuel price increases and the global impact of changing food consumption patterns in China and India. Another part of the problem was the rise of the biofuel sector, which converted grain crops from feed for humans and livestock to fuel. But some of it certainly derived from the reduction in efficient domestic production of food.

As Mbeki entered the last stretch of his tenure as president of South Africa, his much vaunted land-reform programme had sought to pull itself back from the brink of disaster by focusing on the growth of commercial and entrepreneurial black-owned agriculture. The government had accepted the limitations of ideology and turned again to the skills base of the commercial agricultural sector for help. But billions of rands had been lost and food production affected in the interim.

More to the point, the cost of the exercise was rapidly becoming un-affordable within the existing constitutional restraints. Land prices had moved up sharply and claims had increased. To meet its objectives, the government would have to turn to expropriation at less than market prices. The impact on both internal and external investor perceptions would be measurable.

There was a final concern. The land-reform programme had dragged on for virtually the entire life of the ANC incumbency – fourteen years – and seemed to have no end. Cut-off dates were extended, *post facto* claims accepted, rejected claims reinstated and decision-making was perilously cumbersome. Within some of the projects there was a dreadful circularity: communities paid out financial compensation for their land spent the money and returned, demanding their land back once more. Land in-vasions – and in one case murder – occurred. Like so much else on the reform agenda, it seemed to just drag on and on …

And while it did, South Africa was falling behind the world in its capacity to produce food, both for itself and the world. The UN Food and Agriculture Organisation's National Production Index tracks the perform-ance of every member country in the world on an annual basis. It starts from a baseline of one hundred in 1980.

In the 2005/2006 yearbook, the world index had climbed to 180. India was at 200. Brazil reached 260 and China stood at 340. South Africa managed 125. More alarmingly, South African production had remained stagnant in the mid-120 range for the entire period from 2000 to 2005, while world production had increased by 12.5 per cent.[13] In 2008, South Africa became a net importer of food.

South African agriculture had also failed to produce jobs. In September 2002 the sector employed 1 420 000 workers. Five years later, it supported 1 164 000, according to Statistics South Africa. One could have hoped this was a result of workers moving from employment to self-employment through the government's rural reform programme. But it was not. Informal agri-cultural jobs decreased from 551 000 in 2002 to 343 000 in 2007. Both gross agricultural production, as measured by the UN Food and Agriculture Organisation, and employment in the sector had come to a halt for the five-year period coinciding with the most active land redistribution. With a growing population and stagnant agricultural production, food security inevitably becomes an issue.

CHAPTER 14

The rise of the proxy state

The instant formal government is abolished, society begins to act. A general association takes place, and common interest produces common security. — THOMAS PAINE[1]

THE PRECEDING DOLEFUL CHAPTERS HAVE RECORDED THE arrest of state formation and the serious degradation in most areas of public administration during the Mbeki tenure. But the picture would not be complete without attempting to capture the response of the society to this withering away of state competence. I have called this the rise of the proxy state.

The proxy state does not run South Africa. It is not some sort of fabulous conspiracy sitting at the right hand of the president. It is not a group of nefarious people who meet once a month *à la* novelist Dan Brown's *The Da Vinci Code*. It does not have a directing body. Most members of the proxy state do not even know they are members and, in most cases, certainly would not know one another.

And yet the proxy state exists: influential if not powerful, effective if not dominant. It can be found at the lowest level in the individual who makes his or her living by helping people acquire identity documents from a failed Home Affairs Department, or facilitating the passage of building blueprints through a log-jammed regional planning department. The proxy state can be found at the highest level where huge corporations undertake what were once state functions on behalf of privileged groups with resources that sometimes eclipse those of the state.

It is important to make a qualification here. This is not about the formal privatisation of state functions which was such a feature of late twentieth-century state evolution in developed countries. Such privatisation has never occurred on a large scale in South Africa, because of a lack of political will and some legitimate concerns about possible outcomes, although commercialisation of key services has occurred. The proxy state is something else: it is the informal assumption of influential roles by private players in interstices of the public administration where the state has ceased to function efficiently.

The philosophy of surrendering chunks of responsibility for state functions to private agency is well established in the ANC and has been for very many years. One of the first promoters of this, if unwittingly, was Nelson Mandela, South Africa's first democratic president. His objective was always the raising of resources for his private projects, mostly involving young people, and his target was the major private companies. In this he was quite shameless, pressing for money and expertise for schools, orphanages, training colleges and other facilities. At one point, one of the major corporations dispatched one of their executives to politely inform the president that it could no longer continue to make such contributions.

'That young man had a cold heart,' Mandela sorrowfully told me.

Yet he understood the issue, and the demands tailed off. Not so for other members of the movement. This process of 'government by beggary' gathered pace throughout the 1990s as the major corporations – and indeed the skilled and resourced minorities – were called upon to assist with building state resources in policing, schools, town planning, admin-istration, local government, financial management and a host of other enterprises, over and above their tax obligations.

This was nothing new. The racial minorities had long held a reputation as being communities with among the highest levels of voluntarism in the world, especially during the apartheid years. The difference was that instead of this voluntarism being devoted to *augmenting* state resource, it was now *substituting* for it. Power, meaning the capacity to effect change, was ineluctably drifting away from the formal state into the hands of the proxy state.

The most obvious macro-phenomena of the proxy state are of course private health, education and security. These are the three areas that most affect the lives of individuals and it is from this terrain that the state has retreated most. This is not to say one should not have private enterprise in these areas – it occurs all over the world. It is the *scale* of it and the lack of a countervailing state presence that is at issue. Consider these facts:

- For every rand spent by the state on patients in South Africa's public health-care system, R6.60 is spent by the private system.
- A private school system that delivers only 1.3 per cent of the annual matric output produces 25 per cent of graduates with a university pass rate in science and mathematics.

- The combined strength of the SAPS and South African National Defence Force is superseded by the number of men and women employed by private security firms, and total private security spending is now equal to the SAPS 2008/9 budget – an eighteen-fold increase in a decade, according to research by the South African Institute of Race Relations.

Despite all the rhetoric of the government, all its posturing about extending the reach of the ANC to improve the lives of the masses, despite the grand designs and endless conferences, the reality is that the provision of *quality* care in health, education and safety lies infinitely more in the hands of private agencies at the end of Mbeki's presidential tenure than it did at the beginning. There is supreme irony in all of this. The Mbeki administration endlessly debated the question of the formal privatisation of state resources, and its union partners in its uneasy alliance railed against it, yet huge swathes of public-service *function* have been quietly, indeed clandestinely, privatised as the state system fails.

The legion of consultants, contract and temporary workers who have buttressed the state, virtually since the ANC's accession to power, are part of the proxy state. They include the high-level advisors brought in by new ANC ministers to consult on policy. Most, as I have observed earlier, came from deeply socialist and academic backgrounds and nearly all the advice they proffered has either been quite simply wrong or incapable of execution, given the fragility of the institutions.

Later, as the state departments started showing signs of critical dysfunction, a new breed of technical advisor *cum* operator was brought in. The most obvious example was the Department of Home Affairs. This department, earning the rueful description as the most incompetent and hated in government, had chosen to literally obliterate its institutional memory in the first phase of affirmative action. Five directors-general in eight years failed to salvage a department whose inability to account for its expenses was legion and whose incapacity to meet its mandate was epic. It is probably best remembered as the department where a young man, driven crazy by a year-long delay in the issuing of his ID document on which his livelihood literally depended, took a woman employee hostage with a toy pistol. The kidnapper was arrested and a public subscription netted tens of thousands of rands for his defence. Such was home affairs. In 2007, however, the government suspended its latest director-general and effectively placed the department under the public curatorship of a group of peer directors-general, but in reality under the administration of a rescue team provided by one of the country's top consultancies. The brief was no longer to advise on how to restore the department: it was to actually *do* it.

More important, however, have been the very many private individuals who have been retained by the state, not for expert or specialist reasons, but quite simply to keep the wheels turning. Many of these were white former employees retrenched as part of the 'transformation' policies of the state. By 2007, this layer of non-permanent staff was costing the state in the order of R1 billion a year. This, it needs to be noted, is a charge in addition to the existing cost of maintaining the bureaucracy.

The government has consistently argued this investment is necessary to complete the process of skills transfer from the previously entrenched bureaucracy to the new one. There is merit in the argument if one accepts this was part of a structured, time-limited, coherent programme. No such programme was apparent in any of the state departments until very late in the day. In fact, anecdotal evidence suggests that fourteen years into the transformation, the 'transitional' staff remains in many departments the invisible bedrock of the administration. There has been limited take-up of skills and, for most permanent staff, these 'temporaries' are regarded not as dispensable mentors, but as intrinsic to the continuation of operations.

The elements of the proxy state mentioned above are at least visible, accountable and quantifiable. No more needs to be said about them here.

Operating outside the formal state structures, meanwhile, is the subterranean proxy state, a veritable army of fixers and facilitators. It is impossible to give an exhaustive list of such members of the proxy state, but one can simply observe that in the past decade South Africa has seen an explosion of small businesses (mainly run by former bureaucrats) providing services for the acquisition of passports and identity documents, preparing indictments against criminal employees, undertaking criminal investigative work, licensing vehicles and businesses, recovering monies owed by the local authorities or state, facilitating the passage of tax returns, assisting with estates and shepherding plans through the approval process. It is important to note that, in the main, these facilitators do not merely advise on the content and processes of regulatory compliance or compile the documents. In many instances they assist the bureaucracy with its processing. In other words, they stand behind the counter rather than in front of it.

The most extreme manifestation of the proxy state is the growth of criminal activity arising in place of state function. The most obvious has been the rise of vigilante action in poorer communities against suspected criminals. The incidence of such activity has been recorded in an earlier chapter. The importance of it, though, is the growing willingness of non-state agencies to act on behalf of what is considered to be public interest, even if this means breaking the law. It may be efficacious, but it does not contribute in the long term to state formation.

The question has to be asked whether or not the proxy state serves the long-term interests of the society and the country. The short answer is that its criminal manifestations clearly do not. They further erode state authority. But the facilitation element of the proxy state does: it rolls things forward, gets things done and results in deliverables that usually add up to satisfied citizens and investors. In the short term, then, it is unwound at the state's peril. In the long term, it is deeply questionable whether the proxy state truly serves the interest of state formation.

The first and fundamental problem is that it does nothing to strengthen the innate capacity of the state to fulfil its functions. It is a natural human response that as long as one has a back-up, one is less likely to take full responsibility for oneself.

The second is that it exacerbates inequality in the country and feeds into the current high levels of unhappiness by those who feel marginalised by wealth and power. Nobody who has sat in long home affairs queues can be unmindful of the dislike with which the line regards those who disappear into the side office with a 'consultant' in the lead.

The third is that it serves corruption, as all these facilitating services come with a fee, a portion of which must track back to the bureaucracy. Why else would they do it?

There is an interesting developing-world debate here about the role of 'good' and 'bad' corruption. To Western and developed countries, corruption in the sense of public officials taking undue and hidden personal enrichment from the processes of government is intrinsically anathema and should be routed out. It has led to much misunderstanding between the developed world and some Africans, many of whom have a very different view of these things, and done little more than open the way to the 'badly' corrupting nations that are now very active in Africa.

Peter Berger, a prominent sociologist, once developed what I thought was an interesting way of approaching the issue. He argued that it was possible to differentiate between 'good' and 'bad' corruption. Good corruption was when the cost of corruption was no more than the cost thereof. Bad corruption was when it was more.

To explain: If one paid R100 to a licensing official to register one's car and he in turn did no more than follow procedures, accept one's legal fee of R230 on behalf of the authority and took no decisions that would prejudice the society, then the cost of the corruption was merely R100. If, however, the public servant took the R100 and then issued the licence without charging the legal fee, the cost of corruption was R100 plus the R230 forfeited by the state. The corruption thus cost R230 more than the cost of the corruption. Cumulatively, then, the surplus over the cost of corruption equals the billions of dollars that have been stolen in post-colonial Africa and which has led to its marginalisation for decades.

In many African countries, the greatest weight of corruption is in the category of only the cost of corruption: it is a facilitation fee that is written off from the consumer point of view as a cost of doing business; and from the point of view of the bureaucracy, it is merely an undisclosed component of civil servant remuneration. There are thus two parallel cost structures: the formal one in which the legally prescribed amount goes through to the state coffers, and the informal one, which pays the bureaucracy.

The danger, of course, is that this system becomes embedded as part of the structure of the state and attempts to unwind it have perilous unintended consequences, as Nigeria discovered when it embarked on its anti-corruption drives. Output of service, as bad as it was, was threatened and both consumers and investors found themselves severely disadvantaged. As the free float of facilitation fees dried up, the pressure on the state to pay higher wages increased, as did the taxes. In some of the worst cases, bureaucrats simply swung from 'good' corruption to 'bad'.

Once embedded, this corruption moves with the target host. It may change its contours, but it remains tapped into the mainspring. I well remember a conversation with a very wealthy and successful Kenyan Indian businessman. He lamented thus about the transition from the corrupt administration of Daniel arap Moi to the supposedly clean one of Mwai Kibaki: 'The first thing to get democratised was corruption. This was bad. At least in the old days when you paid for something, you received a benefit. Nowadays you pay and nothing happens, because there are too many people in the loop, all cutting each other's throats.'

South Africa, I believe, is in the incipient stages of creating such a dual structure and such a democratised corruption. While much of it might still be 'good' corruption, the opportunity to regress to 'bad' corruption is immense. The growth of the subterranean proxy state risks facilitating such a move.

There is another area of operation of the proxy state that is as yet imperfectly understood. It stands at the extreme end of the proxy state and consists of the alliance between the formal policing and justice elements and the criminal fraternity. It is disconcerting that a superb piece of investigative writing by Misha Glenny should lump South Africa in the same camp as Colombia, Kazakhstan and Indo-China in terms of its integration into international criminal networks.[2] It is these forces who will take most comfort from the political decision to close down the country's foremost anti-corruption unit just as it is poised to proceed against the highest and the mightiest in the country's political and administrative spheres.

The government's response to the growth of the proxy state has been ambivalent. *In extremis*, it has cultivated it for its own purpose and deployed it to resolve immediate, pressing concerns. And yet it is fully aware of the dangers – hence attempts to curtail the role of the private medical aid societies and its deep suspicion of the private security companies.

The risks attached particularly to the latter become apparent when we consider what the effect would be should renegade elements of the private security corps choose to ally themselves with criminal elements. There is mounting evidence that this might well have happened after the bitter 2007 security guard strike, leading to the surge in robberies at residential and business premises.

The proxy state puts the government in a quandary. The criminal wing of this state clearly does not serve the interests of state formation. But what about the element happily entrenched as the facilitator of service? If the government reduces the proxy state, it courts the certain consequence of a further decline in service output. If it allows it to grow, it cedes greater influence and power to external authority and further challenges the way in which it has implemented its affirmative action policies.

It is this challenge that the ANC will have to confront in the years to come. In many ways South Africa has been more fortunate than the post–Soviet Union countries of Eastern Europe. There, power passed effort-lessly from corrupt party bosses to consortiums of gangsters, fixers and security bosses. South Africa at least had the bulwark of existing institutions during the transition. But as these institutions are weakened by the hammer blows of political criminality the birth of a fully fledged gangster state becomes a possibility. Thus the dangers in ANC Classic's decision to close down the Scorpions.

PART III

The Social Kingdom

CHAPTER 15

A new client class

In general, the art of government consists of taking as much money as possible from one party of the citizens to give to another. — VOLTAIRE[1]

THE GREATLY IMPROVING FINANCIAL SITUATION OF SOUTH Africa in the five years prior to 2007 led to a parallel and acrimonious debate about the fairest and most effective way to disperse its benefits. From this arose the centrepiece of the Mbeki administration's programme of racially based economic and social engineering, which is not significantly different from those that had gone before in other parts of the post-colonial continent: Africanisation, indigenisation, affirmative action. In South Africa, it has been broadly termed black economic empowerment, later prefixed by broad-based, although it travels in many guises and has many similarities to the programme of economic empowerment adopted by the ANC's predecessor, the National Party, in uplifting white Afrikaners in the years from 1950 to 1990.

In a noteworthy speech to parliament in 2004, Mbeki talked about two nations: one rich and one poor, one white and one black. It was an evocative and necessary speech, although the appealing simplicity of the proposition would become blurred in the years to come, as many blacks became rich and some whites poor.

There was widespread sympathy for Mbeki's position. He had, after all, been elected by a party that was overwhelmingly supported by poor black people. Should he walk away from that, he would be betraying his constituency and putting at risk the advances of this fragile democracy. A large, dispossessed and aggrieved constituency was of no benefit to either Mbeki or the white minority. Apart from a small group of extremists, whites thus generally accepted that the political liberation of black South Africans would inevitably entail the surrender in some measure of their privilege, wealth and opportunities. The how, the when and the how much would always be the issue.

The ANC positioned its affirmative action policies on three grounds, two pragmatic and the other moral. It argued that an economy without significant black participation would eventually be strangled by social and political tumult among the dispossessed. It also argued that companies with a significant representation of the majority racial group would be able to do better business with like South Africans.

It argued on the moral front that there was an imperative to set aright the centuries of discrimination and denial by whites. The argument was thus simple and seductive: share now because it is necessary, profitable and right. Fail to share, and we will have to take. Underlying the ANC assumption, and tacitly if reluctantly accepted by the business community, was the view that the market itself would not be able to correct centuries of structural distortions created by white domination.

Thus emerged a process that eventually amounted to one of the largest and most rapid reallocations of wealth, income and opportunity outside revolution between one sector of the society and another. It was effected within the law and peacefully. In this sense, it was a quite remarkable achievement.

The tragedy is that the objectives, methods and time-frames for the project were never clearly established. What began as a widely supported concept of economic rectification ended as an open-ended programme of expropriation, which raised the racial temperature, incited manipulation and cronyism, and led to profound disillusionment for all parties. More remarkable still, the financial cost of this vast programme of social and economic engineering was never once quantified or even discussed. The moral rectitude of the programme swept all arguments before it, and as the main beneficiaries of the scheme came to hold sway over the process, rational economic debate retreated even further.

The booming economy during the first years of the life of empowerment initially went some way to assuaging the concerns of the white and other racial minorities. Ironically, it was the white and Asian minorities who were the greatest beneficiaries of the political liberation of black people. Freed of sanctions and travel restrictions, they joyfully sallied forth and, being skilled, entrepreneurial, confident and hard-working people, they did extremely well for themselves and their companies amid conditions of great international investment liquidity.

The acute skills crisis also ensured that in the short to medium term, they benefited at home. Even when offered packages to leave the public sector to make way for black replacements, they did not fare badly. Some were taken back as consultants at fat salaries to help the inexperienced new incumbents. Others started their own small businesses: the profusion of new enterprises filed with the company registrar attested to this.

White unemployment never exceeded 4 per cent (better than many European Union countries) compared to between 23 per cent and 40 per cent of blacks, depending on the measurement. The labour-absorption rate of white tertiary graduates was some four times higher than that of blacks in general, although black absorption in critical skills areas like accounting and engineering was much better than for whites, because of affirmative action pressures.

Higher levels of disposable income led to materially higher standards of living. The second home for holidays became *de rigueur* for many. Luxury car sales soared, as did those of pleasure boats, motorcycles and all the other toys of the well off. Being white in Africa, even after a huge political transition, appeared not bad at all.

But not even a higher standard of living could offset what would become a decline in quality of life. Rampant crime and the collapse of the post-liberation public educational system drove many abroad. As affirmative action changed its nature from a guiding to an imperative force and the targets shifted upwards, many left the country to find another home. Those who came back usually did so as contractors in short-term employment. Some did not even have to leave the country. They simply chose to become contractors within their companies. Thus was created the inward expatri-atisation of a generation of skilled white workers.

Yet it would be naïve to suggest that it was only affirmative action or Afro-pessimism that drove out skills. Amid a worldwide shortage of skills, there was an insistent and seductive pull effect for whites to migrate. In-creasingly, they were joined by fellow South Africans from all racial groups, to the point where it became a national crisis and the finance minister railed against the unfair poaching of home-grown talents. At a time of acute internal skills shortages, however, affirmative action as conceived by the Mbeki administration added a further, in some cases crippling, challenge to the long-term interests of the country.

BEE was a cornerstone of the ANC's redistributive policy and will probably be one of Mbeki's most enduring legacies. It is now important to consider its intellectual origins, legislative framework, implementation, achievements and limitations.

There is some dispute over definition and numbers regarding what constitutes a 'black middle class' in South Africa. A University of Cape Town Unilever Institute research project in 2006 put it at roughly two million souls.[2] The South African Institute of Race Relations estimated in 2007 that the core black middle class, as opposed to a broader 'lower middle class', consisted of 322 000 adults. This represented an astonishing 74 per cent growth in the number of 'middle-class' blacks in two years.[3] The purchasing power of this group, meanwhile, had grown from R130 billion in the last quarter of 2005 to R180 billion in the first quarter of 2007.

Further research by the Centre for Development and Enterprise estimated that if the past rate of growth could be maintained, the core middle class would number 916 000 black people, equal to nearly 70 per cent of the white middle class, by 2013.[4] Although still small in number – about 11 per cent of the total population – it would constitute an influential and even powerful political component of South African society. Whether it can ever grow to that size is debatable, given the catastrophe that was to befall South African public education under Mbeki.

How did this significant redistributive achievement come about, and at what cost?

The core of Mbeki's Economic Kingdom was to encourage growth through domestic and foreign investment and export. Handled correctly, argued the ANC theorists, the economic growth rate would be enough to placate old money and accommodate the aspirations of new. To use the cliché, the growing pie would feed all. It did not work out quite like that. Growth failed to keep up with the objectives of the programme, the process became increasingly a zero-sum game with significant transfers of wealth through direct and indirect taxation, equity and employment appropriations from the traditional wealth-holding classes to the new middle class and the welfare population.

Mbeki's programme was thus not a rampant free market as suggested by his opponents. It was a highly directed combination of racial cronyism and social welfarism, underpinned by good macro-economic management and a fortuitously benign international economic environment. It was not at all dissonant with ANC policy through the years. Indeed, a reading of the tenets of the Freedom Charter leaves one marvelling at the extent to which Mbeki succeeded in keeping to the core redistributive elements of the charter, at least for the favoured classes, while appearing all the time as a liberal free marketeer.

The intellectual mainspring for the ANC's affirmative action programme can be found in the policies of the Malaysian majority, the Bumiputera, after 1969, the policies adopted by the United States from 1968 onwards and the Indian anti-caste projects dating back to the 1950s.

These policy initiatives have drawn fiercely partisan evaluations. Revisionist writers in the three countries have argued that the policies did little more than facilitate the entry into the economic mainstream of the elites who were poised to move there anyway, while condemning the remainder to a pitiless cycle of poverty and dependence.

In Malaysia, the policy has indisputably spawned cronyism on a scale so massive as to draw the censure of the European Commission and an admission by one of the earliest protagonists of the policy that it had failed. Bumiputeran Anwar Ibrahim, a former deputy premier and now the opposition leader, argues that it has benefited only the Malaysian political establishment and its cronies. Even the current prime minister, Abdullah Ahmad Badawi, has urged the Malaysian indigenous people to 'throw away their crutches'.

The 2008 Malaysian general elections saw a huge reversal of the fortunes of the Bumiputera as the ethnic minorities and a broad slate of marginalised Malaysians revolted against a policy that had done little for them. The parallels with South Africa were inescapable.

This is perhaps the most important lesson for South Africa: thirty-seven years after its implementation, the Bumiputeran policy was so entrenched that it appeared impervious to change, despite its failure to meet its objectives. Its continuation perpetuated deep racial tensions and denied Malaysia the competitiveness needed to enter the front ranks of the developing nations. In the end, an alliance of wealth-creating elites and the marginalised united to severely challenge the orthodoxy.

The risks of such racially engineered economics are being felt in another populous, successful country. In India, attempts by successive well-meaning governments to change the caste system have seen a rise in the number of jobs and opportunities 'reserved' for the lower castes, with no evidence that these previously disadvantaged communities are getting richer any faster than other castes. The rise in the number of 'reserved' positions, meanwhile, has led to serious riots and continuing tensions between the lower castes and the rest of the society.

In South Africa, the emergence and growth of what could be called the black middle class was the result of an unwritten and probably not even acknowledged compact between the Mbeki administration and what, for want of a better term, could be called 'big business'. Both parties had a vested interest in the outcome. Mbeki needed a pliant and dependent political class that would support him in what he instinctively knew from post-colonial African history would be a showdown between the beneficiary elites and the black working and peasant classes – what I have described as the clash between ANC Classic and ANC Lite. Big business believed it needed a black middle class as a buffer against populist revolt. It needed to show that capitalism could work and radical change was unnecessary.

What emerged was the surrender of what in normal societies would be considered inherent and inviolable prerogatives of capitalist management: whom to employ, when, where and how; whom to take on as partners and under what conditions. This process can best be described initially as a guided diversion of private wealth. Only in the end did regulatory prescription come to supersede the negotiated surrender by instalment of private-sector prerogative. As the programme gathered momentum, so too did the insistent pressure on the administration by the entitled classes begin to take its toll. The process was ratcheted up and what began as a series of gentlemen's agreements about ways to empower black South Africans in the mainstream of the economy ended up in diktat, threats and hectoring by those appointed to oversee the process.

The essential pillars of this process fell into four areas: population of key posts in the public and private sectors, accession to ownership of equity, awarding of contracts and the establishment of minimum wages. The key legislative enactments were the Employment Equity Act of 1998 and the Black Economic Empowerment Act. It is important to understand the intent of both.

The preamble of the Employment Equity Act sets out clearly the objectives of the measure: to eliminate unfair discrimination in employment, implement employment equity to redress the effects of discrimination and achieve a diverse workforce broadly representative of the people of South Africa.

The purpose of the Act was to achieve equality in the workplace by implementing affirmative action measures to redress the disadvantages in employment experienced by 'designated' groups. These groups were defined quite simply as 'blacks, women and those with disabilities'.

The measures that were to be taken by employers included steps to identify and eliminate employment barriers, put in place measures to increase diversity in the workplace and to make reasonable accommodation for people from designated groups in order to ensure they enjoyed equal opportunities. Employers had to draw up and submit to the Department of Labour a plan as to how they intended improving racial representation in their organisations. These plans would be monitored going forward.

The Act noted that no employer was obliged to take any measure that would result in an absolute barrier to the advancement of a 'non-designated' person.

This exemption, however, was subject to the overall objectives of the legislation. Again, no person was entitled to discriminate against an employee on any grounds involving race, gender, sex, pregnancy, marital status, family responsibility, ethnic or social origin, colour, sexual orientation, age, disability, religion, conscience, belief, political opinion, culture, language or birth. But the kicker was that it was not unfair discrimination to take affirmative action measures consistent with the purposes of the Act. The mishmash of good intentions, necessary legislation and contradictory provisions kept the courts and legal profession busy through the years ahead.

The first celebrated cases were, not surprisingly, about what could be considered 'fair' as opposed to 'unfair' discrimination. The rulings, including Constitutional Court judgments, came down firmly against any specific act against a 'non-designated' person (i.e. white) from being refused employment or promotion purely because of skin colour. These judgments constituted a temporary setback for the governmental and parastatal entities as they embarked on a massive and wholesale clearance of white people from positions in state employ.

Unable to move legally against incumbents, the state simply focused on restricting new employment opportunities and promotions to 'designated groups' and paying the older ones to leave. The provision of attractive severance packages persuaded many senior and skilled people to depart in a rush. Inexperienced new appointees battled with the triple obstacles of unfamiliar jobs, lack of a supporting infrastructure and a raft of new laws, regulations and expectations. Small wonder, then, that the casualty rate among these first waves of incumbents was high, a number being fired for incompetence or corruption or collapsing with physical and physiological ailments.

The ANC referred to this process as the 'redeployment' of party cadres to national service. It was an apt description: the challenges and burdens carried by this frail first line of 'deployees' were among the heaviest borne by the whole liberation movement. By 2002, mental disorders such as depression and post-traumatic stress were accounting for 36 per cent of the disability pay-outs at one of the country's largest insurers. Many of the recipients were deployees or retrenchees.

The consequences of this programme were of course mostly unexpected and unintended. It is mischievous to attribute the crisis of 'delivery' of public services exclusively to affirmative action. The hugely expanded remit of the public service, new regulations, consolidation of structures and the international skills crisis all played a part. But it is indisputably true that the departure of high-level white skills and the admission of inexperienced black personnel contributed greatly to a decline in the capacity of the state and parastatal entities to meet their new tasks. This affected all agencies and all institutions across the board and was immediately felt by the public. The poisonous cycle of inexperienced leadership that was created led to failing public entities, which led in turn to public anger, which put pressure on the failing leadership, which led to the further weakening of the entities.

The management of continuity and institutional memory in organisations is the subject of a vast array of academic studies. Most show that successful companies are those that have the ability to attract new ideas and leadership, while still retaining a core of experience and maturity in the organisation. Only in revolution and war does one set out deliberately to completely rupture the organism. The manner in which the ANC government has implemented its affirmative action policies in public entities has done partly that, with long-term implications for Mbeki's legacy.

In the first waves of affirmative action employment in both private and public sector, there was undoubtedly a huge leap in the number of black employees in middle to senior positions. This was the bedrock of the new black middle class and contributed to the rapidly changing socio-economic profile. The rate of this absorption was profound, and the fact that the country could continue its growth path despite this massive institutional discontinuity was a reflection of the buoyant financial situation.

But by 2007, the process had begun to slow. The demography of middle and senior managements was stabilising. The country had simply run out of enough qualified black people to be appointed. With the white skills exodus, the lack of new black applicants, failing educational institutions and a deep initial reticence by the government to encourage imported skills, the country found itself in a largely self-induced skills crisis for most of the Mbeki administration's existence.

The shortage of skills is universal, but in South Africa it has reached dire levels. All state departments were reporting vacancy levels ranging between 25 per cent and 40 per cent in total and up to 80 per cent in some of the specialised disciplines by the end of the Mbeki era. Such levels of vacancies would be challenging in even established and developed bureaucracies. In South Africa, they were the kiss of death.

The private sector is similarly hamstrung, although its capacity to moderate the pace of institutional discontinuity has saved it from the sort of crisis experienced in the public sector. Yet a fierce ideological dispute has arisen over the very existence of such a thing as a skills crisis. The private sector and the less ideologically minded of the ruling party admit the shortage. The proponents of an unrestricted and expanded affirmative action programme insist that the reason the skills shortage exists is that there is a latent racial bias towards the employment of black people. They point to the high levels of absorption of white university graduates and the continuing underemployment of black graduates as proof.

The foremost proponent of this view that the skills crisis is an 'urban myth' is Jimmy Manyi, chairman of the Employment Equity Commission, a state-recognised institution created to ensure compliance with the objectives and targets of the legislation. Mr Manyi, it must be noted, is also the chairman of the Black Management Forum, whose members are the main beneficiaries of affirmative action, and is therefore hardly a disinterested party.

The extent to which state policies in education have contributed to the failure to provide the legions of skilled black people to fill the posts created for them by suasion and legislation has been discussed. Suffice it to say here that of all the most misconceived grand projects of the Mbeki administration, the racial engineering of the national workforce to meet arbitrary numbers must count as the gravest misjudgement. From it flowed many of the travails that were to befall the administration, and from it grew some of the direst challenges that will dog Mbeki's successor.

Worse, as in Malaysia and the United States, there is every indication that what began as a short-term 'rectification' programme has embedded itself as part of the very fabric of South African society. Thus the architects and beneficiaries of the scheme have vehemently opposed any suggestion of a sunset clause to phase out the programme, despite the fact that increasing numbers of people who qualify as 'disadvantaged' will in the future be the children of wealthy and accomplished black parents and will inevitably constitute a self-perpetuating class of the 'over-advantaged'.

In 2006, a senior Department of Labour spokesman declared that the affirmative action programme would be abandoned only when inequality was ended: a manifestly unattainable goal in the most utopian society, and one guaranteed to keep the official and his succeeding generations in employment forever.

The scope of the programme has also shown signs of narrowing. The definition of 'black' and 'women' in the legislation has been reworked in practice. The first to find themselves *de facto* excluded from the 'designated' groups were the Indian and coloured communities. On the premise that the children of these communities had not really suffered under apartheid, and the belief that they were better positioned to get ahead on their own anyway, the level of discrimination against this category has slowly risen or, put another way, advantage has been steadily whittled away. It is felt most intensely at university-level admissions and in the public service.

The goalposts were also shifting. When the Financial Sector Charter Council reported in 2007 that it had accounted for 26 per cent of affirmative appointments in its executive positions, thus exceeding its 25 per cent target, it was summarily dismissed by the Equity Commission, which said it fell short of the 40 per cent long-term objective.

The debate had also moved from the class of person who should be employed in organisations to the individual. When a major South African insurance and brokering company made an appointment that led to the resignation of a senior black executive, the Black Management Forum mounted a sustained attack on the appointee and the company on racial grounds. It was no longer a question that black people should be appointed: it was a question of *which* black person should be appointed and where.

By 2007, the government had achieved and exceeded all its employment targets in its public service, but there was no indication of a slowdown in the headlong zero-sum numbers game that constituted government policy. Long after reaching its targets, available skills in the 'non-designated' groups and abroad were shunned, and the bureaucracies continued to limp along with ineffective leadership and gaping holes in the ranks.

It was thus apparent that less than a decade after the introduction of this 'rectification' action with all its fine intentions, it was in danger of becoming exclusive, embedded and as impervious to economic rationality as were apartheid's job-reservation policies of three decades earlier.

The warning shot was eventually fired by the Public Service Commission, the independent body charged with overseeing the public service, in its 2008 report which observed: 'The implementation of affirmative action is fraught with tension which compromises the capacity of the Public Service to implement recruitment standards in a situation of open competition' and that 'the current recruitment practices need to be augmented and complemented by objective, competency-based testing as a determiner for employment'.

If affirmative action had created a dire situation in the public service, at last acknowledged by the Public Service Commission, it had quite simply become unworkable in the private sector.

In the sixth Commission for Employment Equity's annual report in 2006, the minister of labour, Membathisi Mdladlana, referred to the declining number of reports submitted by the private sector and railed at the slow progress made in appointing black people to senior positions: 'We must all remember that barriers to employment and the work environment were in most cases not there – we put them there!'[5] The sentiment would no doubt have been endorsed by South African industry, which could point with some emotion to the employment barriers erected by the state's failed educational and skills policies.

But, it was true, the report by the Equity Commission showed wholesale contempt for the legislation by the private sector which, in many cases, despairing of ever acquiring or retaining sufficient black skills to meet the growing affirmative targets, had opted to risk the fines for non-compliance. By 2007 the number of senior black managers had settled at 22 per cent – an astonishing fourfold increase in a decade – although it was becoming increasingly apparent that it was not going anywhere upwards fast.

A major employment placement agency, Jack Hammer Executive Headhunters, reported in 2008 that more than half of its senior appointments in 2007 had been white. This, the agency pointed out, was not because clients were not desperate for affirmative appointments, but rather because the dire skills crisis was forcing them to give priority to skill and experience.

PE Corporate Services, a remuneration analysis organisation, counted another feature of the skills crisis. In 2006, only two-thirds of the 850 companies in its survey would have considered counter-bidding for a staff member wishing to resign. By 2007 it had risen to 80 per cent as corporations desperately held onto their skilled staff.

By the end of Mbeki's rule, then, the helter-skelter process of appointment by quota was at an end. Neither public nor private sector could heedlessly pursue an ideologically based numbers game at any cost. Something had to give.

The ultimate cost of affirmative action as envisioned by the ANC may be even more deeply rooted than imagined. The unintended consequence may not be the economic liberation of black South Africans that is so rightly deserved, but their continual dependence.

An insightful piece of research by the South African Institute of Race Relations argues that, far from improving the creation of a classically mature middle class, this form of affirmative action merely increases its dependence.[6] The burden of being classified 'affirmative' weighs heavily on the multitude of talented black managers who would have qualified on merit for an increasing role in a rapidly opening market. More, an insidious mindset of dependence on government largesse is embedded in the class. It thus becomes inextricably bound with the success or failure of the government and its willingness to accommodate this expectation.

And herein lies the irony. Many of the whites dispossessed from public or private life because of affirmative action have left, either to fulfil themselves in foreign countries or to start again from the ground up by establishing their own small businesses. While this category has thus increased its independence and mobility, the reverse has happened to those who have filled the gaps: they are in thrall to a policy resting on the grace and favour of a governing clique and a surging economic growth rate.

There are some indications of a changing groundswell. A new generation of young black entrepreneurs and professionals are actively kicking back against any imputation that they are affirmative action employees and that their appointments are based on anything but merit. Black professional groups are drawing the line against missionaries like Jimmy Manyi and argue that the means is in grave danger of destroying the end.

In 2007, Solidarity, the predominantly white trade union movement, drafted and proposed a code of good practice in terms of the Employment Equity Act. It suggested that the affirmative programme should have a time limit; that white first-time job seekers be exempt from the provisions of the Act; and that when a black person is evaluated for a post in terms of the legislation, the candidate's real disadvantage, as opposed to the disadvantages experienced by his or her group, be considered.

The response from Manyi, ostensibly the independent and non-conflicted curator of the equity process, was as predictable as it was depressing. He said the proposals were fraudulent and criminal.

Ironically, the splendid Springbok victory at the Rugby World Cup in 2007 seemed to seal some sort of tipping point. The team, largely white but with some brilliant black players in the back line, brought home the greatest accolade to South African sport in a decade (the previous being yet another Rugby World Cup triumph). Immediately after the victory in Paris, the ideologues, represented by the minister of sport, began talking about the need for more transformation, which, reading the shorthand, meant exiting some of the white players and bringing in more blacks.

The response from the country was astonishing and, to the ideologues, deeply disconcerting. From all quarters, including respected members of the black elites, came a howl of indignation. It was as if the very suggestion of racial quotas was seen as a slur on a national achievement. Mbeki, arguing that in the pursuit of transforming the sport a few lost games here and there were unimportant, was by force of popular emotion converted to wearing the rugby jersey for his next cabinet meeting and talking about the unifying nature of the sport. Three weeks later, he announced the end of quotas in sport. Few, however, were convinced that this would extend to a phasing out of quotas in the engine houses of the South African economy.

CHAPTER 16

Share of the spoils

A government that robs Peter to pay Paul can always depend on the support of Paul.   — GEORGE BERNARD SHAW[1]

PARALLEL TO THE DRIVE FOR AFFIRMATIVE ACTION IN EMPLOY-ment was the vital initiative to ensure greater participation of black South Africans in the ownership and direction of the economy. This concept had a ready-made model. The development of Afrikaner capital from the 1920s onwards had, to a material extent, been based upon the growth of cooperatives in the agricultural sector and equity holdings, however small, in the major Afrikaner business entities. In 1963, the front-running Afrikaner private-sector company Federale Mynbou bought out Anglo American's General Mining and Finance Corporation in what today would be called an empowerment deal. This marked the Afrikaner's definitive breakthrough into sustained capital accumulation.

Economic empowerment for black South Africans was driven initially by the private sector as various initiatives were undertaken to assist black business leaders to become self-sufficient. The programme had mixed success. While a number of black South Africans did undoubtedly become very wealthy, the sustainability of many of the projects came under question. In some cases, too, there were blatant examples of self-enrichment under the guise of empowerment, with no discernible advantage to black South Africans or the country.

The next wave of empowerment was on a slightly more organised basis. It consisted largely of deeding chunks of equity to various consortiums of black shareholders, on the understanding that they would redeem the purchase price at a later stage through growth in the share valuations. There was one problem: most of these projects were launched into a languid stock market and, in some cases, were in highly volatile sectors like media and information technology. As the debt mounted and the shares stagnated, many of the beneficiaries of these deals lived by the charity of the other shareholders and the banks. It was hardly a formula for a long-term inroad of black enterprise into the market.

These failures prompted the Mbeki administration to decide on a more concerted, coherent and sustainable strategy. The driver of the government's redistributive capital programme was the Broad-Based Black Economic Empowerment Act of 2003.

Its goals were set thus: 'To increase broad-based and effective participation of black people in the economy and promote a higher growth rate, increased employment and more equitable income distribution.'

The Act created a Black Economic Empowerment Advisory Council to advise on the best methods to implement the policy. The legislation envisaged the publication of codes of good practice and, crucially, the agreeing of 'transformation charters' for each major business sector.

These charters were to become the battleground on which South Africa's private sector fought its rearguard actions against the proxy expropriation of significant chunks of their equity. Eventually, the generally agreed quantum of privately held equity to be surrendered was in the order of 25 per cent, although an arduously negotiated charter for the finance sector put it at 10 per cent direct and 15 per cent indirect investment. It was also agreed that businesses with a turnover of less than R5 million a year and employing fewer than fifty people would be exempt from the terms of the BBEE project.

From 2003 onwards, the business of empowerment consumed much of the imaginative and productive corporate resources of the country. Hundreds of deals were announced with a variety of parties. Various funding devices were found for each one as the incumbent shareholders struggled to find a way to ensure a sustainable transfer of wealth in a way that was affordable, while the aspirant shareholders jostled to get in line for the largest cut possible, at the least investment feasible.

Manipulation inevitably arose. One prominent black businessman made an estimated profit of more than R70 million during an eight-month period, merely by acquiring equity as an empowerment partner and then on-selling it to a non-empowerment party. This was not the first time he had done it. In 2002, he acquired 'empowerment' shares and sold them on at a huge profit to another buyer. It was as cynical a manipulation of good intentions as could be imagined, and an early warning of the risk to which racial economic engineering lends itself.

As the process unfolded, however, it became apparent that three things were happening: a disconcertingly few black South Africans always appeared to be at the head of the queue, most of them senior serving or former members of the ANC; the costs of the transactions were high; and, finally, the returns in terms of identifiable benefits to the economy and the broader society were elusive.

None of these shortcomings, however, was allowed to stand in the way of the process, which had assumed such a sanctified and missionary status under the Mbeki administration that the slightest challenge was greeted with outrage by the ANC leadership and, above all, the new beneficiaries. South Africa's business community grumbled privately, but cooperated. They had learnt the art of accommodation under apartheid.

Like affirmative action in employment, however, the programme of enforced distribution of privately held equity had adopted a life of its own by 2007. The charter agreements were hardly dry when BBEE advocates were calling for their scrapping on the basis that the private sector had failed to live up to the expectations of the beneficiaries. It was clear that the idea of a limited accession to equity would be ditched in favour of a surge to acquire as much as possible from wherever possible. A showdown was inevitable.

This came in 2008 with that most conservative of sectors, the financial institutions. These bodies let it be known that billions of rands pending in various empowerment deals, and indeed an ambitious programme to extend banking facilities to the very poor, were threatened unless the government gave a clear answer to what its expectations were. The institutions, at huge cost and time, had negotiated sector charters for 10 per cent direct black ownership in their institutions and 15 per cent indirect. Amended government guidelines had, however, put the target at 15 per cent direct investment. The pressure was now on to scrap the sector charter and adopt the departmental guidelines. The sector pointed out that this was not an academic issue of percentages: the value of the shares affected had increased by up to 187 per cent from 2004 and 2005, when the deals had been concluded, to the end of 2007.

The costs of new empowerment buyouts at any percentage had become, quite simply, too expensive – both for the aspirant new black share owners and the old shareholding classes, which usually ended up underwriting the deal in some form or another. Economic reality had at last overtaken ideological imperatives.

The difficulty of measuring the extent of empowerment within sectors was meanwhile vividly illustrated when the Investment Management Association of South Africa reported in 2007 that the asset-weighted level of direct black ownership of the industry was 22 per cent. The Association of Black Securities and Investment Professionals immediately rejected the report and claimed ownership was at 16 per cent. It was a harbinger of the effort, energy and time that would have to be put into keeping the record straight – let alone advancing the programme or even running the businesses.

By the end of 2007, the proponents of BEE were arguing a range of punitive measures to force compliance with this programme of enforced wealth and opportunity transfer. Business Unity South Africa suggested that only empowerment-compliant companies be allowed to list and that companies would have to report on compliance at the time of their annual reports. The proposal, imposing as it did yet another layer of regulatory requirements on investors, was hardly geared to ensure improved competitiveness or acceleration of South Africa's growth requirements.

Indeed, key figures in the mining and manufacturing sector were warning by late 2007 that empowerment policies were acting as a clear disincentive to further investment in South Africa.

In all cases, the government made clear that its objective was to ensure that previously disadvantaged communities should be the first to benefit – a laudable objective, but one that inevitably would lead to much division and dissension by the new beneficiaries.

Among the more notable examples was the awarding of the contract to run security at South Africa's airports. The contract was granted to one entity that proved so incompetent that it had to be re-awarded. Somebody, allegedly with high-level police connections, was so incensed that they took their venom out on the hapless chairman of the Airports Company of South Africa. He was arrested for allegedly being an illegal immigrant and his home shot up by mysterious gunmen.

The awarding of the contract to run the multibillion-rand South African lottery followed a similar path of severe dissension, court challenges, delays and confusion. For eight months the country was without the Lotto, the major source of funding for a number of beneficiaries. At the heart of the matter was a resolute view by the losing consortium that the winning one had no right to the opportunity.

A third, even more ominous example of such public–private sector initiatives was South Africa's attitude to development of a new undersea fibre-optic cable along the East African coast, intended to relieve the country's acute lack of broadband. Considerable agreement had been achieved between the major African and multilateral backers when the minister of communications threw a spanner in the works. She insisted that South African shareholders should hold the majority stake in the South African entity. It would be charitable to think this was a decision taken purely from the noble if mistaken objective of growing the South African economy. The reality was that it was aimed at securing yet another chunk of the economy for a favoured few.

The costs of this empowerment are enormous. The advocates of BEE have consistently resisted attempts to quantify these costs, insisting that the initiative serves a higher national benefit. It fell to Ernst & Young to publish in its 2005 annual review of mergers and acquisitions the fact that of the ten BEE deals surveyed, the cost of the transaction amounted to an average 3 per cent of market capitalisation of each company.[2]

The BusinessMap Foundation extrapolated the numbers and came to the startling conclusion that if every listed South African company was to be involved in a BEE initiative, a quantum of R711 billion in equity would have to be transferred at a cost of R85 billion. If one considers that there are many other non-listed companies, the cost of the exercise would be much higher; some estimates put it at R150 billion. Placed in perspective, the cost of the project would be equivalent to 35 per cent of the entire infrastructure spend for the government over the next ten years.[3]

But that was only part of the cost. The same analysis by BusinessMap estimated that wage premiums for affirmative appointments could be 40 per cent above market rates for the very high skill levels. There would also be a 7 per cent premium on the wage bill for skills development. In procurement, empowerment policies would add approximately 20 per cent to the value of tenders.

Totted up, and even making allowances for what would have had to be spent on skills and enterprise development in any case, one is looking at a mega-billion rand investment by a developing country, in what is still essentially an ideological project until its material benefits to the country and the society are demonstrated.

In comparative terms, BEE must rank with the costs of Franklin Delano Roosevelt's New Deal in the US in the 1930s, the Marshall Plan for Western Europe or – dare one say it – the cost of implementing grand apartheid in South Africa. It is a truly massive investment and one that any country would have to weigh very carefully in terms of costs and benefits.

There has been no indication that such an exercise was ever undertaken: indeed, the reverse. But the issue will not go away. Accountants insist that these deals are not investments but costs, according to generally accepted practice. The consequence took an interesting turn in 2007 when Mvelaphanda, a major South African private-sector company owned by black interests and led by the charismatic Tokyo Sexwale, a former ANC guerrilla, was forced to enter a R544 million charge in its books for a share-and-options issue to an empowerment company.[4] A major South African electronics company, Reunert, was only one of dozens of companies that took severe knocks to earnings in concluding charter agreements in 2007. In this case, the loss was a 48 per cent fall in headline earnings.[5]

The cost of maintaining the programme could be even higher than expected. Most of the deals are highly leveraged – anything up to 100 per cent – and, with rising interest rates, a serious question arises as to whether these deals will be affordable in the long run. Vuyo Jack, the chief executive of the BEE ratings agency Empowerdex, was warning in late 2007 that the project may end in a 'huge crunch'. If so, there are enormous political ramifications that Mbeki's heir will have to manage.

In 2008, amendments to the Companies Act came into effect that would make it easier to facilitate empowerment deals. The most important element was the relaxation of rules preventing a company from providing money for the purchase of its own shares in a limited liability company. The reason for the rule was simple: in the event of somebody having a financial case against the company, the claimant could at least look to the contributed capital for recourse. By weakening this section, the government may have been facilitating empowerment and reducing the heavy costs of the transaction, but contrary to the direction of the international business environment since the Enron collapse in the US, they were vitiating creditors' interests. Thus the unintended consequence: while pushing for banks, insurers and medical aid schemes to increase their reserve ratios for the comfort of creditors and members, they were doing the opposite in regard to capital to ease empowerment.

The returns from the empowerment exercise are difficult to quantify at this stage. The project has certainly brought many more black South Africans into senior positions within South African companies and ensured a greater spread of equity outside the traditional wealth-owning classes. Black ownership had increased variously to 12 per cent or 22 per cent of the economy by 2007, depending on the measure. It is also true that some black enterprises have benefited from contracts that might otherwise have been denied. But it is a moot point whether those beneficiaries would not have benefited in any case from an unfettered, high-growth economy in which skills and resources were at a premium.

Certainly, there is little indication as yet that empowered companies perform better than non-empowered ones, or that consumers get a better deal from empowered companies than they do from non-empowered ones. In 2008 a clear example of the conflict of state objectives arose in the Eastern Cape, where spending on desperately needed housing has consistently been 50 per cent less than budget. An investigation gave the answer: the small 'empowered' contractors preferred by the state could not do the job efficiently. The jury is out on whether empowerment equity transactions engineered under these circumstances have strengthened or weakened the internal cohesiveness and external competitiveness of South African companies. By 2008 the first of the divorces from these shotgun marriages were beginning to come through the courts – mainly existing shareholders suing empowerment ones for failure to perform, but a few the other way around.

Black small business, supposedly the driver of Mbeki's new economy, has not benefited to any substantial extent from these new opportunities. Despite the allocation of billions of rands to assist small businesses, the results have been meagre. Lack of skills among recipients, bureaucratic delays, wholesale corruption in some agencies like the Land Bank and a culture of the short term have all contributed to a deeply disappointing outcome. These same small businesses are now also expected to carry a heavier cost for verification of their equity status from 2008 onwards, adding another burden to an already struggling sector.

The lessons have been reinforced at a global level. The pursuit of greater access by South Africa to European and US markets on behalf of the African continent, entirely laudable in itself, fails on a single point. In the event that all trade barriers were dropped tomorrow, it is highly unlikely that any African country, other than a very few with a developed industrial and commercial agricultural sector, would materially benefit immediately. It is not just the *access* to the territories that is the issue: it is the *quality* of the product, the reliability of the logistics and the willingness of the supplier to abide by contractual obligations.

This is no idle speculation. When the Africa Growth and Opportunity Act was passed by the US Congress in May 2000, precisely to give easier access to their markets, it was primarily the large commercial agricultural, manufacturing and industrial entities in the targeted countries that bene-fited. Although 98 per cent of African goods are imported to the US under these beneficial terms, there has hardly been a huge increase in agricultural or finished imports from the exporting beneficiaries. The problem lies in US sanitary and phytosanitary requirements and the difficulty many African markets have in matching them.

The brutal lessons are that not even the best-intentioned legislation can make up for inexperienced management, poor product, lack of entre-preneurial skills and the lack of an enabling environment. To believe that magic legislative wands and racial engineering can change that in and of itself is, frankly, delusional.

Since 1994, R300 billion in equity has been transferred in terms of the empowerment project, yet the edifice now faces severe challenges through changed financial circumstances. Already, the beneficiaries are arguing for even greater subsidy and support from the sponsoring corporates to 'tide them over' and 'consolidate the gains'. This is short-speak for perpetual indebtedness.

Ten years after the launch of its growth and redistribution programme, the Mbeki regime presides over a country undergoing an expensive exercise in racial economic engineering: a programme that began without clarity, proceeds in confusion and offers uncertain ends.

Could it have been handled differently given the self-evident need to ensure black South Africans had both economic as well as political citizen-ship? The last section of this book will suggest some alternatives. Here it needs simply to be noted that the empowerment project as conceived and implemented by the Mbeki administration has to date had limited success and indeed has courted major diversions of energy and resources.

It has advantaged the few rather than the masses by risking private and public funds, diverted capital from productive pursuits, added little to the competitiveness of South African industry, not improved the life of the consumer, done very little for the creation of an indigenous small-business sector and not enhanced services and delivery. There is no evidence it has improved job creation, nor that it has, in and of itself, advanced any of the objectives of the 2003 Act which an unfettered economy would not have achieved in any case.

CHAPTER 17

The hidden classes

Generosity is giving me more than you can and pride is taking less than you need. — KAHLIL GIBRAN[1]

THE GROWTH OF THE WELFARE CLASS IN SOUTH AFRICA HAS been perhaps the most under-reported aspect of the Mbeki tenure. Under pressure to deliver rapidly to the poorest of society, the ANC government embarked on a massive programme of social relief that is now more extensive than in any other middle-income or developing country. It has also become so expensive that the finance minister has on more than one occasion been moved to observe that the country cannot afford it. Hitherto, it has been largely funded by the surplus tax revenue collected in the boom times and savings made by materially reducing the government's external debt-servicing charges over a decade. As the boom winds down and the national debt cranks up towards 2010, the wherewithal to pay for this welfare class becomes a critical point of debate.

In 2001, there were 3.4 million beneficiaries in the South African public welfare system. By 2006 this figure stood at 10.9 million. A year later, it had increased by another 21 per cent and was 12.8 million, which was 7.5 per cent above the medium-term expenditure framework. By October 2007 it was 12.3 million, the weeding out of fraudulent cases having taken it off its high point.

Average monthly payments had meanwhile increased from R462 per grant to R903, and by 2008 consolidated welfare and social security expenditure stood at R105 billion or 4.6 per cent of GDP. The grants had also been tied to inflation and, as pressure mounted, the Treasury had to return to parliament in late 2007 to ask for additional funds to cover rising food prices. The Mbeki administration had undertaken a fourfold expansion of the public social security net, doubled the levels of payment within five years and increased the proportion of the state budget devoted to welfare from 10 per cent to 17 per cent in ten years. By any token, this was an astonishing example of populist government.

The main grants were for care dependency, child support, disabled persons, foster children and the elderly. The biggest increase was in child-support grants, which soared from less than one million to more than seven million in five years, while the age cap was pushed from seven to fourteen years.

The reasons for the massive spiral in qualifying grantees were diverse: more categories of grants being created, reduction in the criteria for quali-fication, expansion in the qualifying period, better knowledge among the public and an expanded administration.

A research project commissioned by the government in 2006 revealed the startling fact that 36 per cent of South African households received one type of social grant, while 31 per cent received two. More than 16 per cent received more than two, while 9 per cent received four each. Without these grants, the survey found, 94 per cent of recipient households would fall below the poverty line.

'Should the grant income of household members be terminated,' the survey warned, 'the majority of all beneficiary households would be unable to cover their expenditure on food.'[2]

The impact of the system was immediately apparent in the number of people living on less than one US dollar a day. From 1996, the number of South Africans falling below this benchmark rose steadily from approxi-mately 1.8 million to more than four million in 2002. At that point, the full impact of the expanded welfare net kicked in and it stabilised at four million, although the exact numbers are a source of endless dispute between the administration and its detractors.

But by 2006 the government was beginning once again to feel the effect of the unintended consequence. Not only was the take-up much higher than expected, but all sorts of desperate side effects were developing. A mass of anecdotal evidence suggested that the grants were fostering rather than alleviating social ills, with widespread abuse of the system and massive corruption. Worse still, there was ample evidence that the social support system had become nothing but a vast aid enterprise, with nearly a third of households living primarily on handouts from the state and lapsing further and further into a state of workless dependency.

The government's response, predictably, was to commission a research project on whether there were any 'perverse incentives' from the scheme. Were young girls getting pregnant to receive a child grant? Were parents disavowing their biological children to re-register them as foster children for grant purposes? Did people deliberately avoid taking medication so as to prolong temporary disability grants?

The research gave some comfort.[3] There did not seem to be any empirical evidence to suggest wholesale and intentional abuse of the system, but there was plenty to worry about. There did appear to be people who refused medication in order to continue claiming disability grants. This, of course, had an impact on the government's AIDS and TB campaigns. The temporary disability grants also had a worrying tendency to become permanent.

The criteria for qualifying for grants also appeared to have slackened. In 1997, 8 per cent of applications were rejected. By 2005, this had fallen to 1 per cent. Other research carried out by the Community Agency for Social Enquiry (CASE) in 2004 had already pointed to the fact that public officials universally regarded these grants as nothing more than poor relief and were in many cases loath to disqualify beneficiaries and thereby return them to abject poverty.

The report confirmed a huge increase in the number of child-support grants and an increase in teenage pregnancies between 1995 and 2005, but there was no evidence that this was as a direct result of the more widely available grant. High rates of teenage pregnancy, CASE observed rather chillingly, had long been a feature of national demographics.

Administrative gaps also existed in the system regarding foster grants and child-support grants. In many cases beneficiaries were claiming both, although the foster-care grant was never intended to be additional to the child-support grant.

Management of the system also tended to encourage foster support, supposedly a temporary relief, into becoming permanent, meaning that a whole class of parents was absolved of any responsibility to ever care for their offspring.

Not surprisingly, given the scale of expansion of the system, corruption became endemic. In 2007, the special investigative unit set up to crack welfare fraud reported that it had saved the state R7.7 billion. The unit estimated that up to one million of the twelve million grants were illegal – 8.3 per cent. Nearly 22 000 public servants had been convicted of fraud. None went to prison. A further 140 000 government employees were recommended for removal from the system. Astonishingly, more than 120 000 beneficiaries had stopped making claims while still under investigation, one step ahead of the law.

The opportunities for syndicate crime from such a porous and corrupt system were not to be resisted. One syndicate that was exposed had already scammed more than R700 000 from the system – and this was only the public sector. Estimates by the unit were that another 500 000 illegal claimants were to be found in the private sector. When the minister of social development, Dr Zola Skweyiya, briefed the parliamentary cluster on social security in February 2007, he confirmed that of the 500 000 private-sector grants, 200 000 had either lapsed or been cancelled.

In October 2007, the KwaZulu-Natal Social Welfare Department confirmed that in that province alone, losses of R440 million had been uncovered due to fraud. The biggest culprit was a 'ghost children' fraud in which R170 million had been skimmed from the system to pay for tens of thousands of non-existent children. The scam, officials alleged, involved eighty-five public servants.[4]

All the evidence pointed to a precipitously introduced system that had run out of control, costing the state hundreds of millions in pointless expenditure.

It was not surprising, then, that the Mbeki administration began to turn its mind to longer-term ways to deal with poverty. Grants on this scale may have temporarily held a further slide by many South African households into dire poverty, but this came at an enormous price, as the trade unions were quick to point out. The costs of the programme robbed other equally deserving causes of funds; the grants led to a general dependency cycle; and the whole programme was critically dependent on economic growth. From 2006 onwards, the discussion was increasingly about a comprehensive social security plan for those earning under R3 000 a month – estimated at 43.2 per cent of the population. This scheme would include basic retirement savings and coverage for death, disability and unemployment benefits.

One of the proposals was to shift the onus of welfare payments away from general poverty relief towards an expanded public-works programme. If households were to be subsidised by the state through their sick, pregnant and juvenile, argued some, let the able-bodied in those households do some work for the benefit of society. Attention was thus turned to the employment guarantee scheme piloted in the Indian state of Maharashtra and later extended to the whole country, in which households are guaranteed at least one hundred days of work a year at a set rate of pay. The government also renewed its attention to an integrated food-security and land-reform programme, an initiative that has thus far failed spectacularly.

The combination of new support for the poor and working poor is likely to feature heavily in ANC planning in the immediate future, given the socialist orientation of the new party executives. The exact contours and costs of the scheme are unknown, but already concern has been raised that this will place an additional heavy burden on the formally employed. As only a comparatively small component of the society was in formal employment and the tax base was even smaller (five million individuals or 10.6 per cent of the population), it appeared that yet another heavy burden of contribution was to fall on the shoulders of this small and non-subsidised wealth-creating class.

The previous two chapters have examined the two key thrusts of the Mbeki administration's wealth redistribution programme. The one created an almost instant black middle class. The other gave rise to the largest welfare class in any developing or middle-level country. Both classes, as argued earlier, were critically dependent on state policy and economic growth for their survival.

But what were the material consequences of these initiatives?

It is hard to convey the essence of the social, economic and political change wrought on South Africa by macro-economic stability, massive state consumption spending and the Mbeki administration's programme of racial economic engineering unless one takes the time to travel this twenty-first-century country. From the largest cities to the smallest *dorps*, there has been an almost ceaseless flurry of building for nearly a decade.

Between 1994 and 2007, 2 355 913 small houses have been built by the state for the poor, services laid on, roads upgraded, toilets erected, telephone lines installed, power points embedded and water mains connected. Informal settlements – otherwise known as squatter camps – have been upgraded, painted, extended, paved and electrified.

The old, classic South African 'townships' such as Soweto, Orlando, KwaMashu, Gugulethu and Alexandra have been given facelifts. In some, private housing initiatives have created clear social distinctions between the wealthy middle class and poorer neighbourhoods: the old monolithic uniformity of the apartheid visionaries has been swept away in a riot of enterprise and house pride.

In the previously whites-only suburbs, the change is equally remarkable. On any weekday morning the cars coursing down the highways from these suburbs are populated by the black middle class. Their children attend the local state schools (in many cases they are almost entirely black) or, if they can afford it, go to expensive private schools. The high-level shopping malls that have mushroomed during the boom years are crowded with a very multiracial clientele, as are the restaurants, bars and cinemas.

It is naïve to suggest all have benefited equally or to deny the reality of dire poverty. But it is also indisputable that things have moved on a dramatic scale. One can always regard South Africa as the glass half empty or half full. The Mbeki administration would claim it is half full, and it is to filling the rest that it is committed. Its opponents argue the opposite: the glass is half empty, and in that half live the millions of poor and dis-possessed.

The essence of this socio-economic change is captured best in South Africa's All Media Products Survey (AMPS) 2006, a database comprising 24 000 weighted respondents, published by the South African Advertising Research Foundation. The foundation is an independent body funded by the South African media and marketers. Having previously served on its board for a number of years, I can vouch for its meticulous attention to technical and data credibility. Its index of development in South Africa is regularly quoted by government, and as regularly challenged by its oppon-ents. The index, factoring in all elements with a baseline of one hundred in 1994, had increased to 125 by 2006.

The income surveys showed that those households earning less than R2 499 per annum dropped from nearly 75 per cent of all households in 1994 to half in 2006. In the income category from R2 500 to R5 999, the number of households increased from 16 per cent to 22 per cent. Those with incomes of R6 000 a month and above increased from 10 per cent to 26 per cent. Breaking this group into rural and urban components, rural households went up from 4 per cent to 11 per cent and urban households from 16 per cent to 40 per cent. Overall, then, the survey showed a significant improvement in the income base of a very large number of South Africans.

No less riveting are the statistics regarding hard services and consumer possession.

The survey showed that home ownership had increased from 64 per cent of the population in 1994 to 73 per cent in 2000 and 78 per cent in 2006. The provision of water to households had increased from 68 per cent of households in 1994 to 74 per cent in 2000 and 75 per cent in 2006.

Broken down into its rural and urban components, water provision in rural areas increased from 40 per cent to 53 per cent between 1994 and 2006, and in urban areas from 97 per cent to 98 per cent during the same period.

In 1994, nearly three out of five households had electricity. By 2006 it was more than four out of five. In rural areas it more than doubled from 30 per cent to a remarkable 74 per cent and in urban areas from 88 per cent to 96 per cent. The use of electric stoves improved from one-fifth of households to one-third in rural areas and from 64 per cent to 74 per cent in urban areas. Electric refrigerator usage doubled from 24 per cent in rural areas in 1994 to 52 per cent ten years later. The use of hi-fi systems increased from 24 per cent in rural areas in 1994 to 53 per cent a decade later. In urban areas it increased from 54 per cent to 74 per cent. Only 27 per cent of rural dwellers had television in 1994. A decade later, the figure was double at 60 per cent. In urban areas it ramped from 79 per cent to 89 per cent. Landline telephones showed a decline across the period, but this was offset by the exponential growth in mobile telephony from 17 per cent in 2000 to 49 per cent in 2006.

Many of these findings were reinforced by a community survey by the Department of Statistics, based on 284 000 randomly selected households and released in October 2007. The 2008 Statistics South Africa Income and Expenditure Survey revealed that the per capita income of the poorest 10 per cent of the population had risen by a staggering 79 per cent between 2000 and 2006.

By the fourteenth year of ANC rule and the eighth of Mbeki's tenure, huge strides had thus been made by the president in meeting one of the foremost objectives of his administration: an aggressive redistribution programme aimed at creating a pliant middle class and helping the indigent. The costs were high and might well prove to be unsustainable, the long-term risks to the country significant. But nobody could deny what had been achieved, and in a very short period of time.

And yet the Mbeki administration has received scant credit for this victory from its beneficiaries. Why?

Part of the answer is undoubtedly the phenomenon of rising expectation. The average ANC supporter is not the person he or she was in 1994. People have savoured the excitement of the political transition and drunk deeply from the cup of ANC promise. The very principle of affirmative action implies advantage and advancement on the basis of race. The fact that both have been unequally apportioned, as is always the case, has merely served to sharpen expectation and deepen disillusionment.

Behind the undoubtedly impressive statistics in the South African Advertising Research Foundation report and the expansion of the social welfare net lies the cold reality that wealth has not been equally or even proportionately distributed under the Mbeki administration. The Gini coefficient, the measure of inequality in South African society, has hardly changed other than in its composition. By 2007, the levels of inequality once dividing black South Africa from white, so rightly condemned as a product of an unjust system, had been neatly replicated in the divide between wealthy and poor blacks. While income inequality within the white and Indian minorities had remained relatively constant between 1996 and 2005, inequality within the black majority had grown from 0.52 on the index to 0.64.[5]

Further research by the South African Institute of Race Relations revealed the disturbing fact that inequality among the black community was growing faster than in any other sector. It also revealed that whereas the average increase in black income between 1996 and 2005 was 20 per cent (7 per cent more than the rest of the country), inequality between black people had equally grown by 20 per cent in the same period. Thus, while South Africans were generally growing richer, they were not growing more equal. South Africa was not unique in this. The World Bank research on inequality published in 2007 showed that with economic growth, income inequalities within countries in sub-Saharan Africa had worsened, not lessened. The wealthiest 10 per cent of these economies increased their wealth relative to the poorest 10 per cent from tenfold to twentyfold between 1975 and 2005.

But that was not the point. Nobody in Nigeria, for example, would argue that the country was anything but a deeply unequal society. The ANC, however, had been elected on its platform of egalitarianism. That was now under threat.

In a sense, then, Mbeki has become the victim of his own success: affirmative action is proving indivisible and racially porous. The politically nurtured sense of expectation and increasingly of entitlement held by some in the black elites against the racial minorities is as fierce (perhaps more so) among less advantaged black communities against the more advantaged ones. Obversely, by 2007, the first wave of business beneficiaries of the empowerment programme were bewailing the fact that the very rules applied to predominantly white businesses to ensure compliance with the state's affirmative action policies were adversely affecting their own businesses.

Whole new terrains of battle opened up, and, in this process, who paused to consider whether they could now watch television in their own home and trip to the toilet down the corridor, whereas they could not do either ten years ago? The world has moved on, but Mbeki, by his year-after-year recital of the number of toilets built for poor communities, misses the point.

A second part of the answer to the question why Mbeki is not enjoying just acknowledgement is to be found in two words: growth and jobs. While the statistics show impressive development in a number of areas, the central determinant of any successful society, the proportion of its citizens retained in productive and sustainable jobs, is lacking. As we have seen, South Africa's growth rate under current constraints is insufficient to sustain a significant reduction in joblessness and, even if it were, the distortions in the labour market created by past apartheid policies and equally restrictive post-apartheid regulations will ensure it will remain largely jobless growth.

The third answer as to why Mbeki has not enjoyed full recognition for these achievements lies in the political terrain. As the influence of the Mbeki presidency waned within the ANC, so grew the power of the populist wing. It was not in their interests to give praise, nor even address the facts. The ANC members who voted to halt Mbeki's continued leadership of the movement were inflamed by grievance, not informed by facts.

The final answer as to why poor communities do not feel any sense of real satisfaction from the rosy statistical picture painted in surveys by organisations like the South African Advertising Research Foundation has already been covered. It lies in the incapacity of the state to deliver in key areas on its promises to the poorer communities, because of the systemic erosion of the integrity and efficiency of important state entities and institutions, primarily law and order, education and health.

It was this bundle of factors that would lie at the heart of Mbeki's defeat at Polokwane.

PART IV

The Future
Kingdom

CHAPTER 18

Mbeki and demodernisation

The great thing in the world is not so much where we stand, as in what direction we are moving.

— OLIVER WENDELL HOLMES[1]

IN FEBRUARY 2008, PRESIDENT THABO MBEKI DELIVERED HIS eleventh State of the Nation address to parliament. It was significantly different from the previous ten in that there was little reference to his past achievements, no long lists of toilets under construction and no vaunting promises.

Instead, he spoke quietly and convincingly about the many problems that beset the country and concerned its citizens, although he could not quite avoid his old habit of referring to the doubts that assailed *them* – the public – as opposed to the concerns *he* might have. As always, there was the distance. Absent was any reference to black empowerment and his usual chiding of the minorities for not more rapidly surrendering more. Remarkably, he conceded that there had been serious errors in state planning. For the president who had staked his reputation on his technocratic abilities, this was an enormous and painful step towards humility.

He concluded with fourteen 'apex priorities' that had to be addressed. Given that only three years earlier the accelerated growth initiative had narrowed priorities to six, the increase indicated that in the interim little had been achieved or, conversely, there were twice as many crises. Whichever, it was an admission of how much still had to be done, and perhaps an acknowledgement of how little of substance had been achieved.

Still, Mbeki concluded, South Africa was on track to the future and there was no need for concern. His speech was creatively themed 'business unusual' and was the best I had heard him make, for one reason only. Despite the glossing over of major issues and the tiresome repetition of all the plans still in place to bring the country its long-delayed future, it captured nothing so much as the impression of a person suddenly caught by the dreadful realisation of how solemn a burden he has to carry.

During the subsequent week of debate on his address, the president's own party remained strangely mute before the sustained onslaught of the opposition on the administration's demonstrable record of mismanagement – quite unlike the baying and heckling that usually greeted opposition criticism.

Part of this was undoubtedly because many members of the ANC caucus had an eye on the new management of the party and were anxious not to be seen as being too cosy with Mbeki and his Lite ministers. But part, hopefully, was a realisation that the country was indeed in trouble, and not even the most short-sighted parliamentarian could or should distance him- or herself from that reality and that legacy.

Four weeks later, finance minister Trevor Manuel delivered his twelfth and probably last budget – a consummate and stylish affair that seemed to satisfy everybody except, inevitably, the communists and unionists. He warned that stormy times were ahead, but was pleased to confirm that with an international reserve of $35 billion in the hold, the result of the Mbeki administration's financial prudence, he was confident the ship of state had enough ballast to weather the turbulence. It was a pleasing performance and well received, and Mbeki could justly feel that it was the culmination of the sound macro-economic management that had characterised his tenure.

But that, sadly, is about where it ended. By mid-2008, nine years into the Mbeki presidency, South Africa was in trouble on just about every other front.

A series of reversals had struck the ANC and the country, most of them in the short period of two years between mid-2006 and mid-2008. The international economic weathervane had swung sharply around. Credit crises across the globe, slowing international growth, a cooling of Asian demand for raw commodities and the fears of a US recession all had their effects on the South African economy. Oil and food prices had soared – global food prices had increased by 65.4 per cent from April 2007 to April 2008, pushing South African food inflation to 15.6 per cent, while oil touched $140 a barrel. Not surprisingly, consumer-price-index inflation was 11.6 per cent in June 2008, thereby culminating a full twelve-month run outside the inflation targets set by the Reserve Bank. Economists expected it to stay at 9.1 per cent for at least two years. Internally, the national power crisis, with promises of more shocks in water and transport infrastructure, had shaken investor confidence in the planning and maintenance capacity of the state and would undoubtedly have an impact on economic growth.

Mbeki had become even more erratic and inscrutable, firing good ministers and officials while protecting the worst. The levels of vitriol and abuse against his critics had increased, commensurate with the rising tide of public concern and distaste. Then he was ejected from his party power base and the country experienced a power vacuum, in which various organs of state went to public war against each other. The victor, ANC Classic, celebrated its accession to power by demanding closure of the one anti-corruption unit that was showing its mettle by pursuing suspected criminals right up to the top leadership of the party and the highest-ranking officer in the SAPS – this despite the fact that public opinion polls showed the country was 70 per cent in favour of retaining the elite unit.

The reason was not long in coming. Gwede Mantashe, newly appointed secretary general from ANC Classic, said the Scorpions had been infiltrated by 'former apartheid agents' intent on destroying the ANC elites. In fact, less than a sixth of the unit's members were former policemen and only a handful of these had anything to do with the old security police. The public could be forgiven for suspecting the real reason behind calls for closure was that the ANC elites were tired of being caught stealing and wanted to get rid of an inconvenience. By closing down the unit and handing such cases over to the SAPS and its ANC deployees, those opposed to the Scorpions no doubt felt assured of a more understanding audience.

Those with a more intimate knowledge of South Africa were bracing themselves for more shocks during 2008 in virtually all spheres of government: education, public health and food security. The skills crisis, now driven to the point of national emergency by government policy, was no longer academic: it confronted the citizens, the state and the business community at every step of the way. And the crime situation, despite some improvements in the most violent categories, continued to reap its usual grim harvest of the dead, dying, wounded and mentally scarred. In May 2008, rolling xenophobic violence across South Africa left scores dead and tens of thousands homeless. The violence was a direct result of Mbeki's failed regional and domestic policies, but the response was typical – inaction and the assertion that this was all the work of sinister right-wingers set on embarrassing Mbeki.

This combination of factors had turned investment attitudes from positive to lukewarm. By 2008, they were teetering on the edge of becoming cold. Money started to seep and then flow out of the country – R33 billion disinvested between Polokwane and Trevor Manuel's budget presentation in February 2008, although how much of this was part of a global trend of withdrawal from emerging markets, and how much South Africa specific, is hard to say. The risk premium assigned to South Africa by foreign investors had risen fourfold in a quarter, according to one investment manager index.[2]

Incoming funds slowed from the requisite R6 billion a month to cover the balance-of-payments deficit. By April it had swung back slightly, although it was a touch-and-go business. Standard & Poor's, the international rating agency, ranked South Africa the eleventh most-at-risk economy of forty emerging markets, largely because of the deficit on the balance of payments. This deficit began to swell to uncomfortable levels and then subsided slightly on the back of an export surge induced by a weaker rand. Still, whereas 70 per cent of the deficit was financed by portfolio flows in the good days, this had dropped to 13 per cent by the first quarter of 2008.

The currency weakened – a dramatic 20 per cent against the euro over eight weeks in early 2008 alone. Household debt had risen to 77 per cent of average annual income and debt servicing soaked up 12 per cent of private income. More rate hikes were in the offing. The impact on that mythical creature, the ordinary South African, was severe. Defaults on credit cards as a percentage of the book were up 50 per cent and on car finances 45 per cent between December 2006 and December 2007, although the year-on-year comparisons in default judgments still looked manageable, largely because the full impact of the rising interest rates, inflation and the credit legislation had not yet been fully brought to book.[3] But insolvencies had still risen 37 per cent for the three months ended January 2008 compared with the same period in the previous year. The January-on-January increase was 58.1 per cent. By February 2008, company liquidations had increased by 23.2 per cent and compulsory liquidations by 117.9 per cent as opposed to twelve months before. And there was no relief in sight.

Property prices stabilised and then began to drop as homeowners unloaded their properties on the back of rising interest rates, a credit squeeze, higher electricity charges and soaring municipal taxes imposed under the new rates regulations. Emigration was increasingly cited as the reason for sales: the First National Bank Residential Property Barometer showed this factor up from 9 per cent of sales in 2007 to 12 per cent in 2008. In high-net-worth households it rose from 13 per cent to 18 per cent. One in five of the South African elite was preparing to bail in Mbeki's ninth year in office, one survey showed.

There was some talk of recession, but many economists still believed the country's economic fundamentals were robust enough to prevent it. Yet the atmosphere was one of free fall: economic, social, political and, most serious of all, moral.

And so somewhere between the earliest and headiest days of the Mbeki tenure and the point when he stood, greying and sombre, to deliver his State of the Nation address in 2008, something profound had happened. That something, I would argue, was the beginning of the demodernisation of South Africa and its recasting into what East Europeans used to wryly call 'a newly under-developed state'.

Choose the moment when that happened. It could have been when the Mbeki Ascendancy refused to confront the arms scandal openly and went into defensive mode, with all its long consequential chain of dissimulation, deceit, crisis, dismissals and eventual schism. It could have been when the national capacity to fund and support the ambitious affirmative action objectives exhausted itself, but nobody really noticed or cared. Perhaps it was when the nation suddenly woke up to the fact that children from the poorest communities who were about to 'matriculate' were largely unable to read, write or add. Or might it have been when, at last, the country discovered it had only enough skilled people left to service a mid-sized US city?

Was it when the nation realised that one-third of its households were dependent on state handouts and that it had created the most expansive non-contributory welfare state in the developing world – *without the long-term capacity to fund it?* Or was it when most people decided that the small child killed by violent crime was one too many? Perhaps it was when the public learnt that some parliamentarians were defrauding the very chamber that was the repository of the nation's values and democracy, or when they learnt that directors-general and ministers were racing through revolving doors between public and private office, taking personal handfuls of cash for their own enrichment each time, often illegally.

Conceivably it was when the last ordinary South African rebelled against the last outstretched palm of a corrupt public official; when the last modern person was revolted by a president who retained a health minister who had allegedly once stolen from her patients; when the countless victims of crime rejected a president who had knowingly kept a police commissioner in office, despite the most damning evidence of corruption against him, collected by the country's most senior prosecutorial arm. Maybe it was simply when the lights went out in the national electricity emergency of 2008 and everybody suspected the country had finally missed the boat for a modern destination.

The answer, of course, is that it was a little of all of the above.

The Institute for Justice and Reconciliation is a reputable NGO which, since the inception of the South African democracy, has produced a Reconciliation Barometer that measures the extent to which the environment is supporting or hampering the cause of racial reconciliation.

The 2007 survey came out just as Mbeki was making his State of the Nation speech. Perhaps he had been given a preview of the report. Perhaps that accounted for his sombre tone. The report showed that every indicator of social and political confidence had gone negative compared to the same time a year before – in some cases, dramatically so.[4]

The greatest victims were the institutions of state: the presidency, parliament, political parties – all the bodies of representative government that had been born in such hope and had been so diminished over the years. These were the representatives of the majority of the people of the country – yet they were increasingly rejected. When it came to key indicators for public performance – service delivery – the declines in public confidence were even more marked.

Topping the list with a decline of more than 20 per cent compared to the previous year were transparency and accountability, correct appointments, cost of living, implementation of affirmative action, controlling inflation, reducing crime, narrowing the income gap, fighting corruption and retaining skilled people.

The net effect of all of this was that by 2007 the majority of South Africans indicated in the Reconciliation Barometer for the first time that they had more faith in religious institutions than in presidents, parties or governments. In this, of course, they were merely joining the majority of people on the rest of the continent, who had long since chosen to put their faith in God before their politicians and relied on the deities rather than their governments to make tomorrow happen. It is not by chance that Africans are the most religious and hopeful people in the world.

The Justice and Reconciliation findings were confirmed, if any verification was needed, by the South African Social Attitudes 2007 Survey by the Human Sciences Research Council. The survey, tracking attitudes from

1998 to 2007, showed a general rising public confidence and trust in public institutions from 1998 to 2005. Then there was a precipitous plunge.

Public trust in national government had risen from a factor of forty-seven in 1998 to sixty-nine in 2004. By 2007 it was fifty-two. Parliament peaked at sixty-five in 2004 and was at forty-six in 2007. Local government, at fifty-five in 2004, was at thirty-four in 2006. Political parties stood at forty-two in 2005 and at twenty-seven two years later. The police fell from forty-six to thirty-nine in the same period.

The churches, the Independent Electoral Commission, big business and the courts all retained or increased their trust levels during this period. Only two conclusions were possible. First, everything outside the control of the ANC mostly kept faith with its public; everything within the control of the ANC mostly lost faith. Second, the tip-over point correlated almost exactly with Mbeki's second term of office.

Does all this mounting evidence of arrested state formation, failing public confidence and political factionalism mean that South Africa's inevitable destination is a failed state? The answer is no, with the enormous caveat that, unless a sea change of attitudes occurs within the ANC and those who support it, the country's existing process of demodernisation will simply accelerate.

One of my former political science teachers, subsequently killed by apartheid agents, hated loose terminology, so let me hasten to define what I mean by demodernisation. It is the process whereby the key pillars that support the development of a modern state are weakened and the society begins a reversion to an earlier form of social, political or economic order. This collapse can come about through outside intervention, natural catastrophe or merely the slow erosion of the pillars themselves through neglect, criminality or unrestrained contestation.

What would be those pillars?

- first, a human infrastructure able to support the growth of an economy to a level where it can deliver material and incremental benefits to a broad mass of the society;
- second, a physical infrastructure built in tandem with the first pillar and able to achieve the same goals;
- third, a level of internal social cohesion whereby the component elements of the society may not like each other but are prepared to work together for the broader good;
- fourth, a public trust in institutions; and

- fifth, a public trust in leadership, at least to the point where people believe that even if that leadership is sometimes wrong, even incredibly wrong, it is still acting in good faith and transparently.

If all or most of these pillars are in place, the country can see generally positive progress towards the virtuous circle of higher economic growth rates, more efficient distribution of benefits and growing social harmony. Intrinsic to this healthy macro-economic status are a few vital indicators. Debt, both public and private, must be in check; inflation controlled; balance of payments of an order that they are coverable by inflows; the currency reasonably stable; and the cost of money proportional to investment returns. With all this in place, any nation can expect growing fixed direct investment and yet another step change in national prosperity.

This does not imply that all the elements need to be in place simultaneously. But it does mean that they must at least be moving forward in terms of an identifiable objective, and that no one pillar is being reinforced through policies that weaken another.

I will argue that each of these pillars is now under pressure, and the next years will be decisive in deciding whether South Africa survives as a growing and competitive country or continues its retreat from modernity, increasingly uncompetitive even with a number of the players on its own continent. From a position in which there was a comparatively harmonious constellation of factors that created a general forward impulsion during South Africa's modern decade, there is now material disharmony between policies and players. This has led to a slowing of progress and, in some areas, stagnation and regression. The state response has been to increase the activity (conferences, strategic papers, speeches) while falling short on the action (outcomes).

Worse, it has resorted to the tiresome belief so beloved of the old apartheid regime: that if only all this could be *explained* to everybody, they would immediately understand. Thus the ANC under the Mbeki administration has created a range of promotional bodies dedicated to carrying a message of hope and resolution to the world through the simple expedient of excising all the bad news. Needless to say, it has not worked.

The $35 billion in reserves that Manuel hoarded until 2008 was a significant achievement. But he knows that the country faces a severe disconnect in the relationship between its macro-economic form and its real-economy substance. Wisely, he warned the country to brace for difficult times.

The reality is that vital economic drivers at play in South Africa are going the wrong way. Hopes that the country's inflation rates will fall back into the initial targeted band within a year or so are delusional. How can inflation subside, even in the medium term, when oil prices have entrenched themselves at historic highs, food prices will continue to rise on the back of biofuel-induced shortages and changed Asian consumption patterns, internal inflation will be driven by the high costs of labour (compounded by affirmative action, emigration and the demands of the massive infra-structural development programme) and administered costs are set for quantum leaps because of neglect by the government to maintain and expand the country's hard-service platform over a decade and a half? A careful analysis of South Africa's inflation components shows that even if one strips out fuel and food, core inflation is materially growing.

Growth rates are falling back from recent historic highs of 5 per cent plus as the impact of the energy crisis and the slowdown in the short-term credit-led consumer boom begins to bite. Whether they can recover in the medium term to the good-time highs is a moot point, but even if they do growth will be nowhere near the 6 per cent benchmark set by the government's own economic experts as the very minimum needed to reach the millennium goals for poverty reduction by 2014.

Unemployment rates fell in early 2008 to the lowest level in eight years (down from 25.3 per cent in September 2006 to 23 per cent in September 2007), but this was largely driven by a surge of domestic workers being taken on by the new black middle classes and a jump in community workers – this last partly associated with an increase in police and nursing recruit-ment. But this could only be short term. Sadly, it did not translate to an increase in the labour participation rate in the economy. This rate fell from 57.3 per cent in September 2006 to 56.6 per cent a year later.

With the slowdown in the economy post-2008 must come increased levels of unemployment. The mining sector, deeply sensitive to cost vari-ations, was already beginning its retrenchment programmes in early 2008, and the withholding of power sources by Eskom for new projects prom-ised even more job losses in the construction, tourism and manufacturing sectors.

Agricultural employment, which has shown no growth since 2001, has been affected as the small, labour-intensive farms are driven to the wall by both economic and ideological pressures in favour of the major agribusinesses, which already employ 78 per cent of agricultural labour.

Ironically, this may be the area of greatest employment growth in the short term, despite state failures in the land-reform programme, as agribusiness scrambles to catch up with the global food price bonanza sparked by Asian consumption. Generally, however, with the skills crisis deepening and incapable of resolution in the short term, the job creation potential of the infrastructural programmes, punted by the government as the short-term answer to unemployment, must thus be questioned.

In this condition of high inflation, lower growth and a short-term deepening of unemployment, the state is forced back on what it has already used extensively – populist relief spending. Here is the rub. With the government incurring mounting debt to finance its urgent capital infrastructural development, the savings that have been made in government debt financing over the last decade of prudent fiscal management will diminish. But it is these savings, created by lower debt, that have been used to finance the Mbeki dependency society – South Africa's finance minister has warned of this many times.

No rocket science is needed to complete the equation. Falling growth plus rising debt-financing costs equals reduced state social spend – unless the post-Mbeki state chooses to ignore all the most elemental rules and pushes for massive state consumption spending, and damn the debt. Reduced social spending increases internal disequilibrium. The very basis of South Africa's leap to modernity in the last decade of the twentieth century and the first years of the twenty-first is challenged. Demodernisation looms.

But to determine a process of demodernisation there must be two things: a previous state of modernity from which one retreats and a new state of pre-modernity towards which one declines.

I have sought to demonstrate in earlier chapters that South Africa's era of real modernity probably began with the political liberation of all its people, the adoption of a modern constitution with its heavy emphasis on human and environmental rights and, finally, the tabling of an economic and social policy by the ANC, which balanced the needs of a growing economy with the obligations to tackle the unacceptable disparities in wealth, income and opportunity between sections of the society.

In these years the checks and balances of the infant state were more or less applied and the democratic project was sufficiently advanced to record rising levels of public compliance and respect for institutions and leadership – itself a remarkable achievement, given the deep historic divides in the country and the fragility of the institutions.

It would also be that brief moment in time when the country disposed of the skills, resolve and resources to match its rhetoric with effective action. The electrification of millions of homes and the provision of telephones to millions more was achieved before the ANC government and the parastatals had wound down the technical resources of the state and local authorities through a combination of ignorance and ideology. There was thus both the will and the capacity to ensure delivery of social good on a fairly wide scale.

In terms of time, this would be the period stretching from the release of Mandela and the legalising of the ANC to roughly the end of Mbeki's first term in office in 2004 – in other words, the period from conceptualisation of South Africa's programme of modernisation, its negotiation, implementation and first fruits. That era, subject to what the future holds, may yet be remembered as the high water mark of the modern and free South African state in the first decades of the twenty-first century.

Thereafter, as the public attitudinal surveys show, the country moved onto a path of declining trust and confidence stemming from the Mbeki administration's style of governance and leadership (or lack of it) and the first impacts of earlier errant policy decisions, some dating back a decade.

What would the demodernised version of South Africa look like?

It would be a reversion to a state in which a small and self-electing elite would hold all effective political and economic power, no matter what clever devices are erected to hide it. The state would be an arm of the party and the primary source of wealth accretion by the elites. It would be corrupt and self-serving and, increasingly, the real work would be done by expatriates.

Income inequalities between rich and poor would deepen, not lessen, and the country would be in a permanent state of political and social instability between urban and rural communities, classes, ethnic and tribal groups, locals and foreigners, and rent-seeking factions. The economy would limp along with suboptimal growth rates. The private sector would be subject to endlessly predatory incursions by the politically connected to acquire equity or opportunity, coupled with massive corruption of state agencies.

Talented young South Africans, black and white, would leave in huge numbers for better opportunities abroad. In this regard, South Africa would be no different from the rest of the continent, which has seen legions of its best and its brightest living abroad, not because they want to, but because as modern and moral beings, they simply cannot tolerate the incompetence, corruption and despotic style of their ruling elites at home. South Africa's high-level skills base would shrink to a handful of native-born citizens, complemented by a number of expatriates. Foreign capital would be either short term and adventurist or tied up in ruinously prejudicial terms. Increasingly, the country would revert to being a primary commodities producer and the entire state would limp along with inadequate infrastructure, held together by endless patching, pinching and prodding.

With this as backdrop, it would be small wonder that South Africa would lose its pre-eminence as the continent's most modern country to peers such as Nigeria and Kenya in the medium term, Angola and the Democratic Republic of Congo in the longer term. The country would consequently no longer speak with its current unique authority on behalf of the African continent: that golden moment, too, would have slipped away. In this scenario, South Africa would become marginalised, patronised and dismissed by the developed world.

If this picture looks vaguely familiar, it should. It is a composite of what the old apartheid state looked like, contains elements of what the current state looks like and, finally, includes chunks of what it could look like in the future. But – and this is the crucial point – it is *not* what South Africa is now, *nor need it become.*

South Africa is not comprehensively dysfunctional, and there are indeed positives in the current scenario.

The first is that South Africa still has a strong and resilient economy. The Heritage Foundation's Index of Economic Freedom for 2008 is a useful guide. Every year the foundation assesses all the countries in the world in terms of ten variables and then comes to a judgement as to how economically free they are. The ten variables or 'freedoms' are business, trade, fiscal, government size, monetary, investment, financial, property, freedom from corruption, and labour.

In 1995, the second year of ANC rule, South Africa was ranked at forty-four. In 2008, it was at fifty-seven in a larger number of assessed countries. It was the difference between being with Italy and Greece then, Albania, Bulgaria and Jordan now. Yet the country *had* shown an improvement in most of the freedoms.

Most importantly, the survey indicated that South Africa had made progress in a number of areas of its economic liberalisation programme and, at an overall measure of 63.2 per cent, it can be considered a reasonably competitive country with a largely benign investment and regulatory regime. Indeed, given the inevitable tumult of a major political and social change, compounded by some appalling policies, it has stood up remarkably well against the index.

But the assessment also sent some serious warnings. Government regulatory conditions have worsened, not improved, the country's business-freedom index. Here, inevitably, constantly changing regulations that seek to put more power back in the hands of the government or advance its redistributive programme are an issue. Because of that, investment is not where it could or should be – it is grouped with the likes of Albania and Costa Rica instead of the next band of Singapore, Australia, Chile, Israel, Jamaica and Germany.

Prudent macro-economic management has ensured the country is sitting with material reserves which can, in the finance minister's meteorological idiom, weather the storm created in the short term by international turbulence. The government's debt-servicing burden fell from 23 per cent of GDP in 1995 (the apartheid legacy) to 12 per cent in 2007. The ratio of government debt to GDP is a relatively modest 30 per cent.

And even worrying factors like the deficit on the current account of the balance of payments can, in the great swings and roundabouts that is world economics, be offset by the steeply rising exports suddenly made more competitive by a weakening rand. In short, by the beginning of 2008, South Africa was better off in terms of its currency, GDP growth, inflation and reserves than it had been in the hairy days of 2001. There was also still a lot of private and state infrastructure spend in the wings between 2008 and 2010 – if only the skills were available to properly deploy it.

The second positive is that, unlike some of the seriously conflict-ridden societies in the world, there is still a remarkable degree of agreement among South Africans about the desirability of creating a single, inclusive society, albeit one with its continuing deeply contoured cultural differences. This is a precious commodity that has, to a large extent, survived even the divisiveness of the Mbeki tenure, although towards the end there were increasing examples of interracial exasperation, often precipitated by a relatively minor incident – an attempt to impose racial quotas on the national cricket team; four idiotic young Afrikaner university students humiliating black women cleaning staff in a mock initiation ceremony; a surpassingly insensitive piece written by a conservative white newspaper columnist.

Finally, technology might yet create the small gap needed by South

Africa to make a step change in its prospects. Cheap electricity was for decades the differentiator in South Africa's bid for industrial investment. That is gone – snuffed out by the Mbeki state's inability to maintain and sustain its power-generation platform, which now has to be replaced by the massive deployment of state subsidy in order to be revived.

A highly productive commercial agriculture sector for decades held out the opportunity of relative food security as a key differentiator in post-liberation South Africa. The Mbeki state's grotesquely bungled agricultural reform programme has now put that on the critical list, but a recovery is possible through the improvements in crop yields thanks to genetically modified crops – provided the ethical and environmental issues are dealt with.

There is also the imminent expansion of cost-effective broadband internet through new underwater cable and a roll-out of a new digital communications platform within South Africa. The first opportunity was not brought by the state – it was brought by resolute private players *despite* the state and all its delays and demands for the enrichment of local players. But it was, ultimately, brought. The second opportunity is within the remit of the state, which has been trapped for years in the web of enrichment, bureaucracy, delay and confusion that has become the natural character of public organisation in South Africa. These opportunities offer a chance for the growth of a whole range of new high-value businesses.

There is another potential positive. The Mbeki era, no matter what its successes in redistributing wealth and opportunity, failed to build a unanimity of objectives, let alone tactics, between the three columns of the modern state: government, business and labour. The consequence was a rolling series of conflicts between the state and the unions, culminating in the public service strike of 2007 and collateral damage to private sector–union relations. The removal of the Mbeki Ascendancy from the equation does hold out the hope, faint though it may be, of a return to some sort of normality in the relationship. After all, the country was doing pretty well in getting to know itself before the Mbeki Ascendancy arrived with all its imported airs, demands and angst.

This proposition will no doubt be tested to the utmost in the coming years as the unions seek to make up for comparatively nominal wage increases over a period of time by demanding inflationary increases going forward – the Polokwane dividend. The unions are themselves very vulnerable, despite crowing a pyrrhic victory at the December 2007 conference. The reality is that they have been losing members in all sectors except the public service, which has grown in both numbers and in confidence, the latter served by a sense that low-hanging fruit is there for the picking from a cowered, ineffectual and divided state employer.

ANC Classic purports to represent the working people of this country. If so, what better challenge can be put to it than to persuade members to focus on the central task of creating a dedicated, hard-working, committed, professional and honest cadre of storm troopers serving a modern, successful and effective state machine?

The exit of the Mbeki Ascendancy has also triggered a resurgent independence and vigour in the once supine ANC-dominated legislature. That is to the good. Whether it is a short-term bloodletting by ANC Classic against Mbeki's ministers, as appears the case, or a genuine change of institutional culture remains to be seen – but at least it is there.

There is a final positive. The ANC is attempting to row back from some of its more egregious policy failings – belatedly, perhaps desperately belatedly, but at least it is happening.

The emphasis on preventative policing has now swung back to restoring the obliterated detective capacity. In April 2008, the minister of health announced a R2 billion refurbishment of major state hospitals that had been allowed to decay while state resources went to create rural preventative medicine centres.

The Department of Land Affairs announced in 2007 that the focus of land reform will henceforth be on productive usage of land and job creation rather than quota-based land transfers. In public education a 'Foundations of Learning' programme is attempting to rectify some of the mischief caused by outcomes-based education and there is talk of re-establishing the old teachers' training colleges to produce solid nuts-and-bolts educators.

The Public Service Commission warns of the dangers of unrestrained race-based appointments and Eskom, exemplar of just about everything that can go wrong when inexperienced ideologues gain control of a major utility, is wrenched back on track by brutal reality. Only in the housing arena do we await a recantation of the government's ideological position, insisting on expensive formal housing provision rather than relying on the explosive innovativeness of informal settlements.

And yet, positive as all this may be, there still remains the dangerous overhang of ideological overreach.

The South African parliament entered its session in 2008 with more than ninety pieces of legislation, a limited number of which had any chance of being effectively implemented. The reality is that the country is groaning under a weight of legislation that it cannot currently apply – and yet by early 2008 there were promises of even more regulations and requirements, from testing vehicles for roadworthiness every two years to introducing additional regulatory requirements for listed companies.

This legislative overreach has been a feature of the Mbeki tenure. He is the father of the grand design and the unfulfilled hope. Now that he has lost control of the party, the offspring continue this dangerous tradition. The parliamentary legislative programme for the first post-Polokwane session was an uncomfortable mishmash of hope, expedience, naïveté and make-work. Some, not all, of the proposed laws would add to the burden of ill-considered measures that will remain a millstone around the neck of Mbeki's successor.

But there is a more disturbing component to all of this: the clear intention of the ANC state to address failed and implausible policy with costly, illusory and wrong remedies. A few examples suffice.

An earlier chapter on health demonstrated how the government's failure in the management of the public health system has driven millions into the private health system, where they should never have been in the first place – even the state sends its lower-level workers to private hospitals. Here they face the high costs of the system, much of this itself the consequence of another failure by the state – to produce and retain trainable, professional and cost-efficient health professionals.

Instead of addressing the core issue – the failure of public health systems – the government instead seeks to expand its remit of incompetence into the private health system. As this system is primarily a contractual relationship between private citizens and private companies, it should theoretically have nothing to do with the state. But in early 2008, the state moved to introduce what amounts to price controls on private medical care rather than using its enormous arsenal of powers, through competition and other regulations, to manage what might be considered exploitative and abusive trading practices in the sector.

Indeed, the minister of health chose to devote almost her entire budget speech in 2008 to the private medical-care system, in which she should have the least interest, rather than deal with the manifold failures of the state system, in which her interest should be paramount.

The second example relates to food security. The effect of the failed agricultural reform programme has been to threaten small commercial farmers in favour of large agribusinesses, drive down long-term investment in the sector and deliver stagnant agricultural productivity for more than five years, as tracked by the UN Food and Agriculture Organisation.

The core problems have been tediously identified in collapsed scheme after scheme: bureaucratic delays, lack of extension and financing support, the weakness of the cooperative and syndicate systems that take over the farms, the unwillingness of beneficiaries to actually farm the land, corruption, sloth and incompetence.

Rather than facing up to the problems, the state now proposes to genuflect towards the skills issue by bringing in 'mentors' – read 'white commercial farmers' – and jacking up support systems. But it remains committed to demonstrably failed communal ownership models for the farms and the acquisition of land that it cannot afford at market prices. Worse, it retains a utopian view that large numbers of poor black people just cannot wait to get their own piece of land so as to be able to toil from sunup to sundown for a pittance. They aren't and they won't. This view, in fact, is the nearest parallel to the old colonialist stereotype of the 'happy native'.

Instead of admitting the faulty premises on which the policy is based and looking at other more creative options such as leasing the land from white commercial farmers on behalf of trained black commercial farmers and then assisting them to buy the land over time, the government intends expropriating commercial and productive land at less than market value, something that might require an amendment to one of the founding principles of the 1996 constitution and will certainly threaten food security.

Another example of this grafting of hopeless remedies on failed policies is to be found in the towns and cities. The biggest problem confronting the government here is mismanagement and the debt for services incurred by municipalities that they cannot or will not collect from residents. Instead of dealing with the problem at source, something that requires political will, systems and perseverance, they instead change the rates formula. The short-term benefit will be a huge surge in revenue for local authorities to offset their debts. The long-term effect of these increases on commercial property will be a turbocharged level of national inflation, while it will also lead to a decline in residential property prices. With the current state of high indebtedness of the society, particularly the black middle class, the inevitable end result will be more negative equity, foreclosures and severe political consequences. As these rates are now also to be rolled out to agricultural land, expect more wholesale destruction of the small farmer and higher unemployment in the agricultural sector.

A last example suffices. Earlier chapters highlighted the major disparity between per capita input for social services relative to output. On international scales and measured against peers, the disparities are in some cases ludicrous. The key reason for this, I have argued, is the failure of the ANC government and the Mbeki state to create a professional service culture. *That* is where the problem begins and largely ends. Instead of dealing with the issue, the government continues pumping resources down this very leaky pipe. The result is diminishing returns and frustrated expectations. Nobody in the ANC has had the courage to stand up and say to its union partners: you cannot have service delivery to the poor *and* the very low levels of professionalism protected by you through your public union membership. Make the choice.

These examples were chosen at random from many possible candidates to make a few introductory and cautionary points about the current state of the country. The ANC government – whether Classic or Lite – has not made a fundamental shift of mindset in regard to its policy making. It remains committed to ideological outcomes and is quite prepared to compound the consequences of bad decisions by imposing even worse remedies. The unintended consequence, like a virus in a complex IT system, thus simply rolls forward, transmuting itself into ever worse outcomes.

In forcing reality to fit ideology, the ANC is prepared to venture ever further from what it incessantly claims are its market-based fundamentals. These include the introduction of regulatory price determination in private-sector enterprise, prescriptive shareholdings for international entities and the expropriation of privately held property in contravention of one of the base elements of the country's consensual founding constitution. All this points in the direction of centralism and away from free markets. It is all a mindset of demodernisation.

The ANC's almost knee-jerk response to policy failure is: if it ain't working, drown it in money. That, at its heart, may be the defining weakness of the ANC and Mbeki in power: an extraordinary capacity for spending money on the short term, the ideological and the populist and the inability to establish the conditions for long-term wealth creation, retention and equitable dispersion.

All of these elements, this thoughtless expedience, are so deeply ingrained in the ANC way of doing business – business unusual – that it will be an extremely difficult mission for any new leadership to change course. This is particularly so with a notably divided party and in conditions of a deteriorating economy marked by declining growth rates, rising inflation and swelling unemployment. It is not an enviable position for the ANC and it is only the malicious who would find any satisfaction in it.

In the chapters that follow, I will address each of the key pillars needed to reverse South Africa's incipient demodernisation and propose a possible way forward that surrenders none of the gains made by the democratic state but confronts the grave challenges that have arisen from bad policies, bad implementation or simply bad attitudes. I do so with all due caution and humility, aware that despite repeated calls by the ANC for white South Africans to propose creative alternatives, those who do are too often reviled as being racist, destructive, anti-patriotic, anti-poor or nostalgic for apartheid. Still, it is a country for which it is worth taking the risk.

CHAPTER 19

The balancing act

To be conscious you are ignorant is a great step to knowledge.
— BENJAMIN DISRAELI[1]

THE SOUTH AFRICAN STORY IN THE FIRST DECADES OF THE twenty-first century will essentially begin and end with one word – skills. Everything that has faltered since the advent of the ANC to power has been because of the country's inability to retain, find, nurture and grow its skills base. Because of this, it has failed and continues to fail in effectively serving the expansive social platforms and modern expectations it has created.

The term *skills* needs to be defined in its broadest sense of information, knowledge, experience, application and culture. This is not simply a process of teaching someone how to make something happen, but of inculcating the attitudes and habits that make it possible to keep making it happen. Information is easy to transfer. Understanding the context within which it can be used on a sustainable basis is far more complex.

The country's high crime rates are a consequence of skills shortages in the police and justice chain. The ailing public education and health systems are similarly afflicted. The inability to support the physical infrastructure is related to a skills crisis. The capacity to expand that infrastructure is haunted by it. Financial administration of the state, documentation of citizens, expansion of agricultural potential and the attraction of appropriate levels of investment all depend on one thing: skills.

Mercifully, South Africa has moved beyond the treasonous assertion by some of the leading empowerment beneficiaries that the skills shortage is an urban myth, a patently self-serving proposition designed to maintain an artificial shortage of skilled labour to drive up the price of affirmative posts. It was the oldest trick in the book, but the country now seems firmly apprised of the fact that at least a decade of hard work lies ahead to rebuild the state's weakened mass educational systems and its failed skills-development programmes.

In March 2008, a report on three hundred privately held companies made it official: the shortage of skills was now the single greatest constraining factor to business growth in South Africa.[2] In the same month, a listed South African company formally attributed its drop in earnings to the loss of high-level staff who were emigrating to escape crime. It was a first. In its inaugural National Scarce Skills Master List released in April 2008, meanwhile, the Department of Labour gave the cheering news that the country was short of 420 chief executives and managing directors; 13 525 general managers; 3 570 engineering managers and 6 675 information and communications technology managers. This was widely held to be a grievous understatement of the real situation.

What are the country's immediate needs in its skills programme?

The first is a consistent and higher-volume output of pupils from public secondary schools with the requisite literacy, science, maths, business science and business culture skills. The government's attempts to meet its 50 000-a-year target for science and maths graduates has failed for a single reason – refusal to let go its delusional ideological position that the whole failed educational system can be uplifted simultaneously. Thus it begins with a pilot project to upgrade science and maths marks in nineteen schools, and when that shows signs of working, it expands to 529 schools – and then wonders why the project yields diminishing returns as the finite pool of effective teaching skills is diluted, proportionate to the growing number of pupils.

The Khutsong model offers a solution. It derives its name from the remarkable successes achieved by the North West provincial education department, which took 173 struggling matric pupils from stressed communities in 2007 and achieved a 73 per cent pass rate through concentrated instruction in a boarding-school environment. The state should identify the best and the brightest in its public school system and place them in stand-alone, high-quality secondary educational facilities where they can be boarded, instructed by the best available talent (importing teaching resources, preferably from African or Asian countries, if necessary) and primed to pass meaningful examinations that deliver substantive outputs. Khutsong has proved what everybody knew: talent is not the issue – a failed home and school environment is.

The target should be 50 000 graduates a year, increasing to 100 000 in three years and 150 000 in the fifth year in each of the disciplines – a sixfold increase in current output. Thereafter, it must increase by at least

20 per cent a year for five years. It is not a cheap option, but it is certainly more cost-efficient than the numerous broad-based upgrade schemes that have so uniformly failed. The cost of producing qualified and capable graduates through this system would be less than that currently incurred by producing large numbers of under-qualified people who fail repeatedly at the tertiary level.

The scheme is doable and affordable and very, very urgent. All that stands in the way of unblocking this essential channel for high-level skills is the lack of political will. Given the crisis, it would probably be advisable to start these 'apex' schools immediately with the current crop of matriculants and Grade 11 pupils. They could be undergoing post-matric training by 2010. The rest could be phased in retrospectively until a full five years of tuition was offered in these institutions. The first crop of fully educated graduates would thus come on stream in 2014, which is about when the government's current 'foundation of learning' scheme is mooted to produce its first results.

But well-educated secondary school graduates are not going to go anywhere if they are denied further appropriate avenues of development. This is where the whole elaborate, confused, bureaucratic and self-destructive skills-development project needs to be scrapped in its entirety and all its sinecured servants retired as soon as possible. Mbeki, fond of English quotations, would be wise to invoke Oliver Cromwell's address to England's Rump Parliament in 1653: 'You have sat too long here for any good you have been doing. Depart, I say, and let us have done with you.'

What South Africa needs is short-term, practical bridging qualifications for graduates of its public education system in both the business sciences and technical arenas. In short, those graduates should be able to qualify for bursaries to obtain basic *practical* post-matric qualifications, enough at least to get them into reasonable employment, where they can later improve their qualifications to the highest level through existing professional bodies and institutions on a part-time basis.

The most important thing is to move them from the academic environment into the working arena as quickly as possible. One of the most debilitating features of the current situation is what can be called the culture of permanent tutelage. Because of the poor quality of instruction in our secondary and some tertiary institutions, many young South Africans are entering employment not as productive elements of those operational environments, but as ill-equipped bystanders and photocopier minders.

Locked into a process of almost permanent instruction courses, upgrade programmes, training, mentorship and sabbaticals, they become distant from the *job* and slaves to the *training* – thus the endless demands for more and more training, with ever-diminishing results, the bane of every South African business. Worse, they become regarded in the workplace as perennial students, unworthy of being entrusted with anything serious. Not having proper responsibilities, the employee enters another round of insecurity and dependency. And so the cycle goes, sometimes for years.

Two-year intensive post-matric courses with very high levels of practical content will help counter this culture of permanent tutelage. After graduating from an apex school, or from any other school, and having passed through the intensive post-matric training courses, the successful graduate will be in an entirely different position from the current candidate who emerges from a shaky secondary school environment and a dodgy 'learnership' to end up frustrated and sidelined – or worse, unemployable.

But there are a few vital ingredients in this mix. Without them, the system will collapse back into its current state of inertia, confusion and failure. The most vital ingredient is *simplicity*. That means the academics and bureaucrats need to take a back seat and the technicians and business people need to step forward.

The bridging qualifications must be basic in content and limited in numbers. I cannot imagine more than ten base courses being needed, sufficient to head-start the next generation of artisans, farmers, engineers, nurses, accountants, technicians and professionals into meaningful employment from which they can gain experience, contribute to the employer and start the process of longer-term upgrading of their skills *in situ* if that is required or what they desire.

Encouragingly, much of this is already the basis of the government's Further Education and Training (FET) colleges, products of the Joint Initiative on Priority Skills Acquisition (JIPSA) project. Of its first graduates in 2008, from eleven new vocational programmes, one-third dropped out and only half the rest passed. The results show the dreadful impact of failed state secondary education, decimated teaching skills and learner irresponsibility – but it is a start.

This is where the role of the private sector becomes important. The current SETA system has placed a labyrinth between the requirements of the employer and the acquisition of the employee. Both parties have suffered. In some cases, like the regional master-builder associations in a number of provinces, the industry has set up training centres at its own cost to produce the desperately needed artisan skills for the booming industry that the accredited education and training authority cannot. The duplication of costs and the pressure on scarce training resources can be imagined.

The SETAs should be scrapped when their terms expire and they should be replaced by the old industry sector training authorities. The relationship in these bodies should be directly between the employer associations and the training institution in regard to the skills that are required. Who better, after all, to determine the skills need of a growing economy than those people in direct interface with the demands of the market? All other parties have value only if they bring cash or have technical expertise.

Employers would need to be levied a basic fee (not a percentage of payroll) to cover the training council's fixed costs and make an additional per capita contribution to the training of each individual they subsequently employ or send for training. Ideally, the sectors should arrange job markets on an annual basis to allow businesses to recruit candidates from school and undertake to pay the cost of their tuition, subject to the necessary contractual relationships and terms being established. The risk, as always, is of breach of contract, but that already happens to a great degree because of the skills crisis.

So who would run this enterprise?

Clusters of government ministries do not work. They never have and never will, for the simple reason that departments have an organic life of their own and rarely like collaborating. They are not fusible amoeba. If one wants proof of that, it is worth reading the comments of Shaun Liebenberg, the outgoing chief executive officer of South Africa's Denel armaments company. Liebenberg had been brought in to rescue the state-owned manufacturer after it had plunged from being the fourteenth-largest arms manufacturer in the world to near bankruptcy under the stewardship of ANC deployees. He warned about the lack of 'horizontal stakeholder' buy-in and recounted the lack of communication between all state departments involved in the business. It was to be a common theme under Mbeki's 'technocratic' leadership.

If the government is determined to address its middle- to long-range skills crisis, it has to treat it like a crisis. The Joint Initiative on Priority Skills Acquisition, set up in 2006, has made some progress in this field. It set itself modest targets – to increase the output of engineers from 1 400 a year to 2 400, with a cumulative target of 12 000 by 2010, and to bump artisans from 5000 a year to 12 500 a year, up to a cumulative 40 000 by 2010. These targets in and of themselves greatly understate the real needs of the country if it hopes to support a 6 per cent growth rate, but they are a start.

Despite some fine features and a measure of real momentum, the programme has a problem in that it is just what it proclaims to be – an emergency measure aimed at priority skills acquisition. It does not have a seamless skills-development trajectory anchored in the state schools, running through bridging tuition into internships in industry and on to skills upgrade *on a broad front*.

JIPSA does commit itself to addressing the 'mismatch' between the products of tertiary education and the expectations of employers. This is exactly where a combination of a post-matric practical bridging qualification and a structured internship programme within employing entities could work. These are crucial moves towards helping nurture more skilled and confident young people to take the daunting first steps in the private sector (or on the way to an entrepreneurial career).

One of the most interesting things to emerge from the JIPSA process, however, is the beginning of some very effective private- and public-sector cooperation in skills development. This, of course, belies the claim that the private sector is intrinsically hostile to skills development. It is not. But it has little truck with monstrously bureaucratic and misdirected ventures like the SETAs.

It is necessary to create a new department of national skills development with a lifespan of exactly ten years. It should be staffed by professionals, imported if necessary, and its head should report directly to the presidency. The function of apex schools and training institutions, along with management of the certification for short-term training qualifications, should be lifted out of the existing, failing departments and managed autonomously. This department would certify certain institutions to run the short-term courses or, if the sector agrees, industry colleges could be set up.

The programme would have its own budget voted by parliament and partly subsidised by reductions in the budgets of the existing departments of education and labour. Once functioning and delivering, it is a certainty that it will attract large amounts of private and donor support here and abroad, which over time would help relieve funding pressures. The staff who run the special schools, technical programmes and certification processes would not be part of the national teacher cadre, would be recruited separately according to strict criteria of excellence, would stand outside existing terms and conditions negotiated with unions and would function according to a charter of performance excellence.

This corps of instructors would not need to be trained, thus obviating the huge diversion of energy and time currently spent in the national and provincial education departments as they attempt to bring the mass of educators to the level where they can at least do the jobs for which they are paid. The apex school instructors would instead be able to give their full attention to teaching their wards.

The recruitment process for teachers would be undertaken by a commission of external and independent experts, who would focus exclusively on teaching competence. There would be no role played by government, the private sector, parents or unions. The presidency would have the final say on the selection criteria and delegate responsibility to the commission to ensure they are met. Ideally, existing teaching staff should be given the opportunity to apply, but if the complement cannot be met, the balance would be recruited externally.

The programme would run according to very strict and narrowly defined objectives relating entirely to quality of output. Again, as these instructors would be assumed competent to begin with, there would be no need to set endless targets for their training and upgrade, which so dominate current departmental functions. Benchmarks would have to be met every year and the teaching staff incentivised to reach them. At the end of ten years, the programme would be wound down and the schools and training colleges returned to the various education departments and the labour department respectively.

By that time, the country would have produced 1 745 000 competently trained artisans, professionals and technicians and the nation's long-term growth prospects could be assured. By that time, also, one would hope that the national educational system would have been able to pull itself back into some sort of productive order.

Now, the foregoing is complete and utter anathema to just about every party with a vested interest in the current chaos. The bureaucrats will oppose it because it means losing control; the teachers will resist because it will highlight their incompetence; unions will complain because it reduces their role; and the academics will shout because it puts power back in the hands of the practitioners. The scheme, it will be claimed, is elitist, exclusivist, authoritarian and content based. Exactly. It is a crisis response, an emergency fast-tracking of the essential skills required by the country while the fixing of the rest of the educational system takes its ponderous, generational course. South Africa has tried the other way and it has landed the country in an awful mess.

There is, however, a more legitimate concern. This scheme would suck out approximately 10 000 of the best teachers from the system in the first year, growing to approximately 40 000 in the final year. This would be a major burden on the balance of the educational system, which would still be battling along to improve educational levels for those who do not qualify for the apex schools, producing, as it currently does, the next generation of the unemployable. The impact could be partly ameliorated by importing teachers and better use of teaching aids in the apex schools. It would most certainly be lessened by dumping the preposterously ambitious outcomes-based education 'statement' in public schools and reinstating basic disciplines that teachers can teach and pupils can grasp. This, in fact, is already happening as the education authorities reimpose a 'foundations of learning' programme, which, if it was honest, the department would have branded 'back to basics'. But, it is true, there may be some fall-off in the output from the national and provincial education systems. This is a risk that would have to be taken to kick-start the national skills revolution. After all, how much worse can it get?

The above proposal addresses the medium- to long-term issue of the skills crisis. What about the short term? The critical immediate requirement for the country is the identification, recruitment, retention and growth of high-level skills. All else is secondary.

The national educational systems cannot produce sufficient graduates to support the government's target growth rates. Ironically, the slowdown in economic growth caused by a multiplicity of reasons may be a blessing in disguise. It may create breathing space for the country to reorganise.

There is a limited stopgap opportunity for skills importation. But it is not the cavalry over the hill. Talented people will not be attracted here in the short term and skilled native-born South Africans will not be persuaded to remain in the long term unless a host of other unrelated issues are dealt with – security, cost of education, career progression and so on.

The seriousness of the situation was captured by a 2007 international survey of countries most likely to attract high-end skills. South Africa came last of the thirty countries surveyed, behind Nigeria, Ukraine and Iran. Without the ability to pay the very high expatriate earnings and benefits of these countries and without an adequate support structure in terms of education, health and security, South Africa pulled the short straw.[3]

The Home Affairs Department's 35 200 vacant posts for 'critical foreigners' attracted precisely 1 123 foreigners in 2007, despite a major marketing effort. Considering all other forms of permits, no more than 5 000 foreigners were lured to South Africa. If the country wishes to solve this crisis, it will have to be done internally.

This goes directly to the heart of the government's affirmative action programme, arguably the most sensitive in the national discourse, redolent as it is with notions of equity, restitution, fairness, opportunity and the future. This is understandable. The topic certainly deserves to be treated with more respect than has currently been shown by the opportunists and ideologues who have seized it for personal enrichment.

But there is a compelling reality: successful countries are created when people are involved in managing the future, not the past. There is a rational limit to how far one can use subvention to advance one group or another without damaging the very basis for the future prosperity of the country as a whole.

Eskom and the country's municipalities followed a determined policy of affirmative action for more than a decade, regardless of its effect on the operational efficiency of services. The consequences contributed to an avoidable national energy crisis that will most certainly result in thousands of lost jobs and a slowdown in both fixed foreign investment and GDP growth. In early 2008, Eskom was hiring seventy-year-old retired white engineers to come back and help out, and inviting 561 white technical candidates for interviews from a list provided by the extreme right-wing political party. This was undoubtedly expedient, but should never have been necessary. It was humiliating for Eskom and ultimately an embarrassment to the whole affirmative action project. It proved exactly why such delicate social engineering projects should be managed technically, not ideologically.

The argument is not that affirmative action or empowerment is not necessary. It is very necessary. But the Eskom case illustrates the dangers of allowing the process to run away from reality. The fact of the matter is that by 2008 affirmative action as conceived and initiated by the Mbeki government was a dead letter. No funeral had been held. No wake was called. But the government, business, unions and the public knew it was no longer possible to continue in terms of the objectives and targets established. There were just not enough qualified black people to employ, largely because of the failure of the state educational system to produce them. Implausible policies eventually have a habit of writing their own death warrants, and so it is with Mbeki's style of affirmative action.

In essence, the government conceded the point when it granted permission for 35 200 foreigners to be appointed to key positions in South Africa. But the point was made: the government was prepared to seek external skills, even if this meant unbalancing the equity numbers. And why should it support the employment of a German or American while discouraging the appointment of a white South African?

But how to proceed? The one option is to do nothing. Just let the policy whither away, ignored and unmentioned. There is a difficulty with this approach. First, it is bad for law in general to have some legislation not applied. Second, once appointed to do a job, bureaucrats will do it. Third, tendering and other business in the country is still dependent on various empowerment criteria. That cannot be ignored, as it affects the profitability and competitiveness of business. Fourth, it is bad policy to run a country on the basis of exemptions that become the rule.

There is a way out of the morass. Reimagine the affirmative action process *now*. Invite South African companies to submit a current audit of the status of their workforces on a voluntary basis and revisit it every two years. If companies have improved their status, they should be rewarded by a simple credits system, which is counted as a weighting factor up to 20 per cent when being considered for state tenders. At the maximum incentive level, such companies will be competing equally with black empowerment companies. No targets. No compulsion. No public hysteria to offend employers and discourage investors. No monstrously burdensome paperwork. No opportunity for the drivers of empowerment to bludgeon a crony into a top position. No chance for a disreputable politician to make some populist gain from an ignorant speech.

A company that goes the extra mile gets the benefit at state-tendering stage. Every company will quickly make its own assessment as to what makes economic sense. It will have the same result, but much less of the aggravation, bureaucracy and cost. This will be crucial for small businesses and in particular empowered businesses, which will soon face the crippling weight of auditing and reporting their progress in terms of current legislation.

There are other issues relating to empowerment – ownership and black business development – that I will deal with in a later chapter. Here, let it simply be noted that unless the Mbeki Ascendancy or his successor acts pre-emptively to refashion affirmative action, they will be left with a legacy of historic embarrassment. The first step to wisdom may be a revisiting of the Equity Commission's composition, so as to weight it with technical expertise that can at least be aware of the fine equilibrium that needs to be kept between growing black share of the economy and its management versus the critical skills needs of the country.

So much for the regulatory side. On the development side, the state needs to massively commit its resources to developing the virtuous chain of skills acquisition from school level, through tertiary training and into the workplace. This, as suggested earlier, requires special schools and bridging, work-focused training qualifications to at least get young people into the work environment. The government's role in this needs to be further refined. Currently, as we have seen, the government provides a number of bursary opportunities at significant cost to the taxpayer. The payback, sadly, is less than impressive. Completion rates are low and the spread of skills inadequate.

Criteria for the awarding of these bursaries need to be tightened and aligned with the chain of skills acquisition. Preference should be given to those pupils from poor communities who have qualified for apex schools and have either opted for short-term bridging qualifications or have qualified to move directly into the tertiary institutions.

It is essential to place young people with potential from poor communities on a clear growth path from an early age. It is vital to support them at each level of their progression from special school through bridging training and into employment, and from there to higher levels of skills acquisition – indeed, to the highest level. The acquisition of these skills is currently the preserve of the richest and most privileged, white and increasingly black. It should not and must not be so for the future. One of the greatest challenges facing South Africa is the high drop-out rate at each level of the educational process, particularly in the year preceding the matric examination and the FET colleges. Between the first and ninth grade, there is a 95 per cent retention rate. In the final grade, matric, there is inexplicably a 10 to 15 per cent drop-out rate. Why?

Without a clear progression chart and the reasonable certainty of support, the temptation to surrender to the pervasive culture of dependence is overwhelming. The annual ritualised campus protests by students refused readmission because of serial failure in their examinations or the inability to pay university fees is merely symptomatic of the broader problem of systemic underachievement – a function of both quality of services and the lack of a learning culture.

Those with a realistic chance of success from the poor communities should be at university. Those with a secure line of support should be there, too. Anything less is simply a cruel tease. It is not beyond the capacity of states and institutions that both those prerequisites are met and that deserving students should be allowed to progress through the portal of learning to the rich and rewarding life to which they are entitled by their work and talent.

But it is a beginning, an attempt to focus the national resource and innovation on the achievable and to move away from the illusory, the populist and the faddish, everything that has wasted a decade and cost the country so dearly.

CHAPTER 20

A double-edged sword

The chief obstacle to the progress of the human race is the human race.
                                        — DON MARQUIS[1]

THE POST-MBEKI SOUTH AFRICA REVEALS AN INTRIGUING MIX of the positive and the negative in regard to physical infrastructural development. On the one hand, it shows a dramatic expansion of infrastructure geared towards the needs of the poor: housing, electrification, telephony, potable water, roads, schools, community halls, sporting facilities and clinics. It also boasts many new urban developments for the middle classes and the rich. Commercial properties like hotels, shopping malls, offices and industrial sites have all grown exponentially with a booming economy and a major reallocation of national wealth. This is all to the good and is demonstrable evidence of the bright side of the Mbeki legacy.

Sadly, most of this populist investment has been at the cost of the sinews that make for modern states. The power generation and distribution crisis has been discussed at some length. Similar concerns were being expressed in 2008 about the water, rail and road systems. Expert analysis indicated that without major investment in new dams and reticulation systems, the country would be facing a power-like crisis in its water provision by the year 2014. The government has denied this, as it did the electricity crisis only a year before it all fell apart. Ministerial assurances, sadly, are now regarded with the same weight as confetti at an Italian wedding.

The degeneration of the road systems – other than the toll roads – was self-evident to all South Africans. The South African Rail Commuter Corporation reported to parliament in early 2008 that an infrastructure backlog of R25 billion was compounding its failure to deliver services effectively. Its ability to raise the capital – let alone the skills – to deal with this was affected by the ambitious Gautrain rapid transport system, for which the initial cost of R20 billion in 2005 had risen to R25 billion by 2008. In the same month, the environmental authorities confirmed that only two of Durban's eight beaches had been able to retain the 'blue flag' of water and environmental purity – all the others had been contaminated, possibly by endemic leakage from crumbling sewerage mains.

Compounding the problem was the country's commitment to host the FIFA Football World Cup in 2010. The honour was very important for South Africa and evidence exists that such events, if properly managed, have a material impact on tourist and investment potential going forward – *provided the supporting environment is conducive to such growth.*

This last proposition, however, was dealt something of a challenge when the World Economic Forum's Second Annual Travel and Competitiveness Report (2008) came out. South Africa was ranked sixty-first out of the 130 countries surveyed, just beating Montenegro and Uruguay. The survey covered ten indices. South Africa's closest rivals in each category were: Montenegro (policy rules and regulations); Canada (environmental sustainability); Nepal (safety and security); Sri Lanka (health); Uzbekistan (prioritisation of tourism); Taiwan (air transport infrastructure); Saudi Arabia (ground transport infrastructure); Serbia (tourism infrastructure); Guatemala (information and communications technology infrastructure); Taiwan (price competitiveness).

There is a point to all of this. In order to stage such a prestigious event as the World Cup, let alone capitalise on its legacy, considerable effort and funding are required to bring the country to host status, quite apart from the cost of the event itself. These costs are at present unquantifiable. By 2008, initial state investment of R20 billion in the World Cup had grown to R30 billion. There is no reason to think it will stop there – in fact, rising power, oil and labour costs guarantee that the final cost will be higher.

South Africa *will* hold the event. The ANC government would rather bankrupt the country than see it fail: too much in terms of national and even continental pride is riding on this. Whether it will be a *successful* tournament that will refute rather than reinforce the stereotypical view of African efficiency lies in the hands of the legions of people working day and night to make it happen. It also remains to be seen what benefit the new stadiums will be in a country with a limited number of people who attend public events and few real revenue-generating sporting codes.

The important point, however, is that the World Cup has significantly diverted national resources away from other and more pressing pursuits. This is not simply in terms of money but – and more importantly – in terms of scarce skills. Between the demands of the World Cup requirements, the limitations imposed by the energy crisis and the paucity of appropriate skills, there is now a forbidding question hanging over the government's ability to roll out its R563 billion (and rapidly rising) capital programme by 2010.

'I love the South Africans' spirit of can-do,' a senior World Bank official once remarked to me, 'but I wish they had a better sense of the don't-do.'

All of this raises critical questions about the deployment of national resources in the capital programme in future. The first challenge is effective prioritisation, while the second is efficient roll-out.

Given a decade and a half of spending on establishing facilities and housing for the urban poor, it is now vital that the state rebalances its efforts between the populist (and popular) on the one hand and the needed (and critical) on the other; that it directs its energy towards the infrastructural platform that is the mainspring of any successful economy. This is clearly understood by those in power and is the basis of the infrastructural regeneration of the country.

Of necessity this implies a focus on power (generation, transmission, distribution, alternative sources), water (storage, purification and distribution), roads (provincial, urban and peri-urban), ports, railways, airports and communication (broadband). Nearly all of these are addressed in the government's capital roll-out, but it is essential to say again that this is the heart of South Africa's twenty-first-century economic platform. Nothing should detract from its importance.

This inevitably raises the question of South Africa's commitment to the region and to the continent. From its earliest days, the ANC has taken on an additional responsibility to foster and represent the interests of the rest of Africa. This role, not always welcomed by other Africans, has led to the commitment of huge amounts of the country's scarce resources, not least of all prodigious time from Mbeki himself, to a damaging level.

The country's technical base has been drawn into multilateral projects such as NEPAD and a host of regional and continental activity. Its parastatals have invested heavily and with little or no return in service platforms across the continent – returns, particularly on capital, are pathetically low. Now, surely, is the time to review that and decide whether Africa's long-term interests are best served by such dispersions of South African–based skills and resources or whether they should rather be harnessed for the stabilisation and growth of South Africa as a first step towards a better subcontinent. This is not a call for a Monroe Doctrine for South Africa, but it is a caution about the limits of the doable.

The question of effective roll-out is crucial, and here one issue must dominate: the effective utilisation of resources. The South African Treasury has already raised its concerns about the monitoring, evaluation and reporting of this very significant spend. The auditor-general, still battling to institute acceptable standards of financial reporting in routine administration and crippled by staff vacancies, must be doubly concerned. This scale of spend is just too big to be left to an already fragile auditing service and a manifestly ineffectual Public Protector's office.

The government should consider the creation of a stand-alone risk-management unit comprising technical, investigative, prosecutorial and forensic auditing expertise, with no other function than the constant evaluation and investigation of these major projects. We have seen what the benefit of focus has been in units such as the Scorpions.

This macro-project risk-management unit should be involved in every major project from the date of inception and should stay with it until completion. That way, it can forestall problems and save the auditor-general enormous headaches when his staff is inevitably called upon after completion to unravel what actually happened. South Africa's history of tender irregularities, corruption, private-sector malfeasance, poor performance and political interference is too well documented for us to have any illusions: the government's capital-development programme is one huge siren call to every crook and chancer in town.

The South African business community is rife with anecdotes about how empowerment tendering is working: a legion of stories exists about established companies losing out to affirmative tenderers who, within days of the award being made, are at their door asking to buy their products or services at more than the price they originally and unsuccessfully bid.

This will be the acid test of the ANC government. Is the infrastructure-development programme intended to lay the foundation for South Africa's surge into the twenty-first century and ensure job growth for the future? Or is it yet one more elephant to be killed for the eating by a small and connected group of insiders?

CHAPTER 21

Getting back on track

Experience teaches slowly and at the cost of mistakes.
— JAMES A FROUDE[1]

S OUTH AFRICANS ARE NOT A VERY TRUSTING BUNCH. IN FACT, research in the *World Values Survey*[2] shows that Africans have the lowest level of trust of their compatriots of any group of people in the world. There may be good social and historical reasons for that, but it is also true that trust becomes even more impaired when it is overlaid with racial tensions, income inequalities, arrested state formation and weak leadership.

South Africans have emerged from the Mbeki era more distrustful of those that rule them than when they entered. Most of this distrust is directed towards the political parties and state institutions at present, but it cannot but have an effect on relationships between communities and individuals.

Remarkably, and as a testament to the good sense of most South Africans, the levels of racial tension within the country as measured by numerous polls show that the overwhelming pool of sentiment is *for* a unified, non-racial and fair society and *against* discrimination, racial hatred and retribution. In this general paradigm there are differences: blacks and the coloured community tend to be more hopeful about the future and trusting of the state, while the white and Indian minorities show themselves to be more sceptical. But none of this signals irreversible divides which are on the point of degenerating into open conflict, although the xenophobic violence of mid-2008 gave a chilling foresight of what could happen in a scenario of complete breakdown of trust.

Equally important, evidence suggests that tribalism, a major constraint on African development, is an existing but not hugely divisive force in the national life, despite desperate efforts by some hostile agencies to read tribalism into every political spat in the ruling party.

Taken as a whole, then, South Africa can confront the future with a measure of confidence. More than five years of a growing economy and a major dispersal of wealth through the various layers of society have created a general sense – more, a reality – of an improved standard of living among millions of South Africans. The left wing of the ANC would dispute this, but it is the truth.

This has probably helped to smooth some of the rougher edges of the transition, at least for the white community, who have done comparatively well in the post-liberation era, as well as for the new black middle classes, who have achieved an economic status on a scale and scope unimaginable to their parents. But it is naïve to think that this would be sufficient to carry the country through indefinitely. The boom times are over, and in an environment of fiercer economic competition, there must be an impact on class and racial tensions. It is therefore important to understand the main socio-economic underpinnings of the society.

If one were to seek to summarise the major points of tension between the former wealth-holding and new wealth-seeking classes, it could probably be put thus: the wealth holders believe they have made significant sacrifices of power and opportunity, but this has not been matched by returns in the form of effective governance and a productive society in which all elements contribute to their fullest ability. To them, the ANC's programme of redistribution appears a one-way street with nothing except exit signs at the end for them.

Conversely, the wealth-seeking classes feel they have not benefited adequately from political liberation, are still fobbed off with sub-standard public services and are patently way back in the queue when it comes to jobs, opportunities, wealth and dignity. To them, the ANC's programme of redistribution has been a cosy deal between various factions of the new and the old beneficiary classes.

Both groups feel betrayed by the quality of governance – the black elites in both private and public life are therefore in the crossfire from the old elites and the traditional poor and working classes.

The clue to unlocking the impasse, thus, must be a system whereby the wealth-holding classes are seen to be demonstrably contributing to the advancement of the broader society (not just the elites) while the wealth-seeking classes are perceived to be making serious efforts to use opportunities not simply for egregious self-enrichment, but for the benefit of the broader society.

There are two particularly at-risk communities in South Africa in this time of slowing economy and falling employment.

The first is the new black middle class, which is vulnerable because of its short-term personal debt and the fact that it has not had time to accumulate significant wealth to cushion the impact of rising interest rates on one of its key asset classes – property. Mercifully, South Africa is not confronting the scale of meltdown mortgage default as has occurred in the United States and to an extent in the United Kingdom, but it is worrying enough when one considers the huge number of first-time buyers. Severe economic pressures on this group can only be alleviated by higher salaries, again inflationary, or state attempts to control prices, a dramatic step towards the controlled economy.

How, then, does one seek to defend the advances made by the broad band of the black middle class without resorting to the most destructive form of subvention and dirigisme?

The concern here should not be the black elites who have by now well entrenched themselves in the mainstream of South African capitalism – in some sectors they *are* the mainstream – but rather in genuinely empowering the aspirant black entrepreneur and spreading the benefits of equity ownership to the widest possible group. The new elites – and their children – are already embedded as a self-perpetuating class of the over-advantaged, the inevitable consequences of free-market economies (and indeed communist ones). There is nothing to be done about this and neither should there be – it would be naïve to ask this class of newly enriched to adopt a moral posture different from wealthy classes around the world. But neither is there any reason why the state should continue to protect their interests at the cost of the broader society. The focus of the state should, and must, be on the poor and the dispossessed.

One of the benefits of the Polokwane conference was the clarifying of this distinction between the advantaged (white with increasing numbers of blacks) and the disadvantaged (black with increasing numbers of whites) as opposed to Mbeki's constructs, which were based on blood and race. Whether the leadership of ANC Classic will continue to advance the interests of the disadvantaged or will itself become corrupted is a moot point. Betrayal of the African people by its leadership is a depressingly familiar feature of modern history.

Empowerment as pioneered by the Mbeki administration has had a rocky start, as discussed in earlier chapters. It has certainly facilitated a material increase in the number of black South Africans in senior positions in public and private life and given black-owned entities entrée to state contracts. But it has failed to significantly expand ownership of the country's wealth to a broad range of people, grow indigenous businesses or create self-sufficiency among the black community. In fact, it has done the reverse. Too many black entrepreneurs have quickly worked out that the shortest route to wealth is not through starting one's own business but by sashaying one's way into some 'empowerment' deal that inevitably ends up with a minority stake in a largely white-owned business. Such stake, meanwhile, is all too often subject to the vagaries of the share market price or the charity of the host company or lending institution.

There is also a growing indication that even where empowered companies are created, the challenges of managing modern business entities often prove tougher than expected for the new management. Then follows another round of expectation and demand for subsidy or subvention – either from the state or the private sector. Unwillingness by the private sector to respond is then characterised by the empowerment lobbies as 'a reluctance of big business to transform'. This in turn sparks another round of state activity, more private-sector resistance, deeper disillusionment.

The reality is that shotgun marriages are rarely happy. This is particularly true in business. The weight of evidence, rarely publicly articulated by the private sector for obvious reasons, is that far too many of these empowerment deals are delivering less than expected benefits. The most common complaints relate to issues of funding (or lack of it); contractual breaches; failure to deliver what is promised; attempts to interfere in management prerogatives; and difficulties when new rights issues are made to expand the business.

At the heart of the problem lies a simple issue: for the old guard there is an expectation that empowerment deals must have a rational and economic basis. For many of the new guard, bolstered by the Mbeki Ascendancy's rhetoric of redistribution, the exercise is purely ideological. There are exceptions, of course – some of them stunning. But this programme has generally not been a happy one, and in some cases it has been very destructive. In any case, this is not, and never can be, the way to create a robust indigenous business class such as one finds in West and East Africa. We have wasted precious time.

It is too late to change the paradigm. The dislocations caused to South African investment and competitiveness by the process thus far would be nothing compared to the havoc were it to be summarily terminated. The existing sector charters need to be completed and current agreements

concluded to the extent that economic realities will allow. This in itself is
a doubtful proposition, as rising market valuations, compounded by escalating interest rates from 2007 onwards, make equity expensive and money
costly, no matter how honeyed the sweetheart deal. In some cases we have
seen a reverse effect – by early 2008 the first of the empowerment deals
were being canned because in some sectors a weaker economic climate no
longer made it possible for the equity acquisitions to be funded on the
basis of future earnings.

The refusal of the banking sector in early 2008 to increase its agreed
ceded equity share to align with new state-prescribed quotas and a raft of
court actions by disappointed shareholders against first-wave empowerment partners in early 2008 were a sign of the times.

In its place must come a new view on how to advance black ownership
and a robust indigenous business culture. The argument has been raised
before that, given the huge historic and cultural imbalances between white
and black South Africa, it is naïve to rely merely on impersonal market
forces to drive towards some sort of final moment of equalisation in the
distant future. Neither economies nor humans wait for such moments
of truth.

If one accepts that truth (itself hotly debated) the next obvious question
has to be *how*?

The Mbeki strategy of relying on the private sector to subsidise the
major part of the cost for this reallocation of wealth has not succeeded. It
has not brought material advantage to the many and has, in fact, critically
diverted South Africa's business community from its core function of being
globally competitive, profitable and tax-paying. It is, in fact, a tribute to
the remarkable resilience of the private sector that it has been able to keep
the country's ranking in the middle-tier countries of the world for the last
decade and a half in terms of per capita GDP and business efficiencies,
despite plunging competitiveness indicators for the factors under the control of the public administrations, roughly termed 'enabling factors'. When
one captain of South African industry was asked at a conference abroad
what he spent most of his time doing, he replied: 'Managing history'.

What is in fact needed is a direct transfer of wealth from the wealth-
holding communities into the hands of the marginalised: no fancy footwork
and billions of rands paid to corporate mergers and acquisition experts; no
army of sinecured beneficiaries sitting in existing companies; no alienation
of foreign investors.

The state urgently needs to create both the structure and the funding to achieve this. Current systems are clearly failing. The two key areas in which the government undertook to enhance entrepreneurship and job creation – agriculture and small business – have been failures. Little wonder that there is no faith they will do any better in the future.

What went wrong?

Certainly, there was no lack of money. It was, instead, a series of mis-judgements and errors that led cumulatively to systemic failure. In order of importance: lack of mission; no coordination of state functions; frag-mentation of institutions and funding; corruption; no effective business support; and inappropriate choices of target beneficiaries – too many inexperienced, mismatched or simply political people.

How to remedy this unconscionable waste of time and money?

First, all public funds targeted at small-business development should be aggregated from all departmental budgets and parastatals – and put under a single locus of control.

It may be necessary to augment this with additional budgetary appro-priations. This may take the form of a national wealth tax of some sort for a limited duration – say, a decade. The consolidated public money, together with any new funding raised from taxation, should finance a new, unified development and empowerment trust. There would need to be certain critical elements in the scheme:

- The funds raised would have to be ring-fenced and placed under the control of an independent trust, with a board of impeccable South Africans.
- The trust would report to the presidency and parliament.
- The operational staff would be appointed on merit and, as a specific condition of their employment, would not be associated with any political party, pressure group or institution advancing sectarian inter-ests. Given the skills crisis, it is possible that foreign talent could be recruited.
- It is possible to consider requesting one of the existing development agencies to act as managing agent for this programme subject to the trust's mandate – perhaps the Industrial Development Corporation or the Development Bank of South Africa. The Land Bank, its past now rotten with corruption and mismanagement, should be closed and its functions transferred to the Development Bank.

- There should also be a review of South Africa's multiplicity of development agencies with a view to incorporating them into one or transferring their roles to a single existing institution (probably the best option) which could be selected by inviting the relevant agencies to bid for the brief. Regional development bodies can be converted to regional offices of this one development entity. The efficiencies would be inestimable.
- The trust would be responsible for investment in indigenous start-up businesses through seed capital, business planning, feasibility, mentorship and the development of cooperatives for securing best advantage on capital goods, supplies and distribution.
- It would also be responsible for aligning the whole function of the trust with the new skills-development programme of the state and with a new system of preferential state tendering, to be discussed later.

What sort of funds are we envisaging?

If one were to consolidate all existing annual development investment from state institutions at all levels of government, the figure would come to approximately R13.7 billion a year. An additional R7 billion a year from a further tax appropriation of 1 per cent on personal and corporate taxes would amount to approximately R20.7 billion for investment in micro, small, medium and large entities. Taken over the ten-year life of the wealth tax, this would mean about R207 billion at present value. That is by no means small change.

It is also suggested that there would be a second leg to the function of this development and empowerment trust. It should allocate resources from its budget to buy equity in existing listed South African companies on behalf of the qualifying poor. If half of the budget were used to purchase equity for the poor and that number was estimated at two-thirds of the population, it would mean every adult person would qualify for a tranche of shares worth R1 000 per year for life at 2007 values. This is not a huge amount, but it would be a first step towards genuinely empowering the poor.

Management of the small-business development programme is, as usual, critical. The sad fact is that literally billions in state, donor and private money has been blown on exactly these schemes for small and medium enterprise (SME) development. Repeated analyses of South Africa's capacity to grow its small and medium indigenous enterprises show the country is among the worst performers in the comparable tier of developing economies. In all cases, the failures outweigh the successes.

Inevitably, the failure rate results in a paroxysm of finger-pointing. The beneficiaries claim they were inadequately supported by the funding agency. The funding agencies claim that the recipients failed to exercise the most basic of business discipline. There is, of course, truth on both sides.

It is undeniable that state effort to support the growth of small business, identified way back in 1996 by the ANC as one of the big potential growth opportunities, has failed to meet its objectives. Indeed, the thrust of state investment in business during the Mbeki era appears not to have been towards the small and micro-sector at all, but towards strengthening wealthy consortiums of black entrepreneurs operating in the formal, high-sized sector. The Land Bank is merely the most egregious example. The reality was again highlighted by Statistics South Africa findings in early 2008 that of the two million non-agricultural jobs created since 2001, less than 7.5 per cent were in the informal sector. Formal employment had increased by 1.7 million jobs, while informal employment rose by only 200 000. Agricultural employment, meanwhile, remained virtually static.

The parameters of such small-business development assistance need to be clearly established. The first is some serious skin on the table from the entrepreneurs in terms of pledged assets – even if it is only a motor vehicle. It is also essential that recipients have basic business-management skills. Certification from one of the two-year bridging business-training courses with heavy emphasis on business culture, together with one year's experience in the chosen field of investment, would suffice. Finally, pre-scribed levels of surplus reinvestment in the business, subject to the penalty of an immediate withdrawal of the loan and forfeiture of the pledged assets, would help to deal with the tendency among small businesses to instantly monetise surplus. Again, management of this exercise should be in the hands of independent overseers who are incentivised on the basis of performance of their units.

There is a very powerful tool that the state can use to assist the develop-ment of small business – preferred state tendering. This brings us back to the state's failed empowerment initiative. The current state empowerment tendering processes are operating suboptimally, to put it politely, yet this is undoubtedly the most powerful tool in the state's armoury to advance an indigenous business culture.

The major state enterprises currently operate in terms of prescribed tender qualification processes. In reality, they are widely ignored. The result has been an explosion of fraudulent tendering to the point where illegal tendering processes are by far the largest component of corrupt and fraudulent state activity by value – and growing. The introduction of affirmative action, which allows a high discretionary element in terms of weighting of competitive bids (lawfully up to 20 per cent but often five times as much), has merely exacerbated the situation, as it always will.

Worse, the process has introduced major distortions. A new class of '10 per centers' has emerged – affirmative operators who act independently or on behalf of white entrepreneurs to secure contracts at inflated rates, then outsource the execution back to the white company that would have secured the contract in the first place, at a lower rate. The state's threats to act against 'fronting' of this nature ring hollow for two reasons: policing of these scams is almost impossible in such ideologically engineered economic transactions and, given the acute skills crises in the country, any effective implementation of such a policy would only lead to further catastrophic losses of state resources. In other instances, now commonplace, empowerment tenderers are securing contracts and then, in order to make their margin, sourcing products from China, thus sidestepping opportunities for local suppliers.

Assuming these anomalies can be dealt with, in itself a major assumption given the fragility of the state entities, the system of preferred tendering could yet give aspirant black entrepreneurs the opportunity to make significant progress. But, and this is a defining but, the systems *have* to be tightened to ensure that only deserving entities can qualify. This goes back to the question of the expertise, funding, track record and management of these entities.

The proposal here is thus one of a long chain process that converts the current short-term attitude to the building of long-term capacity and resource in an indigenous business sector. The process begins with graduates of priority or apex schools with business and business culture skills. It proceeds to bridging practical training courses and then to internships at existing corporations, where candidates both build experience and (hopefully) add to their skills. Once through this process, the candidate, now at least able to put a basic business plan together, approaches the development and empowerment trust for assistance in refining the business plan, accessing funding, joining cooperative ventures for procurement of supplies and services, and beginning the process of qualifying for the state database as a potential preferred supplier of goods or services. The end point is a competent and confident entrepreneur, backed with the necessary range of support and experience to at last go out and make the difference. Crucially, it will no longer be a case of the taxpayer subsidising the entrepreneur's lack of skill and knowledge in the hope that at some future point the entrepreneur will actually deliver value on his or her tender.

There is, of course, one major disadvantage to the ANC from such a programme. It takes time. The ANC is ideologically a millennialist movement, as are all parties whose roots are in socialist and communist ideologies. It believes change comes with the wave of a wand, in an instant epiphany. It fails, as all pre-modern organisations always do, to understand that building a modern state is, to use the cliché, a process and not an event. Everything the ANC has done so far is based on the assumption that the intent will always determine the outcome. It is this belief that has led South Africa to its current level of arrested state formation. If no other great leap of imagination by South Africa's rulers is made, it should be that, sadly, things take time.

The implementation of a long-haul and integrated vision of empowerment at the outset of the Mbeki era a decade ago would have meant the first beneficiaries of the scheme would have been through the chain by now and formed the basis of a resilient, sustainable and confident indigenous business sector, along the lines of the West and East African models. It is late in the day. Only since 2006 has the state begun addressing itself to even vaguely appropriate and coordinated policies such as JIPSA. There has been much and conspicuous destruction of wealth and time. But it is not too late. If implemented promptly, we can look forward to the day when black entrepreneurship is not measured by a perpetual 25 per cent handmaiden status to white-owned businesses, but as major private-sector players in their own right.

The white business sector will undoubtedly be concerned by suggestions that an even greater emphasis should be placed on preferential tendering for small and preferably black-owned companies. In early 2008, the Department of Land Affairs was considering favouring 100 per cent black-owned firms over even suitably empowered white ones. Not surprisingly, the proposal raised the question as to why white-owned companies should have even bothered to go the distance with new equity deals and empowerment transactions if they were going to be discriminated against anyway – a classic case of the remorseless logic of unlimited entitlement. If indeed, the department – or the state – proceeds with such a policy without tightening pre-qualification rules for tendering, it will most certainly lead to yet another wave of loss and disillusionment.

In terms of the proposals advanced in earlier chapters and here, it could, however, be beneficial. It has already been suggested that all current equity legislation be dumped, after the completion of deals that are under way, and replaced with a fully developmental model. In that scenario, companies that comply with voluntarily established affirmative action targets for employment would gain credits for state tendering. To the extent that they comply, they could gain a status equal to a fully black-owned company – in other words, they would compete on equal terms. This would further encourage companies to increase their proportion of black senior staff.

Even if they do not achieve equivalence in empowerment ratings, the scrapping of the current highly regulated environment would remove one of the biggest impediments to companies that cannot achieve staff empowerment targets – the insistence by other private-sector companies that they show empowerment credentials before being considered for work. In other words, even as the space to tender for public-service works closes slightly in favour of fully black-owned firms, the opportunity to tender in the private sector opens.

There are two immediate risks to the proposals so far presented. The first is that the ANC state will choose to adopt the new taxation levels *and* proceed with its current and failing empowerment programme with all its many perverse incentives. This would be fatal. The very purpose of the trust is to create a path for the establishment of an independent and efficient indigenous business sector, to unchain the existing South African private sector from the restraints of onerous and ideological empowerment requirements and partnerships. It can be done. There are already examples of black-owned, long-standing portfolio management companies with diverse and broad-based black shareholdings, survivors of the first wave of empowerment initiatives, which are operating on their own feet and with their own resources. Intriguingly, it is these companies that are increasingly being chosen by major corporations for empowerment deals rather than polyglot consortia of businessmen, operators, politicians and hastily assembled 'disadvantaged' groups.

The ANC would have to be aware that attempts to prolong the current form of empowerment would create major risks to the fragile economic recovery and already cautious foreign direct investment. The trust offers a way to engage a wide range of sponsors from the private sector, multilateral organisations and the public in building a new indigenous business sector.

The second risk is that the programme will fail merely *because* it is in government hands. With an unbroken string of failures in building entrepreneurial entities in the small and agricultural sectors, it is hardly surprising that the business community is sceptical that anything undertaken by the ANC government will work.

This is a risk. But the purpose of the trust operating independently under a strong mandate would be the best defence against ANC deployments and the snout-in-the-trough culture that characterises many of our public (and some of our private) organisations.

But why should South Africa's wealth-holding classes agree to a voluntary increase in levels of taxation? The answer is simple. It would mean an end to systemic discrimination in terms of opportunities and jobs as entailed by current empowerment legislation. It would free the private sector to pursue competitiveness and profit. Finally, it would imply a massive reinvestment in the South African equity markets by the trust, with enormous benefit to South African business and shareholders, whether direct or through pension and retirement schemes.

There is a second at-risk community in South Africa: Mbeki's dependency class. Earlier chapters have discussed the exponential growth of the welfare classes to the point where 25 per cent of South Africa's citizens are welfare recipients and one-third of households claim they are dependent on such pay-outs for basic survival. The government has already accepted the principle of linking social welfare payments to food inflation, running at 36 per cent a year in 2008, and in the early months of the same year was facing court challenges seeking to compel it to increase its child-support grants from the capped limit of fourteen years to the age of eighteen. Having been created, the welfare state was doing what welfare states always do – grow like Topsy.

The state also underwrites the cost of water and electricity provision for a significant element of the society. There is a high level of illegal tapping into the power channels – estimated at 10 per cent of all residential electricity supply. With the imminent exponential increase in the cost of basic services because of the government's failure to anticipate the crisis, these costs will rise proportionately and dramatically. The fiscus, in short, is on a hiding to nothing.

And so the government faces a difficult balancing act. It can pull back on its infrastructural spend to reduce public debt, and thus afford its current scale of social spend, but this would forever destroy the country's long-term growth prospects. It can attempt to reduce its social spend and court a huge popular backlash. ANC Classic, having just been elected as the 'pro-poor' representative, would be very loath to take this burden on at this time. Its most likely route, then, would be reduction of its spend on other governmental activities – education, health, policing, defence and so on. But this holds its own dangers. The withering away of the state capacity, the demodernisation of South Africa, will simply accelerate, creating its own downward spiral of lowered growth and employment.

The essential challenge confronting the ANC, then, is how to ensure that more benefit attaches to the massive investment it is making in the expansion of this social welfare network.

Current government thinking is to administer all the separate social security funds through one entity, supporting all forms of state assistance to its citizens – old-age pensions, medical, child-care and unemployment grants, industrial compensation, payments to wards of the court and even injury payments to road-accident victims.

The argument is that the new system will save costs and improve service. This is a bureaucratic response and entirely misses the point. The real problems with management of the social welfare net are threefold. The public service is incapable of running it efficiently; the flow of welfare payments into recipient households is leading to alarming growth of a dependency culture; and, finally, the state's attempt to create meaningful and sustainable job opportunities for those wanting to get out of dependency is floundering through incompetent administration and a lack of interest from the target audience.

The extent of bureaucratic ineptness was captured in early 2008, when a KwaZulu-Natal judge took it upon himself to convene a meeting of the major parties involved in litigation emanating from the Community Social Agency's failure to pay consistently or on time. The agency receives about 3 000 summonses a month from claimants due to inefficiency and delays. The judge's concern was that these claims were inevitably removed from the court roll, drifted around for a while and then were settled by the state, which also picked up the legal costs incurred. The cumulative effect was that hundreds of millions of rands were wasted because of the agency's inability to get it right first time around – and a lot of very happy, very rich lawyers.

The above example merely serves to underline a broader reality: the failure of the state to maintain a public-service culture that ensures effective 'bang for the buck'. This failure is measured in countless ways on a daily basis and inevitably feeds into the public lack of confidence in authority – a key ingredient in failed state formation. It also accounts for the apparent anomaly whereby huge state investment in welfare services is not matched by a commensurate public sense of value from those services; nor does it stand up to per capita comparisons with other developing countries. The reason for this was dealt with in an earlier section of the book when looking at public security, health, education and infrastructure. Putting this right is probably the most important challenge facing the government, and I will suggest some options when looking at the crisis of institutions in a later chapter.

An inevitable consequence of the flow of state resources into the hands of the poor is a misguided belief by both state and recipients that this is something that is *normal*, not something that occurs only when a society fails to meet the basic needs of its people for sustainable and meaningful employment. Any head of state in the developed world who had presided over a fourfold increase in the size of the welfare class would be adjudged to have run a failed economy and would have been dispatched in the tumbrels to the guillotine. The ANC government, conversely, takes pride in the number of people now living on state handouts and grants.

This is not to say support for the poor is not necessary. It is, for the simple reason that employment growth in both the formal and informal economy has failed to keep up with the job seekers in the market. A populist government like the ANC cannot simply stand by and watch such large-scale poverty. But it must be aware of the consequence – the growth of the dependency society.

The research shows that state grants are not received in the average South African household as an entitlement for an *individual*, but as a contribution to the aggregate income of the household. Maximising the number of grants therefore makes sense to the household: it creates annuity income for the household sufficient to support not just the recipients, but indeed everybody under the communal roof.

The consequence, I strongly suspect, is that large numbers of households now focus their attention not on seeking work, starting informal businesses or advancing themselves educationally, but on maximising the number of grants that can be claimed. If this is correct, and it is a hypothesis, it would explain the worryingly low rates of take-up or completion in state human-development programmes. It would also explain the intriguing fact that, although the population growth rate is declining, the number of members of households is increasing – from 4.8 to 5.2 in five years – which suggests that more dependents are being cared for in a single household. This is partly the result of the incidence of AIDS orphans, but it is also bolstered by the adoption of other people's children, so as to be eligible for child-care grants – a form of grant farming.

Even accepting the extremely low levels of state 'capacity' to make any of these programmes work, there must be concern in the fact that the expanded public-works programme had been able to create only 348 900 short-term work opportunities by 2008 – 4 per cent of the unemployed and well short of its target of one million – despite a material deployment of state resources. The failure of state attempts to promote an informal business culture among indigenous poor South Africans – much of the country's informal business is in fact carried on quite robustly by African immigrants – points again to a crisis of take-up.

It should also be a concern that for no ostensible reason, large numbers of school-goers drop out in the ninth grade instead of completing matric. Again, the low completion rate for apprenticeship training, the disturbingly low output from the national literacy campaigns and the low pass rates from state-funded students at tertiary institutions and FET colleges in-dicate a systemic problem in either resource or commitment. As financial resource is clearly not the problem, it can only be commitment – or the lack of it – on the part of the service provider, the recipient or both.

I would argue the perverse incentives of the national welfare system have not been accurately detected in the research that has been done to date. This research has focused on specific maladies flowing from particular types of grants, not on the cumulative impact of the welfare flow on individuals, households and society.

So, taken in its entirety, the welfare net extended at such great cost by the Mbeki administration is flawed in its conceptualisation, execution, outcomes and consequences. At most, it has to be viewed as a short-term intervention to stabilise poverty levels while the state seeks to rebuild its capacity and the economy enters a new phase of growth. Anything beyond that courts the danger of embedding forever a sense of entitlement and abdication. While the modern world is struggling to undo the worst effects of decades of overpriced and over-intrusive welfare systems, South Africa has gone the reverse route – building dependence into the very bones of the society. In this, there is a dreadful irony. If apartheid said to poor black people, do not worry about your future, you do not have one, the Mbeki legacy is a society that says, do not worry about your future, we will give it to you. Both propositions are cruelly wrong.

So what is to be done?

The facile answer is that we should create more permanent, meaningful and sustainable jobs. Indeed we should, but we all know that unemployment is likely to grow rather than shrink in the medium term, unless long-term jobs can be created that will survive the end of the state's infrastructure mega-spend in 2010. I have advanced some ideas as to how we can boost an indigenous business culture and thus create jobs – but this is a long-term prospect.

The short-term answer, then, is to make the welfare system work towards the enhancement of self-sufficiency rather than the reverse. In the absence of the ability of very poor people to contribute financially to the funding of these schemes, their contribution needs to be in another way. A possible solution lies in the idea of a family responsibility package grant. It would have the following elements:

- Assess the needs of households rather than individuals on the basis of child, old age, sickness and unemployment requirements.
- Determine the number and capacity of individuals in that household to undertake remunerative work.
- Ensure work guarantees are provided to those households for a specified number of days each month.
- Expand the eligibility for relief work to range from sixteen years up-wards, with no age cap.
- Ensure a spread of opportunities in the work-relief programme, ranging from manual labour to light duties such as janitorial or craft work, so that as many members of a household as possible may qualify for some work opportunity.
- Remunerate households to the extent that they comply with their work guarantees.
- Build in additional incentives for households that meet and exceed their work guarantees.
- Further incentivise families to the extent that individual members achieve improvements in personal development such as pass rates among children, technical qualifications achieved by young people or even improvements in healthy lifestyles.

- Reward households that achieve their work guarantees with tranches of equity from the state equity trust, discussed earlier.

The benefits of the proposed system are that it becomes a family initiative to ensure a degree of self-sufficiency and independence of individual members of the household. This is an essentially African concept. Through generations, working members of black households have contributed to the support of the extended family. Elements of the suggested scheme have been successfully implemented in India and Mexico. The system also ensures that there is kin pressure on household members to actively pursue work through the various schemes.

Obviously, the system will stand or fall by the quality of its administration, which is a major challenge. The government may consider appointing independent community agents to manage a specific number of households, subject to rigorous auditing of disbursements and fulfilment of work obligations. This would in itself create another layer of remunerated individuals.

This system may just save the welfare net in South Africa and help redress the ever-deepening culture of dependency.

But all of this is a stopgap. The central challenge to South Africa remains its capacity to create employment for as large a number of citizens as possible. It is pointless to raise tax rates to create a pool of funds to establish black small businesses or to put the welfare system on a more contributory basis, if at the end of the day there are simply no jobs available for the unskilled or semi-skilled. In this regard, serious challenges confront the country, not least of all the destruction of its low and middle educational levels and its skills-development base in the last decade and a half.

The creation of small businesses and the development of state-relief systems will assist, but we are living in a fool's paradise if we do not accept that one of the greatest constraints on the growth of employment in this country is the stranglehold the union movement has been able to develop over the years on access to employment opportunities.

This is not to argue for the diminution of union presence in the country. The movement could play a vital role as one of the main pillars for modernisation of the country. Neither is it to deny the important role the unions have played in highlighting the inequalities of society or the alarming growth of political centralism during the Mbeki tenure. Nobody will dispute the sense of moral pride most South Africans felt in April 2008 when the unions prevented the landing of weapons meant for the Zimbabwean regime to repress its citizens, while the Mbeki administration was quietly ushering the consignment through the back door.

But the brutal reality is that the trade union movement, as currently oriented, constitutes one of the biggest obstacles to the growth of low-skill employment in South Africa. The point was emphasised in the official government employment statistics for the first quarter of 2008[3] which showed growth in formal employment, but almost none in the informal sector – the very sector which the ANC has been punting since 1996 as the saviour of South Africa.

Onerous employment conditions have ensured that millions of poor South Africans who could have secured full-time work are left out in the cold or in temporary or part-time work. Many of these, understandably, have now turned to the welfare system as their only source of income.

The ANC is reluctant to confront organised labour on this issue, particularly post-Polokwane, and whenever it has arisen there has been a storm of protest from the unions – most recently over an ANC proposal to create a bifurcated employment market with less onerous conditions for small businesses. Recent resolutions of the Congress of South African Trade Unions returned with a vengeance to the question of what it calls 'atypical' work – contract and casual, in which half of South Africa's workforce resides – and promise further measures to force permanency in such jobs.

But we have now passed the point where the government, any government, can ignore the impact of these restrictive and self-serving limitations. To the extent that a new order may reopen this debate between the government, labour and business, and to that extent alone, one can look forward to a significant reduction in unemployment levels.

The reason why these initiatives have become so critical is obvious. The impending economic dislocations in South Africa, brought on by internal and external factors, will sharpen all the points of tension through the whole social landscape in the country. What was once tolerable by one or other sector of society may become less so in the years to come. Growth and redistribution will not salve this issue as has partly happened in the past: without growth there can be no redistribution, unless it becomes the zero-sum type that inevitably leads to extremism.

South Africans have to move smartly within the limits of the possible to maximise their resources. There is a civilised trade-off between an agreement that demands more sacrifice from the rich, black and white, for the benefit of creating a job-rich small-business sector on the one hand and, on the other, an insistence that the representatives of the labour elites sacrifice something to broaden the employment net, enforce public-service accountability and make it easier for the small-business operator, particularly black, to prosper and grow jobs.

Ironically, this may be the time to commence if not conclude the discussion. The absence of the Mbeki Ascendancy might precipitate such a debate, although the current fluidity in the leadership core of the ANC would make it impossible to conclude – at least not immediately. Yet it could be a new beginning.

If one accepts that job creation is also one of the key fulcrums on which the modernisation of South Africa will again have to be kick-started, then one cannot overlook the importance that agriculture can still play in job creation. The sector has remained resolutely stagnant in terms of job creation during the Mbeki era, due largely to changes in tenure, water rights, security, tenant rights, minimum wages and a host of other economic factors that have crushed the small commercial-farming sector to the point of virtual extinction. The decline in investment in their farms by landowners is currently running at 8 per cent a year, despite record international food prices, according to Land Bank statistics.

The government insists that its new land-reform programme, with its heavy emphasis on redistribution, will improve agricultural output by approximately 15 per cent. Of all the many unmet ANC promises, this surely has to be the most delusional, as time will undoubtedly tell, unless the ANC reviews this flight of utopian madness. The reality is that communal farming models are not conducive to the very high levels of demand of a globalised food-production network.

At the very moment when South Africa should be benefiting from historic high food prices because of changing Asian consumption patterns, the country is enduring stalled productivity and job creation due to the state's failed rural reform programme. In this, it is no different from the mining sector, which has seen investment worth billions available in the good times redirected to other destinations because of concern about the endless internal debates on new-order mineral rights. In this last regard, a poll by Canada's Fraser Institute found South Africa's attractiveness as a mining investment destination had fallen from twenty-fifth out of sixty-eight countries to fiftieth in five years due to the new-order rights regime.

Retrospectively, in future times when a wider perspective is available, I would suggest the Mbeki administration will be debited with having destroyed the greatest number of *potential* job opportunities in the history of the country, through ill-timed and inappropriate ideological interventions at precisely the moment when the greatest opportunities opened up.

Current agricultural reform programmes will have one inevitable result. The sector will be reduced to large agribusinesses, prone to endless labour cutting to remain internationally competitive on the one hand, and a failing 'indigenous' farming sector comprising tottering cooperative systems subject to limitless feuding, discord and unproductivity on the other. The net result, apart from food-security issues, will be a continuing winding down of employment in the agricultural sector.

Still, not all is lost. The opening has been created for the state to lease productive agricultural land from commercial farmers on a ten- to fifteen-year quitrent basis, with both the rental and purchase price being amortised over the period. That means the state can subsidise qualifying black commercial farmers to acquire the land and farm it under the joint tutelage of the exiting commercial farmer (if available) and a properly functioning state extension service (something that still has to be rebuilt). This will obviate having to buy the land at current prices. The key risk will be that the buyer defaults, but suitable guarantees, performance expectations and call options can be structured to reduce the risk.

But the single most important benefit will be the creation of real and sustainable agricultural jobs through small-scale farming, which historically has proven itself a great employment multiplier through the entire production chain. Indeed, accounts of black farmers in the nineteenth century show them capable of highly successful enterprises. It is necessary to wipe out the damage of the apartheid years and get us back to that stage.

A last issue remains. Mountains of reports have been written about what is euphemistically called the lack of internal social cohesion in society. There is very little doubt that on the basis of the simple numbers, South Africa is an ailing society with disturbing pathologies in terms of indiscipline, violence, rape, assault, fraud and a failure to accept personal accountability. Much of this was undoubtedly scripted during the apartheid years, with their appalling toll on social and family structures. Part was also written in the years since, with the ANC's heavy emphasis on a rights-based society being unbalanced by a duty-based one, by its lapses in moral leadership, by its political expedience at time of national crisis and, primarily, by its underlying philosophy of expropriation, redistribution and retribution. Here, then, the rub. While the Mbeki administration has preached a political philosophy of African independence and renaissance, it has practised a social philosophy of entitlement, subsidy and dependence.

This will not correct itself quickly, but some of the remedies suggested above may at least create a stabilising moment, with the opportunity for poor people to obtain a stake in the national economy, creation of more jobs (no matter how menial) and the growth of a proud indigenous business class. The longer-term solutions will have to await a resumption of the country's path to modernisation.

But there is something that can be done in the short term to cool temperatures and focus minds as we enter an undoubtedly supremely difficult time for the country – possibly the most difficult since political liberation. All South Africans need to take a deep breath and step back from the national pastime of attributing racist motives to everything that happens.

Ironically, the broad mass of South Africans, including the white minority, are quite prepared to accept that apartheid was a crime against humanity, and there is a considerable degree of forgiveness from those who were oppressed towards those who committed the crime. But the latest South African Reconciliation Barometer reflects a disturbing trend: the levels of interracial understanding are declining, not improving. In other words, racial tensions are rising rather than diminishing.

Why should this be so?

The most obvious answer is that the parties do not feel satisfied with the status quo. Whites look at the deterioration of capacity in the country and fear for the *future*, while blacks look at the increasing income inequality in society and are angry at the *present*. Whites generally believe blacks have done little to rise to the challenges of modernisation. Blacks, conversely, believe whites have never properly repented for the iniquities of the past. Neither group pauses to consider the considerable benefits both have derived in the post-liberation years: the former in terms of business growth and wealth and the latter in terms of infrastructure and opportunity, if only imperfectly seized.

This negative tendency is also subject to two predatory groups. The first is that band of politicians who are prepared to seize on ethnic mobilisation as the easiest route to power or influence. There are many of them and, in a number of instances, the Mbeki era has done much to legitimise, indeed sanctify, the dangerous emotionalism of this strain. This mobilisation has

proved time and time again in Africa to be of seductive power and devastating consequence. Literally, as we have seen most recently in Kenya and
South Africa, one plays with fire. Indeed, one can construct an argument
that the xenophobic attacks by South Africans on foreigners in 2008 are
nothing more than the extreme end of an ideological spectrum that begins
with a state-sponsored programme of expropriation of private wealth held
by one sector of the South African population.

The second predatory group lies in some among the array of NGOs,
media and governmental bodies set up with a vested interest not in
ameliorating the issue, but keeping it aflame. It is major business, this race-
and-misery industry, with significant revenues. Compromise, reconciliation
and reasonableness are mortal threats to the business plan and need to be
opposed at every turn – and thus every possible avenue for seizing upon a
supposedly racist incident becomes grist for the industrial mill.

There is a great danger here. For every black person assaulted by a white
person, there is an equal and possibly greater number of white people
assaulted by black people. Should every assault across the colour line be
interpreted as a racial incident, South Africa would soon have all the
appearances of the sort of racial holocaust that the country's direst sceptics
have long anticipated. It is urgent that all South Africans should step back
from this precipice: accusations of racism are double-edged swords.

There is another compelling reality. From 1998 to 2008, fully 20 per cent
of the country's white community emigrated. In the wake of Polokwane,
the power crisis and generally high levels of disillusionment with ANC
governance, there was anecdotal evidence of another wave of disillusioned
émigrés joining the diaspora. Certainly, bank statistics on the reasons
for the sale of homes indicated that another 20 per cent of the country's
remaining high-net-worth individuals, nearly all white, were on the move.
This is a scale of exodus proportionate to any of the great migrations of
the nineteenth century – the Irish to America or the movements from
central and eastern Europe. The difference, however, is that South Africa's
emigrants are not the poor and the dispossessed. They are the skilled and
the talented. But there are others who cannot emigrate for whatever reason:
financial, age or a sense of belonging. The mood here is changing. In the
same way that my black colleagues assured me that Jacob Zuma's election was an aberration, I have a distinctly uneasy feeling when my white
Afrikaner colleagues assure me that the spirit of Boer rebellion is a myth.

It is not. The popularity of the folk song 'De La Rey', now an iconic symbol of Afrikaner protest and nostalgia, is testimony to a deep sense of loss, isolation and anger. This is not a spirit one wants to court by an insistence on reparation, apology and humiliation. It is not something one wants to inflame by reckless intrusions on religious and cultural values – and sport, believe it or not, is a cultural value among many white South Africans. Many young whites today were never party to apartheid and had no responsibility for it. The demands for a perpetual state of intellectual, material and emotional repentance and reparation by whites can have only one consequence, as it did eventually among third-generation post-war Germans – blowback.

Should such a blowback occur it will be unfortunate. The Afrikaner is not an isolated or stranded minority as in the rest of Africa. This is a significant, influential and potentially very disruptive force. Ironically, it is the peer-review mechanism instituted through NEPAD, Mbeki's brainchild, which has identified the alienation of South Africa's cultural minority as a danger. Those other African countries know from bitter experience the consequences of alienating key minorities, which is why the rest of the continent stands head and shoulders above South Africa in acknowledging the value of skills and experience – no matter provenance.

South Africans will thus have to exert extraordinary skill at guarding against the predatory forces of ethnic mobilisation and the vested self-interest of the race-and-misery industry. They will need, in the immortal words of one of South Africa's titans of business, to check first who is 'stuffing the duck' before coming to a conclusion on the merits of their arguments. Easier said than done. In a country with a limitless capacity to misunderstand itself, the attractions of simple conspiracy theories, lazy prejudices and cheap passions are vast.

CHAPTER 22

Strangers abroad

Here is my first principle of foreign policy: good government at home. — WILLIAM E GLADSTONE[1]

NO BOOK THAT PURPORTS TO CONSIDER THE LEGACY OF Thabo Mbeki can avoid a consideration of his role and influence in the broader world. This is particularly true because Mbeki was called upon to lead the most modern state in sub-Saharan Africa and was, in any case, intrigued by and infatuated with the world of international affairs.

But an enthusiastic pursuit of reputation on the global stage is often a risky path to popular support, as so many world leaders have found: Winston Churchill in 1945, General Jan Smuts in 1948 and George W Bush in 2008 spring readily to mind. No less so for Mbeki. Indeed, his foreign-affairs persona is so inextricably enfolded into his presidential one that they are virtually inseparable. It was once said that under the apartheid regime, South Africa's domestic policy *was* its foreign policy. During the Mbeki tenure, one could argue that foreign policy was his domestic one – they were identical in principle and vision.

What was the basis of the Mbeki foreign policy and to what extent did it succeed? What does he leave of value for the future?

The driving vision behind his external and internal policies was to challenge the stereotypical view of Africans as incapable of managing their own states or solving their own problems. His mission was to build the institutions, values and outcomes that would once and for all signal that this vast continent had come of age in the international sphere and could rightfully claim its place at the top table of nations. It was his intention to wring out a better deal for the people of Africa in economic and trade terms. It was a vaunting and courageous vision, and his determination in tackling it should never be underestimated.

But it ran into the same headwinds as his domestic endeavours, and for virtually the same reasons.

Mbeki's grand foreign policy failed largely because it over-elaborated structures, underestimated resources, ignored continental sensitivities, became wedded to a highly personalised and in some cases paranoid world view and, in the last instance, foundered on Mbeki's inability to make bold and decisive decisions regarding the toughest foreign policy issues confronting him. If this sounds familiar, it should. All these frailties lay at the root of so many of his problems in rolling out a sustainable legacy in the domestic sphere.

One of Mbeki's greatest practicable foreign policy achievements was undoubtedly the reshaping of the moribund Organisation of African Unity (OAU) and the African Economic Community into a modernised and vibrant African Union (AU). This new body was established in July 2002 from the fifty-three member states. The new body envisaged a Pan-African Parliament, an African Court of Justice and a Peace and Security Council that subsequently oversaw the deployment of AU peacekeepers into the Democratic Republic of Congo (DRC), Sudan, Burundi and Somalia. In a further elaboration, plans were made for an African Standby Force – a rapid-reaction unit to forestall threats to regional peace and implement the much more aggressive intervention mandates of the AU as compared to its predecessor, the OAU.

From the OAU the AU adopted NEPAD – an ambitious programme to eradicate poverty, promote sustainable growth and development, integrate Africa in the world economy and accelerate the empowerment of women. One of its chief instruments was to be the African Peer Review Mechanism (APRM), which effectively required every member to submit itself to an assessment of its governance practices on a regular basis.

Leadership of the new organisation became a tussle between Mbeki, the new kid on the block, and Libya's Moammar Ghaddafi, who had long treasured a desire to become the leader of the African bloc. Mbeki won and Ghaddafi retreated into pursuing his objectives on a different stage. The Pan-African Parliament was inaugurated on 18 March 2004 with forty-one of the AU member states agreeing to participate through 202 legislators. Its new R1.5 billion headquarters outside Pretoria was under construction soon afterwards.

The result of all this Herculean effort, much of it driven by the South African president, is an almost classic Mbeki paradox. Africa now boasts a potentially viable institutional infrastructure in the form of the AU and a nascent Pan-African Parliament. It has an active if not yet effective peace and security regime. It has a raft of protocols and principles culminating in the ambitious and worthwhile APRM, and it has an institution in NEPAD that seeks to advance the interests of pan-African infrastructural development. In short, it is all there in terms of institutions and principles and intent.

And yet it has not all quite come together. In the last years of the Mbeki administration the continent witnessed deeply contra-indicative political events in two of the three major partners in this initiative: Nigeria and Kenya. Both experienced flawed elections – in the latter case leading to violent ethnic clashes that set back by decades a carefully nurtured national consensus.

Peacekeeping operations have not been an unqualified success. One of the biggest challenges to the peacekeeping mission of the AU's aggressive 'responsibility to protect' mandate was in the Darfur region of Sudan from 2005 onwards. The African Mission in Sudan (AMIS) failed in its primary objective, largely due to the lack of equipment, funds, personnel and expertise for the 7 000 AU peacekeepers. They were later augmented by UN forces. Equally, an operation by the African Mission in Burundi (AMIB), begun in April 2003, can claim only slender returns. Both operations have locked material numbers of African peacekeeping forces in place for unpredictable periods of time. It is unfair to blame the AU for this – one only has to look at the length of time NATO forces have been deployed in the Balkans to understand how painstakingly long such missions historically tend to be. But the point remains: the AU has not *succeeded* in two of its first peacekeeping deployments and for a fundamental reason – it simply does not have the capacity to sustain such projects over the long haul.

By 2007, disturbing reports were being tabled about the weakening discipline of South African troops on peacekeeping operations, with a number of reported murders, assaults and rapes directed at local populations and a substantial loss of weapons – in one case, the armaments of an entire patrol 'lost' to rebels in the DRC.

The NEPAD legacy is now also under threat. It was always a controversial project, with challenges by various civil rights groups that it was a collusion between the African elites and the developed world and ignored the real issues on the continent. As most of these bodies had been left out of the process, one can easily detect an element of self-interest in all this – it has been my experience that there is nothing more embittered than an NGO cut out of the funding loop. Less easy to dismiss, however, were the words of one of the founder members of NEPAD, Senegalese President Abdoulaye Wade, whose Omega project for African growth had been fused into NEPAD. He told a West African television channel in 2006 that millions of dollars had been wasted achieving nothing: 'I have decided no longer to waste my time going to those meetings where nothing ever gets done.'

There is truth in this. Apart from one major and very disputatious underwater fibre-optic cable project – which did not need a whole institution to effect – little of material impact has emerged from all that time and expense. Serious doubts exist whether NEPAD will survive Mbeki's departure. In all likelihood, the first initiative to go will be the APRM, which has already had a very lacklustre take-up by the majority of members.

Yet South Africa will undoubtedly continue to fund much of this extensive institutional infrastructure and its operational costs, given the notorious reluctance of African governments to pay their dues to multilateral organisations. The government has been remarkably coy in telling the South African public what its exact share will be – questions in parliament have been met by emotional responses that the mission far outweighs any crass concerns about costs. This hardly reassures a society and an economy already accommodating another vast and uncosted ideological project – Mbeki-style empowerment. The proposed African Standby Force will also have to rely heavily on South African logistical and technological support.

The net result of all this effort by the Mbeki presidency to reshape the architecture of intra-African and extra-continental foreign relations is not too dissimilar from his experiences at home: a wealth of institutions and intentions, but a dearth of capacity to support them and a disturbing willingness to ignore their principles when expedience demands.

This brings us to the two parallel issues that most severely challenged the Mbeki foreign policy legacy and displayed all the darker characteristics of his management of domestic policy: intransigence, defensiveness and paranoia.

The first manifested itself in a range of positions at the UN on human rights issues which, even if defended to the last breath by the Mbeki administration for a century, are still explicable only in terms of a bitter hatred of the United States and the West, a willingness to surrender the most basic principles of the country, and indeed those of the fine multilateral constitution partly created by Mbeki, in pursuit of an ideological posture, much of it driven by a deeply pro-Palestinian, pro-Islamicist lobby within his own presidency and foreign affairs ministry.

The Geneva-based UN Watch, an NGO set up to monitor the voting record of member states in regard to human rights issues (albeit with a strong emphasis on issues affecting Israel), reported in late 2007 that South Africa had one of the worst human rights voting records in the UN. It charged, specifically, that South Africa had:

- voted with China and Russia, the only other members opposing a Security Council resolution urging the Myanmar military junta to free political prisoners and end sexual violence;
- voted to discontinue scrutiny of human rights violations in Iran and Uzbekistan;
- encouraged the UN's Human Rights Council to block surveys of country infractions of human rights;
- as a direct result, been responsible for scrutiny of human rights violations in Cuba and Belarus being withdrawn from the UN mandate; and
- voted against accreditation of a Canadian gay-rights NGO.

The charges led to an immediate response in South Africa. In a statement issued on 18 November 2007, the Department of Foreign Affairs reaffirmed its commitment to human rights, but accused the UN of double standards in not addressing human rights abuses in developed countries; said the choice of issues was biased and that a holistic view of South Africa's record would look better; demanded the UN should not simply condemn abuse but should do something concrete about it; claimed the resolution on Myanmar was opposed because it was in the wrong forum rather than because of its content; and so on.

The justifications quickly placed South Africa in an intolerably contradictory position. It had been the main protagonist for a more aggressive policy of interference in the internal affairs of African states through the AU and had instituted a formalised process of scrutinising governance among its members through the APRM. Yet here it was at the UN, doing all in its power to balk at that body's powers of scrutiny and reprimand regarding member states that abused human rights in the rest of the world.

Not surprisingly, seasoned members of the UN looked for a more plausible reason for this bizarre record. They marked it down to the intractable suspicion and antagonism of Mbeki and his presidency towards the developed world, and moved on to other things.

The second major challenge to Mbeki in the international terrain, of course, was the festering wound of Zimbabwe, which, like the arms scandal internally, dogged him for every step of his presidency and eventually came to be one of the sources of his greatest humiliation on the international stage he had so much wanted to bestride as the African Kemal Atatürk.

The Zimbabwe story is briefly told. South Africa's northern neighbour was a British colony and entered a bitter civil war between 1967 and 1979, after an intransigent white minority under Ian Smith refused to accept the principle of black majority rule. Independence had been unilaterally declared in 1965. The war had claimed more than 20 000 lives before the then South African prime minister, John Vorster, intervened with the support of neighbouring African leaders.

He cut off military support to the Rhodesian security forces, withdrew helicopters and his paramilitary units from the Zambezi Valley, suspended fuel supplies (as Rhodesia was under international embargo, this was serious), closed the borders to traffic and cut electricity. Within eighteen months, Smith and his black nationalist foes were at the negotiating table from which eventually emerged the modern (now previously modern) Zimbabwe.

Vorster's actions were decisive and courageous. He did not believe that the white minority in Rhodesia had a viable policy to find an accommodation with its black majority (his own policy of separate development proved no more viable, but that is another story) and he anticipated a continuing escalation of violence across the whole sub-region. His actions had a price, which he had fully anticipated. It brought about a schism in his white nationalist Afrikaner party and led to the birth of an enduring ultra-right-wing element that was a factor in his country's politics right up to the democratic elections of 1994 and indeed claimed the life of Chris Hani, one of the icons of the ANC resistance struggle.

The victor in the 1980 Zimbabwean elections, Robert Gabriel Mugabe of the Zimbabwe African National Union – Patriotic Front (Zanu-PF), began promisingly, with an appropriate rhetoric of conciliation and support for market economies. This quickly soured. A rebellion by the Matabele people, constituting 16 per cent of the population and concentrated in the south-western regions, supported by South Africa's newly militarised leadership under PW Botha, was brutally crushed. A land-reform programme underwritten by the United Kingdom was halted because of widespread corruption on the part of Zanu-PF. In 2000, amid an already declining political and economic environment, Mugabe went to the country in a referendum to give him more power. He failed. Then the wheels came off.

Elections were rigged, unionists repressed, opposition members in the Movement for Democratic Change (MDC) under Morgan Tsvangirai assaulted and arrested, bands of state-sponsored vigilantes (called war veterans, although most had not even been born when Rhodesia was at war) roamed the countryside, attacking any perceived enemy of Mugabe. Huge tracts of productively farmed land owned by whites were arbitrarily seized and handed to cronies of the regime or the veterans. Poor urban dwellers, supporters of the opposition, were driven from their homes by bulldozers. As the economic situation deteriorated, Mugabe imposed price restrictions. The economy went into free fall. By 2008, 80 per cent of Zimbabwe's population was unemployed, inflation was in the millions per cent and life expectancy at birth – 39.5 years – was one of the lowest on the continent.

Watching this precipitate fall from grace of one of Africa's once most prosperous countries were Mbeki and his Ascendancy. It is tiresome to go into the details of his engagement with Mugabe. Let it simply be noted that in pursuit of 'quiet diplomacy', Mbeki forbore to take any decisive steps to oppose Mugabe publicly or to impose deterrent restraints such as sanctions or other measures. He gave scant comfort to the constitutional opposition in Zimbabwe or to a world increasingly appalled by the human rights violations in that country.

On the contrary, he defended the process of quiet diplomacy in public and mounted a campaign against the West on the basis that it should leave Africans to sort out African problems. Typically, Mbeki steadfastly ignored the irony of Africa insistently demanding Western intervention in terms of peacekeepers and aid to sort out the consequences of man-made disasters on the continent, while simultaneously opposing the West's right to challenge the political leadership that caused the crises in the first place.

Suffice it to say that Mbeki's quiet diplomacy yielded little for eight years. Zimbabwe slid inexorably towards catastrophe. A million refugees fled across the border to South Africa, adding to further problems of crime, unemployment and a rising mood of xenophobia. To save the village, it appeared, Mbeki's strategy had first to destroy it.

In 2007, Mbeki was mandated by SADC to mediate between the competing factions in Zimbabwe. Here, at last, was some progress. He managed to persuade the octogenarian Mugabe to hold the 2008 elections in conditions of reasonable fairness and to publish the results at each polling station as they became available – crucial to avoid the vote rigging that occurs in so many African states immediately after the polls close. He also pushed for constitutional changes to remove the thirty nominated seats in the legislature, by which Mugabe could have expected to retain power. These were material advances, which, had they been immediately honoured, would have vindicated the Mbeki legacy despite the inordinate length of time taken to resolve the issue and the effective destruction of the Zimbabwean economy in the interim.

Such vindication, tragically for the besieged Mbeki presidency, did not come. The polling had no sooner closed in Zimbabwe than it became abundantly clear that Mugabe had lost – contrary to his delusional expectations.

The central tallying of votes was abruptly moved from its pre-arranged spot to a secret security force headquarters; opposition members were illegally denied access to the tallying; a number of Zimbabwe Electoral Commission officials were arrested for allegedly under-counting Mugabe's vote; a recount in twenty-three parliamentary seats was ordered by Mugabe – suspiciously akin in numbers to the nominated seats Mbeki had persuaded Mugabe to forfeit – *even before the results were out*; the presidential results were delayed for weeks and then Mugabe demanded a run-off election, again contrary to the very electoral laws Mbeki had sponsored. Finally, the army, police and militias swarmed back into the streets and remote rural areas to intimidate the opposition, and the New York–based Human Rights Watch reported that 'detention camps' were being set up for opposition members.

It was clear that Mugabe had no intention of going, and as he had neglected to follow the first rule of an outgoing despot, namely to make a deal with the incoming regime, he had little room to manoeuvre. Intelligence reports to the South African government indicated that the Zimbabwean police and military leadership, deeply involved in human rights abuses and widespread corruption during the entire tenure of the Mugabe regime, were bunkering down for a shoot-out.

The SADC monitoring team, under South African pressure, announced the electoral process to have been free and fair, as they had done on every previous occasion, and went home even before the votes were counted – not unlike watching the first forty-five minutes of a World Cup football match and then unilaterally declaring the final result at half-time. Mbeki courted disaster by visiting Mugabe in Harare on his way to an emergency SADC summit (boycotted by Mugabe) and being photographed hand in hand with the culprit. Asked if there *was* a crisis in Zimbabwe, he said no.

A few weeks later, a Chinese ship carrying seventy-seven tons of ammunition and support weapons for the Zimbabwean military arrived in Durban to offload its cargo, preparatory to sending it to Zimbabwe. Despite being in flagrant breach of its own National Conventional Arms Control Committee rules forbidding dispatch of weapons to countries with a record of human rights abuses, neither the committee (chaired by an Mbeki loyalist) nor the government did anything to prevent the consignment reaching its destination. It fell to church organisations to get a court order and union threats not to unload the cargo to prevent this lethal gift from the Chinese government from further adding to the crisis. The ship subsequently sailed away.

And so this great tragedy moved to its final tableau in the Security Council of the UN on 14 April 2008. Here Mbeki was called upon to chair the Security Council's deliberations on relations between that body and the African continent. It had been Mbeki, after all, who had been most zealous in securing a non-permanent seat on the Security Council for Africa, and it was he who had defeated Nigeria's Olusegun Obasanjo as the first African two-year member. By all measures, this should have been the apogee of his career, the crowning moment in his attempts to be seen as the embodiment of African modernity, the colossus straddling an uncomprehending developed world and a resurgent Africa, the swansong that would have emblazoned the Mbeki legacy as one of progressiveness and modernism. It was a disaster.

Mbeki failed to address the most pressing human rights issue on the continent in his twenty-minute address. If he hoped this would dissuade discussion among his peers, he was mistaken. The other members of the council called for the urgent release of Zimbabwe's election results and even the mild-mannered UN secretary general, Ban Ki-Moon, all but gave Mbeki notice that the world was tired of waiting for African leaders to resolve the problem. The next day, the Group of Eight most industrialised nations issued a statement expressing their concern about the situation in Zimbabwe.

Mounting violence eventually forced the MDC to withdraw from the 27 June presidential run-off elections and Mugabe declared victory to outrage among a range of Western and African leaders. Mbeki, under intense pressure from all quarters, fought off further sanctions and put his faith in a power-sharing deal between Zanu-PF and the MDC, thus effectively seeking to reward electoral theft, as had happened in Kenya.

In late July 2008, South Africa managed to kick-start a round of direct negotiations between the parties with the aim of crafting a transitional power-sharing agreement leading eventually to MDC control. By this stage even Mugabe could read the signs. His country was in economic ruins, international pressure was intense and both the UN and AU had sent their own envoys to 'support' Mbeki. He at last grasped that his main champion and protector, Mbeki, was himself under enormous pressure and that the process might soon be prised from his friend's flaccid grip. With suitable guarantees for him and his henchmen in regard to indemnities from prosecution for crimes and human rights violations over decades, he indicated he was at last prepared to contemplate the end of his despotic tenure. For some it was a glorious justification of Mbeki's policy of quiet diplomacy. For others that was as absurd as calling the German surrender in 1945 a vindication of Neville Chamberlain's policy of appeasement in the 1930s. In both cases the consequences had been incalculable, needless human suffering.

The only question that remains in regard to the Zimbabwe situation is whether Mbeki could have averted the protracted and devastating impasse earlier. During his tenure he and his apologists endlessly sought to reduce the argument to the absurd – either full-scale military invasion or nothing.

Of course, the alternatives were many, on an escalating scale of public condemnation, targeted measures against senior government officials, selective non-humanitarian embargoes, sporting and cultural bans, transport interdictions, power interruptions and, finally, total isolation. None of these tacks were ever attempted. Indeed, the Mbeki administration went out of its way to rally African opinion in an anti-West front on the basis of a spurious African solidarity, a sort of giant racial partners-in-crime project that did nothing to enhance either Mbeki's international image or that of Africa. Mugabe's sense of impunity, not surprisingly, grew until it was indeed impregnable. He had become the ultimate self-fulfilling prophecy.

When I had debates on this issue with senior ANC members they would ask what options there were. When I reminded them gently of John Vorster's solution to Smith's intransigence, they regarded me as if I had shot their favourite dog. Whether it was from the memory of that hated apartheid figure or a recoil from the thought of actually having to *do* something about the growing Zimbabwe crisis, I could never quite work out.

There is an even better example of successful African intervention in a continental problem area. In February 2005, Gnassingbe Eyadema, president of the West African country of Togo, died. In terms of the constitution, leadership of the country went to the Speaker of the legislature until elections could be held. The military, however, opted to illegally install Eyadema's son, Faure, as president.

Within two days the pretender had been summonsed to Abuja by Nigeria's President Olusegun Obasanjo, acting on behalf of the AU. A person involved in the process told of how Obasanjo warned Junior that if he went ahead with the plan, Nigeria would cut off every resource to Togo, and Faure, his wife and children would be 'walking the streets of Lomé without shoes'.

On 4 May 2005, elections were held. Faure, it must be observed, still won, allegedly by vote rigging, but the point was that Nigeria had used its considerable weight and authority to halt at the outset this challenge to constitutionality and human rights. The pride of the new Nigerian modern middle classes at this intercession in favour of democracy was palpable.

All this leads to a consideration of what future international role South Africa has in the wake of the Mbeki era.

The first point is that the institutional edifice created by Mbeki with such care and cost will survive – but only just and probably for no longer than a new South African government is prepared to make the necessary huge financial and human resources investments to keep it alive.

The reality is that although the African continent has enjoyed a significant economic growth path in the last five years, this has largely been on the back of three factors: soaring commodity prices; step-change opportunities created by new communication technologies; and some smart macro- and micro-economic management in some countries (Nigeria's consolidation of its banking system is a stellar example).

None of this yet adds up to a sustainable growth path. Neither does it deal with the reality that increased wealth in West, South and East Africa has simply translated into yawning and growing income and lifestyle inequalities, with the attendant risks of social upheaval à la Kenya. In the short term, all the powerhouses of Africa will have their major challenges: Nigeria's is the physical and security infrastructure to manage its key export commodity, oil, and the stemming of truly awesome levels of lost national income through theft; in South Africa it is a rebuilding of the physical, human and institutional infrastructure, systemically weakened during the Mbeki years; in Kenya it is managing the political landscape and resurgent ethnic tensions.

None of this is to say that the pan-African institutions so caringly nurtured by Mbeki will collapse. They will not – but they will, I fear, simply limp along, the home of nothing more than a stream of good intentions and hopes, the resting place of those numerous politicians dissuaded from considering illegal challenges to adverse electoral outcomes at home. In other words, no change there.

At best, we can say that Mbeki was a prophet before his time. That time, though, will surely come, although when is anybody's guess.

The second point is that South Africa has lost its moral and technical pre-eminence in regard to its position on the continent. Again, qualifications are necessary. It is not that South Africa will not continue for a considerable time to be the economic powerhouse of the continent, nor dominate in terms of all the key indices of power consumption, GDP per capita, industrial output and so on.

What it has lost is the almost mythical aura it had in the immediate post-liberation phase as the saviour of the continent. Part of this was due to the unethical and buccaneering attitude of some of the South African companies and entrepreneurs that first entered the continent after liberation. Much damage was done before the serious players emerged after doing the requisite analysis and scoping. But it is also true that South Africa's public service hardly helped. Over the years – and here anecdotally – I have witnessed the slow creep of cynicism on the part of my African social and business partners about the South African 'miracle'.

The weakening of the criminal justice system in South Africa threatened the life and property of African expatriates in South Africa. African visitors to the country were subjected to the most humiliating insults and bureaucratic obstacles, the like of which few South Africans have experienced in, say, Nigeria or Kenya. South African state departments, trade and industry in particular, failed to match their promises. Bilateral trade agreements remained unsigned (granted, huge disputes exist as to who was to blame); highly qualified African technicians and academics were refused access to South Africa while all sorts of criminals, gangsters and hucksters were waved through, and grassroots xenophobia has grown. This process will be inevitably compounded by the crisis in internal energy generation due to bad planning and management, which must result in a South African retreat from involvement in major African power projects for some time. Again, although South Africa has taken a vociferous role in campaigning for a fairer international trade regime on behalf of the continent, it has in reality yielded little.

Many progressive Africans, not surprisingly, have begun an inexorable process of discounting South Africa as a significant player on the continent and, for both practicable and chauvinistic reasons, have begun challenging South Africa's self-appointed role as the voice of Africa. The xenophobic violence in mid-2008 – anticipated in NEPAD's African Peer Review Report on South Africa in 2007 – hardly helped. This opens up intriguing new possibilities in regard to major African power alliances, none of which are of comfort to South Africa.

The aggressive attempts by France's President Nicholas Sarkozy to court the Mediterranean rim countries in a new political and economic alliance may yet work. If so, the nominal and unconvincing Arab solidarity with sub-Saharan Africa may diminish. The war between the Arabic north and African south in Sudan has generated its own, if understated, tensions. With the extraordinary rate of globalisation and modernisation of the North African countries, the attraction of an emotional and largely historic association with its South becomes less important. Only Ghaddafi is out of step with this initiative.

West Africa is looking increasingly West for technology and capital and East for markets. South Africa is still important for its investment in the telecommunications, financial, manufacturing, agricultural and retail sectors, but as it has no specific expertise or presence in the dominant oil upstream and downstream markets, it is not a major player. The Chinese, by comparison, are players simply because they are voracious consumers of all base and fossil commodities and will do anything to acquire them – going indeed to lengths no listed South African company would countenance.

East Africa is exactly what its name suggests. Its focus is massively directed towards India, strengthened by the historic ties between the vibrant Asian-descended Kenyan trading community and the Indian homeland and by the exploding trade with China. The major trading entrepôt of Dubai has also opened a huge opportunity for East African trade at a material disadvantage to South Africa, which has been pretty roundly defeated in its heartland expertise – retail and tourism – although its financial sector is still quite active.

Increasingly, South African intra-African trade is being characterised by three features.

Apart from some very dominant plays in the financial and telecommunications space, South Africa's major involvement in the African markets in the future will be in mining in the toughest and least hospitable parts of

the continent. The country's mining industry is well placed to do this –
the ultimate toughies – but let us not fool ourselves that this is going to
create Africa Inc. for South African enterprise.

The second feature is the move by South African companies to take
their operating entities offshore and to access funding from foreign sources.
This is partly for tax benefit reasons (increasingly closed down by South
African authorities) but also because it is actually easier for South African
companies to operate in Africa by appearing as little South African as
possible, for reasons of both national pride in the target market and the
endless obligation to defend what the country is doing in terms of its
international politics.

Third, the real African demand from South Africa is not for capital (in
the recent era of liquidity excess, money has been begging to find a roost
in safe harbours in Africa) but for skills. Most of the skills moving north
are white, many of them refugees from affirmative action. The loss of
these skills obviously impoverishes South Africa, but one can at least take
comfort in the fact that it is contributing to a growth of African industry
and skills.

This is not to say that when deployed in the target market these skills
all fit in immediately. A whole new process of acculturation takes place,
worthy of a book in itself.

What does this all mean?

Firstly, the ability of South Africa to impress its African neighbours
with its assumed right to be regarded as the pre-eminent sub-Saharan
African country is rapidly eroding. This is because South Africans, in the
view of many Africans, have not proved themselves more successful at
running a modern state than has the rest of the continent. We are just
coming off a higher base and therefore have longer and further to fall is
the common view. That we have fallen under Mbeki is no longer a subject
of debate among most Africans.

Secondly, the view that South Africa is the repository of all skill and
wisdom is dead. Most South African multinationals operating in Africa no
longer regard South Africa as their primary source of skills, given the poor
quality of educational output. They recruit from abroad and increasingly
from India, the Middle East and South-East Asia. In a particular quirk, many
are recruiting South Africans off international databases and agencies and
not directly from South Africa at all.

Thirdly, the treasured South African view that there is some intrinsic solidarity between all African countries based on a shared sense of deprivation and marginalisation is challengeable. The South African attempt to create a common front in regard to the European Union–African partnership agreements in SADC has ended in discord. South Africa's aggressive posture at the World Trade Organisation's Doha round of talks is attracting concern from other African states. Zimbabwe opened serious cracks in the façade of SADC unity and raised concerns by other African countries about the damage that was being done to its attempts to project its modernist image.

The bottom line is that South African dominance on the continent, the earlier and very chauvinistic South African view that it was uniquely placed because of its economic dominance and its history of anti-apartheid struggle to engage the multilateral agencies on behalf of the continent, is now under threat. As South Africa inevitably turns more inwards to resolve its fractious political and weakening economic conditions, it is unlikely that its ability to project its external influence will grow. The reverse is true. Mbeki's defeat at Polokwane and internationally over the Zimbabwe debacle will discount him and, tragically, the country for some time from having any major moral, economic or political influence in the region or abroad.

This reality seems not to have been brought home to most South Africans. There remains either a white hubris that the minority group will sally forth to save Africa, or a black consensus that, as the victims of the longest enduring form of foreign domination on the continent, the majority group is anointed with a particular victim status, allowing members to speak for oppressed Africans. I have sat through too many meetings and dinners with black South Africans and other Africans to have illusions any longer. The majority of Africans who are not from South Africa are appalled by the decline in the country's infrastructure and bemused by the lack of willingness of the indigenous people to rise to the manifold opportunities created by the liberated South Africa.

This was best summarised at one dinner party that I hosted where a Nigerian entrepreneur, goaded by the endless plaints of the South African guests about the iniquity of apartheid, observed (as best I recall): 'My parents would have praised God for what you have received. You have infrastructure, political power and great economic influence. You have the ear of the world, which we never had. You have not had civil war such as we endured. What more, in God's name, do you want?'

This will be the big question to be answered by the Mbeki succession.

It will have to seek to meet Mbeki's extravagant promises without losing focus on the many domestic challenges; it will have to rebuild bridges with the continent and the world; it will have to reposition itself in terms of its human rights and environmental policies through balanced, consistent and predictable policies; and, finally, it will have to signal to all parties that the protocols and documents signed with such abandon by the Mbeki administration and then so lightly ignored have meaning. South Africa and Africa's integrity depend upon it.

CHAPTER 23

Saving the institutions

We must accept finite disappointment, but we must not lose infinite hope. — MARTIN LUTHER KING JR[1]

AMID ALL THE GLOOM AND DOOM, IT IS EASY TO FORGET HOW fortunate South Africa is in having such broad areas of consensus between the majority of its people. Inspired leadership pulled the country back from the brink of racial implosion at the critical moment in the early 1990s, and a benign financial environment for most South Africans has since seen the entrenchment of a core set of values supportive of a modern and democratic state and society – even if current political leadership shows itself in serial breach of these values.

The 2007 South African Reconciliation Barometer[2] shows that the glass is still half full as regards interracial reconciliation, and there is thus an important platform on which to build future confidence and internal cohesion.

A previous chapter sought to focus on the economic levers that can be used to establish a baseline stability within the society to accommodate the two most at-risk communities. Now we will look at how institutions can be strengthened to support that baseline.

The overwhelming advantage South Africa has is a constitution that enjoys wide legitimacy and was the creature of genuine national engagement. The South African Opinion Leader Survey 2007, for example, found that 88.4 per cent of the respondents had a great deal of confidence in the constitution, versus 32.3 per cent who had confidence in the public service. It set a modern yardstick by which to measure the society and thus presents all elements of society with major challenges. Nothing can be more important in the coming years then protecting the integrity of both the constitution and the court that interprets it on behalf of the society.

During the tumult caused by the fracturing of Mbeki's *de facto* one-party state, the role of this court and its officers has been bandied about as if they were disposable elements in some church raffle. Granted, most of these attacks have come from the ANC's youth wing, arguably the most pre-modern element in South African politics, but they nevertheless constitute an attack on the integrity of the one remaining institution of the country that had escaped the insidious influence of the ruling party's toxic politics.

The second important institution to have thus far remained reasonably inviolate is the judiciary. This institution has experienced its own travails, brought about by skills shortages and inexperience, but it has generally shown a strong independence in its decision-making. This has not saved it from the ire of ANC Classic and those in its leadership most subject to its scrutiny. As Zuma's trial date approached in August 2008, the attacks on both the Constitutional Court and the judiciary by ANC Classic increased in intensity and recklessness to the point where even the supine ANC Lite cabinet was moved to express its concern about these challenges to the constitutional order.

The key to the integrity of this system remains the Judicial Services Commission, which is ultimately responsible for appointment of the country's judiciary. Sadly, a half-baked resolution to a case in 2007 involving *prima facie* evidence of irregular conduct by a judge in a senior position has called into question the ability of the commission to make firm, concise and appropriate decisions. This institution, more than any other, needs to be urgently reviewed by presidential commission to determine if it is competent in its membership and function to fulfil its awesome responsibilities at this crucial juncture in the country's history.

The South African parliament, as observed earlier, has undergone something of a metamorphosis since the defeat of the Mbeki Ascendancy. On no less than seven occasions in the first two months of the 2008 parliamentary session, a non-partisan consensus was reached in the committees about the failure of government ministers and state functionaries. This was an almost miraculous event and an indication of the capacity of the institution to establish its independence and fulfil its watchdog role.

But beware of hubris. The ruling party is in a state of considerable flux and the warming show of independence in parliament at the beginning of 2008 could merely be just another terrain of battle for the protagonists in the internal party struggles. The fact that the ruling party opted to convert the latter part of the parliamentary session to only fifteen plenary working days so as to allow parliamentarians to 'concentrate on constituency work' is an indication both of the deep confusion within the party about who is calling the shots and the willingness of the party to subject the imperatives of the state function to party expedience. Still, in broad terms, the judiciary and parliament are in a reasonably good position to fulfil their constitutional duties.

Where the problem arises, however, is the erosion of capacity within the public sector itself, and I would suggest that some urgent corrective action is needed to restore a sense of discipline and effectiveness in the public service.

The Public Service Commission is the independent body charged with overseeing the administration and integrity of the public service – the board of external directors, if one likes. In its 2004–2007 review, the commission highlights rising levels of corruption within the public service and what amounts to an almost contemptuous attitude by many departments to attempts by the commission to call them to account. In only 36 per cent of the instances of corruption referred to the departments by the commission were responses ever received, let alone action taken.

The charitable view is that it is mere incompetence that prevents the bureaucrats from responding to these queries. The more ominous interpretation is that the departments have no interest in complying – that the country has moved beyond the point where corruption is aberrational, to the level where it is an entrenched part of the culture of public organisations, as it is in many other developing countries. This concern can only be deepened by the blatantly political decision of the ruling party to destroy the one functioning and effective anti-corruption unit in the country.

A starting point, I suggest, would be for the ANC to review its legislative programme. One of the most destructive legacies of the Mbeki tenure is ideological and legislative overreach. By the end of his tenure, the disconnect between the intent of legislation and its practical outcome had reached such levels that Mbeki – and indeed all the institutions of state – had begun to lose the faith of the public at a startling rate.

This, then, is the first point: the urgent need to distinguish between what *should* be done (the preserve of the ideologue and dreamer) and what *can* be done (the sphere of the implementer and the rationalist). The South African political elite is awash with the former and bereft of the latter. With the post-Polokwane ANC's born-again enthusiasm for being 'pro-poor', prepare for an avalanche of deeply ideological, costly and impractical legislative proposals.

It is therefore more important than ever that a rigorous policy-impact approach is applied to all prospective legislation. Such an approach would require all legislation to be submitted to a separately constituted technical committee, comprising representatives of the most affected state departments and external parties, to decide whether the legislation is practicable, capable of implementation and desirable. This must happen before legislation is tabled.

If the legislation is deemed feasible, the technical committee must confirm in writing that it is capable of implementation. By so doing, each director-general confirms that he or she personally underwrites the effective implementation of the legislation and this becomes part of their performance charters. If they refuse to do so, the legislature would know that if the politicians press ahead, they do so against the best advice of the state.

This will not entirely stop stupid legislators making stupid laws. But it would slow down the pace of irresponsibility in our legislature and shift the onus of flawed policies and laws firmly from the directors-general to the ministers and legislature. No more will South Africa have to endure the popular ministerial pastime of blaming its ever-revolving officialdom for failing to implement laws it had no hope of enforcing in the first place.

The next step must be the implementation of performance charters for every public servant, tied to both incentives and sanctions for meeting the objectives or failing to do so. Thus far, the state has made derisory attempts to impose performance charters on its top public servants, the directors-general, and as of 2007 only 27 per cent of these had been signed off.

The astonishing fact, then, is that major sections of the public service are run by officials who have no sanction against them in the event that they do not perform, other than the withholding of bonuses. As this historically does not happen, even for the worst infraction, it is hardly a threat. It is this fact alone that has given rise to the pervasive characteristic of the South African public service – endless turmoil between ministers and directors-general, between staff and directors, between directors-general themselves and between the departments and the public. Underlying all of this is a pervasive culture of smear, backbiting and defamation by anonymity. In many cases these rows end in a settlement with the director-general concerned, often amounting to millions of rands, and he or she being moved on to be replaced by someone else, who goes through the same hoops.

Apart from being enormously diversionary for the official concerned, it does not make for focused and necessary decision-making. Neither does it enhance the credibility of the state: indeed, one of the things that has probably most damaged the Mbeki administration's reputation is this spirit of impunity that prevails at both the party and official level. It is a culture in which hardly anybody is ever called to account for even the most grievous failings, and in even fewer circumstances penalised.

The completion and adoption of these charters at director-general level and a rapid cascading down the ranks to the lowest level are critical to restoring some semblance of discipline, professionalism and care to a public service that is widely regarded as being the greatest single obstacle to implementation of the ANC's redistribution policies and actualisation of some excellent social legislation.

This step will inevitably bring the government into conflict with the public-service unions, which regard such charters as anathema. Here again lies an urgent need for the ANC government to re-engage with the unions in order to establish a *modus vivendi* whereby honest work is rewarded with honest pay. The challenges of achieving this should not be underestimated: not only is the public service battling with a problem of service culture, it is also struggling with a self-induced skills crisis that is now at critical level. In this last regard, establishment of the apex schools and bridging qualifications is urgently required to start normalising the situation.

It is essential that the state should begin a review of all appointments above the level of deputy director-general in national departments and the equivalent grading in provincial and local authorities to determine fitness for office. In the event that the incumbent is unable to match the require-ments, he or she should be immediately recalled and placed on an urgent upgrade programme, returning to an equivalent post only on completion of a suitable skills-based course. A review of public servants' qualifications was in fact authorised in 2005 by the Public Service Commission, but by 2008 it was reporting little progress, due to stiff opposition or indifference from the public service. In a country where an estimated one-third of résumés are fraudulent, the bureaucratic tardiness is perhaps understandable.

In the interim, the government should establish the equivalent of a national stabilisation force of experts, local and foreign, to parachute into stressed public organisations and at least keep the wheels turning. To some extent this is already happening through interventions by large consulting firms in the management of state institutions such as home affairs and various attempts by departments such as local government, Eskom and agriculture to pull together core teams of experts to assist and maintain operations. The Joint Initiative on Priority Skills Acquisition, one of the better state initiatives, is active here also. Sadly, anecdotal evidence suggests that, once compiled, the database of experts lies unused, no doubt awaiting a full-scale crisis such as the one that hit Eskom.

It needs to go further. A model exists in the United Kingdom, where the Department for International Development has created databases of deployable civilian experts in the fields of engineering, law enforcement, accounting and communications. This allows suitably qualified people to be dispatched at a moment's notice to trouble spots. The same principle can be applied in South Africa, but it would need to be done in a coordinated way so as to ensure effective deployment of resources and, critically, that the stabilisation units are provided with cast-iron mandates to get the job done without political interference from local vested interests.

This has to be driven from the top, indeed from the presidency, as the natural inclination of all bureaucrats is to oppose and frustrate the intervention of any other agency in their affairs. The state would be amazed at the corps of high-level skills still existent in the country and how many people would be more than prepared to join such an initiative, were they to be convinced this was a genuine attempt by the government to put South Africa back on track and not just another way to allow its public servants to abdicate responsibility.

The ANC has made no secret of the fact that it regards the party as the true commander of South Africa and its fortunes. Because of that, it is impossible to consider a restoration of integrity in South African institutions without considering the heart of the problem – the party itself. In this sense, then, the ANC's finding of its own moral core is not a party imperative but a national one. In the absence of any likely challenger to its hegemony, the salvation of national integrity can to a large extent proceed only through rather than around the party. And of course, herein lies the irony. The political leadership of the ANC insists simultaneously that the party is both the state and a private organisation. It is part of the enormous confusion in the minds of the organisation about what it exactly *is*, but while the leaders wrestle with the issue, the reality is that the country stumbles further along the path of demodernisation.

The fact that the ANC and its leadership have lost credibility among a material swathe of people should surprise neither the party nor the public. No political movement can make so many mistakes and not expect that there is a price to be paid. Mbeki paid the price for his particular style of leadership at Polokwane in December 2007 and there is little doubt that Zuma will pay a similar price before the next election for his lack of leadership. But it is the ANC, the near-century-old institution, that will pay the overall price in terms of lost credibility at home and abroad.

This is not to say the ANC is in danger of being voted out of office. It is not. The compelling ties of history, nostalgia, legend, patronage and certainly the concrete advances delivered by the party to the poor will ensure it wins a majority at the next polls. The question therefore is not what will replace the ANC, but rather what *kind* of ANC will South Africa inherit in 2009?

By early 2008, the country had entered an uneasy interregnum that had created ominous vacuums in the state function. While Mbeki and his ANC Lite still held power, Zuma and his ANC Classic held influence. These two forces were in constant tension with each other during this period as the camps vied for dominance. No state institution escaped the war: the bemused board of the South African Broadcasting Corporation found itself the object of an ANC parliamentary vote of no confidence in April 2008 – one more skirmish in the battle between Classic and Lite for political control of the state broadcaster. Into this space crept other actors, particularly those who had been held at bay for nearly a decade by the Mbeki Ascendancy: the communists and unionists.

It is important not to become diverted by this situation. It is temporary. Mbeki will depart from office in 2009. Well before then, his doings and those of his associates, while protected by the secrecy of power, will have been dissected, disseminated and deprecated by his political foes within his own party. Almost the first thing ANC Classic did when back in the seat was to call for a full internal inquiry into the arms deal and an audit of the sweetheart deals done through Chancellor House, the party's secretive investment arm. The thrust of this book has been that much which Mbeki did was sound, but that more, too much more, was questionable and indeed deeply damaging to the long-term interests of the country. He and his Ascendancy will limp rather than blaze into history.

Between now and then there will be huge turmoil in the ANC as a new leader and a new ascendancy is found. ANC Classic, as currently constituted, will not govern South Africa for long, and neither, in all probability, will Jacob Zuma. Both are just too implausible.

ANC Classic is made up of too many competing interests. The crisis of power in South Africa has allowed all sorts of unlikely parties – the unions, the communists and even the ANC Youth League – to claim they are, in fact, the inheritors of the ANC's mantle of power, on the preposterous basis of a paltry 2400 votes at a party conference. The constitution is the source of power in this country and whoever is elected to the presidency in terms thereof is, to quote the constitution, 'the Head of State and head of the national executive' – the one in power. Everybody else is but a pretender.

The only option for ANC Classic, if it wants to run the country, is to use its two-thirds majority in parliament to fire Mbeki and replace him. But this they can only do if they can prove him to be in serious violation of the law or the constitution, guilty of serious misconduct or unable to perform his duties. ANC Classic would find itself pressed to make a case on any of these charges without potentially incriminating itself: many are, after all, still part of the government.

And so the country endures the discomfort of a ruling party pretending to be in power and a president pretending to rule. The fact that Mbeki has chosen not to make explicit his constitutional powers, despite the most outrageously provocative claims by ANC Classic and its associates, can only be a testament to his ineffectiveness or impotence.

Zuma was a compromise candidate – the only one who was adjudged capable of challenging the formidable and nurtured ruthlessness of Mbeki. That has been accomplished. If criminal convictions do not get him, internal party politics will. Neither his character nor his skill is adequate for the task ahead and this is widely accepted by even those who were at the head of his battalions in Polokwane. The spectacle of the would-be president insisting that he does not have a single policy idea other than those of his party is hardly the recipe for inspired leadership in these perilous times.

That leaves a compromise candidate like the staid but as yet largely untested Kgalema Motlanthe, current ANC deputy president, or some former outsider like Mathews Phosa or Tokyo Sexwale, key members of the resurgent Coalition of the Walking Wounded. In any event, the individual is probably going to be only as important as the policies he or she chooses and the efficiency with which they are implemented.

The extent to which this ANC leader will turn South Africa away from its current trajectory of demodernisation is dependent almost entirely on the extent to which this person can build on the sound foundations laid during the Mbeki years and roll back the damage caused by unsound policies.

The party and its declining standing in the eyes of both the South African public and the international community will be among the biggest challenges for any new incumbent. There are some simple steps that would go a long way to assisting with this process and restoring the strength of institutions.

The first has to be a review of the current system of proportional representation. The concept was entrenched in the constitution and endorsed by all parties in the quite noble belief that it would give smaller parties a fighting chance of gaining parliamentary influence, rather than being wiped out by a winner-takes-all constituency system.

But the inherent risk from the beginning was twofold. The system places great power in the hands of the party bosses, as they are ultimately the ones who make the call on who goes where. Secondly, it removes parliamentarians from the direct relationship one finds in constituency-based systems. This increases the distance between the elected and the electors. In an ideal situation, the system would self-correct through open, responsive and transparent administration.

As we know, the reverse happened during the Mbeki era. The party became the preserve of the inner circle and critics were sidelined, diminished and destroyed. Accountability between the executive leadership of the country and the ruling party fell apart. The distance between the parliamentarians and the electorate similarly widened. A common refrain from the public has been the inability to find anybody to whom they could complain. This lack of accountability had its inevitable spin-off in plummeting discipline among the ANC caucus: absentee members, defrauding of parliament and disdain for any form of direct responsibility. The whole was exacerbated by the floor-crossing system, which allowed political mercenaries to move from one party to another without forfeiting their parliamentary seats. This worked well for the ruling party, which picked up numbers through offering patronage, but it did nothing for inculcation of a sense of responsibility in parliamentarians.

Mercifully, there are signs that the yawning gap between electorate and ruling party is about to be bridged. Moves are under way to scrap the floor-crossing rules and there is a rising tide of informed non-partisan opinion in favour of an electoral system that combines an element of proportional representation to ensure minority representation while reinstituting a constituency-based system.

Changing the electoral system is a very good way to start the rejuvenation of the democratic project and enhance the image and accountability of the ANC.

Equally important is a clean-up of the Aegean stables that constitute South African party funding. In early 2008 Mathews Phosa, a potential presidential front-runner, called for an audit of the ANC's business activities through Chancellor House, which played a key role in building the party's finances from bankruptcy to a disclosed R1.7 billion (and however many more undisclosed billions). Those with an optimistic bent will see this as a step towards transparency and honesty in the ruling party – something that has been sorely lacking to date. The sceptics will see it as just another front in the war between Classic and Lite to see who should share the spoils of power. Nevertheless, the investigation does open the possibility of a greater understanding of the murky relationships between the business community and the ruling party.

But this would have to be followed by three immediate steps.

The first would be the introduction of legislation requiring all political parties to declare the sources of their income, as is the case in nearly all modern democracies.

The second would be a full public inquiry into the arms scandal that has caused so much pain to the ruling party. This could require some form of truth commission, the opportunity to make a clean breast and move forward.

Third must be an undertaking to act against all parties who have broken the law in any way in regard to the securing of either personal or party advantage from state tenders or influence during the Mbeki era. Clearly, those in the presidency would not be exempt from such action.

Without these steps, the ANC will continue to labour under a cloud of suspicion and an endless dribble of allegations and litigation, which will only damage it further and expose it to the charge that it is among the most venal political movements on the continent. This century-old movement deserves better than that.

The next important initiative by the ANC to establish its integrity and position itself as a modern political movement is to terminate its declared policy of 'deployment'. The concept itself is, frankly, pre-modern. Developed world parties accept that the nature of the societies they govern is one of countless cross-cutting loyalties, influences, forces and imperatives, all brought more or less into balance by good laws, sound institutions, informed and active publics, responsive leadership and responsible economies.

Modern political parties do not 'deploy' people to seize the commanding heights of the economy, control the public service, hijack the judiciary and dominate the cultural and sporting life of the country. Totalitarian states do that. It has been a constant source of bewilderment to me, in debating these issues with modern and deeply intelligent ANC luminaries, that they cannot see the contradictions between their claims to represent a modern party and the essence of the policy of deployment – unless one takes the utterly cynical view that deployment is not a political manoeuvre at all, but one designed to advance naked personal self-enrichment.

No matter. An earlier chapter reported on the disaffection the policy of deployment has caused at local government level among the public and the damage it has done to the integrity of the local government system. That damage is replicated at virtually every level on which the ANC operates and in every sphere, whether it is forcing economic advantage to politically connected cohorts through 'empowerment' or dictating who should play in a cricket team.

There is an urgent need for the ANC as a political party to step back – not just in the interests of decompressing tensions within the society, but also in the interests of its own legacy. Does it really want to be remembered as just another failed party within a failed one-party state? Does it care? These are the core issues that any new leader of the ANC will have to confront if the vision for the party goes further than just the short-term gain of power, privilege and perks.

A first gesture towards acknowledging the eccentricity of its deployment policy is to require all public officials, or those in the parastatals, to resign all political affiliations and take an oath of acknowledgement that their single and undivided loyalty is to the constitution of the country and the protocols of the public service. Breaches would be on pain of dismissal.

The parallel challenge for the new ANC leadership in office is to re-establish the conventional relationship between the executive and the other elements of society. There is good news here. Despite the largely destructive attempts by the Mbeki Ascendancy to diminish the authority and power of just about every other constitutional entity (Reserve Bank and Constitutional Court excepted), most still survive in some form of robustness, other than easily acquirable offices such as that of the Public Protector.

Nothing much requires to be done other than the obvious. Respect the courts and do not attempt to influence the appointments. Comply with the powers given to the statutory bodies even if you do not like their reasoning. Attend parliamentary committee sessions and answer the legislators' questions – all the legislators, for they all represent the public. Disagree as much as you like with the media, but at least do them the courtesy of giving them the truth (they always seem to find out if you do not). Above all, respect the independence of the Reserve Bank, because it is the one thing that marks the difference between a modern state and a grab-what-you-can collective.

If one were to draw up a ten-point action list for the new incumbent it would look something like this: re-establish the integrity of the party and its leadership; secure the constitutional system of checks and balances; maintain prudent macro-economic policies balanced with investments in small-business growth and export opportunities; continue with the infrastructure-development programme (under tight controls); deal with the skills crisis; reset the public service to 'care' mode; reinvent empowerment to make it meaningful to the poor and rewarding to the industrious; sustain the welfare net on a contributory basis; reshape the rural reform programme to ensure food security and employment; open the labour market to the deeply marginalised; and, with all this under the belt, look forward to both renewed economic and job growth when the international cycle turns.

Summarised, the new incumbent will have to deal with three major crises emerging from the Mbeki legacy and the incipient demodernisation of the country: legitimacy, dependency and efficiency.

This book has sought to highlight the challenging situation in which South Africa now finds itself through international economic circumstances and internal problems, many of which are self-induced. The situation is now critical in many respects and only if the government moves to emergency mode, as it has done in the case of Eskom, is there a hope of reversing the country's trajectory of demodernisation. The solutions are not difficult, incapable of implementation or contrary to the broad objectives of post-liberation South Africa. But they do require political will, courage and perseverance.

The legitimacy issue can be dealt with by restoring the ANC's integrity by restructuring the electoral system to compel properly accountable public representation, ensuring transparency in its funding and dumping its anachronistic 'deployment' policy. The legitimacy issue in the state functions can be dealt with by requiring all public officials to resign from political parties.

The dependency issue can be dealt with by converting the current race-based 'empowerment' philosophy into a full-stretch state initiative to support the creation of a robust, indigenous business sector and the spread of even small parcels of equity in existing companies to as many poor South Africans as possible. Running parallel must be a programme to convert the existing open-ended and much-abused state subsidy system into a structure where recipients contribute to the cost of the subsidy through public-benefit work, no matter how menial.

Part of this, perhaps the hardest part, requires a serious re-examination of the role that the small, particularly black, business sector and agriculture can play in job creation – provided the necessary steps are taken to reduce the burden of regulation on the small-business entity and to create a viable commercial farming sector, which would be a major multiplier of jobs. The latter requires a change in attitude by the government from expropriating productive land to leasing it on behalf of qualifying black commercial farmers on the quitrent system.

The efficiency issue is not something that will be resolved immediately. It is the proverbial time bomb that has been ticking away in the hold while all on deck have been enjoying the benefits of South Africa's post-liberation economic boom between 2002 and 2007. The immediate steps to achieve it are the creation of apex schools for critical skills and the introduction of national, post-matric, short-term, experience-based qualifications in the ten key disciplines needed for the restart of the South African economy. The current SETA system needs to be scrapped and replaced by industry training bodies.

Efficiency in the public service, the major constraint on economic development and the support of the poor, needs to be effected by a series of steps, as set out above. Needless to say, political 'redeployment' must be publicly disavowed.

All of this needs to be achieved while maintaining the delicate balance of consensus that has prevented the country imploding since 1994. The trade-off, the new consensus, is not that difficult

The government must admit that the country is in crisis mode and that only extraordinary efforts will prevent it sliding down the path of demodernisation. The acceptance of this point might be easier now than before, given that ANC Classic, bizarrely, appears not to hold itself responsible for the current crises, despite being part of the power elite for a decade and a half. Nevertheless, a gap has been created and new leadership might be able to seize the nettle.

The rich (now both white and black) need to accept that greater contributions will be made through the fiscus in direct transfers to ensure equity acquisition by poor people and the creation of a viable black small-business sector.

Black entrepreneurs will need to accept that wealth will have to be acquired not by unsustainable extorted equity deals, but by industriousness, focus and personal accountability.

The poor would need to know that state subsidy is not a one-way flow but a payment for reciprocal value in the form of public-interest work.

The unions should understand that the legitimate rights and interests of their membership will be respected, but not at the price of protecting a lack of professionalism in the public service and unproductiveness in the private sector.

Finally, the ANC would need to accept that it does not own South Africa or its people and that its resources are not available for the personal enrichment of its cadres. The ruling party is nothing more than the temporary custodian of the hopes and ambitions of all South Africans and, as a servant to the people, it is dispensable at any point. This last obligation on the ANC, will, on past evidence, be the hardest to effect. The spirit of arrogance and impunity is deeply embedded in the culture of the movement: it has learnt at the knee of its master.

The creation of such a consensus is not beyond the reach of this country. Greater compromises were reached in 1994 when the ANC gave up a failed war of insurrection and the white elites gave up political power in an isolated and failing state. Out of that emerged a national consensus based on truly modern principles. Credible and moral leadership took this moment forward and bequeathed it to the Mbeki Ascendancy. Momentum carried the project for a while, but then, like an IT system stripped of its engineers, the initiative began to falter amid withering physical, human and institutional infrastructure. It is not too late. Nothing is ever too late if the moment is seized.

Notes

INTRODUCTION

1. Brian Pottinger, *The Imperial Presidency. PW Botha: The First 10 Years.* Southern, 1988.

CHAPTER 1

1. *Table Talk*, 1830.
2. Sakhela Buhlungu, John Daniel, Roger Southall, Jessica Lutchman (eds.), *State of the Nation: South Africa 2007.* Human Sciences Research Council, HSRC Press, 2007, p. 19.
3. Padraig O'Malley, *Shades of Difference: Mac Maharaj and the Struggle for South Africa.* Viking, 2007.
4. *Ibid.*, p. 233.
5. Mark Gevisser, *The Dream Deferred: Thabo Mbeki.* Jonathan Ball, 2007, p. 650.
6. Richard Calland, *Anatomy of South Africa: Who Holds the Power?* Zebra Press, 2006, p. 129.
7. Xolela Mangcu, *To the Brink: The State of Democracy in South Africa.* University of KwaZulu-Natal Press, 2008.

CHAPTER 2

1. Address to joint sitting of the US Congress on 26 December 1941.

CHAPTER 3

1. *The Rebel*, 1951.

2. Calland, *Anatomy of South Africa.*
3. *Ibid.*
4. *Ibid.*, p. 94.

CHAPTER 4

1. *An Inquiry into the Nature and Causes of the Wealth of Nations*, 1776.
2. Andrew Feinstein, *After the Party.* Jonathan Ball, 2007

CHAPTER 5

1. Letter dated 4 April 1864.
2. 'Government graft surges dramatically', *Business Day*, 22 February 2008.

CHAPTER 6

1. Former US Assistant Secretary of Treasury in the Nixon and Ford administrations.
2. 'Growth, employment and redistribution: The government's new economic strategy', *Umrabulo*, second quarter, 1997.
3. 'The Reconstruction and Development Programme', *Umrabulo*, second quarter, 1996.
4. Alan Hirsch, *Season of Hope: Economic Reform under Mandela and Mbeki.* University of KwaZulu-Natal Press, 2005.
5. No. 25, May 2006.

CHAPTER 7

1. US industrialist, 1863–1947.

2. Mandisi Mpahlwa, 'Proposal to go it alone on trade misreads the evidence', *Business Day*, 7 November 2007.

3. 'State cash cows hamper growth', *Business Day*, 22 November 2007.

4. Statistics South Africa, *Statistics of Liquidations and Insolvencies*, P0043, September 2007.

5. 'Pinched homeowners scramble to sell', *Business Day*, 29 January 2008.

6. 'Beware tsunami of debt', *Financial Mail*, 9 November 2007.

7. International Labour Organisation, *Key Indicators in the Labour Market*, 5th edition, September 2007.

8. Hirsch, *Season of Hope*.

CHAPTER 8

1. www.leskoblog.com, 14 March 2005.

2. Buhlungu et al. (eds.), *State of the Nation*, introduction.

3. 'Fired government official still at work', *Natal Mercury*, 22 January 2008.

4. See Auditor-General of South Africa, *General Reports on National, Provincial and Local Government Audits 2005/06*.

5. South Africa's Five Worst Municipalities: DA discussion documents at www.da.org.za/da/site/eng/campaigns/5municipalities.asp.

6. Auditor-General, *General Report on the Audit Outcomes of Local Government for the Financial Year Ending 30 June 2003*. Pretoria: Government Printer.

7. Centre for Development and Enterprise, *Voices of Anger: Protest and Conflict in Two Municipalities*. Report to the Conflict and Governance Facility, April 2007.

8. *Ibid.*, p. 3.

9. *Ibid.*, p. 56.

10. United Nations Office for the Coordination of Humanitarian Affairs, 'South Africa: Local Government Minister Dismisses Claims of Failed Service', ERIN, 4 January 2008.

CHAPTER 9

1. *The Trial of Gilles de Rais*, 1965.

2. Institute for Security Studies, 'The 2006/07 Crime Statistics', *SA Crime Quarterly*, No. 21, September 2007.

3. Mo Ibrahim Foundation, *Index of African Governance 2007*. www.moibrahimfoundation.org.

4. South African Institute of Race Relations, *Where We Rank for Murder*. Fast Facts, No. 8, August 2007.

5. Crime Information Analysis Centre, South African Police Service. *Crime Situation in South Africa*, June 2007.

6. Crime Information Analysis Centre, South African Police Service. *Crime Situation in South Africa, April–September 2007*, December 2007.

7. Patrick Burton et al., *National Victims of Crime Survey South Africa 2003*. South African Institute for Security Studies, ISS Monograph Series, No. 101, July 2004.

8. 'Johannesburgers still fear crime', *Business Day* survey, 22 November 2007.

9. Burton et al., *National Victims of Crime Survey*.

10. Mari Harris and Stephano Radaelli, 'Paralysed by fear: Perceptions of crime and violence in South Africa',

SA Crime Quarterly, No. 20, South African Institute for Security Studies, June 2007.

11. 'Violence spilling into the work place', *The Star*, 25 October 2007.

12. PricewaterhouseCoopers, *Global Survey of Economic Crime*, 2007.

13. National Non-Ferrous Metal Anti-Theft Combating Committee. Second quarter, 2007.

14. Burton et al., *National Victims of Crime Survey.*

15. Anthony Altbeker, *A Country at War with Itself.* Jonathan Ball, 2007.

16. South African Police Service, *Annual Report 2006/07.*

17. David Bruce, 'Good cops, bad cops: Assessing the South African Police Service', *SA Crime Quarterly*, No. 21, September 2007. South African Institute for Security Studies.

18. SAPS, *Annual Report 2006/07.*

19. Mari Harris and Stephano Radaelli, 'Paralysed by fear'.

20. South African Law Commission, *Conviction Rates and Other Outcomes of Crimes Reported in Eight South African Police Areas.* Research paper 18, project 82.

21. Institute for Security Studies, Monograph Series, No. 64, September 2001.

22. 'Heist gang's history of lawlessness', *The Star*, 17 January 2008.

23. Burton et al., *National Victims of Crime Survey.*

24. Martin Schonteich, 'Does capital punishment deter?' *Africa Security Review*, Vol. 11, No. 2, 2002.

25. Jonny Steinberg, 'Murder unsolved in shadows of the state's shaky edifices', *Business Day*, 20 November 2007.

CHAPTER 10

1. US Secretary for Health, Education and Welfare, 1965–1968.

2. South African Institute of International Affairs, *In Brief: Fast Facts*, No. 7/2007, July 2007.

3. *Ibid.*

4. Global Campaign for Education, *Global School Report 2008*, December 2007, p. 19.

5. Carol Paton, 'Why SA fails its children', *Financial Mail*, 9 November 2007.

6. Brahm Fleisch, 'Primary education in crisis: Why SA schoolchildren underachieve in reading and mathematics'. Quoted *ibid.*

7. Sigamoney Manicka Naicker, *An Investigation into the Implementation of Outcomes Based Education in the Western Cape Province.* University of Western Cape, 2000.

8. Mary Metcalfe, 'Why our schools don't work', *Sunday Times*, 13 January 2008.

9. Anil Kanjee, *Improving Learner Achievement in Schools: Applications of National Assessments in South Africa.* Human Sciences Research Council, 2007.

10. Centre for Development and Enterprise, *Doubling for Growth: Addressing the Maths and Science Challenge in South Africa's Schools.* October 2007.

11. Anil Kanjee, *Improving Learner Achievement in Schools.*

12. Mary Metcalfe, 'Why our schools don't work'.
13. 'Teachers "not coping" with OBE', *Natal Mercury*, 28 September 2007, p. 6.
14. *Ibid.*
15. Centre for Development and Enterprise, *Doubling for Growth*.
16. Prega Govender, 'Studying hard, far from home, pays off for Khutsong matriculants', *Sunday Times*, 30 December 2007.
17. Department of Education, *Strategy Implementation Report April 1 2006 to March 31 2007*.
18. Centre for Development and Enterprise, *Skills, Growth and Immigration Policy: Overcoming the Fatal Constraint*, 5 February 2007.
19. South Africa Higher Education, *Higher Education Impact: Universities in the SA Economy*, December 2007.
20. 'Wage gap due to skills crisis', *Business Day*, 6 February 2008.
21. Centre for Development and Enterprise, *The South African Skills Crisis: A Report from the Corporate Coalface*, 5 February 2007.
22. Centre for Development and Enterprise, *Skills, Growth and Immigration Policy*.
23. Democratic Alliance, *Skills and Vacancies: DA Outlines Problems and Proposes Solutions*, discussion paper 2007 and immigration policy.

CHAPTER 11
1. *Le Crime de Sylvestre Bonnard*, 1881.
2. Department of Health overview, 2006.
3. Karl von Holdt and Mike Murphy, 'Public hospitals in South Africa: Stressed institutions, disempowered managements', in Buhlungu et al. (eds.), *State of the Nation*.
4. Gauteng Provincial Government, Department of Health, *Annual Report 2006/07*.
5. Critical Care Society of South Africa, *South African Medical Journal*, Vol. 98/1, 2007.
6. Karl von Holdt and Mike Murphy, 'Public hospitals in South Africa'.
7. Academy of Science of South Africa, *Nutritional Influences on Human Immunity with Special Reference to Tuberculosis and HIV Infection – Consensus Study*, 2007.
8. Boston University School of Public Health, 'Impact of HIV/AIDS on health service personnel', *South African Medical Journal*, Vol. 97/2, 2007.
9. Collette Schulz-Herzenberg, *A Lethal Cocktail – Exploring the Impact of Corruption on HIV/AIDS Prevention and Treatment Efforts in South Africa*. Institute for Strategic Studies, December 2007.
10. Child Healthcare Problem Identification Programme and Medical Research Council of South Africa, *Saving Children*, 2005.
11. USAID, *Infectious Diseases Report: South Africa*, September 2006.
12. Health Systems Trust, 'The role of the private sector within the South African health care system', *South African Health Review 2007*, 6 February 2008.
13. World Health Organisation, *Index of Key Health Indicators*, 2007.

CHAPTER 12

1. US Army general, 1893–1981.
2. Eskom, *Annual Report*, 2001.
3. National Energy Regulator of South Africa (NERSA), *An Independent Electricity Supply Industry Assessment and Mitigation Strategies: Final Report*, October 2007.
4. Eskom, *Annual Reports*, 1996–2006.
5. Eskom, *Annual Report*, 2006.
6. 'Eskom was right about energy demand, Mbeki admits', *The Weekender*, 12 January 2008.
7. NERSA, *An Independent Electricity Supply Industry Assessment and Mitigation Strategies.*
8. 'Cable theft affects business in South Africa', National Non-Ferrous Metal Anti-Theft Combating Committee, *Newsletter*, second quarter, 2007.
9. Department of Public Enterprises, *South Africa Agency Reviews Security of Electricity Supply*, 6 February 2007.
10. 'Power crisis threatens to sink major projects', *Business Day*, 18 January 2008.
11. Learning Information Networking and Knowledge Centre, *South African Telecommunications Sector Performance Review.* University of the Witwatersrand, 2006, p. 20.
12. 'Millions unspent in drive to bring SA's poor online', *Business Day*, 5 December 2007.
13. LINK, *South African Telecommunications Sector Performance Review*, p. 20.
14. World Economic Forum, *Network Readiness Index*, 2006/07.
15. South African Institution of Civil Engineers, 'South African infrastructural report card', *Engineering News*, 15 December 2007.
16. *Ibid.*

CHAPTER 13

1. US winner of the Nobel Prize for Economics, 1912–2006.
2. Statistics South Africa, *Survey of Large-Scale Agriculture.* October 2006.
3. *Ibid.*
4. Centre for Development and Enterprise, *Land Reform in South Africa: A 21st Century Perspective.* June 2005.
5. Department of Land Affairs, *Annual Report 2006/07*, director-general's introduction.
6. Land Bank, *Annual Report 2006/07.*
7. Philip du Toit, *The Great South African Land Scandal.* Legacy Publications, January 2004.
8. 'Massive fraud programme', *Farmers Weekly*, 17 August 2007.
9. 'A new dawn on land reform', *Farmers Weekly*, 28 December 2007.
10. 'Forestry firms face big land claims', *Business Report*, 14 January 2008.
11. 'Protracted land claims threaten KZN sugar industry', *Natal Mercury*, 18 December 2007.
12. 'Facing up to BEE challenge', *Farmers Weekly*, 18 January 2008.
13. United Nations Food and Agriculture Organisation, *National Production Index*, 2006.

CHAPTER 14

1. English writer, 1737–1809, *The Rights of Man*, 1791.
2. Misha Glenny, *McMafia: A Journey*

*through the Global Criminal
Underworld.* Knopf, 2008.

CHAPTER 15

1. French author, humanist and satirist, 1694–1778.
2. Unilever Institute of Strategic Marketing, *Black Diamond 2007 on the Move.* University of Cape Town, June 2007.
3. South African Institute of Race Relations, *Drivers of and Obstacles to the Growth of the Black Middle Class.* Fast Facts, No. 9/2007, September 2007.
4. Centre for Development and Enterprise, 'Can Black Economic Empowerment drive new growth?' *CDE in Depth,* issue 4. January 2007.
5. Sixth Commission for Employment Equity, *Annual Report,* 2006.
6. South African Institute of Race Relations, *Drivers of and Obstacles to the Growth of the Black Middle Class.*

CHAPTER 16

1. Irish dramatist, 1856–1950, *Everybody's Political What's What,* 1944.
2. Dave Thayer, *Annual Mergers and Acquisitions Review 2005.* Ernst & Young, 15th edition, 2006.
3. See BusinessMap Foundation reports, *BEE 2005 Behind the Deals* and *2006 Charters and Deals.*
4. 'Equity deal not a cost, complains Mvela', *Business Day,* 4 September 2007.
5. 'BEE costs hand Reunert a 48% earnings knock', *Business Day,* 22 November 2007.

CHAPTER 17

1. Lebanese-American poet, 1883–1931.
2. Christell de Koker, Liezel de Waal and Jan Vorster, *A Profile of Social Security Beneficiaries in South Africa.* Department of Sociology and Social Anthropology, Stellenbosch University, June 2006.
3. Geospace International, *Report on Incentive Structures of Social Assistance Grants in South Africa.* July 2006.
4. 'R440 m fraud just tip of the iceberg', *Natal Mercury,* 30 October 2007.
5. 'Income gap "widens" for SA blacks', *Business Day,* 7 November 2007.

CHAPTER 18

1. American poet, author and physician, 1809–1894.
2. 'Institutional investors fighting shy of South Africa', *Business Day,* 19 February 2008.
3. Statistics South Africa, *Civil Cases for Debt,* P2041, January 2008.
4. *The 2007 SA Reconciliation Barometer: Seventh Round Report,* December 2007.

CHAPTER 19

1. British politician, 1804–1881, *Sybil,* 1845.
2. 'Global concern on shortage of skills', *Business Day,* 13 March 2008.
3. 'Anywhere but here', *Financial Mail,* 7 March 2008.

CHAPTER 20

1. American humorist, 1878–1937.

CHAPTER 21

1. English historian, 1818–1894.

2. *World Values Survey 1999–2002.* Wave at www.worldvaluessurvey.org.
3. Statistics South Africa, *Labour Force Survey*, P0210, September 2007.

CHAPTER 22

1. Four-term British prime minister, 1809–1898.

CHAPTER 23

1. American civil rights leader and clergyman, 1929–1968.
2. *The 2007 SA Reconciliation Barometer: Seventh Round Report,* December 2007.

Index

Do you have any comments, suggestions or
feedback about this book or any other Zebra Press titles?
Contact us at **talkback@zebrapress.co.za**